Getting Started in Computer Music

Mark Nelson

THOMSON

™

COURSE TECHNOLOGY

Professional ■ Technical ■ Reference

Educational facilities, companies, and organizations interested in multiple copies or licensing of this book should contact the publisher for quantity discount information. Training manuals, CD-ROMs, and portions of this book are also available individually or can be tailored for specific needs.

ISBN: 1-59200-842-9

Library of Congress Catalog Card Number: 2005929778

Printed in the United States

06 07 08 09 10 PH 10 9 8 7 6 5 4 3 2 1

Professional ■ Technical ■ Reference

Thomson Course Technology PTR, a division of Thomson Course Technology
25 Thomson Place
Boston, MA 02210
http://www.courseptr.com

Publisher and General Manager, Thomson Course Technology PTR:
Stacy L. Hiquet

Associate Director of Marketing:
Sarah O'Donnell

Manager of Editorial Services:
Heather Talbot

Marketing Manager:
Cathleen Snyder

Senior Editor and Acquisitions Editor:
Mark Garvey

Marketing Coordinator:
Jordan Casey

Developmental Editor:
Orren Merton

Project Editor:
Karen A. Gill

Thomson Course Technology PTR Editorial Services Coordinator:
Elizabeth Furbish

Copyeditor:
Brad Crawford

Interior Layout Tech:
DPS

Cover Designer:
Mike Tanamachi

Indexer:
Katherine Stimson

Proofreader:
Gene Redding

} Acknowledgments

A quick tip o' the hat to the fine folks at Thomson Course Technology: Mark Garvey, Orren Merton, Karen Gill, and Elizabeth Furbish. Thanks for putting up with the new guy. Thanks to Reid and Dog for the *kokua* and to the long-suffering Uji and Newt for once again appearing out of thin air when least expected. And let's not forget the press contacts, company representatives, and helpful office staff who took time out of their busy schedules to provide certain pictures you'll find sprinkled throughout the chapters. If I sell enough books, I'll send all of you flowers; until then, I can only send my thanks.

Above all, *mahalo nui* big time to Lanamalie. It's been a long slog; I promise to stop whining now.

About the Author

Mark Nelson has been a recording and performing musician since before he could drive, which was a very long time ago indeed. A masterful player of the acoustic guitar, Appalachian dulcimer, and other folk instruments, he has appeared everywhere from Kansas to Kaunakakai and from Barrow to Boston. (He once worked as a banjo-playing gorilla in Dublin, but that's another story.)

Mark is equally at home on both sides of the glass in the recording studio as a producer, engineer, or musician. He's been writing about music technology since the early days of MIDI and digital audio for such magazines as *Electronic Musician, Music and Computers, Revolution,* and *MIDI Guitar.*

Mark and famed Hawaiian musician Keola Beamer host the Aloha Music Camp, an immersion in the music and culture of Hawaii, held twice each year on the magical island of Molokai. He lives with his wife and various furry and finned friends in southern Oregon's Applegate Valley, where he maintains a small recording studio, creates music, and watches the trees grow.

http://www.mark-o.com

TABLE OF Contents

} Introduction

It is no secret that the personal computer has revolutionized the way we interact with media. In just a few short years, computers have gone from a high-priced luxury for the elite few to a basic household utensil. People everywhere are learning how easy it is to organize their music collections, edit family photos, transfer videos to DVDs, and surf the Internet—all tasks that were impossibly difficult as recently as the mid-1990s.

Even better, the personal computer has revolutionized music. Computers are vital for everything from composing to performing to recording and distributing music. Computers help us create new sounds, restore fragile historic recordings, and perform music in ways undreamed of by the musicians of yesteryear. With the help of a personal computer, learning music has never been easier or more accessible. Guitarists are discovering that they can replace a garage full of high-end boutique amps with a laptop and the right software. Composers no longer have to book a concert hall and hire an orchestra to hear their music.

Nowhere has the revolution reached as far as in the world of recording. Consider this: The Beatles' immortal *Sgt. Pepper's Lonely Hearts Club Band* was recorded in 1967 at the then-state-of-the-art EMI Studios for umpteen thousands of dollars—on the very latest in four-track analog recorders. My first album, recorded in 1979 at a budget 8-track studio, cost me as much as a new car in studio time and tape alone. Yet right now I'm typing this on a $1,200 home computer that recently handled a mix with 48 tracks of uncompressed audio, beaucoup edits, piles of onboard effects, and tons of automation without breaking a sweat. Don't worry if you don't know what I'm talking about. You will by the end of the book.

What's that mean to you? Just this: For a very modest outlay, you can assemble a first-class set of high-quality tools to help you achieve your musical goals.

Getting Started in Computer Music is your guide to the sometimes bewildering but always exciting world where music and computers converge. Enjoy the ride.

What You'll Find in This Book

If you have ever wondered how to record music in your own home, how to hook up a keyboard to your computer to unleash a world of new sounds, how to set up a system to remix a dance track, what software to use to write and print out a song, or where you can learn to hear the difference between an Ebdim7 and an Ebm7b5 chord, you've come to the right place. *Getting Started in Computer Music* gives you a thorough introduction to using a computer to get where *you* want to go with *your* music.

One thing I promise: You won't find math here. This is not a technical manual. If that kind of thing interests you, look in Appendix D, "Resources," where you'll find links to Web sites that will keep your slide rule limber for years to come. Nor is this book an operational guide for a particular platform or software. If that is your interest, I suggest you pick up one of the other fine books in the Course Technology catalog.

What you will find is a good introduction to the many ways your computer will help you create, learn, perform, manipulate, write, and record music. If you've absolutely no idea what the knobs on a mixer do, if you wonder where on the computer you plug in your keyboard, if your neighbors are complaining because your amp doesn't sound good until you crank it up to 11, or if the words "computer" and "music" make your brain hurt ... sit back and relax.

Here's what you'll find:

* Information to help you choose the best tools for your needs
* Tips on buying and setting up your computer
* Information on choosing music software

* Practical advice on choosing audio hardware
* Step-by-step instructions for recording at home
* Tips on selecting and using microphones effectively
* Tutorials on MIDI, looping, and digital recording
* Professional tips for getting the best sound
* Detailed information to help you clearly understand the hardware and software used to create, produce, and record music

Who This Book Is For

Whether you have a computer and wonder how you can use it to further your musical goals or you're a longtime computer user who is looking to get into music, you'll find the answers here. In my experience, the questions most people ask involve basic concepts such as, "How do I record a song?" and "Can I use my home computer, or do I have to buy something special?" You will find the answers here. And you'll find solid, practical tips and techniques for selecting a computer, choosing your software, and buying gear. Plus you'll learn valuable, time-tested techniques for using your new tools.

Here's a short list of who will benefit from this book:

* Music students
* Guitar players
* Singers
* Amateur musicians
* Keyboard players
* Professional musicians
* Remixers
* Acoustic musicians
* Music educators
* DJs
* Electronic musicians
* Composers
* Parents

* Band leaders
* Aspiring recording engineers
* Next year's pop stars
* Last year's has-beens
* Aging rock stars
* You

The Old "Mac Versus PC" Question

Few things in life are as boring as the endless arguments over which is better, the Mac or the PC. Two minutes on any online forum reveal post after impassioned post devoted to one or the other. I guess that's because we just like to take sides, no matter how trivial the issue.

The bottom line is this: You can forge a desktop music monster using just about any machine made in the past few years, running pretty much any operating system you want. If you prefer a Mac, great. PC? Also great. Linux? More power to ya.

That being said, I use Macs exclusively in my studio and business, as I have since the early days of computer music. At that time, if I recall, the big debate was between the Commodore 64 and the Amiga (anybody remember them?), with the Mac taking a distant third. Windows was only a gleam in Bill Gates's eye.

A short time later I dove headfirst into the brave new world of digital audio. A partner and I opened a new 24-track digital recording studio, and I volunteered to build a computer-editing suite, the first one in southern Oregon. At the time, there was only one choice for all practical purposes: Digidesign's Pro Tools. And Pro Tools worked only on a Mac. End of debate. For many years, the Mac remained the system of choice for anyone doing serious work.

That was then, this is now. Today Windows holds the clear lead in software, hardware, and support. A quick flip though any music catalog will show dozens of pages devoted to Windows-only software and hardware. Likewise, pro studios built around the PC far outnumber those using Macs. (Many use both, by the way.)

Still, the Mac continues to attract a hard-core following. I'm one of 'em. I have thousands of hours invested in developing a certain skill set with some very specific software, and I have no intention of changing any time soon. I have used Windows-based systems from time to time in my work. To tell the truth, I can't find a heck of a lot of difference between the two.

Many of the examples and screen shots in this book are from a Mac. If you are among the 99 percent of computer users who favor the Windows operating system, please don't go getting your knickers in a twist if you see a little Apple in some of the illustrations.

And Apple heads, I don't want to hear any whining from your side when I discuss things from the PC perspective. Let's just all try to get along, okay?

Though I'll discuss the pros and cons of each system in depth in Chapter 3, "Choosing Your Computer," the bulk of this book provides practical, hands-on knowledge that transcends the platform wars.

How This Book Is Organized

You don't need to know anything about computers, music, or home recording to benefit from this book. My goal is to provide you with a clear understanding of where the world of computer music stands right now.

Getting Started in Computer Music takes a functional approach through eight chapters and four appendixes.

* **Chapter 1, "Music Making on the Computer"**—First we'll look at all the myriad ways a computer can help you get more out of your music. I'll cover such things as recording, composition, looping, virtual instruments, using a computer as a performance tool, and more. For instance, did you know that you can use the same software to study music theory that is used in university music departments? Or that many professional film composers rely on their computers to hear their music *before* they hire an orchestra? Or that your computer can mimic the sound of a classic electronic synthesizer that would set you back $20,000—*if* you could find one? Or that your computer can help you write lyrics?

* **Chapter 2, "Understanding the Gear"**—Since all of what follows requires some understanding of basic studio terms and techniques, the

second chapter is devoted to discussing the nuts and bolts of recording and recording equipment. After a brief introduction to the recording process, we'll take an extended tour along the recorded signal chain. If you have ever wondered what all those little knobs and buttons do, here's where you'll find the answers. I'll also discuss microphones in some detail, as well as help you set up your room both for recording and playback.

* **Chapter 3, "Choosing Your Computer"**—Here's where you'll get the information to help you choose a computer, understand the basics of hard drives and memory, and find the peripherals that are right for you. Along the way we'll touch on the merits of a dedicated music system and discuss using a laptop as your primary computer.

* **Chapter 4, "Choosing Your Software: What Do You Want to Do?"**—Rather than simply list tons of the latest products, this section is designed to help you decide what software best meets your needs. We'll cover software for audio and MIDI recording and looping, scoring and educational software, software samplers, synthesizers and virtual instruments, and much more. You'll learn what features to look for and what questions to ask in the important task of building your computer music system.

* **Chapter 5, "Track One: MIDI"**—Originally developed to allow on-stage keyboardists to play multiple instruments simultaneously, MIDI (Musical Instrument Digital Interface) has expanded into a powerful tool useful for everything from music education to live performing to audio recording to looping. Even if you have no interest in playing keyboards, MIDI can greatly assist just about everything you do. In this chapter, I'll also talk about the world of alternate MIDI controllers, such as MIDI guitars, wind instruments, and percussion.

* **Chapter 6, "Track Two: Looping Tools"**—It's no secret that a huge percentage of the music recorded in the past 15 years is based on looped beats and rhythms, tiny snippets of music played over and over. What was originally the domain of crazed studio engineers armed with razor blades, splicing tape, and endless patience is now so simple that just about any four-year-old with a PC can master the basics. But there is much more to looping than simply rearranging somebody's prerecorded tracks. We'll look at how to find and manipulate MIDI and

audio loops, how to create your own, and how to integrate looping into live performance.

* **Chapter 7, "Track Three: Digital Recording for the Solo Musician"**— Next we'll explore a very common character, that of the solo acoustic musician or singer/songwriter who wants to record at home. You'll learn how to choose your hardware and software, how to set up your room, what gear you'll need, and where to put everything. And you'll learn solid, studio-proven techniques for recording voice and acoustic guitar and other instruments. Finally, you'll learn the basics of editing and mixing. Don't worry if you don't play guitar; the techniques and tips are the same no matter what style of music you make.

* **Chapter 8, "Track Four: All Together Now: The Desktop DAW"**—The final chapter puts it all together. A DAW (Digital Audio Workstation) is a fully integrated virtual studio incorporating multitrack digital audio, MIDI, looping, virtual instruments, and more. After looking at your system and gear requirements, we'll take a song from conception to completion. You'll learn about integrating MIDI and loops, planning a live session, recording for multiple instruments, using effects effectively, winning mixing strategies, and more.

* **Appendix A, "Glossary"**—Don't know a DAE from a DAO? Find the definitions for all of the technical terms used in the book here.

* **Appendix B, "Buying Used Gear"**—Assembling a first-class collection of gear doesn't have to break the bank. Learn how to shop for used gear without fear: where to buy, what to buy, and when to pass on by.

* **Appendix C, "Manufacturers"**—Here you'll find Web sites where you can check out the software and hardware you've been reading about.

* **Appendix D, "Resources"**—This appendix contains a useful collection of Web sites for further exploration.

1 } Music Making on the Computer

With a quick pass of the magic wand, transform the lowly computer sitting on your desk into your band, your musical instrument, your recording studio, your performing partner, your music teacher, and your inspiration. While we're at it, let's add booking agent, promo manager, fan club president archivist, and record store. Not bad for a little chunk of plastic and silicon.

The words *computer music* used to conjure up weird images of strange sci-fi bleeps and boops, whooshes, and swirly waves of sound perfect for the wild imaginings of the second half of the past century. In fact, music and computers have been linked since the earliest days. Programmers in the 1950s attempted to create music on primitive machines the size of a house. The results, while interesting from an intellectual point of view, would hardly get you dancing. But they're perfectly logical, to quote a certain Vulcan.

Computers are essentially machines to do math, and music is all about math. What is a musical tone but a set number of vibrations in the air? A chord is simply a group of tones a certain distance apart. And rhythm is nothing more or less than a recurring number of beats in a set time period. The hard part, of course, is making it all sound good. That's where you come in.

Fortunately, you no longer have to be a rocket scientist to get music out of—or into—a computer. This chapter will give you a picture of all the different ways your computer can help you compose, study, record, and perform music. I'll also touch on how you will benefit from multimedia, audio restoration and archiving, and networking your music. Later on, we'll look at the hands-on specifics of how to set up the perfect computer system to meet your needs, and I'll discuss the best software for each task in Chapter 6, "Track Two: Looping Tools."

For now, let's concentrate on what is possible. Although you may have your mind made up already, this chapter could show you a few tricks you haven't thought of yet.

Making Music *with* the Computer

In this section, I'll talk about the ways you can use a computer as a musical partner. Wouldn't it be great if you always had a band ready to try out your song ideas? Or could practice to a real drummer instead of a metronome? When you're ready to hit the stage, how'd you like to have a performing partner that knows exactly what you're going to play?

Auto-Accompaniment

Imagine playing with a musician who knows without speaking what key you're in, how to harmonize your melody, and what kind of beat to apply. Even better, your partner will track your tempo changes and tell the band to follow you. Now imagine she'll never clean out your refrigerator, borrow your car, or try to steal your best friend.

Welcome to the world of auto-accompaniment software. Forget about those cheesy pooka-pooka rhythms on your great aunt's keyboard—thanks to the superior processing power of today's computers, real, intelligent auto accompaniment is at your command. Using software like Band in a Box (PG Music) or SoundTrek's Jammer, your computer provides a complete band, with drums, bass, horns, and strings, that listens to your playing and follows your chord changes—or creates them on the fly. The programs generate entirely new arrangements based on your input, perfect when you are fresh out of ideas. Take it from me, more than one hit song has been written this way.

The programs work like this: While you play your electronic keyboard or other Musical Instrument Digital Interface (MIDI) instrument, the software tracks your performance and adjusts the backing tracks as you go. Or manually enter the chords and select the style first. (See Chapter 5, "Track One: MIDI," to learn more.) A few programs don't even require a MIDI instrument, instead using sophisticated pitch detection to track your singing!

At its most basic, the software simply adjusts to your tempo changes, a terrific way to practice without the lockstep limitations of following a metronome. But many programs go far beyond this. Here's a quick breakdown of some important features and their uses:

* **Tempo adjustment.** Automatically speeds up or slows down to keep the backing tracks synched to your playing.

* **Real-time chord recognition.** Creates full chords appropriate to the musical genre based on your one- or two-finger playing. Perfect for those with limited keyboard chops.

* **Intelligent harmonizers.** Creates chords and/or harmony lines from your melody. Some programs generate melodies from chords you input, a great time-saver.

* **Leads and fills.** Great to flesh out an arrangement. Or use the computer-generated leads as study tools.

* **Pitch tracking.** Some software can determine the pitch of simple melodic phrases sung or played into a microphone, much like a digital tuner hears the pitch of a guitar string. Only

works on monophonic ("one voice") sounds like a solo voice or flute. It's very difficult and takes huge amounts of processing, so it's pretty rare.

❋ **Styles.** Here's where you choose your band and the type of music: everything from a piano, bass, and drums jazz trio to a full-blown symphony. Not surprisingly, the majority of the available styles lean toward rock, dance, and pop music. Some programs let you edit or load new styles; some don't.

❋ **Virtual instruments.** While some software simply spits out MIDI, requiring an outboard keyboard or sound module, many programs provide a healthy collection of software instruments. Just about every program can take advantage of the sound sets built into your computer.

❋ **Lead sheets.** Once you've tweaked your composition to you heart's content, print out the chord changes and melody for your band.

❋ **Recording.** Most programs let you record a MIDI file of your performance and the arrangement; a few handle digital audio recording as well.

You'll find that auto-accompaniment software shares many features with the jam tracks discussed in the next section. The main difference is in how the software interacts with you. Auto-accompaniment software can turn any keyboard into an intelligent arranger.

❋ **INTELLIGENT ARRANGERS**

Intelligent arrangers are keyboards or desktop devices that automatically create full musical performances featuring multiple instruments that interact, often in startlingly human ways, with the performer. Once the domain of inexpensive keyboards, intelligent arrangers are cropping up on everything from simple digital pianos to full-fledged music-production powerhouses. Although features vary from brand to brand, most feature some kind of auto-accompaniment with backing tracks, multiple instruments, styles, and chord recognition.

At their best, these devices can create full-featured, realistic accompaniment. At their worst, you can hear them in any hotel bar.

Jam Tracks

As anyone who has spent any time practicing an instrument knows, sometimes you just need to *play* the dang thing. Sure, you could call up all your friends, agree on a time, drive down to somebody's garage, and then wait around for every one to show up. But wouldn't it be better if the band were always tuned up and ready? In a nutshell, that's what jam tracks do—the software becomes your virtual band.

Say you want to work on your soloing chops while playing over a set of difficult chord changes. Or perhaps you have a song idea that's no more than a melody and some chords, and you wonder what it would sound like as a bossa nova.

Software can range from simple MIDI song files to full-out algorithmic accompaniment with multi-part arrangements featuring a rhythm section, strings, keyboards, horn parts, solos, and even melodies. As with the auto-accompaniment programs discussed earlier, you enter chords, choose a style, and sit back while the music unfolds.

Look for many of the same features as in the auto-accompaniment software. In fact, there is often a large overlap between the two—the big difference is in how the program interacts with your performance. Popular programs like Band in a Box create stunningly realistic backing tracks, but they won't adapt to your playing. M-Audio's cool Drum & Bass Rig provides beats and bass lines to quickly get you up and playing. Yamaha's Home Concert software adjusts the backing tracks to your tempo as you play.

What if you want to play along with a real band? The time-honored way is to pop in a CD and wail away, though wouldn't it be better if you could put yourself *in* the mix, so it sounds like you're standing right next to the lead guitar? Even better, wouldn't it be great if you could slow down the jam just a hair and maybe even tune the track to your instrument? You can. Nor do you have to rely on CDs. You can use virtually any music, in any format.

And for you vocalists: Imagine singing along to hit tracks without that annoying diva caterwauling in your ear. Removing lead vocals from a mix is a piece of cake with karaoke software such as PowerKaraoke.

Looping software, such as Apple's inexpensive GarageBand or IK Multimedia's GrooveMaker, offers powerful options for play-along tracks. You are just a few mouse clicks away from a smokin' rhythm track. Repeat to your heart's content and jam away. Just try getting your band to play the same four bars for an hour!

❋ EVERYTHING DOES EVERYTHING NOW, DOESN'T IT?

Due to limited processing power, earlier music software tended to do one thing and one thing only. Now the trend is for every program to attempt to cover every possible use. So expect to find recording features in your notation programs, looping tools in your recording software, and auto-accompaniment features just about anywhere. The downside to all of this overlap, aside from confusion, is that these extra features are not always fully implemented.

That's why it's always best to define what you need to do first and then get the specific software you need. Nothing is more frustrating than discovering the "added features" of your big honkin' software purchase don't really get the job done.

Live Performance

As you may guess, the same features that make auto-accompaniment and jam tracks software useful at home and in the studio will make you shine on stage. Gone are the days when enterprising musicians attached drums and cymbals to their feet, strapped a tuba to their chest, and twanged away on the ol' banjo. You and your trusty computer can sound like an entire stage full of musicians.

It's common in the pro-studio world to mix two versions of each song: the finished mix for the CD and another, special mix without the lead vocal. Why? Because many singers like to perform to the same mix, night after night. MIDI song files let you do the same thing. We'll delve into MIDI in Chapter 5; for now I'll just say that a MIDI song file is a tiny computer file that sends instructions to your keyboard or software instruments to play a song. Song files range from simple, piano-only accompaniment to full-blown orchestrations that come very close to mimicking the original recording. Song files are all over the Web: A quick search yielded 488,000 hits!

As you can imagine, MIDI song files are used extensively for karaoke. But you can do a lot more with them. Got a three-piece Irish band and your agent booked you to play a wedding where the bride's family insists on a certain song? Fire up vanBasco's freeware Karaoke Player on the laptop and dazzle 'em with a full-dress arrangement of "Feelings," complete with schmaltzy strings. I personally guarantee a big tip.

Here's a common scenario: Say you like to sing karaoke, but you can't find your favorite song anywhere. You have the lyrics and chords written down on a napkin, but your keyboard chops are limited to one-finger noodling. Wouldn't it be great if you could enter the information, choose a style, and have the software create the arrangement? Well, of course you can. Even better, if you have a songbook with the notation, scoring programs such as MakeMusic's Allegro make it easy to copy the music by selecting from an on-screen menu. Even if you don't read music, you can easily duplicate what you see. Press play, and the music will play in perfect sync with the lyrics.

One of the most powerful performance partnerships you can make with your computer is in loop-based music. (I'll discuss this topic in depth in Chapter 6.) Thanks to lightning-fast processors and clever software design, your computer can interact with your performance in real time, much like a "real" musician. Unlike static, preprogrammed MIDI files or auto-arrangements, performance-based software, such as the revolutionary Ableton Live, creates dynamic, flowing arrangements that evolve over time.

With a MIDI file or CD, you have to follow the arrangement each and every time—and if you feel like throwing in an extra solo, tough. The robot can't follow you. But with performance-based software, you decide what happens next. If you need to skip a chorus because the stage manager is threatening to lasso you, fine.

At its best, live-performance software is downright inspiring. You'll feel like you're playing with a real musician, not a mindless robot, which is more than I can say for some of my former band mates.

DJ

Using funky vinyl records, old turntables, and rudimentary rhythm machines, mix masters, scratchers, beat mavens, and spinners changed the way music was made well over 25 years ago. Hardware for DJs has been evolving for some years, and they now have a great assortment of digital resources at their disposal: digital turntables, CD players that emulate the sound and feel of vinyl, digital mixers, samplers and triggers, and hardware production workstations. But until recently, computer tools for DJs hadn't really kept up.

That's changing. Software emulations of the hardware devices abound, and new interfaces offer real-time control. Hardware/software bundles like Evolution's X-Session—billed as the "world's first USB DJ mixer"—and the feature-laden FinalScratch let you cue, cut, scratch, and mix digital files with ease. (See Figure 1.1.)

Figure 1.1
Evolution's X-Session turns
your computer into a DJ
mixer.

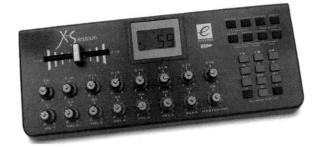

I've only scratched the surface here, but this should give you an idea of some of the ways your computer can become the best performing partner you've ever had.

Making Music *in* the Computer

Here's where we'll look at using your computer to make and transform musical sounds. Open the hood of any electronic keyboard and you'll find a computer, just as you'll find a computer inside any modern effects box, such as the popular Line 6 Pod 2.0 Amp Modeler. Drum machines? Yep, they're computers, too. So are beat boxes, samplers, digital tuners, and a host of other common tools. So why not take advantage of the superior processing power of the home computer and eliminate all of the clutter?

Synthesizers and Samplers

As a college student I had the opportunity to visit the studio of electronic music pioneer Paul Beaver. I remember a large industrial space, one wall stacked floor to ceiling with electronic gear connected by miles of wires running who knows where. Row after endless row of knobs, switches, meters, and blinking lights attested to the precise manipulation you needed to make a single, solitary sound on the tiny keyboard. In order to produce a complete song, the synthesizer operator had to record countless individual tracks, each the product of hours of painstaking work.

Synths have come a long way since then. Just about any discount mall keyboard has infinitely more power than the behemoths of yesterday. But why use an external device when your computer can handle the computations needed to synthesize musical sound without batting an eyelash?

The earliest synthesizers, like the monster living in Paul Beaver's studio, were analog devices. Musical sounds were produced via a complex interaction of electronic tone-producing circuits ("oscillators") modified by voltage-controlled filters, voltage-controlled amplifiers, low-frequency oscillators, and other modules, all connected together via short wires called "patch chords." To this day, a particular sound on a keyboard, sampler, or synthesizer is still called a patch.

> ❄ **WHAT'S A SYNTHESIZER?**
>
> A synthesizer is a device that produces sound purely by electronic means. Special circuits produce tones, which are modified in various ways to create "synthetic" sound. Why call it synthetic? I don't really know. Maybe it was to differentiate between the synthetic electronic sounds and the "real" tones produced by "real" musical instruments.
>
> While some synthesizers are capable of astonishingly lifelike simulations of "real" instruments, their power lies in creating sounds unlike anything else in the universe.

Digital synthesis uses mathematical routines (called *algorithms*) to create and modify the tones. As a result, digital instruments are smaller and far more stable than their analog forebears. We'll discuss the various kinds of synthesis in greater detail in Chapter 3, "Choosing Your Computer."

While a synthesizer creates musical tones electronically, a sampler starts with a short recording. In effect, samplers are digital audio recorders. These audio bits, or samples, may be further processed using synthesizer-like filters and oscillators, layered with other sounds, or processed with effects before being mapped to a keyboard or other controller for playback.

Software synthesizers and samplers come in many shapes, sizes, and flavors. Some are stand-alone programs so complex they take over your computer. Others operate from inside a host, such as a digital recording studio or looping program. All sound far better than the rudimentary noise machines you used to hear in video games. (See Figure 1.2.) As with romplers (see the definition that follows), programs may include a large collection of instruments:

❄ **Virtual instruments** are software models of actual (or imaginary) musical instruments. Take it from me, it's a heck of a lot easier to tote a virtual Hammond B3 organ than it is to move an original. If somebody plays an instrument, chances are there's a virtual version of it.

❄ **Soft-synths** let you program your own sounds from scratch. Some, like Native Instruments' FM7, are re-creations of hardware used in actual instruments. Others take a more general approach.

❄ **Software samplers** are exactly like their hardware cousins: programs that record and play back sampled sounds. Some offer an enormous degree of control, others less so.

❄ **Rompler** is a new term for a sampler that plays back prerecorded samples. The term comes from hardware instruments such as E-MU's Proteus series that stores samples in read-only memory, or ROM. Romplers often have extensive collections of instruments to choose from.

❄ **Drum libraries and rhythm sequencers** are specialized applications for programming and playing back percussion parts. Many also have bass sounds, handy for quickly dialing up the underpinnings of your song. Almost all recording and looping software has built-in drum programming of some sort. And there are many, many third-party programs that work with, or within, your recording tools. Extensive sample libraries of real drummers playing real drums are a cost-effective way to lend polish and realism to your mix. And no one will complain about all the racket at four in the morning.

Figure 1.2
Now you can fit a modular synth on your computer's desktop! Used with permission of Arturia.

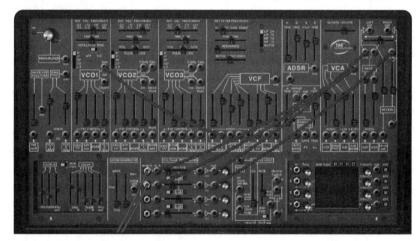

Effects

Ever notice how good your voice sounds when you sing in the shower? That's because your voice reverberates off the tile walls, making it sound fuller. Another common effect you can hear in the real world is the echo, a delayed return of sound.

Guitarists are famous for pushing their amps past the breaking point, distorting the nice clean signal into a snarling brown fuzz. That's another effect. So's the weird way your voice sounds when you hold your nose, believe it or not.

Basically, an effect is anything that affects the sound. In the early days of recording, engineers discovered that they could simulate the sound of a large room by feeding the recording through a large steel plate. Or they would run their thumb alongside a reel of tape to slow it down and speed it up, creating a whooshing effect called "flanging." Delay effects involved running a loop of tape back through another tape recorder. By the time it got back, the original sound had an echo. Some effects work to flatten out the loud bits so you can raise the overall volume. Others keep anything but the loudest sounds from getting recorded. And some effects just have to be heard to be believed.

Digital effects are one of the greatest changes wrought by the PC revolution. Big-time recording studios used to be known for rack upon rack of specialized effects costing thousands of dollars. Now you can put the same amount of power—or more!—inside a laptop.

Almost every bit of recording or looping software made comes bundled with a plethora of effects. For basic uses, most will get the job done. But why stop there? Software emulations of classic effects modules can be yours for a fraction of the original's price, if you could actually find the original. Not everyone has the luxury of recording in a European concert hall, but thanks to your trusty computer, you can sound like you did. And some digital effects are almost like musical instruments in themselves, supplying lush, ever-evolving washes of sound throbbing to the beat of the song.

We guitarists haven't been overlooked. If you're anything like me, you've bought and sold dozens of stomp boxes, effects pedals, and amps in your search for "the Tone." Studio guitarists have been known to hire cartage services just to deliver the truckload of effects units, amplifiers, and speakers they may need to please a picky producer.

Digital modeling technology re-creates the sound, look, and feel of classic amplifiers and guitar effects. Amp modeling is one of the hottest developments in computer music, and I'm here to tell you that it's getting better all the time. (See Figure 1.3.) This die-hard tube-head is convinced.

One of the odder uses of digital effects is adding noise to a pristine, digitally recorded sound. Yep, you can make your brand-new, state-of-the-art recording sound like a worn-out old phonograph record complete with hiss, crackles, pops, and skips. Ain't science wonderful?

Actually, adding noise to the mix makes a lot of sense. Say you've found the perfect beat on an ancient LP. You record some hand percussion, wah guitar, and vocals to add to the mix—but the pristine new tracks sound out of place. Dial up a lo-fi effect like Digidesign's D-Fi, add a dash of surface noise, and *voilà*! Who said disco was dead?

Figure 1.3
AmpliTube Uno not only looks like a huge stage rig, it also sounds like one. You can download it for free. See Appendix C, "Manufacturers."

Sound Design

Picture this: You and your family are watching videos from last summer's trip. On the screen, Uncle Billy mugs for the camera, takes a bite of Grandpa's chili, and lets out a scream that sounds like a Tyrannosaurus Rex being eviscerated by a fleet of mutant space weasels. Welcome to the wacky world of sound design.

Sound designers use every trick in the book to come up with the soundtracks you hear every day. By combining the recording, sampling, synthesizers, and effects tools inside your computer, you can, too. Home movies will never be the same.

Professional sound-design applications are well beyond the scope of this book, but I'll list some anyway just to whet your appetite. Who knows? Maybe you'll find your calling.

- Special effects for film
- TV commercials
- Radio
- Theatrical sound
- Electronic games
- Recording
- Cell phone ring tones
- Electronic novelties
- Halloween haunted houses

Recording Music

The single most-asked question I hear at parties, the most popular topic on chat rooms, the number-one query to salespeople in music stores is this: "Can I record a song on my computer?" The answer is an unqualified "Yes." You can record a song on just about any computer made in the past five years. Period.

What *kind* of recording you can do is another story. Digital audio requires huge amounts of processing power and storage; MIDI files are so small you can store thousands on an old-fashioned floppy disc and record huge multitrack projects on a Stone Age computer like the Commodore 64. Loop playback and manipulation falls somewhere in between.

We'll cover exactly what you need for each application in later chapters. For now, let's look at the different types of computer recording to give you an idea of what's possible.

MIDI

As I said earlier, MIDI is simply a bunch of code enabling digital devices to communicate. Like all digital code, MIDI is ideally suited for the computer. One of MIDI's most common uses is passing performance information from a keyboard controller to a synthesizer, either virtual or actual. The MIDI data from the keyboard tells the synth which key (or keys) you pressed, how hard you pressed it, and how long you held it. Then that MIDI data not only plays the sounds on your synthesizer or computer, it can also be recorded for later playback.

Keyboardists were the first to reap the benefits of the computer revolution. MIDI files are small, and sequencing programs relatively uncomplicated, so even the most sluggish computer can handle multiple tracks of MIDI data.

MIDI information is treated just like the text in your word processor: You can cut, paste, and duplicate blocks of data and move stuff from place to place. You can speed it up, change the key, or change the instrument it's played back on. Ever wonder what a drum part would sound like played by a clarinet quartet? May be just the ticket to spur your creativity.

But you don't have to be a skilled keyboardist to get in on the action. Legions of one-finger players take advantage of MIDI recording's powerful data manipulation to enter complicated drum and bass parts one note at a time. You don't even need a keyboard: MIDI rhythm sequencers, beat boxes, and drum machines get you rocking in no time with no more than your mouse. If you can point and click, you can record a song.

Even if you never have the slightest intention of using synthesizers or samplers in your music, MIDI sequencers offer tremendous power for your recording and performing chores. Most effects programs respond to MIDI automation, letting you make dramatic, real-time changes in your sound. And wait until you discover the joys of mix automation using a MIDI control.

But I'm getting ahead of myself.

> ❄ **WHAT'S A SEQUENCER?**
>
> The first real synthesizer designed by Robert Moog had circuitry to record and play back the control actions that defined the sounds in sequence. Thus the operator could set up a short musical loop that repeated over and over. As the technology matured, hardware sequencers were developed that stored more information.
>
> MIDI made it all easier, of course. It wasn't difficult to devise a program that would record the sequence of MIDI keystrokes you played, note when you played them relative to a timing standard in beats per minute (BPM), then play them back in the same order. In fact, when you play back a MIDI sequence, the computer and your instruments are literally re-creating the performance.
>
> MIDI sequencers do not record actual audio, but many programs combine both MIDI and digital audio recorders.

Loop-Based Recording

A *loop* is a short snippet of prerecorded audio or MIDI intended to be played over and over. For instance, you can take a couple measures of a drums playing a groove, add a simple repetitive bass line and guitar blast, and voilà! Instant funk!

I've already mentioned looping tools a number of times in connection with jam tracks and live performance, but did you know that it's easy to record your mixes and create your own loops?

All looping software lets you save a recording of your finished mix, though in some rare cases it's a platform-specific format that can be played back only on the original program. MIDI-based mixes may be saved as a specialized type of file called an SMF (Standard MIDI File) that is playable on any MIDI sequencer. Most Web browsers feature helper applications for playing SMFs, making the format one of the easiest ways to share your music on the Internet.

Audio looping software often can save completed songs in one of the standard audio file formats: WAV, AIFF, or MP3. Users of Apple's GarageBand (see Figure 1.4) have the option to export songs directly into iTunes, handy if you're one of the millions with an iPod.

Why be content to simply rearrange existing loops when it's so easy to record your own? Almost every looping program supports either MIDI or digital audio recording, though implementation and features vary wildly from program to program. The best programs approach the power of full-featured digital audio workstations.

Looping has come a long way from the early days of analog synthesizers playing short sequences. Many genres of music, particularly in the dance world, are extensively based on loops—whether that's a good thing is up to you. But loop-based recording has powerful applications in traditional recording, too.

Consider this: You have just about finished recording your new song. All that's left is to record the perfect solo. The old way took a lot of steps: reach for the mouse, hit "record," grab your

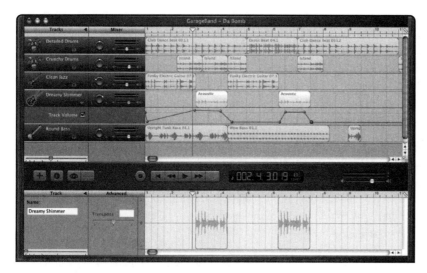

Figure 1.4
Apple's easy-to-use GarageBand loop arranger is included with every new Mac.

instrument, play the solo, put down your instrument, grab the mouse, stop the recording, roll back, and listen. If this sounds like a great way to kill creativity, you're dead right.

Why not set up a loop around the solo section and just play take after relaxed take, letting the software take care of saving each pass? With looping software, you can. Then just go back and choose the best one.

Digital Audio

The digital audio home studio is without a doubt the single most powerful change in the history of recording. Inexpensive digital studios have enabled legions of musicians who formerly would never see a recording contract to get their music heard. Even major artists use home studios to record demos or to track parts when inspiration strikes. Combined with the power of the Internet, the digital home studio has completely changed the way music is made, distributed, and enjoyed.

Sure, major record labels will always be around. *Somebody* has to design and market the next teen sensation. For the rest of us, independent is the way to go.

Because digital audio and recording are such huge subjects, much of this book is devoted to tips, tutorials, and techniques for recording at home. It doesn't matter if you can't tell your aux from a hole in the ground. You'll find the answers in Chapters 2, "Understanding the Gear," 6, and 7, "Track Three: Digital Recording for the Solo Musician."

WHAT'S DIGITAL AUDIO?

What we think of as sound is nothing more or less than waves of moving air. Pluck a guitar string. Immediately the string begins to vibrate. The vibrations are carried to the guitar's top, which then starts to vibrate itself. As the top moves up and down, it pushes against the air, creating a series of ripples, or waves. The waves move outward through the air, just as ripples spread across a pond when you drop a pebble.

Our ears are marvelously adapted to gather and focus sound waves, transmitting the energy via the eardrum and specialized hairs, bones, and other structures to nerve endings, which send bioelectrical information to our brain. We then decode the electrical impulses as the sound of a guitar string.

Analog sound amplification uses a smoothly variable electrical voltage to exactly mirror the air pressure changes of a moving sound wave. So we say that the voltage is *analogous* to the original changes in sound-pressure level, hence the term "analog" recording. Old-fashioned recording tape registers these continuous electrical changes as changes in magnetism. Picture a light bulb connected to a dimmer switch: As you turn the switch clockwise, the light gradually gets brighter; turn it counterclockwise, and it dims. You could say that the brightness of the bulb was an analog to the movement of your finger on the switch. Now contrast that to a standard wall switch. There are only two choices: The bulb is either on or off. We call that a binary system because there are only two ways to describe the light bulb's condition at any point in time.

That's the way computers work, too: They are really just a mess of switches that are turning off and on. So how do you convert a smooth sound wave into an on-or-off digital signal? You take a "picture" of it by reducing the frequency of the waves and their height to a single point on a graph. (See Figure 1.5.) Of course, one or two samples aren't going to tell you much—your nice smooth sound wave now looks like a bad drawing of the New York skyline. But if you take thousands and thousands of measurements each second, you can describe the shape of the original wave quite accurately. That's what digital audio's all about: taking a constantly variable sound wave and rendering it as a set of discrete measurements. By the way, the nerve cells in our ears and brain are binary, too: They are either sending a signal or resting. So you could say that digital audio has been around as long as we have.

Figure 1.5

Digitization changes a nice smooth audio waveform into a stepped approximation. The higher the sample rate (measured in kilohertz), the more accurately the digital recording will reproduce the original waveform.

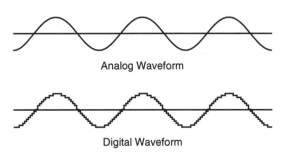

Analog Waveform

Digital Waveform

Digital recording used to be the domain of expensive pro recording studios and equally expensive home studios. Today you can build a dandy little home system capable of recording a fully produced, professional-sounding CD for well under a grand, *including* the computer and outboard gear! And digital recording is not just for experienced tech heads recording weird hyper-electronic-trance-fusion-bebop—I have heard very fine home recordings of unaccompanied cello and classical guitar made by musicians with absolutely no studio experience.

Later on I'll discuss exactly what you'll need in the way of a computer, microphones, and other gear in order to record both solo and groups. And we'll take a trip along the signal chain in Chapter 2. Chapter 7 talks about recording for the solo musician and singer/songwriter, whereas Chapter 8, "Track Four: All Together Now: The Desktop DAW," discusses recording groups and setting up what's called a project studio.

For now, let's look at some of what you can do. There's more to digital home recording than slamming out the next big hit. That's nice, too, though.

❋ **Practice.** When learning an instrument or perfecting a new piece, there is simply no better way to gauge your progress than to hear a recording of your playing. For most people, renting a studio is out of the question. Plus playing in front of strangers when the clock is ticking isn't exactly going to make you feel relaxed. When you are learning a new musical skill, the tendency is to think you cannot possibly sound any good. I always tell my students to listen to what they have *played*, not what they intended to play. Hearing yourself quickly points out any timing or intonation problems and focuses on areas that need improvement. And sometimes it's great to find out how great you actually sound! Keep a mic set up and connected to the computer where you practice, and you'll always be ready.

❋ **Archiving.** Several years ago, the last living player of a rare and beautiful South Pacific guitar style lay sick in a nursing home. Neither his children nor his grandchildren nor his great-grandchildren had learned to play his music. To them it was old-fashioned. And besides, as his grandchild told me, "I can always ask Grandfather to play for me." Then the old man died, and a type of music unique to that island died with him. What had been passed down from generation to generation will never be heard again. No one will ever again play the guitar the way the old man did. No one will ever know the joy that his music brought to the faces of the little children each morning when he walked to the fishing boats playing his "Patapata Maniata," his "Dawn Song," as the sun rose higher in the tropical sky. Maybe you don't think your music is worth preserving, either. But maybe, just maybe, it is.

❋ **Collaboration.** In the business world, there's telecommuting. Why go to the office when you can stay connected at home? We musicians can do that one better. We can record a musical idea on our computer in Des Moines and zap it across the planet to a drummer in Istanbul. He adds his ideas to the mix and shoots it to a keyboard ace in Paris, who sends it to a singer in Oz, on to a bassist in Barrow, and then back to you for the next round.

❋ **Fun.** There's no getting around it. Hearing a song take shape as you add each part and try out different mixes is a ball.

- ❋ **Band rehearsals.** Tired of waiting around while your guitar player tries to figure out the chords to your new song? Record it at home and send a CD a week before you get together. A swinging band is a happy band.

- ❋ **Demos.** A demo is a recording to show what you can do. Bands use them to get club gigs; songwriters send them out to swing a publishing contract; everybody uses them to try to get a record deal. Demos are also great to try out your ideas. You can record demo versions of every song and live with them for a couple of weeks. *Then* you'll be ready to record the finished masterpiece.

- ❋ **Sharing.** I have a friend who sends out a dandy new song each Christmas. Beats the heck out of those annoying, long letters. Or share your newfound musical skills with a group of like-minded people. Several online groups have started doing this. It's a great way to connect.

- ❋ **Fame and fortune.** Okay, the main reason we want to record at home is to let the whole world know just how amazingly amazing our music is. Yes, you can record a CD at home, get it played on the radio, get it played in dance clubs, sell it over the Internet, sell it in shopping malls, develop a fan base, go on tour, get your picture on the cover of *Rolling Stone*, and make millions and millions of dollars (well, hundreds of dollars, anyway). Others have, so why not you?

Combining MIDI, Loops, and Digital Recording

This is where the big dogs hang out: the digital audio workstation, or DAW. You've already read about how each of these elements can enhance your recording experience. Why not combine them all in one seamless recording environment?

When you get right down to it, a computer doesn't really know the differences in MIDI, loops, and digital audio. It's all ones and zeros as far as the CPU is concerned. So it makes a great deal of sense to incorporate all of the recording tools you'll need—a MIDI sequencer, loops, and digital audio recorder, plus software instruments, drum machine, effects, editing, and more—into a single program.

Powerhouse DAWs such as the Cubase family of products, Mark of the Unicorn's Digital Performer, Apple's Logic Pro, and Digidesign's flagship Pro Tools line let you work intuitively, jumping from one task to the next as your mood and needs dictate. Grab some beats and loop 'em for a rhythm bed, lay down sparkling MIDI keyboards and bass, trigger horn samples from your virtual instrument collection, dial up a snarling, overdriven amp for your guitar, and then add vocals. Add some effects to taste, try out a couple of mixes, mix it all down to stereo, and burn a CD. All with the same program.

Complex? You bet. Powerful? Absolutely.

Of course, not everybody likes to work that way. If you've been working with one particular program for a while, why dump all your skills and start over? That's why a number of interfacing protocols have cropped up. You can loop in your favorite looping program, sequence in a dedicated sequencer, and record digital audio in a third program, all synchronized perfectly behind the scenes.

As you can tell, I'm enthusiastic about recording on a computer. It is one of the most fun things you can do in your bedroom, though if I told you about the others, I could sell a lot more books....

Writing Music

So far we've talked about using your computer as a performance partner, a musical instrument, and a recording studio. So it should come as no surprise that your computer excels as a scribe, as well. But you probably didn't know that it could help you come up with lyrics or even inspire your creativity.

In fact, composers use computers in every part of the writing process. We've touched on using auto-accompaniment and looping tools to help write music. And for many, composing and recording go hand in hand. In this section I'll discuss the physical process of writing music with a computer. I'll get into specific software in Chapter 4, "Choosing Your Software: What Do You Want to Do?"

Scoring

Pity the music copyist of a few centuries ago. Every time the composer had a brainstorm, the poor fellow had to laboriously ink the score, note-by-note, staff by staff, page by page. And then he had to make a clean copy for each and every musician in the orchestra, carefully transposing for certain instruments and adding the proper number of rests for others.

Imagine how much faster it would have been if the composer could have made the changes directly into the computer, had the program automatically extract each part, correctly transposed and annotated, and then printed them out. Well, it's not only possible, it's also commonplace. Somewhere, there must be some lonely school band director who's still copying and collating music by hand. If you know of one, please tell him that there's hope.

But you don't have to be a composer or band director to take advantage of the power of a scoring program. In fact, you don't even have to know how to read music!

Let me hip you to a dirty little secret: Lots of musicians who can't read music use scoring programs to hear what an unfamiliar piece of written music sounds like. It's simple: Copy the notes one by one with your mouse or keyboard, and the program will play them back. Even better, many scoring programs support optical character recognition so you can scan in the music.

So how do you get an electric guitar player to turn down the volume? Put a piece of music in front of her. Okay, it's an old joke, but there is a grain of truth in it. Reading music for a guitar is difficult; you've got at least six different places to play middle C, for instance. That's why tablature was invented; it's a simplified musical notation that shows you exactly where to fret each note. Many scoring programs can generate tablature from written notation, which is great for learning new songs, and some will generate written notation from tablature, as well. Guitar-specific programs such as Finale Guitar or Sibelius' G7 are great choices.

Many sequencers and DAWs spit out written scores from your input, with varying degrees of success. But if you want real control over the final look, pick up a scoring program. You may choose to have your score look like it was professionally engraved or opt for the casual, hand-written look common in jazz. Scoring programs range from relatively simple shareware such as TablEdit and easy-to-use entry-level programs such as MakeMusic's PrintMusic! all the way up to richly complex work environments such as Finale and Sibelius.

One more thing: Just about any scoring program worth its salt speaks MIDI. So all you have to do is play your keyboard, MIDI guitar, or whatever, and out comes a perfectly formatted piece of music.

Lead Sheets

Essentially a type of score, a lead sheet usually has the lyrics or melody written out along with the chords and any instructions specific to the song. (See Figure 1.6.) Lead sheets are handy for everything from compiling fake books to band practice to teaching guitar to leading campfire sing alongs.

Often the lead sheet will contain nothing more than a bunch of chord symbols with slashes to indicate the rhythm. Studio musicians in Nashville, who may play on a dozen songs a day, developed a numbering system to quickly communicate the chord changes and make rapid adjustments in case the singer needs to change the key. Singer/guitarists often like to see the lyrics with chord symbols written directly above the words.

The time-honored way to write one is on a napkin while drinking coffee late at night in a greasy spoon. You can do better than that. Most scoring programs support different kinds of alternate notation, including the Nashville Numbering System and percussion notation. Even better, the same auto-accompaniment tools that helped you write the song often can print out a basic lead sheet for you.

Figure 1.6
A lead sheet is a valuable tool for rehearsal or performance.

Lyrics and Songwriting

Writing lyrics can be a lonely job. If you are anything like me, you have dozens of notebooks and file folders stuffed to the gills with illegible scribblings, crossed-out lyrics, hastily inserted additions, and obscure lyric fragments.

Help is only a mouse click away. Songwriting sites have proliferated on the Web: You can find everything from online courses offering step-by-step guidance to sites that will randomly generate lyrics in the style of popular songwriters!

If you're serious about songwriting, you need serious songwriting software. The best combines such word processing features as a spell checker, dictionary, and thesaurus with tools to help you quickly shape your creation. Programs such as LyricPro even include tools to help you create a bio and promote your new creations! Many will scan your lyrics to ensure that your syllables fit the beat and check your rhymes, suggesting alternate words when you get stuck. A database function keeps track of your changes so you can resurrect that perfect lyric you discarded three months ago. A few full-featured programs, such as MasterWriter, include tools for generating and recording melodies, beats, and chords. Some even bundle digital recording functions so you can burn your song to a CD complete with vocals!

Or maybe you just need some help with certain parts of the process. Rhyming and slang dictionaries can help you find the right word. Phrase databases suggest new lyrics and point out clichés.

Or you can get help finding the right song form, fire up an interactive arranging tool, or learn tips and techniques from the pros.

When you're done, check out a database of publishers and bone up on the ins and outs of songwriting contracts and music law.

Inspiration

A recent clever TV commercial showed a frustrated composer struggling at the keyboard, his studio floor littered with crumpled paper. As he stared out his window, a flock of birds landed on nearby electrical wires—black shapes lined up on five parallel lines. With a flash of inspiration, he recognized the shapes as music and played the melody.

Sometimes inspiration springs from unlikely places. Why not see what your computer can come up with? Although there's no telling what may inspire you, consider these suggestions a starting point:

* **Automatic composition.** Let the computer come up with the music. If it sounds good, make it your own.

* **Granular synthesis.** Generate entirely new sounds by running an audio sample through a freeware granular synthesis generator. I can't describe the arcane mathematical process that makes it work, but you've never heard anything like it.

* **Effects tricks #1.** Legendary reggae producer Lee "Scratch" Perry let his vocal delay effects run wild over basic bass and drum tracks, inventing a whole new genre of music. You can, too.

* **Found sounds.** Who says you can't harness the rhythmic power of your household appliances? More than one great song started off by jammin' with the Maytag.

* **Picture this.** The old song says, "A pretty girl is like a symphony." Run a digital picture of her through an image synthesizer and you'll hear it for yourself!

* **New sounds from old sources.** Experiment with unlikely sounds triggered from your sequencer—send drum sounds to a pitched instrument, or see what happens when your horn parts are played as a New Age pad.

* **Effects tricks #2.** What happens when you run your voice through every effect in your arsenal?

* **It's not stealing, it's research.** Inspiration is yours for the asking online. Any number of musicians are willing to share their coolest loops, samples, and standard MIDI files.

❄ **Train wrecks are beautiful.** Try fooling with the styles in your auto-accompaniment program. Who knew your sensitive ballad would make such a great polka? For more weird fun, merge two or three completely different songs into one polyrhythmic, harmelodic monster.

❄ **No solo mio.** Lonely? Uninspired? Find a writing partner online. The Web is a beautiful thing.

Learning Music

Computers delight in repetitive tasks. They never get tired, they never complain, they are endlessly patient. A computer will never cancel a lesson because a better gig came up. A computer can listen to you massacre "Little Wing" ten thousand times without ever speculating on your parentage or comparing you to an unsavory bit of human anatomy. In short, a computer is the ideal music teacher.

Schools know this, of course. Or at least, schools in counties that haven't entirely eliminated music and art from the curriculum do. If you're a parent living in one of those school districts, run, don't walk, to buy your child a computer and some basic music-education software. It has been proved time and again: Music is an essential part of any child's development and leads to success with reading, mathematics, writing, and social skills. Give your child music, and you'll prepare her for life.

Educational programs run from point-and-play games for toddlers all the way up to university-level music courses. No matter what the instrument or skill level, there's bound to be software to help.

And don't overlook the tremendous potential of the Web. With just a few well-placed queries, I've found everything from interactive guitar-tuning applets and string-gauge calculators to online lessons, sound clips of unfamiliar musical styles, and advice on how to avoid repetitive stress injury.

Music for Children

A few years back, parents began playing classical music to their newborns in the hopes of boosting their children's IQ. Whether or not the "Mozart Effect" was real, it did boost CD sales and no doubt helped a few fussy babies drift off to sleep.

There are children's music programs to cover every age and ability, from hearing and repeating simple patterns for preschoolers to learning to play the piano. Some take a creative approach, encouraging children to make new sounds and explore the worlds of melody, rhythm, and harmony. Some teach specific skills, such as reading music or playing a particular piece. Kids love looping and DJ programs because they can instantly create music that sounds just like what they hear on TV.

Even if you don't want your precious baby to grow up to be a musician—or, God forbid, marry one—do yourself a favor and look into what children's music software offers. Early music education reinforces other important learning skills. Kids find it fun. Music is healthy, intellectually stimulating, and calming all at the same time. And it's so much better that watching Junior morph into a game-playing, TV-addicted couch blob.

Learning an Instrument

I've already said that your computer may be the most patient music teacher you'll ever know. But one thing a computer can never do is inspire you to excel at music the way a sympathetic human can, right? Well...

Learning any musical instrument involves a number of discrete steps. First you must learn to produce sound on your instrument (easier on some than others!), then become familiar with the basic repertoire, develop your technique as you explore more challenging music, and finally, make the instrument an extension of your soul. I have taught music to adults and children for many, many years, and I can say that your computer can be of invaluable assistance through all of these steps—even the last. For what do we musicians desire above all things but to be able to play music freely and effortlessly, as if our instruments were hard-wired to our brains and fingers?

I'll let you in on the Big Secret: You reach that stage through practice, evaluation, more practice, refinement, and yet more practice. There is simply no substitute for putting in the time, even when you are just starting out. So wouldn't it be great if the process were fun? How about if you could get instant feedback on your performance so you could correct your mistakes before they become bad habits? Or play a video game that actually taught you to read music? What if you could play along with a band or orchestra, no matter what your proficiency? Or make a recording to showcase your new skills? While we're at it, why not start playing music in weeks instead of years?

This is where computer-assisted music education excels. Your computer will speed up the learning process big time, no matter what your level. In fact, beginners can make real, satisfying music right from the start.

Since MIDI was originally developed for electronic keyboards, it will come as no surprise that keyboard and piano tutors abound at all levels. If you don't own an instrument, look for a system that bundles software with a keyboard. Lessons come tailored for young children, middle and high school music students, advanced players, and adult beginners. Always wanted to play the piano, but were afraid of failure? Pick up the eMedia Piano and Keyboard Method and worry no more.

Almost all keyboard-instruction software comes loaded with features designed to improve your playing without the frustration of trying to learn on your own. Interactive tutorials monitor your progress and suggest new lessons based on your ability. Sight-reading and ear-training games make these important tasks fun. Scale- and chord-study modules help you drill without tedium. Many programs automatically generate backing tracks so that you can hear your music in the proper context. Most will let you concentrate on just the right or left hand part.

Like a million other nine-year-old kids, I dropped out of piano lessons after only one year because I couldn't relate to the boring little ditties foisted on me each week. I wanted boogie-woogie, and dear Mrs. Ladyslipper taught only "Three Little Lamby-kins." You have it so much better. Choose from a wide variety of popular, rock, and blues styles. PG Music's popular Pianist Series makes it possible to master Latin music, get greasy with some New Orleans funk, or get inside an Oscar Peterson jazz solo. And let's not forget the classics! Ah, if only Mrs. Ladyslipper were around now.

Guitarists and electric bassists have a large range of choices, from play-along jam tracks to DVD lessons with split-screen video and scrolling tablature and fingerboards to full-blown interactive tutors. As with the keyboard instruction, the lessons include numerous modules to speed the learning process and make it fun. Expect to find a tuner, animated fret boards, video with close-ups of right and left hand positions, chord charts and dictionaries, backing tracks, and more. With products from eMedia, PG Music, SDG Soft, and many others, you can learn note-for-note solos from such great players as Jimi Hendrix and Eric Clapton, study the classics, learn the secrets of jazz soloing, or just improve your technique.

Several excellent guitar-to-computer interfaces have come on the market in the last few years, making truly interactive lessons a reality. And don't overlook the myriad lessons and tablature sites on the Internet. You can even find lessons to help you set and repair your axe or get the most out of your effects pedals and amp. If you want to learn guitar, your wait is over. (See Figure 1.7.)

Figure 1.7
The Line 6 GuitarPort
makes it easy to connect
your guitar to the Internet.

Drummers and percussionists haven't been forgotten. Software lessons feature step-by-step in-struction, video lessons with master drummers, scrolling notation, jam tracks, help with reading, tips on setting up your kit, and more. Develop and improve your rhythm and time by playing along on any MIDI instrument or drum pads. Even if you don't play the drums, you can find lessons to help you program realistic parts on your drum machine or rhythm sequencer.

No matter what your instrument, there's probably instructional software. Harmonica? Yep. Cello? But of course. Voice? Naturally. I have even found resources for bagpipes.

Although nothing can take the place of a qualified music teacher, your computer can greatly enhance your learning of just about any instrument. And teachers take note: Incorporating computer-based learning will give your students the chance to succeed. After all, one of the greatest joys of being a musician is sharing our knowledge.

Ear Training

Eons before writing was invented, musicians played and sang. Music has always been there: for dancing, for celebrations, or to commemorate a battle, calm a baby, or mourn a death. How did these ancient musicians learn their art? How did they pass their songs and melodies down through generations? How did they know what to play? By listening. All music was played by ear until just a few short centuries ago. And even today, many types still are.

How does a jazz pianist know how to shape her accompaniment? How does a rock guitarist know what chords are being played so he can play his solo? How does a composer know what chords to play behind a brand new melody? How can musicians from different countries and cultures sit down together and create wondrously spontaneous music at a jam session? The answer is the same: by listening. Or, to be more accurate, by knowing *how* to listen and knowing *what* you are hearing.

That's what ear training is all about. Some types of music, notably folk styles such as Celtic or bluegrass, are simply meant to be played by ear. And music with a lot of improvisation, such as jazz, rock, and blues, requires the quick response that can come only from an educated ear.

But why would a piano player who reads fluently need ear training? Well, it really does help to be able to *hear* the music, doesn't it?

Ear training is generally part of learning music in school. In my dismal experience, the instructor stood at the head of the classroom pounding out chords as we laboriously attempted to write them out. The next day we would get our corrected manuscripts and learn how we did. By then, of course, we had completely forgotten what the lesson sounded like. Sorry, Charlie, but that ain't the way.

Guess what? Ear training on the computer is fun. Spend your time playing games while you learn to hear the notes, intervals, chords, and rhythms. See if you can play back a melody the first time you hear it. Learn to hear written music in your head before you play it.

No matter what your instrument or taste in music, your playing will improve with a little time spent learning to hear scales, intervals, and chords using programs like the Personal Ear Trainer and Ars Nova's extensive Practica Musica.

Music Theory

Breathe the words "music theory" to most amateur musicians, and they will run away screaming. Funny thing is, the same words to a pro are, well, music to the ears. Why the difference? Chalk it up to fear of the unknown. Professionals know that having a solid understanding of how music works is as important as knowing the ins and outs of an auto engine for a race car mechanic.

So what exactly is music theory, anyway? And why do you need to invest your time into learning it? Say you've been playing a song for years in the key of E, and you meet a wonderful singer who nails it every time. You realize that the two of you make a potent pair, only he sings the song in A flat. Using a chord transposition chart, you could tediously find each chord for the new key. However, if you knew how the chords of the song related to each other musically, you could transpose on the fly.

Or maybe you want to know how to fit a melody to a cool set of chords you've come up with. Or find new chords to an old melody. Or write something in an unfamiliar musical style. Or build harmony lines that make musical sense. Maybe you simply wish you could read those dots on the paper.

Here's something else to consider: Beginning improvisers all sound the same. Ever wonder why? Their solos wander up and down a simplified pattern they learned somewhere. They may throw in a few hot licks here and there, painstakingly memorized from a book or CD. But there's no sense of connectedness, no soul.

Soloing is not just about scales, licks, and patterns; it's about knowing which notes to play against which chords to create a personal musical statement. And it's about knowing where the music is going next, where it's been, and what it is trying to say.

That's exactly what you'll gain from having a little theory under your hat.

About now, you probably expect me to say, "And your trusty computer will make it fun and fast and exciting as all heck!" Sorry to sound like a broken record (assuming that anyone knows what one sounds like anymore), but, yes, it will.

As with learning a musical instrument, learning theory takes practice and drill. Why not make a game out of it? That's what most of the programs do. Choose to study at any level, with courses geared to real, practical stuff that you need to know. Guitarists: Get inside chords, scales, and soloing. Classical players: Study the history of music, form, and the basics of harmony. Drummers: Learn to read rhythms to expand your horizons. You can take the equivalent of a university-level course in early music or jazz. Kids can get started out in music with a solid foundation. Adults can finally learn how to read music.

And you can do it all in the privacy of your own home using programs such as Take Note's C.A.T.S. software (Computer-Aided Theory Skills) or MiBAC's excellent series of music lessons. Ain't the modern world grand?

So far we've been talking about making music in, on, and with your computer. To round out this chapter, I'm going to discuss a few other things you and your digital pal can do, such as creating multimedia, sharing and enjoying music, and gathering information to help you meet your goals.

Multimedia

Multimedia is one of those things that everybody talks about, but nobody really knows what it is. Take a look at the ads: Billy's Kustom Komputers proclaims, "The New ABZ-3000 is Multimedia Ready!" Crazy Cyd's Compu-Shack shouts, "Blast through Multimedia with the Zyzz 2.4.2.1X!" In fact, you'd be hard-pressed to find a machine that *doesn't* do multimedia, whatever the heck it is.

Or consider this: Everything from interactive Web sites to director's cut DVDs to airport advertising kiosks uses the term. So what is it, anyway?

The short answer is that multimedia is anything that combines two or more processes, such as music, text, pictures, video, animation, graphics, etc. The word combines *multi-*, as in many, and *media*, used in the sense of the physical devices or structures used to record, store, and transfer information. The familiar enhanced CDs combining CD audio with concert footage and band videos are an emerging form of multimedia. Ditto Web sites with streaming audio and Flash animations.

By the way, if you want to be picky about it, reading a comic book while listening to music on MTV is about as multimedia as it gets.

Anyway, if you can imagine it, you can probably do it.

* **Slideshows.** Probably everyone on Earth now knows about Apple's iPod Photo, the portable device that seamlessly integrates your photos and music. Options abound for every computer and budget.

* **Soundtracks for PowerPoint.** Give your next presentation some real punch with a slammin' original soundtrack and watch what happens. Who knew the VP played air guitar?

* **Video.** A surprising number of software DAWs integrate video playback. So you can spot dialog, add special effects, and synchronize music while working inside a familiar environment without the need for expensive external equipment or synchronization.

* **Enhanced CDs.** An enhanced CD acts like a normal CD on a music player and like a CD-ROM on a computer. Compact discs can store a lot of digital information: up to 700MB. That translates to almost 80 minutes of music. Why not use some of that space for video clips, photos, links, or whatever else you can think of? Enhanced CDs are a great promo tool for yourself or your band.

* **Web sites.** Want to grab more attention for your Web site? Adding music is surprisingly easy. MIDI files are tiny and very well supported, making them the universal format of choice, playable on even the slowest dial-up connection. Thanks to the many audio-compression schemes, visitors can hear your baby's first words or your latest song. With a fast enough

connection, you can even set up 24-hour, real-time streaming audio from your Web site: *Radio Free You.*

Sharing and Enjoying Music

Unless you have been living in a cave for the past 10 years, you already know that the personal computer has profoundly changed the way music is distributed and enjoyed. A few clicks of the mouse open up a galaxy of songs from around the world. Listen to music you would never hear on your local radio, discover bands long gone or so new they haven't toured yet, or compare every single version of "Louie Louie" ever recorded.

❄ **THE DARK SIDE OF FILE SHARING**

Unlimited free music—that's what it's all about, isn't it? Cut out the corporados and forge direct connections between the music creators and their public. Hey, radio doesn't cost anything, so why should downloads? Besides, I listen to music only for my own enjoyment. It's not like I'm stealing or anything. After all, if I bought the CD, why can't I share it with my friends?

For some, including this writer, the revolution has been a decidedly mixed blessing. Legitimate digital distribution is a great thing, but sad to say, the vast majority of file sharing is still done illegally. As an independent recording artist and songwriter, I've seen my sales and royalties take a hit with each wave of the sharing phenomenon, starting way back with home taping. Many of my songs and CDs are offered as free downloads without my permission, and I'm too small a fish to be able to do anything to stop it. I have had people tell me to my face that they don't need to buy my latest CD because someone ripped them a copy as a Christmas present or they "found" the song they wanted on a friend's computer.

So what, you say? Isn't it better to get the exposure and let someone hear my music who may not buy it otherwise? Well, as any mountain climber knows, you can die of exposure. But the real issue is this: If I choose to give away my music, that's my right. If someone else makes that choice, it's theft, pure and simple.

For those of you who contend that sharing intellectual property is a god-given right, I'd like to share some of yours. So how about letting me download your credit card numbers, personal info, and bank account records? After all, it's just digital information stored on a computer somewhere. Who could get hurt?

Distributing Music

Digital music distribution takes many forms. Peer-to-peer file-sharing networks bring millions of songs to your desktop instantaneously. (See "The Dark Side of File Sharing" for another perspective.) Online music stores, such as Apple's iTunes, let you purchase individual songs or entire albums. Some services allow unlimited downloads for a monthly fee, while other sites let bands and solo artists offer their music directly.

Take it from me, distribution used to be nigh on impossible for an independent musician. Unless you had the backing of a major label, you could pretty much forget about selling your product in stores outside of your hometown. Ditto getting radio airplay: Even if you were to find a list and mail your CD to every music director in the country, do you really think any of them actually listen to unsolicited material? I hate to break the news, but your precious, unopened CDs are peacefully sleeping in a landfill somewhere.

Getting your music out to the world via the Web is so much easier. For many, it has been the key to making the jump from part-time weekend-warrior status to professional careers. For others, it's just a great way to get their songs heard. And there is something so satisfying in receiving a fan letter from a distant continent.

No matter what kind of music you create, someone, somewhere, wants to hear it. You can find sharing networks devoted to particular regions, bands, instruments, and musical styles. There are even sites devoted to specific software platforms, so you don't even have to worry about converting file formats. Linking to sites like IndieMusic.com helps Web surfers find your site. Other sites will help you create a Web page and make it easy to upload your music. And even the big dogs like iTunes, Rhapsody, Musicmatch, and Napster carry recordings by independent artists.

❋ BABY YOUR MUSIC

Of course, there are now almost as many digital outlets as bricks-and-mortar music stores. So we're right back where we were before: How's a boy to keep track of it all? One word: CDBaby.

CDBaby (http://www.cdbaby.com) was founded by Derek Silvers as a way for a handful of independent musicians like him to sell CDs over the Internet. It has grown into the coolest, most honest, most creative, easy-to-use, widest-reaching, nicest, and possibly best distribution option ever conceived. Besides helping you market, sell, and ship your CDs, CDBaby gets your music placed with dozens of online music stores via an extremely fair digital distribution service. It will even set you up to take credit cards for sales at your gigs!

I know this sounds like an ad. It isn't. I've been in this biz a long time, with the scars to prove it. CDBaby is the only distributor I've worked with who's on the side of music, truth, and justice.

Archiving and Restoring Music...

Sure, digital audio is great. Pop in a CD and rip the music to your hard disc. Compress it and send it off to a portable player. Download a song and burn it to a CD. But what about all that great music on LPs, 45s, and 78s? Only a fraction of what's been recorded will ever make it to CD. Wouldn't it be great to listen to it on your portable? Or maybe you have tons of old records lying around, and you need the space. Or what about all those song ideas locked away on 4-track cassettes, or the ancient audiotape of your grandmother's accordion recital?

If you can still play it, you can digitize it. Hooking up a cassette or reel-to-reel deck is a snap: Just plug it into the proper input on your sound card or audio interface. Phonograph records require a special RIAA preamp, so dig out that old tuner and wire it up. A few sound cards have the preamps wired in, or you can pick up one of the new preamps designed for computer audio; some even have USB ports, eliminating the need for a sound card.

Once you've transferred the music to your hard drive, the fun begins. Audio-restoration software abounds at every price point, from simple shareware and freeware programs to inexpensive consumer choices, often bundled with CD-burning software to complex, fully professional tool kits such as the Waves Audio Restoration packages. (See Figure 1.8.) At the very least, you'll be able to minimize record surface noise and tape hiss, fix turntable rumble, and repair minor clicks and pops. High-end systems will make a worn-out old 78 sound as good as a newly recorded CD.

Need another reason? You can store 10,000 songs on a hard drive the size of a pack of cards. Or you can build a shelf for your records—say 14 inches high by 14 inches deep by 100 feet long, give or take a few feet.

Figure 1.8
Sound Soap Pro scrubs audio until it shines.

And in Conclusion...

As you can see, there is a lot more to music and computers than just downloading the latest Sex Pistols release. Believe me, I've only scratched the surface. After reading this far, I hope you've gotten a few new ideas. Most likely, you've skipped around, just reading about the topics that you're interested in right now. That's cool. As you read through this book, check back here from time to time. Maybe you'll find a new way to approach writing by using algorithmic composition. Maybe you'll find you want to add real instruments to your beats or use virtual instruments in your all-acoustic CD.

To round out this chapter, here are some more ways your computer will guide you on your musical journey:

❋ **Promotion.** I've already mentioned enhanced CDs, digital distribution, and Web sites, but don't overlook the basic day-to-day promo chores you'll need: maintaining fan databases, developing a graphic image and logo, creating press releases, sending out mailings, designing posters and print advertising, coordinating bookings, and producing videos.

❋ **Business.** Keep track of your earnings and your expenses. Then prepare and pay your taxes. Sorry.

❋ **Copyright.** If you write original music or lyrics, you have the right to decide how they're used. The "people's copyright," sending your composition to yourself by registered mail, doesn't do much more than establish the date you mailed the letter. Go to www.copyright.gov and download the forms and instructions you need. Send them to Washington along with a printed score or recording and get some real protection.

❋ **Organizations and groups.** No matter what your interest, there's a group devoted to it on the Internet. Formal songwriters' organizations, such as BMI, ASCAP, and SESAC, maintain an active presence. If you intend to record and release an album that includes one or more cover songs, get the licenses you need at www.songfile.com.

❋ **Support.** You already know that everything related to your computer music system—each software program, each bit of hardware—has online tech support. But you may not be aware that many manufacturers and retailers have set up moderated discussion groups where you can reap the experience of dedicated people like you who are in the trenches. Often these sites are the first to spot potential problems or identify groovy new techniques.

There's more, but that's a subject for another book.

The next chapter looks at the ins and outs of recording and follows the signal chain from the sound source all the way to the computer.

2 Understanding the Gear

Even if you'll never record your own loops or create MIDI sequences, chances are that the software you use incorporates many features and functions derived from the glory days of analog recording. What's more, for the most part, how signals flow from the source through a mixer and on to their final destination is the same regardless of what kind of system you have or what kind of work you do. You can figure out how to use any software by reading the manual and/or fooling around with it long enough, but software is useless if you can't get sound out of it. If you don't know the difference between a track and a channel, think a ground loop is a drum pattern played on a dirty drum, or can't properly set up your speakers, you'll be dead in the water before you even get started.

That's what this chapter is all about. My aim is to give you a solid foundation on how sound travels from point A to point B; how it can be stored, modified, and changed; and how it eventually gets to your listener. I don't expect you to read it in one sitting—in fact, I don't expect you to read any of the chapters from start to finish. That's why I'll be covering some of the same ground from a variety of viewpoints in Chapter 5, "Track One: MIDI," Chapter 6, "Track Two: Looping Tools," and Chapter 7, "Track Three: Digital Recording for the Solo Musician." So feel free to jump around, but come back here from time to time to bone up on some of the concepts you'll find later in the book.

A Brief History of Recording

Music is fleeting; once the sound has died away, it's gone forever. For most of our history, the only way to hear music was to sit in front of someone who was playing an instrument or singing and open your ears. Before the invention of written music a few hundred years ago, the only way to create a *record* of how a song went would be to teach it to someone, who could then pass it down to someone else. So if you were the King High Pooh-Bah, your record collection would be the court musicians and singers and their memories. Not exactly a portable solution.

Over the years, all kinds of fun mechanical contraptions have sprung up to play back music. The one most people are familiar with is the music box. Turn a little crank and a metal drum spins around; little spikes on the drum strike tuned metal bars. What you get is a tinkly rendition of a familiar song. Change the drum and you can play a different song. The Victorian player piano took this approach even further: Long rolls of paper laced with perforations corresponding to the pitch and length of the desired notes fed through a mechanism that played the keys. Piano rolls, which could capture the timing and nuances of individual performers, were cheap and easy to manufacture and became the first popular mass-distributed pop music.

So what does this have to do with recording? Everything. Recording is about preserving and transmitting information. A record is not a flat piece of plastic with a hole in the middle; it's what's stored there. Bookkeepers keep financial data in record books; bankers record a deed when they write it down. Records are information.

That flat bit of grooved vinyl was once called a "phonograph record." Depending on its size and what it was meant to be played on, it may be a 45 (45 RPM phonograph record) or an LP (long-playing 33 1/3 RPM phonograph record). We just got in the habit of shortening the name. Just as a CD could be called a "compact disc digital audio record." So it's really okay to call a CD a record. Not that anyone ever would.

As you will discover, modern MIDI sequencers (a sequencer is a MIDI recorder) and loop-based recording and playback software are the direct descendants of those early mechanical music devices such as player pianos and the classic street-corner barrel organ. Which may explain why I sometimes feel like a monkey when I'm stuck trying to figure out what to do next....

Audio Recording in an Analog World

What MIDI and player pianos have in common is that they are real-time performance technologies. In other words, a piano roll and a MIDI sequence are both a set of instructions telling a musical instrument how to play; run the instructions and you'll hear the music played back in the present moment. (You could even say that memorization and written notation work the same way.)

But what if you want to hear an original performance played by the original musicians? Thanks to some clever folks who lived in the late nineteenth and early twentieth centuries, you can.

A little background: Sound is basically vibrations moving through the air, sort of like the way waves move across the surface of the water. When the sound waves strike your eardrum, a thin membrane stretched across your ear canal, the eardrum, starts to vibrate, too. (See Figure 2.1.) The vibrations are picked up by nerves and transmitted to your brain, where they are decoded into what you hear as sound.

In fact, any drumhead will vibrate when you direct sound waves at it. So what would happen if you attached a thin needle to the drum's surface and traced the up and down movements onto something, a rotating wax cylinder, say? You'd get a groove whose depth mirrored the vibrations

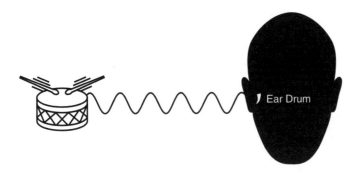

Figure 2.1
Sound moves through the air the same way waves move through water.

Ear Drum

of the drum over time. (Engineers would call the groove an *analog* of the original sound's vibrations because it mirrors one process—changes in air pressure caused by sound waves—with another—changes in the depth of a groove spiraling around the cylinder.) If you then reversed the process, you'd make the drumhead vibrate again. And since sound is just vibrations moving through air, you'd hear a reproduction of the original.

That's exactly how audio recording was born. There's some question about who thought it up first, but that's not important. By 1894, a German named Emile Berliner had the bright idea of cutting the grooves into a flat rubber disc that could be mass produced, and the world has never been the same.

Electronic amplifiers that replaced the mechanical process brought gradual improvements in recording technology throughout the early years. But there was one basic drawback: Everything had to be recorded "live" in a single take. Records were still made by cutting a groove directly onto a disc. There was no way to go back and fix a blown note, or to add instruments one at a time, or to splice together pieces of several performances into a single flawless version.

Thanks to the invention of magnetic tape shortly before the Second World War, all of that changed forever.

Multitrack Basics

Magnetic tape is another analog medium. You may even say it's a two-stage analog. First an amplifier translates the air pressure differences from sound waves into a constantly variable current. As the tape passes over an electromagnetic record head, magnetic particles on the surface are then realigned to reflect the changes in the electrical current.

It didn't take long for someone to figure out that you could cut and splice magnetic tape as easily as you could paper. All of a sudden engineers could take the best bits from multiple performances and join them into one perfect take or create new arrangements from the original material. If you set up a second recorder and sang along to the playback from the first machine, you could record a duet with yourself. Record your normal voice with the tape running slower than normal, and it would sound unnaturally high-pitched played back at normal speeds. Run a section of the tape through a second recorder with the record and playback heads widely spaced, and you could create a delayed echo effect.

Since we use two ears to locate sounds in space, it was only natural to want to reproduce sound coming from two speakers instead of one. That led to the first stereo, or two-track, recorders. But why stop there? If you can squeeze in two record heads, why not four? Or 8, 16, or even 24? Indeed, if you can get the machines to start and stop together, why not chain multiple recorders together for megabuck, megatrack recording projects? Welcome to the '80s.

WHAT'S A TRACK?

The electromagnetic impulses from the record head cause magnetic particles on the tape to shift position. Since the tape is moving, the disruption leaves a path, or track, sort of like when you run a single finger through wet sand at the beach. Multiple record heads create multiple tracks. Open your hand, and you'll leave four tracks in the sand from your four fingers.

Each record head has a corresponding playback head that reads the information stored on the tape. So a four-track recorder will handle four separate inputs at the same time. It's become common to use the term *track* as shorthand for what's recorded, too. So you may say, "Daddy-o, that conga track was smokin'!" And the process of recording is sometimes called "tracking." Even though computer data is not written as tracks, we still use the term in digital audio and MIDI recording.

Multitrack recording fundamentally changed the way music was created. Instead of recording an entire song in one take, the artist could build things up one track at a time. The recording studio became a creative tool for experimentation and composition.

The first digital recorders—the descendants of digital video recorders, believe it or not—also used tape for the simple reason that computer storage and memory was simply too expensive. A book published as recently as 1992 estimated that setting up a basic 8-track digital audio and MIDI computer workstation with a couple of synthesizers and a sampler would set you back an astonishing $45,000! Today you can do 10 times the work on a system that costs one twentieth as much. And you'll do it faster, better, and more reliably.

The Analog Legacy

But even with all of this brave new technology, we still use lots of terms and concepts from the old days. Here are a few oldies you should know, along with some terms unique to digital recording.

* **Arm.** To ready a track for recording. Also called *record enable*.

* **Destructive/nondestructive recording and editing.** With tape, the only way to re-record a part was to write the new one over the old, effectively erasing the original. Since digital data isn't written in a straight line, the new material won't erase the old. The same thing

goes for editing: Cutting a section out of a taped recording meant physically taking a chunk out of the tape. Not any more.

✳ **Edit.** To change something after it's been recorded. Digital data, both audio and MIDI, is sublimely easy to edit.

✳ **Engineer.** Once upon a time, recording engineers were real science-whiz engineers—pocket protectors, white lab coats, and all.

✳ **Fast forward.** The opposite of rewind. Quickly moving forward through the song by speeding up the tape machine's motors. Since random-access recorders have the ability to instantaneously jump to any point, it doesn't make a whole lot of sense to have fast forward and rewind functions, but there you go.

✳ **Flange.** A "whooshing" sound effect. Originally created by running your thumb along the flange of a tape reel during playback. Now the effect is created electronically.

✳ **Locate point.** A user-defined location to begin playback at some point other than the song's beginning. Handy to define parts of a song, such as a verse or chorus, to set punch-in and punch-out points, or to set the beginning and ending points for edit regions. Sometimes called *markers.*

✳ **Loop.** An old tape trick. Cut out a small section of tape and attach the two ends together to form a loop. The looped section will play over and over, endlessly. Nowadays the term refers either to a short repeated section of time within an arrangement or to a chunk of MIDI or audio data intended to be repeated.

✳ **Overdub.** On analog recorders, overdubbing meant adding a new track to a tape that already had recorded material. So a vocalist could overdub a part on track 4 while listening to playback of the band on tracks 1, 2, and 3. With computer recorders, overdubbing writes new material to an existing track without erasing what's already there.

✳ **Pre-roll.** If you select pre-roll, playback will begin a set amount of time before the locate point. Useful to give you time to get ready for a punch-in. Post-roll lets the transport move a set time past the stop point. Comes from the practice of manually "rolling" the tape reels backward or forward slightly.

✳ **Punch-in/punch-out.** A recording technique where you record over a small bit of pre-recorded material, say, to fix a flubbed note.

✳ **Rewind.** Reversing the motor on the tape transport to wind the tape backward. Many software recorders still use a rewind button to slowly move backward through the song.

✳ **Rolling.** An engineer's exclamation to let everyone know that the tape was moving and set to record. Obviously, hard-disc recorders don't "roll," but you'll still encounter the term.

* **Scribble strip.** An area on a mixer set aside to write notes and track assignments. Software recorders usually let you name your tracks directly.

* **Scrub.** Tape engineers would manually rock the reels back and forth while listening to the playback to precisely determine an edit or punch-in point. Most DAWs and MIDI sequencers support scrubbing, in essence playing back the data very slowly over a user-specified area.

* **Splice.** The art of joining two sections of tape together; also the name of the joint. Software still uses the term to represent lining up two chunks of audio one after the other.

* **Take.** Each recording pass is called a take. Sometimes it takes multiple takes to get a keeper.

* **Track.** A linear representation of a place to store recorded data. Computers differ from tape recorders in that you can have many non-playing virtual tracks, each storing a take, for each track.

* **Transport.** The motors, gears, and spindles that would spin the reels and move the tape across the record and playback heads. Also, the collection of switches that controlled those functions. Most software still uses tape-style transport controls such as stop, play, rewind, fast forward, and record.

As you can see, the legacy of the early days of recording is still very much a part of making music on a computer. Open up just about any musical software program, and you'll find many of these terms and practices in use, ranging from transport controls to flange effects to looping to various kinds of cutting and slicing operations.

Digital Audio Basics

Modern digital recording has one huge advantage over both analog and digital tape: flexibility. Once the audio data is digitized and stored inside a computer, you can do amazing things with it. Digital storage media such as hard drives or SmartMedia cards are random access—meaning any chunk of data stored anywhere is instantly accessible. And since digital audio is really just a bunch of numbers, you can make all kinds of fundamental changes to it simply by applying some simple math. Or, more to the point, by letting your computer do the math. But first we need to get the sound into the computer. We briefly touched on the difference between analog and digital audio in the previous chapter. Let's take a closer look at the distinction.

Sound moving through air causes waves of high and low pressure to spread out from the source like ripples on the surface of a pond. (See Figure 2.2.)

Sound waves vary smoothly over time, rising to a peak of high pressure and then falling to a trough of low pressure. The time interval between two peaks or troughs is called the *frequency* (see Figure 2.3) and is measured in cycles per second—also called Hertz, or Hz for short. Sound waves with a low frequency are perceived as bass tones; the faster the frequency, the higher the tone. On the average, we hear sounds between 20Hz and 20,000Hz (or 20kHz (kilohertz)).

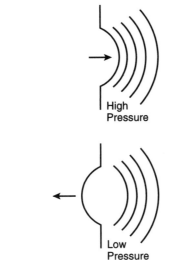

Figure 2.2
(Top) When a drumhead or speaker flexes outward, it pushes against the air in front of it, forming a wave of high pressure.
(Bottom) As the surface pulls back, it creates an area of low pressure.

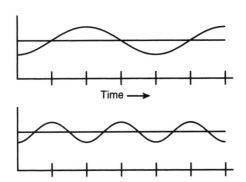

Figure 2.3
The sound wave on the bottom has twice the frequency as the one on top. We would hear the bottom wave as a note one octave higher.

We perceive the amplitude, or height, of the wave as loudness. So a very soft flute sound would look like a gentle wave with a low amplitude, while a snare hit would appear as an abrupt spike. (See Figure 2.4.)

As you learned a little way back, electrical audio signals translate the smoothly variable sound pressure changes into smoothly variable voltage. We call the process analog because the changes in voltages are analogous to the original sound wave.

Digital devices, however, operate differently—instead of smoothly flowing electrical current, they are made up of minute electrical switches. A switch has only two possible "states"—it's either off or on. Computers use two numbers, 0 and 1, to express whether the switch is off or on. (*Bit*, the smallest unit in a binary system, is short for *binary digit*.) Obviously, a single bit is not going to convey a great deal of information, so computers string a number of bits together to form words.

Figure 2.4
(Top) A soft flute slowly
falling in volume. (Bottom)
A snare drum.

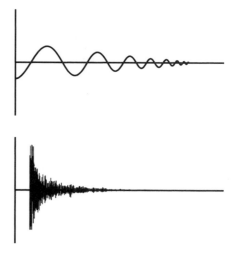

With two bits you have four choices—00, 01, 10, and 11—which can convey twice as much information as a single bit. With eight bits (commonly called a *byte*) you can express 256 numbers, with 16 bits you get 65,536 different values, and so on.

Digitizing an audio signal involves taking a "snapshot" (called a *sample*) of it at a particular point in time and plotting the value. The greater the number of samples you take in a given time period, the more accurately the waveform will be rendered. (See Figure 2.5.)

Figure 2.5
(Top) Analog sound waves
are encoded as digital data
by taking instantaneous
measurements of the amplitude called samples. If the
wave were sampled at a
low sample rate and then
rendered back into the
analog domain, it would
appear as a series of
jagged steps—and sound
ugly, too. (Bottom) Higher
sampling frequencies do a
better job of describing the
original wave.

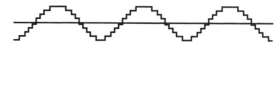

❄ THE NYQUIST FREQUENCY

At its most basic, it takes two samples to describe one cycle of the waveform. Therefore, the highest frequency you can reproduce is half of the sample rate. Engineers call that the Nyquist frequency, after a gent named Harry Nyquist who figured it out.

Since the upper limit of our hearing is around 20,000Hz (20kHz), we'd need a sample rate of two times that, or 40kHz, to render that frequency, hence the 44.1kHz standard, which can reproduce sounds up to 22.05kHz, just above our threshold.

You'd think that would be enough; after all, why worry about sounds we can't hear? There are a couple of reasons to record at higher sample rates, actually. For one thing, many engineers believe we can perceive sounds higher than 20kHz, though we don't recognize them as tones. Rather, these super-high frequencies, which may appear as harmonic overtones, seem to lend a sense of spaciousness and believability to recorded music.

The other reason for using higher sample rates has to do with a nasty kind of distortion called *aliasing* that creeps in when you attempt to digitize a signal that is higher than the Nyquist frequency. Analog to Digital Converters (ADCs) and Digital to Analog Converters (DACs) have antialiasing filters to tame the beast. Many engineers like to oversample—record at a higher sample rate than will be used to reproduce the signal to further reduce aliasing.

The relationship between bits and sampling frequency is complex. Briefly put, the sample rate involves the frequency of sound that can be rendered digitally, while the number of bits relates to the sound's dynamic range, or amplitude relative to absolute silence. All you really need to know is this: More bits mean greater dynamic range, and that's a good thing. Higher sample rates mean higher frequencies, and that's also a good thing. However, higher bit depths and increased sample rates also mean more computations for your computer, and the files will take up a lot more storage space.

The CD audio standard is 44,100 samples per second (44.1kHz) at 16 bits. These days, it's almost universal to record at 24 bits and higher. Raising the sample rate to 48kHz or even 96kHz may pay off for you, or it may not, depending on your equipment and what you're recording. Bluntly stated, most non-pro gear simply isn't capable of reproducing frequencies above 20kHz.

Sample rate and bit depth come into play whether or not you plan on recording your own audio. For instance, it usually isn't possible to mix different sample rates within a song, so you'll need to be on top of it before you start grabbing loops. Likewise, software set at 16 bits will simply cut off the extra bits from any of your 24-bit files, trashing all that extra resolution. Software samplers and sample-playback instruments generate audio at various sample rates and bit depths, too, so you need to be sure everything matches up all down the line.

While I'm on the subject, let's take a quick look at some of the common audio file formats. (See Table 2.1) Professional-quality files are at least 16-bit, 44.1kHz uncompressed audio. A stereo file at that bit depth and sample rate requires 10 megabytes of storage space per minute, so a number of file-compression schemes have cropped up to make the files smaller. Most use "lossy compression," which means some data is irretrievably lost in the process.

Table 2.1   Common Digital Audio Formats

Name	Platform	Used For	Compressed/ Uncompressed	Notes
WAV	PC	CD-quality or better audio	Uncompressed	Format for audio CDs, virtually identical to AIFF
AIFF	Mac	CD-quality or better audio	Uncompressed	Format for audio CDs, virtually identical to WAV
SD II	Mac	CD-quality or better audio	Uncompressed	Format for Digidesign Pro Tools and MOTU Digital Performer
ATRAC	N/A	Mini-disks	Lossy compression	Used only on MiniDisk players
MP3	Mac/PC	Portable players, Internet	Lossy compression	Various levels of compression. Quality ranges from "yuck" to quite good
WMA	PC	Portable players, Internet	Lossy compression	"Windows Media Audio" says it all
RA	Mac/PC	Streaming audio	Lossy compression	Requires RealAudio player
AAC	Mac/PC	Portable players	Lossless compression	Format for Apple's iTunes and iPods

MIDI, or Musical Instrument Digital Interface, is sometimes listed as a digital audio file format. But MIDI doesn't really include any audio; rather, it's a set of instructions telling an electronic musical instrument, such as a synthesizer or sampler, what to play. I'll cover MIDI in Chapter 5.

That wraps up our quick tour through the history of recording. As I said, the purpose isn't to get you up to speed—that's what Chapters 5–8 are all about—but instead to give you a basic understanding of some of the concepts and terms that continue to be used in computer music.

Now let's turn our attention to how sound moves from one place to another.

The Signal Chain

No matter what kind of computer music you'll be making, if it involves creating sound, you'll need to be aware of the signal chain. What's that? The signal chain is the path that the sound, or its electrical or digital representation, travels from the source to your ears.

At its most basic, consider what happens when you hear a friend sing: Her voice is produced by the interaction of her vocal chords, air passages, and mouth. The sound waves pass through the air and reach your ears. You could say there are three links in the chain: the singer, the air, and you.

Now let's look at a more complicated example: Your friend sings into a microphone in one room while you listen on headphones in another. (See Figure 2.6.)

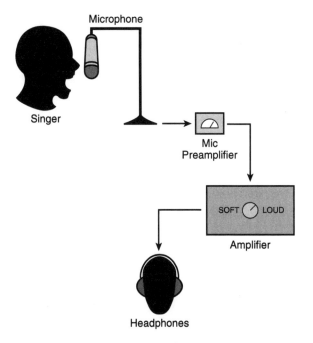

Figure 2.6

The signal chain consists of four elements: a microphone to translate the singer's voice into electrical impulses, a preamplifier to boost the mic's signal to the amplifier's operating level, an amplifier to further boost the signal, and a set of headphones, which changes the electrical signal back into audio.

In this example I used a singer, but the idea would be exactly the same if the sound source were a bunch of loops or the output of a software sampler.

At the center of any studio is the mixer—that humongous chunk of real estate bristling with knobs, push buttons, blinking lights, and row after row of sliders. (See Figure 2.7.) A mixer is a device for moving signals from one place to another, combining or splitting them as needed. Mixers exist in various guises—multichannel analog mixers designed for live sound or recording, computer interfaces with two or more inputs and outputs, control surfaces that interface with software, and

Figure 2.7
The mixer is the nerve center of a recording studio. Digital mixers, such as the TASCAM DM-3200, combine many of the features of large-format analog consoles with the flexibility of software mixers. Used with permission of TASCAM, 2005.

software "virtual mixers" to combine and adjust internal audio. The chances are very good you've got half a dozen or more lying around and don't even know it. If your computer can produce sounds, it has a mixer somewhere inside it. Understanding how a mixer works is crucial to mastering the art of making music with your computer, so let's get started.

Basic Mixer Functions

A mixer takes a number of inputs and routes them to one or more outputs. (See Figure 2.8.) Along the way, you can change the relative levels, diddle with the tone, and mess with the left/right balance, among other things.

Figure 2.8
This simple six-in/two-out mixer combines the six inputs (mic, guitar, stereo keyboard, and stereo turntable) into a left and right output feeding a pair of powered speakers.

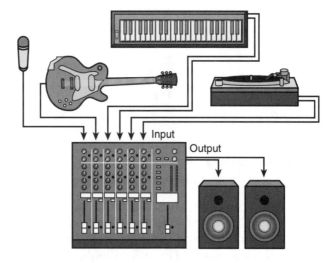

The Input Section

Studio mixers and audio interfaces can handle a variety of input types—microphones, outboard gear such as effects units, instruments such as electric basses and keyboards, and the playback from various kinds of recorders.

✻ MIC LEVEL? INSTRUMENT LEVEL? LINE LEVEL? WHAT'S THE LEVEL ON THAT?

Level is just another word for voltage, signal strength, power, or volume (as in, "Back off on the level of that tambourine, will ya, Ace?"). Different types of electronic devices generate different outputs. Microphones generally output signals around –30 dBu. (A dBu is a unit of measurement of audio signal level in an electrical current.) We use two slightly different measurements for line level. Consumer gear operates at –10dBV. Professional gear is rated at +4 dBu. Although the scales are different, they are related—dBu is referenced to .775 volts, while dBV is referenced to 1 volt. Practically speaking, you don't really have to worry about it as long as you make sure your gear is wired correctly. Instrument-level signals can be very hot, up to +30 dBu.

Generally, you can guess the level of a particular piece of gear by the kind of connector it uses. Microphones operating at mic level use three-pin XLR connectors, while those at line level will generally have ¼-inch plugs. –10dBV line-level gear uses either ¼-inch phono plugs or RCA-type connections. (See Figure 2.9.) Professional audio gear that operates at +4 dBu usually uses XLR connectors.

Because of the differences in level, you can't plug a microphone into a line-level input and expect it to work. Electric instruments operate at higher impedance (also known as *resistance*) than line-level gear, so they require special inputs on your mixer.

One more thing: Audio circuits come in two flavors—*balanced* and *unbalanced*. Balanced circuits do a better job of rejecting noise and avoiding grounding problems than unbalanced circuits do. However, most consumer gear is unbalanced.

✻ PLUG THIS, JACK

Electrical connectors have a *plug* on the male end and a *jack*, or receptacle, on the female end. You *plug* the plug into the *jack*.

Microphone Preamps

As I mentioned, microphones require special preamplifiers to boost their low output to something the mixer can work with. Don't assume that a piece of gear has a mic preamp just because there's an XLR jack! The quality of microphone preamp is one of the most important links in the signal chain. Simply put, a great mic through a lousy mic-pre will sound lousy. The Mackie Onyx series of mixers is renowned for its excellent mic-pres; likewise, high-quality mic preamplifiers are available in audio interfaces by Presonus, Digidesign, MOTU, and many more.

Figure 2.9

XLR connectors are used for microphones and balanced +4 dBu gear. ¼-inch TS phone connectors are found on electric instruments and unbalanced audio gear operating at –10dBV. ¼-inch TRS (tip-ring-sleeve) connections are used for stereo gear such as headphone cords, and balanced audio equipment operating at either consumer or pro line level. RCA ("phono") connectors are usually used for consumer CDs and recorders. Turntables, which also use RCA connectors, require a special preamplifier to operate properly. RCA connections also carry digital signals for some audio and video gear.

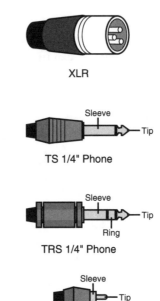

XLR

TS 1/4" Phone

TRS 1/4" Phone

RCA Phone

PHANTOM POWER

Condenser microphones (more on them later) require a small electrical charge to do their work. A few operate from batteries, but most require what's called phantom power. Phantom power is sent back down the mic's cable. If your mixer or interface supports phantom power, you'll find a switch somewhere to turn it on and off. The best designs have individual switches for each mic in; it's more common for phantom to be applied globally or in banks.

HI-Z INPUT

Although instrument inputs look just like ¼-inch line inputs, they don't act the same. Some gear has dedicated—and labeled—high-impedance instrument inputs for guitars and basses. Sometimes you'll see a small switch that converts the jack to high impedance (also called Hi-Z). When in doubt, place a device called a DI (short for *direct injection*) between your instrument and your mixer or audio interface to match the levels.

ON THE SOFT SIDE

The input section of a software mixer is where you assign your various audio and MIDI tracks. Sometimes the interface will use virtual patch cords so you can "wire up" various sound modules and effects devices. Or you may see small boxes with pull-down menus. Either way, the result is exactly the same as in the "real" world.

The Channel Strip

Once a signal gets into the mixer, it follows a path through various switches and circuits that shape it, send bits of it off to do some more work, and make it louder or softer. Welcome to the world of the channel strip. A channel strip is a physical or virtual representation of the path the signal takes through all the circuitry. On most mixers, it's a long vertical strip of buttons, knobs, and sliders.

Although a huge studio mixer looks intimidating, it's really just a number of identical channel strips. Learn one and you've learned 'em all. Audio interfaces tend to be laid out differently, but you'll find most of these same functions on just about any mixer you encounter, hardware or software.

Let's start at the top. Refer to Figures 2.10 and 2.11 as we go along.

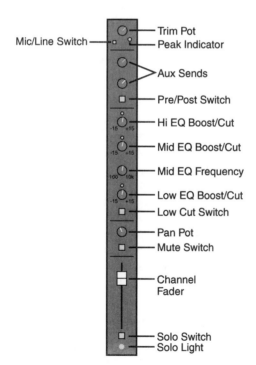

Figure 2.10

The channel strip represents the signal patch along a single mixer channel.

Figure 2.11
Software mixers often re-
tain the look, if not the feel,
of their hardware brethren.

Mic/Line Switch

If a mixer has both mic and line inputs connected to the same channel, use the mic/line switch to set the proper level. Some inexpensive mixers and interfaces dispense with this switch, relying instead on the trim knob to set the level. Even though it may look like you can plug both a mic and a line input at the same time, that's a really bad idea. At the very least, you'll have no way of controlling both sources, and you run the risk of degrading the sound or damaging your equipment.

Trim or Gain Knob

This is the first stage of amplification for the signal. The purpose of the trim control—sometimes called "gain" or "input level"—is to boost or cut the input's strength to match the mixer's optimum operating level. Set the trim too low, and you'll be forced to boost the signal later, which can add noise to the mix. Set the trim too high, and you overload the input, causing ugly distortion.

Peak Indicator

The peak light warns that a signal is approaching—or exceeding—the maximum allowable level. On hardware gear, such as mixers, mic-pres, and audio interfaces, the peak light usually starts to glow several decibels below the ceiling. You can use this to help adjust the input trim: Raise the trim until the peaks just start to light up, then back down a bit. Experienced engineers know just how much headroom is built into their gear. You'll also see this called "clip" or something similar, mostly on software mixers. When a signal hits the ceiling, it's called "clipping."

With digital audio, hitting the ceiling is bad. Clipped digital signals get flattened out and sound absolutely horrible—and they can seriously damage your playback speakers. What's worse, there's no way to fix the problem. So don't let those peak lights come on in your software, ever.

AUX SENDS

Auxes (short for auxiliary sends) split off a portion of the input signal and send it to auxiliary gear, such as effects processors and headphone mixers. On mixers with internal effects, such as the Samson MDR10, and some software mixers, one or more of the auxes may be labeled "Effects" or even "FX."

By using aux sends, you can route signals from a number of channels to a single effects device or effects plug-in. To send some of the input to an effects processor, simply connect the mixer's aux outputs to the effector's inputs and increase the aux level on the desired channel. Don't forget to connect the effect's outputs back to the mixer!

Software mixers usually operate exactly the same way, with one important exception. A hardware mixer will have only so many auxes; with some software mixers you can create as many as you need.

Why use the auxes for headphones? Even though your mixer probably has a headphone jack, you may run into a situation where whoever is doing the recording wants to hear something different from the whole mix. By connecting a headphone amplifier to one or more aux outs, you can dial up a custom headphone mix.

> **GET ON THE BUS**
>
> A bus is a path common to several signals in a mixer. In the illustration at the beginning of this section, each aux send is a bus, as is the main stereo output. Mixers often have a number of busses—sometimes called sub-mix outs—used for creating special live mixes or feeding each track of a recorder, plus various other paths for, say, a CD recorder, control-room speakers, or a digital mix-down recorder. Flexible bussing assignments are one of the great features of digital and software mixers.

Aux sends can operate independently of the final channel gain set by the channel fader, or they can operate after the fader level. What difference does that make? If you were sending some of the signal to a headphone mix, you'd want the level to be independent of whatever's going to the recorder. The opposite could be true if you are using the aux to feed an effect such as reverb. In that case, you'd want the effect to follow changes you make with the channel fader. Otherwise the balance between the effect and the dry (unaffected) signal would be off. Use the "pre/post" switch to select how you want the auxes to operate.

> **WHAT'S AN INSERT?**
>
> Auxes are great for sending portions of multiple signals to a single effect. But what about effects such as compression or EQ that you want on only one channel? Simple. Use an insert, a special circuit on hardware mixers that taps the input, shunts it off to an external device for processing, and then brings it back

to the channel strip. Inserts typically use special Y cables with a single TRS plug on one end and two TS plugs on the other—one for the device's input and one for the output.
Software mixers typically have slots for inserting effects plug-ins.

EQ

Think of the EQ section (short for equalization) as tone controls for the signal. EQ knobs operate like the bass and treble controls on a boombox, but with much greater precision. Hardware mixers may have two, three, four, or more EQ controls to cover various frequency ranges—typically expressed as hi, mid, and low bands. At its simplest, the EQ knob will cut or boost everything above (or below) a given frequency. For instance, a hi EQ knob with a frequency set at 12kHz will affect all frequencies at or above 12kHz, with no effect on lower frequencies. Similarly, a low EQ centered at 80Hz will affect only sounds at or below that frequency.

For even greater control, parametric EQs use three controls: one to select from a range of frequencies, one to dial in the width of the frequency range affected (called the Q), and one to adjust the boost or cut. To save money and space, many hardware mixers only offer semi-parametric EQ consisting of two knobs—a boost/cut control and sweepable (changeable) frequency range with a fixed Q.

Software EQ plug-ins can be even more flexible than their hardware counterparts, affording extremely accurate control over the sounds. (See Figure 2.12.)

Figure 2.12
The Waves Renaissance EQ plug-in is a fully featured stereo parametric EQ. The shape of the graphs gives visual feedback of how each EQ band is operating. Note the extremely narrow Q (the width of the selected frequency range) of the cut just above 2kHz.

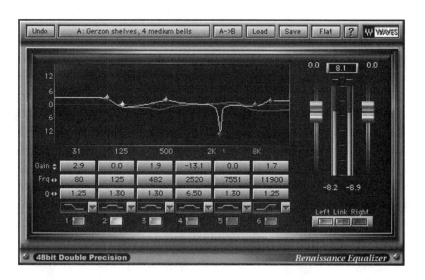

A low cut switch attenuates (lowers the level) everything below a set frequency range. Low cut switches are handy to quickly remove hum or turntable noise from the signal path. For this reason, the switch is sometimes called a "rumble filter"—which I've always thought would make a pretty good band name.

Mute
The mute button removes the signal from the main bus. In other words, it turns the channel off.

Solo
Pressing the solo button mutes everything but the soloed channel. Use it to quickly make tonal adjustments or check levels. Generally, you can set the way the solo function behaves. "Solo in place" (a.k.a. "after fader listen") preserves the channel's EQ, pan, and level settings. In contrast, pre-fader listen (PFL) taps the signal before the pan and fader settings. Use it to set trim levels.

Pan
Stereo uses two speakers to simulate the effects of sound in three dimensions. Use the pan to set the channel's left/right balance. If the pan is set straight up, the sound will appear to come from a point directly between the two speakers. Software mixers generally feature a numeric readout of pan values, with 0 being hard left and 127 hard right.

On two-channel interfaces, the pan determines the output to which the signal is sent. So, if you want a signal to appear in your software at input number 2, pan it hard right on the interface.

Fader
The last level control in the channel strip. Faders have a mark somewhere near the top—sometimes labeled 0dB—to indicate the point at which the signal flows through with no change. When the fader is set below this level, the signal becomes quieter; move it higher to make things louder. Move the fader down to lower the volume and up to raise it. It ain't rocket science.

Channel Meter
Indicates the relative level of the signal.

Automation Controls
Most music software supports MIDI automation data (see Chapter 5) so you can make and record dynamic changes to a sound's volume and panning as it plays. Software mixers may include mini-transport functions to record and play back the automation data.

The Master Section
While the channel strip controls signals coming in to the mixer, the master section deals with what comes out. (See Figure 2.13.)

Interfaces may skip the master section altogether, or they may give you a single knob to set the output level. In software, the various bits may be spread all over the interface—meters in one window, effects returns in another.

Aux Send Level
Sets the overall level going to the aux sends.

Figure 2.13

A typical mixer's master section. Refer to the text below for a description of the various functions.

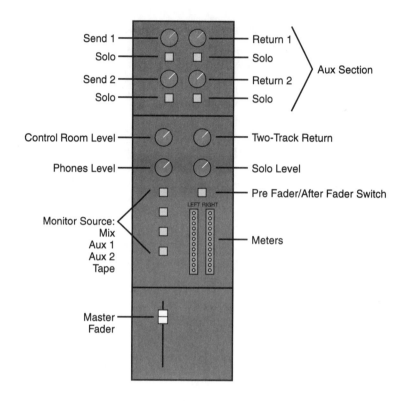

Aux Returns

Often called "effects returns" or something similar. Sets the level for signals coming into the mixer's auxiliary inputs. Some people prefer to bring the effect back to one or two mixer channels for better control.

Control Room Level

Adjusts the level going to the mixer's main speaker outs. If you are using a mixer to feed your audio interface, use the main outs for the interface and the control room outs for your monitor speakers.

Headphone Level

Sets the headphone level. Use it when you want to listen on 'phones. Some old studio dogs call headphones "cans." Just another useless bit of trivia you can throw around to impress your friends.

Monitor Source

Determines which signals appear at the control room and headphone outputs.

Two-Track Return

Also known as tape return. Controls the level of the mixer's tape inputs. Sometimes has a switch to add this signal back to the main mix bus; be very careful you don't set up a feedback loop when you use this feature. See Figure 2.14 for information on hooking up a mixer and your computer.

Meters

Show the level at the main left and right outputs. Sometimes includes a row of switches to select what gets metered.

WHY DO I NEED A MASTER INSERT?

Just like channel inserts, the master inserts let you patch in a remote piece of gear, only this time it affects the whole mix. It's mostly used for dynamics and/or EQ for the final stage of the mixing process, called mastering (or, more properly, premastering). Novices sometimes use the master insert for reverb or other effects better handled by aux sends and returns.

Master Fader

The final, last, and ultimate place to make level changes before all of the various channels and auxes appear at the main left and right outputs. Actually, you shouldn't ever touch the master fader except maybe to fade out the end of a song. Set it at 0, and adjust everything else so the main output meters light up nice and strong without clipping. Then make all your gain adjustments to the individual channel faders.

The Signal Path in Other Gear

I'll round out this discussion by pointing out how you may encounter some of these same mixer functions in other gear. The more you understand the signal flow, the better you'll be able to make great music.

Guitar FX and DIs

Electric guitars and basses have one or more volume knobs to adjust the signal appearing at the output jack. Plug in an effects unit, and you'll need to properly match the levels. Multi-effects devices such as the popular Digitech RP300, Line 6 POD, or Boss GT-8 have extensive software-mixing and tone-shaping controls.

Active DIs such as the Sans Amp Acoustic DI add tone-shaping and volume control in addition to matching your instrument's output impedance to the mixer or audio interface. Once again, it's important to know how to set the levels all along the signal chain.

Figure 2.14
Two ways to route sound between a computer audio interface and a mixer: (Top) The interface is connected via the mixer's tape inputs and outputs. Select the mixer's two-track return to hear playback from the computer. (Bottom) The mixer's input channels are split between instruments and microphones on one side and the outputs from the interface on the other. Signals flow to the interface via the mixer's sub-mix busses. Take care you don't accidentally route the outputs from the audio interface to one of the sub-mix busses; otherwise you'll create a feedback loop.

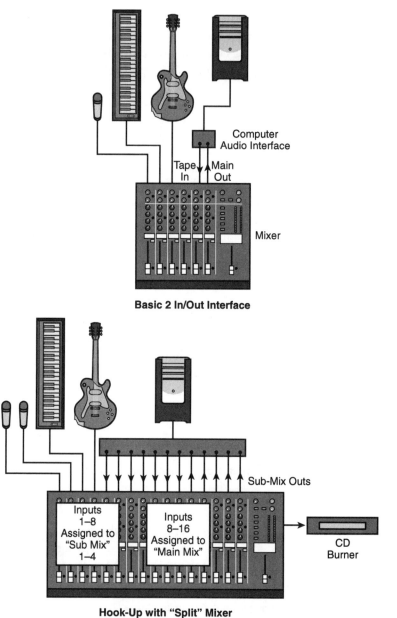

Basic 2 In/Out Interface

Hook-Up with "Split" Mixer

Mic-pres

Stand-alone microphone preamplifiers and channel strips (a mic-pre with EQ and dynamics processing) have many of the same trim and level controls as a mixer.

KEYBOARDS AND SOUND MODULES

Keyboards and sound modules capable of reproducing sounds on many channels simultaneously always have extensive software mixers buried deep inside the user interface. And sometimes making simple changes to the EQ or effects send of a particular sound will be all it needs to go from ho-hum to wow.

The same goes for software synths and virtual instruments. Even though you may be sending the output through another software mixer, check that the individual instrument is sending a good, strong level.

❋ WHAT'S GAIN STAGING?

You've probably noticed that I keep harping on being aware of the level at each and every part of the signal chain. Engineers use the term "gain stage" to describe each amplification point in the signal chain. Since the overall gain of the signal is the sum of all of the various gain stages, it's vital that each be set to its optimum. For instance, if your keyboard's output level is too low, you'll have to make up gain somewhere down the line. That could end up raising the overall level of noise from the cables, hum, or amplifiers. On the other hand, if one gain stage is set too high, you risk clipping the signal.

Gain staging is the process of setting each point in the chain to the proper level. It's the same in the analog and the digital worlds. The trick is to treat each piece of the chain individually. Use the device's meters to set the output at its optimum level before moving on to the next part of the chain. In some cases, you may have to refer to the manual to determine the best output level.

Here's how it works with a microphone, a mic-preamp, and a mixer: First, set the input level on the mic-pre so the clipping indicators just begin to light up on the loudest signals, then back it down a bit to give yourself enough headroom to handle loud singing. Next, adjust the trim on the mixer so the input from the preamp peaks around 0dB on the input meters. Set both the channel and master faders to 0dB and adjust the input trim on your interface so the peaks come in around –4db in your software.

So that's how we get a signal from one end of the signal chain to the other.

❋ HOW DO I GET SOUND FROM MY COMPUTER INTERFACE BACK TO MY MIXER?

Good question. There is no single answer that works for everybody. Many people send the left and right outputs from the computer back to a mixer's tape inputs. For multichannel interfaces, it may make sense to split your mixer into two sections. For instance, on my system, channels 1–8 handle inputs from my microphones, keyboard, and synth modules, while 9–16 are reserved for the eight outputs of my FireWire interface. The interface's inputs are fed via my mixer's sub-mix outputs. I avoid feedback loops by making sure channels 9–16 are not assigned to a sub-mix bus and sent back to the interface. (See Figure 2.14.)

Okay, now that we've looked at how a signal moves through a hardware mixer and its digital simulation, let's take a look at the tool that changes sound waves into electricity: the microphone. If you're planning on working only with prerecorded loops and MIDI, you can skip this bit, and no harm done.

Microphone Basics

A microphone is a device for rendering the changes in air pressure that we call sound into electrical impulses. In one very real sense, a microphone is a speaker working in reverse. The moving parts of a loudspeaker flex in response to changes in the electric current applied to a magnet. As the speaker moves, it gets the air moving, and we hear it as sound.

We'll discuss how to choose and use microphones for very specific tasks in Chapter 7 and Chapter 8, "Track Four: All Together Now: The Desktop DAW." For now, I want to familiarize you with how they work in general.

Pickup Patterns

It may come as a surprise to you that a microphone does not "hear" sound the same way we do. Our external ear, all of that rubbery flesh around the ear canal, is finely tuned to capture sound coming from all around and route it down to the eardrum. Because the ear faces forward, we are more sensitive to sounds coming from in front of us. In fact, thanks to our two ears and their funny shapes, we can pretty well pinpoint exactly where a sound originates—useful if the thing making noise is a large lion looking for a snack.

Microphones are sensitive to the placement of sound as well. For instance, the long shotgun microphones you see on the sidelines at sporting events are extremely sensitive to sounds coming from a very narrow point directly in front of the mic's barrel. One the other hand, the tiny mic built into a telephone answering machine can pick up sounds from anywhere in the room.

We call this sensitivity the microphone's pickup, response, or polar pattern. The usual way to represent the pattern is via a two-dimensional drawing that graphs how the microphone's element (the bit that does the work) responds. Microphones generally are built to exhibit one of four basic patterns: cardioid, hypercardioid, omnidirectional, and figure-8. Some studio microphones have switchable patterns, which greatly extend their usefulness. Each pattern has its strengths and weaknesses—the key to using microphones successfully is knowing when to choose one over another.

CARDIOID

The cardioid pattern—the name comes from the Greek word for heart (see Figure 2.15)—is a versatile unidirectional pickup pattern well suited to many applications. Because cardioid mics reject sounds coming from the rear, they are often used onstage or in noisy home studios. Cardioid mics exhibit a curious property called the proximity effect—the closer a sound source is to the capsule (another word for the bit that does the work), the more the bass frequencies are emphasized. Lounge singers have exploited this for years: "Thank you, thank you very much."

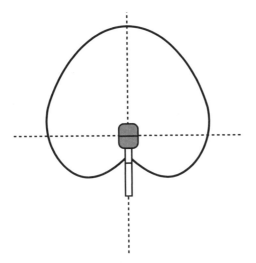

Figure 2.15
The cardioid pattern looks a little like a drawing of a heart. Remember that the pickup pattern extends out in three dimensions!

WHAT'S OFF-AXIS REJECTION?

Directional microphones—cardioid, hypercardioid, and figure-8 patterns—are more sensitive to sounds directly in front of the capsule (or front and back in figure-8 patterns) than they are to sounds coming in from the sides. You could say that the mic is most sensitive to sounds that are lined up on the mic's axis, a line extending straight out from the element. The farther a sound moves off of this line, the less likely it is to be picked up. But the sound won't just get quieter; the microphone's frequency response changes at the edges of its response pattern, too. So it may hear the treble portion of the sound but not the bass, which significantly changes the sound's flavor.

That's why you need to be sure the mic is aimed directly at the sound source and be aware of what may be leaking in from the sides and back.

HYPERCARDIOID

This is basically just a very narrow cardioid pattern. Choose this when you really need to focus a sound and eliminate sounds coming from the sides. The familiar shotgun mic used on video cameras is an extreme example.

OMNIDIRECTIONAL

Omnidirectional microphones are designed to be equally sensitive to sounds coming from anywhere. (See Figure 2.16.) Use them for choirs and large ensembles and in other applications where the sound comes from a wide area. Unlike directional patterns, omni mics are free from the proximity effect, which makes them a great choice for close-miking a musical instrument or vocal. However, be aware that they'll pick up any noise in your studio.

Figure 2.16
Omnidirectional micro-
phones are great for
capturing the sound and
ambience of large
ensembles and open
spaces.

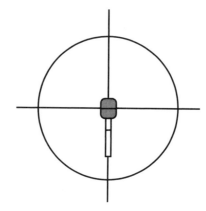

FIGURE-8

Sometimes called a bi-directional pattern, the figure-8 is equally responsive to sounds directly in front of and directly behind the capsule while rejecting sounds aimed at the side. (See Figure 2.17.) Studio engineers often choose this pattern for recording vocal duets, harmony groups, and acoustic ensembles. The proximity effect is not as strong as with cardioid and hypercardioid patterns.

Figure 2.17
No prizes for guessing how
the figure-8 pickup pattern
got its name.

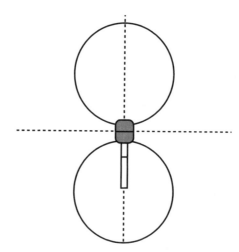

Microphone Types

Not only do microphones differ in how they respond to sound, they translate the sound into electrical current in fundamentally different ways, too. Of the four basic types, you are most likely to use both dynamic and condenser microphones in your computer music applications.

DYNAMIC MICS

Dynamic microphones feature a thin diaphragm attached to a wire coil suspended over a magnet. Incoming sound waves move the coil relative to the magnet, which generates a small electric current.

They are relatively inexpensive and sturdy, making them great choices for the stage—the venerable Shure SM 58 is probably the most familiar vocal mic in the world. Dynamics are great for handling very loud sources, such as electric guitar speakers or Roger Daltrey. However, they generally cannot reproduce high-frequency detail as well as condenser or ribbon microphones, so their use in the studio is generally limited to drums and amplifiers.

CONDENSER MICS

In contrast to the dynamic mic, a condenser uses a very thin electrically charged diaphragm. The diaphragm movement relative to a charged backplate sends variable voltage streaming down the cable. Condensers need a power source, either batteries or phantom power, a small charge sent from mixers and microphone preamps.

Condenser mics are further categorized by the size of the diaphragm. Small-diaphragm condenser mics, such as the Audio-Technica4051, AKG C451B, and Shure SM 81, do wonders with high-frequency sources and are often used on cymbals and acoustic guitar. Large-diaphragm condenser mics with a cardioid pattern, such as the RØDE NT1-A, BLUE Blueberry, and AKG 3000B, are versatile players for both vocals and acoustic instruments.

Multipattern, large-diaphragm condenser mics such as the Neuman U87 and AKG C12 VR are the studio elite. They are used for vocals, pianos, strings, and anywhere highly accurate reproduction is a must.

Although relatively fragile, condenser mics excel at capturing detail and nuance, making them great choices for studio work.

RIBBON MICS

The element on a ribbon mic is a very thin strip of metal that is sensitive to the velocity of air molecules moving past it. (Most mics respond to changes in sound pressure level.) Ribbon mics are capable of great detail and accuracy but tend to be fragile. Most ribbon mics will be destroyed in a flash if you send them phantom power by mistake, but Royer has overcome this limitation with the sensational R-122.

PRESSURE ZONE MICS

More accurately called boundary microphones, pressure zone mics (PZMs) consist of a small omnidirectional condenser microphone capsule mounted on a large, flat surface—the pattern changes to hemispherical due to interference of the boundary, or flat surface. Due to some rather interesting acoustical properties, sound bounces off the boundary and boosts the sensitivity of the capsule significantly. The frequency response of a PZM varies with the size of the reflective surface. PZMs are useful for recording pianos and in some live recording applications.

> ❋ **TU-BE OR NOT TU-BE**
>
> A tube microphone is the Rolls-Royce of the recording world: classy, hand-crafted, flawlessly engineered, and super-expensive. If you want to capture the fluid essence of a fine vocal performance in a well-equipped pro studio, you fire up the tubes. There is simply nothing as warm, detailed, and transparent. And, until recently, you had to be very rich to afford one.
>
> Thanks to advances in both engineering and manufacturing, affordable tube microphones are finally available for the home studio. Check out some of the offerings from RØDE and Studio Projects and the inexpensive MXL 960.

The Rest of the Story

In this chapter, you've learned how the history of recording has influenced how today's software operates, you've followed the signal path through the various pieces of a mixer, and you've learned a little bit about how microphones work.

I'll end this section with a brief look at the other end of the process: how to get the most out of the sound coming out of your speakers and how to set up your listening room.

Monitoring Basics

Believe it or not, your choice of speakers can have a huge impact on your ability to make music. Home stereos or multimedia speakers are designed to color the sound to compensate for limitations in most rooms—usually by increasing the bass and treble components of the source signal.

Studio monitor speakers, on the other hand, are designed to reveal the true sound of the recording. As a wise old engineer put it to me, "You don't want *monitors* that sound good, you want monitors that tell you when the recording sounds bad. So you don't make bad recordings."

> ❋ **WHAT'S A MONITOR?**
>
> To monitor something means to observe, and a monitor is something that reveals what's going on. (Sort of like how the hall monitor back in elementary school would reveal to the teacher that you were filling a squirt gun when you were supposed to be getting a drink at the water fountain.) So the big glowing screen connected to your computer is a video monitor. And studio speakers are called monitors, too.

Prices range from the entry level to the truly extravagant; thanks to the popularity of home recording, we have a greater choice of affordable monitors than ever. Professional studios generally have an assortment of monitors so the engineer can hear how a mix will translate on a variety of speaker systems. Most of us can't afford that luxury, but thanks to some innovative DSP (digital signal processing) technology, the Alesis ProLinear 820 DSP and Roland's DS series model the characteristic sound of a variety of well-known speaker systems.

Monitors come in two basic flavors. Passive designs, such as the Behringer Truth B2031P, require a power amplifier to supply the juice; active monitors feature built-in amps. Many companies, including Alesis, Behringer, Samson, Roland, Event, and Fostex, make active and passive versions of the same speakers. (See Figure 2.18.) While there are strong arguments for either design, active speakers certainly cut down on the clutter. If you opt for a passive design, always buy more power than you think you need: More speakers have been ruined from too little power than too much! Be sure your speakers and amp are well matched.

Figure 2.18
The Alesis Monitor 1 is a popular choice for nearfield monitor speakers.

Stick with a pair of speakers for stereo mixing—a subwoofer may cause you to undermix the bass. (I'll talk about surround in Chapter 8.) Studio speakers are designed for close monitoring. That means you want to hear just the sound coming directly from the speakers without any reflected sound from the walls, floor, or ceiling of your room.

Here's how to place your monitor speakers. (See Figure 2.19.) Sit in a comfortable location where you can reach everything you need to mix. Place the speakers so that the tweeters are level with your ears. You may need to put them on stands or use a shelf above the table where your computer monitor sits. Make sure nothing blocks the path of the sound waves between the speakers and your ears. Place the speakers so that the distance is the same from each speaker to your ear as it is between the two speakers.

Don't put one speaker in a corner; the sound will be skewed toward the bass end of the spectrum. Likewise, try to keep the backs of the speakers at least a foot or two from the wall to cut down on reflections. If you do opt for a subwoofer, you can place it pretty much anywhere you want. Just be sure you can reach the switch so you can shut it off when you want to double-check a mix.

Figure 2.19
Set up your monitors so the tweeters form an equilateral triangle with your ears. That means all three sides are same length, in case you missed that class.

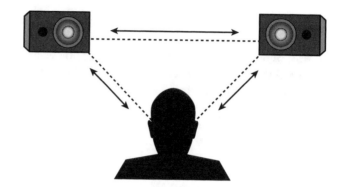

Incidentally, for computer music that doesn't involve extensive use of digital audio, you can get by very nicely with a basic set of multimedia or stereo speakers. In any case, it's a good idea to pick up a good pair of pro-quality headphones, such as the industry-standard Sony MDR-7506 or AKG K-20M.

Basic Room Issues

Sound doesn't really behave like the neat little ripples in drawings and diagrams. It's more like those explosions in deep space you see in the movies—a rapidly expanding ball of energy moving outward in every direction. Every surface that sound touches in a room either absorbs some energy or reflects energy back in another direction, or both. Oh, and different frequencies react totally differently, depending on what they hit and the size of the room. Normally, this isn't a big deal. In fact, we like the way music sounds when it's bounced around a room. But when you are trying to hear what exactly you've recorded, you don't want a bunch of crazy reflected sound fooling your ear.

That's why we take the time to set up our monitors properly. And that's why professional studios are built with no parallel walls or lots of reflective surfaces such as mirrors and windows. The chances are you'll be creating your music at home, in a spare bedroom or in a small section of a bigger room. So it's probably impractical—not to mention way too expensive—to start moving walls around.

No matter. There's a lot you can do to improve the sound of just about any room.

If you can, set up the space where you work well away from any walls to cut down on the reflected sound. In a long, narrow room, set up midway down one of the long walls.

Bare corners amplify bass frequencies. The tried-and-true solution is to purchase acoustic treatments such as Auralex's LENRD bass traps. On a budget? You can help the situation by building bookshelves into the corners; the various-sized books act as great sound diffusers. While you're at it, add bookshelves to break up any long empty walls. (See Figure 2.20.)

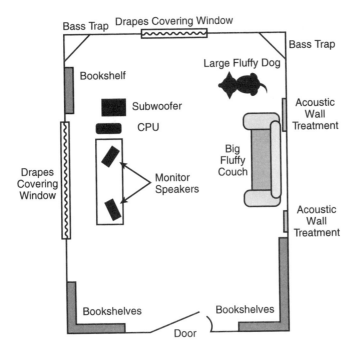

Bass Trap Drapes Covering Window
Bass Trap
Bookshelf
Large Fluffy Dog
Subwoofer
Acoustic Wall Treatment
CPU
Big Fluffy Couch
Drapes Covering Window
Monitor Speakers
Acoustic Wall Treatment
Bookshelves
Bookshelves
Door

Figure 2.20
Tame your room's acoustics by breaking up large flat areas with overstuffed furniture and by hanging heavy fabrics to absorb sounds and building bookshelves to break up the corners. Use bass traps and acoustic foam to fix persistent problems. A large fluffy dog can do double duty as a bass trap or bass drum, depending on your needs and the dog's temperament.

Hang quilts, blankets, or tapestries on the walls to tame some of the reflections. The key is to break up any long, flat areas. Here's a chance to buy that overstuffed fuzzy couch you've always wanted! Carpeting or area rugs on floors are useful, too.

To pinpoint trouble spots, sit at your mix position while a friend slides a small mirror across the walls and ceiling. Mark any spot where you see the front of a speaker reflected in the mirror; that's where the sound will bounce back to you. Stick up some acoustic treatment, such as Studiofoam Wedgies from Auralux, and you're good to go.

Where to Put Everything

No matter what kind of music you make, if you love what you're doing, you'll be spending a heck of a lot of time at it. So invest in a good, comfortable chair. Place your computer monitor at eye level and not so far away that you have to squint. If you'll be moving between a keyboard and your computer, consider a swivel chair. And listen to your mother—sit up straight! Nothing will cool inspiration faster that discovering your work environment is hurting you.

Affordable studio furniture is the greatest thing to hit the home studio world since one-cup espresso makers. Flexible units from Raxxess, QuikLok, and others feature multiple shelves, 19-inch racks and stands to hold your computer, monitor speakers, keyboards, and other gear. There is simply no better way to organize your workspace. And it looks cool, too.

While you're at it, consider some kind of cable management scheme—anything from simply twist-ties to lengths of flexible split tubing, often sold in office-supply stores. Keep like cables together—MIDI with MIDI, audio with audio. And be sure to keep power cables well away from audio and MIDI cables. If they have to cross, make sure they do it at a 90-degree angle to keep the noise down.

If you take the time to set up and organize your workspace properly, you'll find that your studio becomes another musical instrument. And that's what it's all about, isn't it?

That covers the basics. In the next two chapters, we'll look at how to buy and set up your computer and hardware for various musical tasks and consider some of the great software that's available.

3 } Choosing Your Computer

Shopping for the right computer doesn't have to be a scary proposition. Thanks to huge advances in speed, as well as significant reductions in price, today's desktop and notebook computers are cheaper, more powerful, more reliable, and easier to use than ever. In this chapter, I'll focus on what you need to know in order to build the best system for your needs. I'll discuss how the various components work and give you some insight into how to keep everything humming right along. And we'll take a look at some of the other bits and pieces you'll need to assemble for specific musical tasks such as scoring, songwriting, and recording, as well as some tips on setting everything up.

Already own a computer? I'll discuss what you can do to upgrade your present computer so you can run the latest software and hardware.

But first, let's look at the pros and cons of the two main operating systems, Windows and Mac. I'll talk a little bit about Linux, the "open source" operating system, too. Oh, and one other quick thing: Even though PC stands for "Personal Computer," just about everybody uses the term to refer to a computer running some form of the Microsoft Windows operating system. So when you see "PC," think "Windows." "Mac" means a computer made by Apple.

Which Operating System?

A computer is essentially just a pile of electronic circuitry for making mathematical calculations. The operating system contains the instructions for how it does its job. More important for our purpose, the operating system (OS for short) is responsible for the way we as humans interface with our little silicon buddies.

Although intrepid programmers had coaxed music out of computers almost since the beginning, the dawn of the computer-music age pretty much coincided with the development of MIDI (Musical Instrument Digital Interface) in 1983. MIDI is a binary language very much like computer code that was well suited to the Personal Computers of the day. (See Chapter 5, "Track One: MIDI," to learn more about MIDI.)

The first computers to get into music in a big way were the venerable Commodore 64, the Atari—the first computer to sport a built-in MIDI interface—and the amazingly prescient Amiga. The first Macintosh showed up in 1984, and developers were quick to jump on its then-revolutionary graphical user interface (GUI for short) that made it easy for non-techoids to use. The rest of the PC world was firmly focused on business applications and couldn't be bothered with such trifles. By the '90s there really wasn't any choice—if you wanted to do serious musical work on a desktop computer, you bought a Mac. The fact that Macs were more expensive than the PC your cousin used in the office was just something you put up with.

But then something changed. The Windows operating system made computing easy and affordable for the masses. Software developers noticed that Apple's market share was dropping steadily, and all of a sudden you could find real, professional-level music applications for the PC, along with a plethora of programs at the consumer level.

Mac OS

Even though fewer than 10 percent of all computers sold are Macs, the brand has fierce loyalty among its users. The Macintosh was the first computer to use a mouse and a point-and-click user interface with pictures of file folders and icons spread across a virtual desktop. Even more important, Apple was committed to serving the needs of musicians, videographers, and graphics professionals right from the start.

The Mac OS (OS X Tiger 10.4.2 at the time of this writing) contains numerous subroutines such as CoreMIDI and CoreAudio that integrate music at the deepest level. CoreAudio supports 24-bit, 192kHz audio and includes sample rate converters so you can use audio interfaces that do not support this resolution. Even better, CoreAudio lets you use multiple audio interfaces to augment track count—any combination of USB, FireWire, and PCI. (See Chapter 7, "Track Three: Digital Recording for the Solo Musician," to learn more about audio interfaces.) Apple's excellent MIDI and digital audio software, Logic Pro 7, is melded to the interface in ways few third-party programs can be.

The Mac OS is based on the Unix platform, a staple of industrial-strength network servers, so it's robust and stable. Even better, security is unmatched—as of this writing there have been no known computer viruses or successful spyware attacks. Running on a PowerPC G5 system, the current operating system supports 64-bit processing, which greatly speeds up math-intensive tasks such as digital audio and video processing. According to Apple, even 32-bit applications will run faster.

Millions of music lovers have already discovered Apple's easy-to-use iTunes software and the iPod personal music player. And iTunes is but one in a suite of multimedia applications, including iPhoto, iMovie, and GarageBand, a music-production suite, built into the OS. What's more, the

OS includes software instruments that support both DLS (downloadable sounds) and SoundFonts, so you can begin making music right out of the box.

The Macintosh OS has a number of excellent productivity enhancements, but chief among them is the ability to share files with Windows PCs. As an audio professional who often works on music recorded in a variety of project studios, I cannot overemphasize the importance of this feature.

The Mac operating system prior to OS X (yes, they pronounce it "ex" even though it's the Roman numeral for 10) was built on a completely different foundation. Normally in the computer world, this would mean that any software that did not get ported over would be useless. I'm happy to say this is not necessarily the case with OS X. It happily runs "legacy" programs under a version of System 9 called "Classic." That means you don't have to immediately run out and upgrade everything. Even better, it means you can still run older applications. For example, I recently was asked to revise a book I'd written several years ago. The company that created the notation program I'd used has long since left the scene, so there was no chance of getting an upgrade. Thanks to OS X and Classic, I could make the changes without breaking a sweat.

So what's the downside? Why doesn't everyone buy a Mac? The short answer is choice. There simply isn't as much software available for the OS. Although many music programs run on both Windows and the Mac OS, a significant number simply aren't available. (See "Choose Your Music Software First," later in this chapter.)

And many people don't want to learn a new OS or new software. Though, as someone who's worked on both platforms, there really isn't that much difference.

Another argument you'll hear is cost. I'm not 100 percent sure I agree with this one. While it is true you can buy a stripped-down desktop PC for less than $300, if you compare Macs and PCs on a feature-to-feature basis and account for all the hardware and software that comes standard on Macs that you'll pay extra for on a PC, you'll find that the price difference isn't all that great. For example, my Mac iBook includes a CD writer, DVD reader, modem, Ethernet, one FireWire port and two USB ports, a VGA output for an external monitor, and a microphone and audio line out. When I priced out similarly equipped laptops from Sony, Dell, and Hewlett-Packard and added in software for data encryption, editing photos, making PDF documents, and creating audio loops a la GarageBand, the Mac was actually cheaper.

Nonetheless, the only way to use the excellent Mac OS is to buy a computer from Apple. Of course, since Apple is well known for its innovative design and highly rated for customer satisfaction and tech support, that isn't necessarily a bad thing.

Microsoft Windows

The Windows world is all about choice. Not only can you choose from dozens of PC makers and hundreds of thousands of components and peripherals, all of which you may customize to your heart's content, but you can even choose among several different versions of the Windows OS itself. Windows takes its name from the graphical user interface that uses virtual windows with icons and small pictures that are activated via pointing and clicking with a mouse. (Yes, it's just like the Mac's. For the record, the original GUI was developed by Xerox back in the '70s, but no one picked up on the idea until Apple debuted the Lisa in 1983. Bill Gates released Windows 1.0 in 1985, and the rest is history.)

Windows XP (the current version) comes in several "editions," each with its own set of features aimed at particular users. Here's a quick rundown:

* **Home.** As its name implies, Windows XP Home is designed for the home computer. It includes connectivity to the Internet, support for videos and music via Windows Media Player, and other features geared to the home user. Although it doesn't have professional features such as advanced security and access control to seal off important files from prying eyes, Windows XP Home is the best choice for most PC users assembling a computer music system.

* **Media Center.** The Windows Media Center Edition is for a new type of device—the home entertainment center PC. Media Center PCs are designed to play and store home video and TV, play music on CD or MP3, organize and share digital photos, and connect to the Internet. Designed to be the hub of your home entertainment system, these machines feature enhanced graphics, CD-ROM and DVD drives, high-capacity hard drives, and other features that make them excellent choices for computer music applications. That is, if you can get them away from the kids.

* **Professional.** With file encryption, remote access, centralized administration, and other heavy-duty business services, Windows XP Professional is a solid choice for anyone doing work that involves networking.

* **Professional x64.** If you have a computer that supports 64-bit processing, this version of Windows gives you a huge productivity boost. The OS supports up to 128GB of RAM and 16 terabytes of virtual memory (allocating a portion of the hard disk for RAM). That's a lot. Although very few music software titles support 64-bit processing, it is only a matter of time until they all do. In the meantime, all of your 32-bit software will work just fine. Should you make the jump? If you have a dual processor and routinely handle huge audio and video files, sure. Otherwise, it's probably more than you'll need for a long time.

No matter which version of the Windows OS you choose, you'll need to pick up a few more applications if you plan on connecting to the Web. Sadly, hordes of unscrupulous weasels roam the Web, endlessly probing for weaknesses in the Windows operating system. As a result, PCs are famously prone to viruses and spyware. Pick up a firewall and antivirus and anti-spyware programs and keep them up to date by checking the manufacturers' Web sites regularly.

Linux

Linux (pronounced "LIH-nicks") is the first open-source operating system to catch on. "Open source" means that anyone can tinker with it; as a result, the system is constantly improving and growing. (See Figure 3.1.) Originally developed by Linus Torvalds, Linux has many similarities to the Unix operating system underlying the Mac OS. Linux is making inroads into the business world due to its low cost—basically, it's free—and easy customization.

Although some music software is beginning to show up for Linux, its inability to support some of the multimedia formats home users take for granted leaves it not quite ready for prime time. Nonetheless, a goodly sample of music software is already out there, including MIDI sequencers, digital audio recording and editing tools, software instruments, and more.

Linux exists in various formats, called distributions, developed for specific tasks and types of computers. True to its do-it-yourself nature, some versions are designed to run on older computers, breathing new live into obsolete hardware. What's more, Linux can run on Windows machines, so you don't have to give up your familiar desktop all at once.

If you are the type of person who likes to get your hands dirty, or if you want to be on the cutting edge, Linux is worth checking out. Go to http://www.linux.org for more information. Besides, it has the best logo, hands down.

Figure 3.1
Designed by Larry Ewing,
Tux the Linux penguin
projects a friendly image.
Makes you want to try the
Linux OS, doesn't it?

❊ **CHOOSE YOUR MUSIC SOFTWARE FIRST**

It may seem counterintuitive, but the best way to make a decision about your operating system is to decide what music software you'll be using first. Although many software manufacturers create software from both Windows and the Mac OS, some rather significant programs only run on one or the other. For instance, if you are doing large orchestrations and need a huge library with streaming sample playback, one of your best choices is TASCAM's GigaStudio. And GigaStudio works only on a Windows PC. Similarly, Sony's Acid Pro was the first audio looping software to incorporate sophisticated processing to speed up the time-consuming process of matching loop tempos. Yep, it's Windows only. As you'd expect, Apple's terrific digital audio workstation, Logic Pro, works only with the Mac OS.

What's more, certain programs may not support the latest version of an OS. The only way to know is to check a company's Web site for compatibility information. Refer to Appendix C, "Manufacturers," for a list.

You can read about music software in Chapter 4, "Choosing Your Software: What Do You Want to Do?"

Choosing Your Computer Hardware

Now that you've got some idea about the main operating systems, let's take a look at the bits and pieces that go inside the big plastic box we call a computer. In this section, I'll discuss such important topics as processor speed, memory, connectivity issues, and mass storage to help you understand what goes into configuring a computer that best meets your need.

The bulk of this section will look at the Windows-based PC world for the simple reason that these machines are by far the most user customizable. Unlike Mac users, PC customers have a choice of many different makes and kinds of processors, hard drives, video cards, and other hardware. In short, you'll be basically asking the manufacturer to build your machine from the ground up. Have no fear; I will discuss the various offerings from Apple, too.

Once you're up to speed on the terminology and choices, I'll outline some suggested systems for specific tasks.

Processor Speed

Think of the CPU, or central processing unit, as the brains of your computer. The CPU is responsible for the millions of mathematical calculations that go into everything that happens inside the humming block of plastic on your desk. All things being equal, the faster the processor, the faster the computer can do what you want it to.

Processor speed is measured in Hertz, or cycles per second (abbreviated Hz). The speed refers to how fast the CPU master clock is set, by the way. All digital devices require a timing source, called a clock, to operate. Most CPUs now clock in at speeds in excess of 1GHz (gig, for short)—that's one thousand million cycles per second, or 1,000,000,000Hz. Why is that important? Each set of computer instructions requires a fixed number of cycles to complete. The sheer number of calculations needed to boost the volume on an audio file or render the output of a software synthesizer is mind boggling.

One of the fundamental laws of computers is that processor speed doubles every few years. Just a few years ago a 300MHz (a megahertz is one million cycles per second) was so cutting edge that only high-end professional recording studios could afford one.

But don't get seduced into thinking that all you have to do is pick up the fastest chip on the block and you'll be set. The number of bits a processor can handle at once is also a factor. At the time I write this, most computers operate at 32 bits (see the glossary in Appendix A, "Glossary," for definitions of any terms you don't know), which means they can process a chunk of data made up of a string of numbers 32 digits long. Since each additional bit increases the amount of information by a factor of 10, this is a huge improvement over the 16-bit computers of just a few years ago. Sixty-four bit machines are readily available, and both Windows and the Mac OS can take advantage of them. However, until the music software is upgraded, you may or may not get a speed boost that's worth the extra expense.

❋ FASTER IS FASTER, RIGHT?

Everyone knows that a 4-gig PC running Windows is twice as fast as a 2-gig G5 Power Mac. That's a no brainer, right? Well, don't be so sure. I've been surfing computer-geek sites and reading tech journals and computer magazines for years. What I've been able to glean is this: It appears that PCs and Macs are measured using different scales. What is far more important than simple specs is how fast the CPUs actually *work* when doing the kinds of tasks you'd expect in a home studio. The usual way to measure "real-world" computing speed is by setting up benchmark tests with operations such as rendering digital video or altering photos. And here is where things really get confusing. Depending on the test, the "slower" Mac may smoke the "faster" PC.

When you add in other factors, such as the speed of the video card, the number of processors, or the chip's brand and design, it really becomes murky. High-end PCs run blazingly fast. So do top-of-the-line Macs. On some tests, the Mac wins. On others, the PC does. And I'm afraid it depends a lot on who is doing the testing. Yes, a manufacturer will skew its test results to make its products look better.

About all you can say is within the PC world, faster is better. Within the Mac world, faster is better, too. But compare Macs to PCs, and all bets are off.

Processor Types

Spend a few minutes shopping for a PC, and you can't help but be confused by the various brand-name processors. Since things change rapidly in the tech world, I'm afraid I can give you only the most general information. Here's the skinny.

Intel makes two lines of processors that you'll see a lot. The Celeron chips are aimed at the basic office and consumer market. Found in less-expensive computers, they are plenty powerful for home-education programs, MIDI sequencing and looping, and surfing the Internet. Although the rumor that Celeron processors were unable to handle the rigors of digital audio has been debunked, they are best used for projects with small track counts and a limited number of effects.

The flagship Pentium chips are considerably more powerful and have enhanced video capabilities, making them ideal for gamers and anyone doing video editing. They would be the best choice for applications that involve a lot of digital audio, particularly if you'll be running lots of software instruments and effects.

IBM has been in the business for about as long as anybody. Its PowerPC chips are the brains behind the Mac, and for a long time a computer used for business had to have a processor from IBM—period. It makes numerous 32-bit chips, as well as the 970/970FX 64-bit chip.

The other big player is AMD, which sells microprocessors (yet another name for the CPU) under the Athlon moniker. AMD chips have an almost fanatical following among gamers and compare favorably to the Pentiums.

❄ MACINTOSH GOES INTEL

As I was writing this section, Apple made the stunning announcement that it would be switching from the IBM PowerPC chip to a chip made by Intel. The first Intel-based Macs are expected to hit the shelves in the summer of 2006.

Aside from a missed stock opportunity, what does this mean to Mac users? Quite a bit, actually. In the first place, all of the software that runs on a Mac will eventually have to be rewritten. The good news is that a translation application called Rosetta will let legacy programs written for the PowerPC chip work on the new Intel Macs, albeit more slowly than new versions will. That means Mac users will not have to spring for upgrades all at once. The bad news is that Rosetta may not support programs that require the G4 and G5 Altivec engine, which includes just about every music program you can think of. However, given the relatively long lead time between announcing the change and shipping new product, this may be a non-issue.

Apple feels that the move will help it continue to innovate. It may help bring costs down, too, which is always a good thing. In the meantime, there is no compelling reason to avoid buying a Mac if you need one. The machine and software you buy today will operate for years. Besides, it's never a good idea to be the first one to jump on the first release of a new technology. Let somebody else find all the bugs. Whether Macs will be able to run Windows software remains to be seen.

Bus Speed and Cache Memory

Two other numbers to pay attention to are the bus speed and the cache size. The bus refers to the pathway data takes between the CPU and the computer's main RAM (Random Access Memory). The fastest chip in the world is worthless if the flow of data can't keep up. However, don't be alarmed if the bus speed is significantly less than the CPU's clock speed. The CPU's speed refers to how many calculations it can do a second, but the bus speed describes how fast the data moves in and out.

Some processors, including the Intel Pentium, use a dual bussing architecture, with one bus (called the front side bus) moving data to and from RAM while the other (backside bus) serves the L2 cache memory. What's that? Cache memory is a form of special RAM. To save time, the microprocessor first looks in the L1 (Level One) cache, a bit of RAM built into the CPU chip itself. The L2 cache is a separate, static RAM chip. (Unlike dynamic RAM, DRAM for short, static RAM doesn't need to be continually bathed with an electrical charge to maintain its memory. This makes it faster but also much more expensive.)

Okay, so what's it all mean? Basically this: With bus speed, faster is better. With cache size, bigger is better. Are you beginning to see a trend here?

Motherboard

The motherboard is the circuit board containing the CPU chip and sockets for all of the other subassemblies your computer may need. These include such items as the hard drive video card for the monitor, expansion slots to connect PCI cards for sound cards and FireWire interfaces, and much more. You need to be aware of the motherboard's configuration so your system can expand and change to meet your needs. Many motherboards use a ZIF, or zero insertion force, socket to lock down the processor chip. This lets you swap out the processor for a more powerful one down the line—far cheaper than buying a whole new computer! Some good motherboard brands to look for are Iwill, Abit, and Intel.

❀ **WHAT'S WITH THE FANS?**

The CPU works by shuttling electrons around. As anybody who has ever tried to change a light bulb while it's on knows, that can generate a lot of heat.

Perhaps that's not a great analogy, but CPUs do get hot. What's worse, if they get too hot, they stop working. Permanently. So computer manufacturers take great pains to find ways to move hot air away from the CPU. Basically, there are two ways to do it: passively, with metal heat sinks and clever airflow channels, and actively, using fans.

In a system designed to sit under a desk in a noisy office environment, the added noise of one of two tiny fans doesn't amount to much. But in a typical one-room home recording studio, that annoying drone creeps into every track you record.

What to do? One option is to shop for a quiet computer—more and more companies are offering them. At the best, these machines feature sophisticated airflow routing and tiny, low-noise fans that come on only when things really heat up. Notebook computers are often much quieter than desktops, which makes them great choices for the home studio.

Many people place their computers and any noisy peripherals in a room separate from the studio and use extra-long cables to connect the monitor, keyboard, and mouse. Although you can purchase or build an isolation box for the computer, be sure that it is well ventilated, preferably to the outside of the room. Don't be tempted to disconnect any of the internal fans inside the computer's case. Your CPU will melt down faster than you can say "D'oh."

Memory

The CPU uses special chips to temporarily store the operating system, application programs, and data so they can be quickly accessed. It's called Random Access Memory because it doesn't matter where the data is written on the chip's surface; any storage location is instantly accessible. This makes RAM very fast. However, RAM content lasts only as long as the power is turned on. What's more, the CPU is constantly loading fresh information into RAM as needed.

Most computers come with a minimal amount of RAM—256MB seems to be the de facto standard right now. Unless you'll be running very simple applications, this is never enough. Fortunately, even the most basic consumer computers have slots for additional RAM.

How much do you need? Buy as much as you can afford. No single upgrade has a bigger effect on your computer's performance than increasing RAM. As a baseline for light-duty home use such as connecting to the Internet or running simple scoring, sequencing, and educational programs, increase the RAM to at least 512MB. For music applications that use software instruments and digital audio processing, 1 gig is a practical minimum. At 2 to 4GB and above, things really start to hum.

RAM Types

RAM is relatively cheap, but it's worthless if you don't buy the proper type for your computer. Various types are available; I'll talk about the three most common.

SDRAM (synchronous dynamic RAM) is the kind used in most basic computers. It takes its name from the fact that it is synchronized to the CPU's clock speed. In other words, you need to match the RAM to your processor. Luckily, that's pretty easy to do. Most vendors offer tech support or online tables to match your computer's make, model, and CPU with the appropriate RAM chip.

DDR SDRAM (double data rate SDRAM) operates at a much higher bandwidth than SDRAM. This in turn makes it considerably faster.

RDRAM (Rambus Dynamic RAM) is a memory subsystem that replaces both the RAM chips and the bus. It dramatically increases the amount of data and the access speed, making it a potent choice for streaming video and multimedia applications.

Installing RAM

Adding RAM to your computer is something that most people can do on their own. RAM comes in small circuit boards that click into special slots on the motherboard. Depending on your computer, you may need to open the case to expose the motherboard, or you may only have to open an access slot located on the bottom or side of the case.

The first step is to figure out how much RAM is installed in your computer. In Windows, right click on My Computer and select Properties. You'll see a screen full of information about the system, including the amount of RAM. In Mac OS X, click on the Apple symbol at the top left of the screen and scroll down to About This Mac. The window, shown in Figure 3.2, gives you basic system info, including the amount and type of memory.

Be sure to buy the proper type of RAM—mixing different types of memory modules (another name for RAM chips) is a very bad idea. Consult your manual for the correct type, or check the vendor's Web site for compatibility charts. Be very careful when handling the chips—stray static charges, such as those that build up when you walk across a carpet, can destroy them. At the very least, ground yourself by touching a grounded metal object, such as the computer's power

Figure 3.2
My office computer has 1 gig of RAM, enough for most basic graphics tasks and light-duty digital audio work.

supply, before touching the module. Or pick up a grounding strap from an electronics store such as Radio Shack. These typically have an elastic band that goes around your wrist and connects to a plug or clip that you attach to the ground of an electrical switch. No matter which grounding scheme you use, only handle the modules by the edges.

Next, turn off and unplug you computer and place it on a flat, sturdy surface. Now all you have to do is pop open the computer's case and insert the RAM into the proper slots. That may involve a bit of sleuthing, though. Your computer manual—you did save it, didn't you?—can guide you to the proper location. Otherwise, find the motherboard—it's the large circuit board with all the other subassemblies plugged into it—and snoop around for the existing RAM. It'll look like the chips you just bought. You may also see several empty memory slots just waiting to be filled.

If you are simply adding more memory, insert the new RAM into the next available open slots. Otherwise, remove the memory that's currently installed and add the newer, larger chips. If you did it right, the clips at each end of the socket will fasten themselves securely. It takes a bit of pressure to seat the module in the socket, but do not use excessive force. You could break the motherboard, effectively rendering your computer a very expensive doorstop.

If you swapped out your old chips, place them inside the static-free bag that held the new modules. You may need these again if your new memory should fail. (See "All Memory Ain't Created Equal" in the following sidebar.)

Before you button up the computer, plug it back in and power it up. If all is well, your system will run some self-tests and then boot up normally. In Windows, you'll see a screen that shows the new memory; in OS X go back to About This Mac to be sure it sees the new chips. If the computer locks up or fails to recognize the memory, shut down and check to see that the modules are inserted properly. If the computer still refuses to cooperate after you've pulled them out and reinstalled them, there's a possibility you've got a bad chip. That's why you saved the old ones—stick them back and go call the vendor's help line.

❈ **ALL MEMORY AIN'T CREATED EQUAL**

"Chips is chips, right? If they have the same specs, shouldn't a $35 512MB module work just as well as a $59 512MB one? After all, it is a global economy, and all the chips are really made in the same plant, aren't they? The only difference is that the big-name companies charge more because they think we're suckers who will pay for a brand name."

Yes, I have heard these arguments. In fact, I'm ashamed to admit I believed them myself once upon a time. But there is a lot more to the story.

The big difference between the discount brands and the ones recommended by your computer's manufacturer has to do with quality control. Strictly speaking, what you are paying for when you buy a well-known brand is the assurance that they have tested the chips repeatedly, all down the line. That means they are more likely to meet, or exceed, the stated specifications, which in turn means they are far less likely to fail.

Yes, chips do fail. In fact, a senior support technician from a major computer company told me that chip failure caused by third-rate discount memory is the leading cause of serious computer problems. When RAM chips fail, you can lose more than time.

If your digital data and piece of mind are important to you, spend a little extra dough and buy only high-quality memory. Kingston is a good brand.

Virtual Memory

If you don't have enough RAM to run several applications at once, both the Mac OS and Windows automatically take advantage of your computer's virtual memory. What's that? Basically, your system uses a small portion of the hard drive as a temporary storage area, just like RAM. Virtual memory can be as large as the free space on your hard drive.

So why buy RAM at all? Why not just use virtual memory? Because virtual memory is far slower than RAM. Intensive applications, and that includes most music-related ones, may not work properly. This could cause you to lose data or bring the whole system to a screeching halt.

Save up a few bucks and buy lots of RAM. You'll thank me for it later.

Hard Drives

The hard drive is where you keep all of your application files (aka "programs") and data files (aka "stuff"). Hard drives come in two basic configurations: Internal drives are mounted inside the computer's case; external drives are inside their own little boxes and connected to the computer via a cable. Other than the location, internal and external drives are virtually identical.

Internal Drives

Even the cheapest PCs now come with 60 or 80GB internal hard drives. That oughta be plenty, right? Depends on what you'll be doing. If you're the type who likes to store all of your music and home videos on your computer, even an 80 gig drive will fill up quickly.

If multitrack digital audio and/or multimedia is your cup of chai, insist on a 250 gig hard drive or bigger and consider adding a second, either an internal drive installed in an open bay inside the case or an external drive. These days, almost all drives spin at a minimum of 7200 RPM (revolutions per minute). This is a good thing—faster spin translates to faster data reading and writing. And digital audio and video data must be written and read very fast indeed. Drives rated for serious AV (audiovisual) work spin at 10,000 RPM.

If you have an older PC using Windows 2000 or earlier, you may need to update your operating system before you can install a drive larger than 137GB.

External Drives

Most audio professionals will tell you not to record to the drive that contains the operating system. The CPU is constantly performing dozens of chores, ranging from basic housekeeping such as moving data in and out of RAM to refreshing the computer monitor to monitoring the flow of data along the USB bus. That's in addition to any work you've asked it to do, such as recording a vocal take while playing back the backing tracks. And each one of those tasks requires data to be read from and written to the hard drive. So you can imagine that it's not out of the question for something to go wrong and a bit of data to get dropped. Are you sure you want to take the chance that it won't be part of the vocal recording?

The best solution is to invest in an external drive. Here's where you'll need to make another choice. The PC world favors a connectivity scheme called USB (universal serial bus), while Apple went with something called IEEE 1394, better known as FireWire. Both USB and FireWire are *hot swappable*, which means you can plug and unplug devices without turning them off. Both are robust and very well supported—in fact, every Mac comes standard with both.

Of the two, FireWire is by far the better choice for a hard drive—its data-transfer rates are well up to the job of handling multiple streams of video and high-definition digital audio. If you do decide to go with USB, be sure it's USB 2. It sports data-transfer rates up to 480MB per second—that's enough for multichannel audio and video. USB 1 is simply not up to the task. (See "Connectivity" later in this chapter for more about USB and FireWire.)

External hard drives designed for digital audio, such as the Glyph GT 050 (see Figure 3.3), feature rock-solid performance at high data-transfer rates. As a not insignificant extra, Glyph drives are also whisper quiet, something you'll appreciate in a home studio.

Figure 3.3
The Glyph GT 050, an external hard drive, is available in a variety of sizes.

Mass Storage

Although most users treat their main hard drive as the permanent repository for all of their files—photos, music, games, business documents, letters to Mom, and all the rest—you aren't going to do that. Want to know why? Because you are going to be creating music and multimedia, and you know that the data stored on your hard drive exists in the precarious state between being and nothingness. Well, at any rate, you are about to know it.

This is so important I'm going to highlight it. It's called The First Law of Digital Data.

> ❄ **THE FIRST LAW OF DIGITAL DATA**
>
> Digital data does not exist until it is backed up and stored safely. Twice.
> Hard drives sometimes fail. In fact, hard drives fail with remarkable regularity. And when they do, they take all of your data with them. The only way to get it back is to restore it from a copy you stored somewhere else.
> But it gets worse. Much, much worse. Because a million and one things may cause your data to disappear. Your application suddenly decides that a file is corrupted (a nice safe term for #@%$#-ed up). The OS hiccups and forgets to write the contents of RAM to the drive. A power surge blows through the line and zaps the drive motor. Your cat tries to balance on your double mocha latte. Remember that "free" software you downloaded? It was a virus that proceeds to eat your data. Your 11-year-old decides she needs more hard drive space to store a video clip. You've accumulated so many spybots that the only way to reclaim your computer is to wipe the drive.
> And that's not the half of it. Even if you practice safe computing, even if you back up every file to a CD-R on a regular basis, *your backups* can fail. If your songs and other data files are important to you, make backups of your backups and store them in a nice, safe place. Preferably away from power surges, cats, and 11-year-olds.

CD Burners

CD-ROMs (short for compact disc read only memory) have been around for so long they really don't need any introduction. It's nigh on impossible to find a computer these days that doesn't feature a drive that both reads and writes CDs. But, in the event you do, add one. By the way, CD recorders are called "burners" because they work by melting little pits in a dye layer on the disc.

Recordable CDs store up to 800MB of data—enough to handle dozens of stereo audio files, hundreds of MP3s, or thousands of SMFs (Standard MIDI Files). What's more, you can also make *Red Book–compliant* audio CDs. What are those? The specification books for the different types of CDs are bound in different colors. The Red Book relates to audio CDs. If you burn a Red Book CD, it will play on any CD player anywhere. Add some snappy graphics, and you're an independent label.

Of course, depending on your software, your CD burner will happily spit out enhanced CDs with audio and video, video CDs, photo CDs, CD+G (karaoke), and plain-vanilla data CDs. Those are called CD-ROMs, too.

If you plan on producing a number of CDs, consider investing in an outboard duplicator, such as the Microboards QD-2 QuickDisc. Or really automate the process with the Bravo II Disc Publisher from Primera Technology, an all-in-one powerhouse that copies CDs and prints right on the disc.

DVD Reader/Writers

DVDs are good for a lot more than just watching movies. Though a DVD reader in your notebook will let you do just that—handy for those long cross-country flights. Many computers now come with a combination drive that reads and writes CDs and reads DVDs. But hold out for one that writes DVDs, too. Particularly if you'll be generating lots of large files, such as those with multi-channel audio or multimedia. DVDs handle a lot of information; the most common form can store more than 4.7GB.

Like CDs, recordable DVDs come in various types and flavors, not all of which are compatible. Refer to the following list to learn more about recordable CDs and DVDs.

CD and DVD Recordable Types

❊ **CD-R.** A write-once CD format. CD-Rs can hold up to 800MB of data (which works out to about 80 minutes of stereo music). CD-Rs designed specifically for consumer music recorders have copy-protection coding. Various CD standards exist for discs intended for music, data, video, and other applications.

❊ **CD-RW.** A rewritable CD-R.

❊ **DVD-R.** A write-once DVD format compatible with most DVD players. Holds 4.7GB of data.

❊ **DVD-RW.** A rewritable DVD-R. Slightly less compatible than DVD-R; DVD-RWs may be rewritten up to 1,000 times before they fail.

❊ **DVD+R.** A write-once format, similar to but incompatible with DVD-R. Playable only on devices that explicitly support DVD+R and "multiformat" recorders/players. Also holds 4.7GB.

❋ **DVD+RW.** The rewritable form of the DVD+R.

❋ **DVD-RAM.** A form of rewritable DVD, mostly used for recording and playback of TV shows on set-top video recorders.

Memory Cards

More and more computers sport slots for the common flash memory cards used in digital cameras, PDAs (personal digital assistants), and music players. If you use one of these devices, a card reader really speeds up the process of moving data in and out of the computer.

Connectivity

I've already mentioned USB and FireWire in connection with hard drives. Now I want to give you a bit more information on how you can use these and other technologies to interface with other devices you'll be using.

USB

USB is just about the best thing to happen in the Personal Computer world since sliced bread. Even in its original release, USB 1, it made hooking up such useful devices as printers, scanners, QWERTY (standard) keyboards, and mice as simple as plugging in a cable. USB is a true hot-swappable, plug-and-play technology. That means you can start using a device as soon as you insert the cable, and you don't have to power down to exchange it for another. (To be fair, some USB devices require software drivers to operate.) In the crazy world of computer music, where inspiration may come at any time, this is a very good thing indeed.

The downside to USB 1 is speed—it simply isn't fast enough to handle the demands of digital audio and video. So save USB 1 for printers, input devices, MIDI interfaces, and scanners. The good news is that USB 2 is plenty quick. You'll need its 400MB per second transfer rate and data throughput for high-definition multichannel audio interfaces such as the Edirol UA-1000. USB 2 is almost universally supported, but you may still find computers with only USB 1 ports. Pass those by and insist on USB 2 if you'll be doing anything more demanding than playing the occasional game of solitaire.

By the way, you don't need to buy all new peripherals when you upgrade computers. If you plug an older device into the faster USB 2 port, it will work just fine, though at the slower speed. That means you must be wary of daisy-chaining USB 1 and USB 2 devices together; otherwise the whole chain will run at the speed of USB 1.

FireWire 400 and 800

The original FireWire came out of the gate with data transfer speeds around 400MB per second—far faster than USB was capable of handling at the time. Like USB, FireWire is hot swappable and generally does not need special drivers. Thanks to its speed, it has become the standard for transferring huge amounts of data, such as 24 tracks of high-definition digital audio.

The second generation, FireWire 800, is twice as fast. And again, like USB, it is backwards-compatible with older devices.

Many professionals feel that FireWire is the clear choice for demanding audio and video tasks. If you'll be working with high-sample-rate multitrack audio, be sure to outfit your computer with at least one FireWire 800 port.

You will find that many more devices—printers, scanners, digital cameras, MIDI interfaces, and electronic keyboards—support USB than FireWire. FireWire is great for external hard drives, video, and high-end audio interfaces such as the Presonus Firepod or MOTU 896HD. But thanks to the increased throughput, USB 2 audio interfaces such as TASCAM's US-428 and all-in-one devices such as the M-Audio Ozone offer musicians a wide range of choices. (See Chapter 7 to learn more about audio interfaces.)

So which should you choose? My advice is both. USB and FireWire coexist peacefully on the same computer, so you can take advantage of the strengths of each. As a practical minimum, set up your computer with two USB ports for your keyboard, mouse, MIDI interface, and printer and a single FireWire port for a high-capacity external hard drive. Then you can choose an audio interface that meets your needs.

USB and FireWire Throughputs Compared

- ❋ USB 1.1: 12MB per second
- ❋ USB 2: 480MB per second
- ❋ FireWire 400: 400MB per second
- ❋ FireWire 800: 800MB per second

SCSI and IDE/ATA

I would be remiss if I didn't mention these two interfaces. SCSI and IDE/ATA (Integrated Drive Electronics/AT Attachment) are technologies for moving data in and out of hard drives. Both are still very much in use. IDE/ATA is the protocol feeding your internal hard drive. In its various permutations, IDE/ATA is known by many, many other names, including ATA, ATAPI, EIDE, and Ultra DMA. You may run across it as a connection protocol for external drives as well, though USB and FireWire have largely supplanted it.

SCSI (small computer systems interface) is another oldie but goodie. Of the two, many audio engineers consider SCSI the better choice for audio. If you've got a ton of data stored on older SCSI or ATA drives, you may consider adding a SCSI or ATA port when configuring your new computer.

Ethernet

Ethernet connectivity is vital if you'll be using a high-speed Internet connection or connecting your computer to a network. What's that? A network is a group of devices—computers, printers, scanners, hard drives, and others—that is connected together to share resources and files. A LAN (local area network) makes a lot of sense for the increasingly wired home.

> ❄ **WIRELESS CONNECTIVITY**
>
> Wi-fi is all the rage. With a laptop and a wireless card, you can connect to the Internet anywhere—your backyard, the airport, or a park bench. Bluetooth, one wireless standard, is widely supported for PDAs, cell phones, and all new Apple computers and eliminates the wires tying your computer to the keyboard, mouse, or printer. Sadly, wireless data transfer rates aren't up to the demands of video and digital audio, but it's just a matter of time.

Monitors

You use input devices, such as QWERTY keyboards and mice, to communicate with the computer. In the world of computer music, specialized input devices, such as the JL Cooper CS-32 USB Control Surface, greatly speed your workflow. I'll talk about these in Chapter 8, "Track Four: All Together Now: The Desktop DAW."

The monitor is how the computer communicates with you. It can be anything from the tiny 12-inch screen I'm working on right now as I fly across the Pacific to a huge cinema-sized display in a video production studio. Let's take a second to get you up to speed so you can choose the best monitor for your needs.

LCD or CRT?

Basically, computer monitors are TV screens. And just like TV screens, they come in several different configurations. (And, yes, you can connect some computers to your TV.) CRTs (short for cathode ray tubes) are the big boxes that are often as deep as they are high. CRT technology has been around a long time, and the monitors that use it are cheap. Most now have flat screens to reduce glare, meaning the viewing surface is flat and not slightly curved like the older styles. Flat-screen CRTs are terrific values—if you have the space for one. A 20-inch CRT monitor may sell for well under $100.

The terms "flat screen" and "flat panel" are not interchangeable. Unlike the old-fashioned, curved picture tubes, flat-screen CRT monitors have a flat viewing surface to reduce glare and distortion. Flat-panel monitors use LCD screens, a very different and more expensive technology. LCD (liquid crystal display) monitors look great on your desktop and take up far less room than the bulkier CRTs. As the technology matures, resolution (related to how sharp and clear the image looks) is increasing almost as fast as prices are dropping. Still, a 20-inch LCD monitor will set you back around five times as much as a comparable CRT.

Minimum Monitor Size

Monitors are measured diagonally, so a 17-inch screen has considerably more surface area than a 15-inch one. One thing is certain: Get the biggest monitor you can afford. The bigger the monitor, the more information you'll see. Navigating through multiple windows is a heck of a lot easier if they are spread across a nice big display. (See Figure 3.4.)

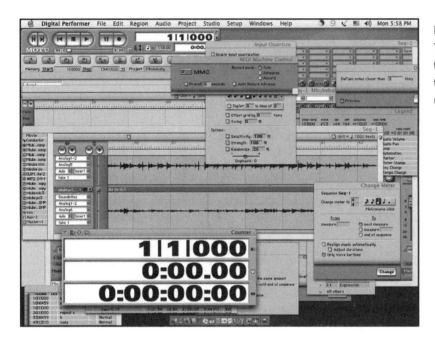

Figure 3.4

There's nothing worse than trying to work on a monitor that's too small for your needs!

Even better, add a second monitor. Not all computers support this out of the box, so you may need to add a PCI video card, such as those from NVIDIA, ATI, GeForce, and Sonnet. (See "What's PCI?" in the following sidebar.) Video cards also increase the video rendering speed, vital for 3-D applications, such as games, and very large monitors. Be sure to do your homework before you buy—there's no sense buying an expensive high-definition 3-D card if all you need is a second monitor to view spreadsheets! Some computers support the Accelerated Graphics Port (AGP), which operates at almost double the bandwidth of PCI. (See Appendix D, "Resources.")

❄ **WHAT'S PCI?**

PCI (peripheral component interconnect) lets you plug special circuit boards (called *cards*) directly onto the motherboard. PCI cards are used to expand the basic functions of your computer. Besides the video cards mentioned above, you can use PCI to add USB and/or FireWire, Ethernet connectivity, enhanced graphics, specialized gaming interfaces, MIDI, and more. PCI cards that add sound-generating capabilities are called *sound cards*. SoundBlaster from Creative Technology is the de facto standard for gaming and basic audio playback. Sound cards designed for serious audio work are called *audio interfaces*.

Laptop owners can take advantage of a similar technology—called PCMCIA (Personal Computer Memory Card Association).

Input Devices

Even though many computer purchases include a mouse and rudimentary QWERTY keyboard, consider going beyond the basics. These days, most computers use USB for keyboards and mice, but you will still encounter some machines with serial ports.

Keyboards

Here's a little-known fact—the familiar layout of the typewriter-style keyboard we all use was actually designed to slow down the rate at which a typist could write! That's right, the first mechanical typewriters couldn't keep up with the speed of early typists, so some clever git thought up the least efficient way to place the letters. And we've been stuck with it ever since. (In all fairness, the inventor, one L. C. Shoales, actually helped speed up typing by eliminating the constant jamming and stuck keys caused by typists using his original, alphabetical key arrangement.)

At any rate, the "universal" keyboard with its linear key layout is not necessarily the best arrangement of keys. If you'll be spending a lot of time typing, consider investing in a curved, ergonomic keyboard to reduce fatigue and lessen the risk of repetitive stress injuries. (See Figure 3.5.) A wireless keyboard is another good idea, particularly in the sometimes-crowded home studio.

Figure 3.5

The ergonomic Maxim Adjustable Keyboard from Kinesis reduces the stress that can cause carpal tunnel syndrome and other injuries. Used with permission of Kinesis Corporation, 2005.

Mice

The mouse—a point-and-click input device—may be the single greatest contribution to computing since silicon. For some reason, Macs use mice with a single button, while the rest of the world uses a device with two buttons. No matter. With a little customization, any USB mouse will work with any computer. Here again, consider a wireless mouse—you'll never know when you may need to grab an onscreen scroll bar while you are seated well away from your desk.

Other Input Options

Since a lot of my work involves graphics and photo retouching, I use a small tablet and pen input device. The pen can handle many of the same tasks as a mouse, and it is far more intuitive when changing parameters for plug-ins and other music software.

If you'll be playing games or sharing your computer with someone who will, it almost goes without saying that you'll need a gaming interface. In some cases, you can use these for your music software, too.

USB or MIDI control surfaces range from simple knobs and sliders found on electronic keyboards to full-featured production tools such as the Mackie Control Universal. Refer to Chapter 8 for a discussion of how a control surface can improve your life.

That about sums up our tour through the various components that make up your computer. In later chapters we'll look at choosing your software and adding audio and/or MIDI interfaces and monitor speakers. But before we move on, I want to talk a little about using a portable computer as your main music machine and discuss the pros and cons of having a dedicated computer for music applications.

Finally, I'll lay out a few suggested systems for various applications.

Laptops and Dedicated Workstations

Laptops have come a long way since the underpowered, heavy machines of a few years ago. For many people, a portable computer is the ideal choice for a music system. Built to withstand hard use, a laptop lets you take your music where you need it—to the stage, on tour, or to the beach. The two biggest drawbacks to portables are the cost—laptops are far more expensive than comparably equipped desktops—and the small monitor screen. That's why many home studio musicians use a *dock*, a device to connect a full-sized external monitor, keyboard, mouse, and other peripherals to a laptop.

Thanks to bus-powered interfaces such as the MOTU Traveler and TASCAM US-122 (see Figure 3.6), laptops make fantastic full-featured remote recording rigs. Gone are the days when you needed a large van to record your band's gig! When shopping for a laptop, be sure it has the connectivity you'll need. Insist on at least one FireWire 800 port and two USB 2 ports. Ethernet and/or a wireless card is essential for high-speed networking. A PCMCIA slot—the portable's equivalent of PCI—is useful for adding options such as an internal audio card or a second monitor. As with desktops, plan on adding lots of RAM.

Figure 3.6
With TASCAM's compact US-122 audio/MIDI interface and your laptop, you're ready whenever and wherever inspiration strikes.

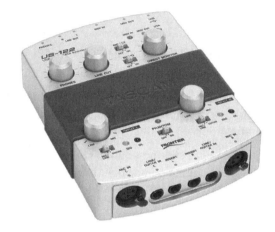

If you'll be doing seriously demanding audio work, consider purchasing a turnkey system designed specifically for computer audio. Dedicated systems by venders such as WaveDigital, Marathon Computers, and Musical Computer (see Appendix C, "Manufacturers") have the advantage of carefully matched hardware and software components, extensive predelivery compatibility testing, quiet operation, and easy integration into your studio.

❄ **ALL-IN-ONE DESKTOP DAWS**

TASCAM began the home studio revolution many years ago with a simple little device that mated a four-track cassette recorder with a rudimentary mixer. Sure, the audio quality left a bit to be desired, but there was simply nothing available that was so easy to use and so dang much fun. Digital descendents of the original PortaStudio are everywhere now. Should you consider buying one?

There is a lot to be said for having everything you need in one small package. Even the simplest devices, such as TASCAM's amazing PocketStudio 5 or the Pandora PXR4 flash recorder, are capable of very high-quality work. The best desktop DAWs, such as Roland's flagship VS2480, the Yamaha AW16G, and the Akai DPS24, rival the features and specs found in professional recording studios. All feature high-quality microphone preamplifiers, internal effects, digital editing, and CD burning, letting you take a song—or an entire CD—from conception to completion in one handy place.

Some people find using a dedicated system far easier than learning their way around a computer DAW. Once you get the hang of the user interface, it makes a great deal of sense to have all of the hardware in one place. And portable systems such as the Fostex VF160EX sure beat the heck out of hauling your computer rig to the gig!

For others, the lack of flexibility and limited upgrade options are a turnoff. Also, editing audio and MIDI data on a desktop unit is not nearly as easy as it is on a computer-based system.

Whatever you decide, integrating a dedicated desktop DAW into your home computer system is generally no harder than hooking up a cable or two and spending a few minutes reading the owner's manual.

Building Your System

Unless you're a dedicated do-it-yourself geek, buy a computer system made by one of the big-name brands. You really can't go wrong with a computer from Hewlett-Packard, Dell, Gateway, or Sony. Of course, if you're interested in the Mac OS, your only choice is Apple.

Do consider buying an extended service plan—three years is the generally accepted life span of a computer. I promise you'll need tech support at some point, and it is nice to have that special comfort of knowing someone will actually answer the call. It really doesn't matter whether you buy online or from your local computer store, though I like to support retailers that employ people in my area. Wherever you buy, don't be seduced into buying more than you need. If you won't be playing games, there's no need for a super high-res 3D video card. And save for the bragging rights, all the power in a top-of-the-line dual-processor machine will be wasted running your MIDI looping software.

What follows is a highly subjective listing of what you may look for in a computer music system.

Education

Just about any basic home computer can handle the software you'll use for music education. No need to spend a bundle; HP and Dell, among others, have recently broken the $300 barrier. You really can't go wrong here, so base your buying decision on your budget and your family's needs.

Be sure to add more RAM—consider 512MB a practical minimum. You may also want to upgrade to a 15-inch or 17-inch flat-panel monitor.

On the Apple side of the fence, at just $499 the new iMac Mini packs a huge amount of processing power into a tiny footprint.

MIDI and Looping

You'll need a little more power, RAM, and hard drive storage space for these applications than you'll find in most basic computers. The Gateway 7310S, with an Intel Pentium D processor, and the Apple eMac are both excellent desktop computers well-suited to MIDI and looping musical production. Both have more than ample speed should you wish to move into light-duty digital audio, such as recording your own loops or adding vocals to a MIDI sequence.

On the portable side, any Apple iBook will more than fit the bill, or check out the Dell Inspiron 2200 notebooks with an Intel Celeron processor. If you think you may step up to digital audio in the near future, pick a machine with a Pentium or Centrino processor.

Digital Music and Multimedia

Digital audio places far greater demands on the CPU and system busses than MIDI. Consider getting a 1 or 2GHz Intel processor with at least 1 gig of RAM, an 80 to 120MB hard disc, and both FireWire 800 and USB 2 ports. At this level of power, you'll find zillions of choices. Or custom-configure a computer from HP, Dell, or Gateway.

Apple's hugely cool iMac has gained a large fan base among desktop studio builders. (On a personal note, I've edited and mixed a number of 24-track CDs on my second-generation 800MHz iMac.) For more power, choose a Power Mac G5.

You'll find lots of laptop choices at this power level. Factors to consider are processor speed (shoot for 1 gig or better), hard drive, connectivity, and battery life. The Compaq Presario V2000 is a fav of the business class due to its low price and long battery life. Apple's excellent iBook laptops offer a terrific value. Consider getting one with a 14-inch screen if you'll be using it as your primary computer.

Multitrack Desktop Recording

Here's where the big dogs play. Basically, buy the biggest, fastest, and most tricked-out computer you can afford. But first do your homework—there is absolutely nothing to be gained by buying a dual-processor computer if your software doesn't support it!

You'll want huge amounts of RAM, several large-capacity hard drives, a DVD and CD burner, dual monitors, and tons of connectivity. Yes, you'll be spending a lot of money—but a couple grand goes pretty far these days.

At this level, the decision to buy a Mac or a PC depends largely on what software you'll be running, as well as what software your associates may be using—many pro studios keep one of each on hand, so they're ready for anything.

Believe it or not, you can do serious audio work on a laptop. Look for the same features you'd expect in a top-of-the-line desktop, load it up with RAM, and hit the road. The HP Compaq Nx9600 boasts a lightning-fast 3.6GHz Intel processor, a DVD recordable drive, and a 17-inch screen, making it an excellent choice for mobile recording. Likewise, any new Apple PowerBook G4 (the PowerBook G5 should be available by the time you read this) has all the features you'll need and then some.

❉ **UPGRADING YOUR OLDER COMPUTER**

So right about now, you may be asking, "Hey, why do I have to buy a new computer? Why can't I just use the same one I've been using all along?" Well, you're right. You don't have to rush out and buy the biggest, newest, flashiest machine. For many applications, the trusty machine you've got right now will work just fine, providing it's not too old.

If you've read this far, you should have some idea of what you'll need to do to get your existing machine up to speed. At the very least, load up the puppy with RAM—nothing will make a greater improvement in computer performance. If you don't have USB or FireWire, consider adding a PCI card and installing the necessary drivers so you can use the new audio and MIDI interfaces. Adding or upgrading a video card can make a huge improvement. Swapping out a small internal hard drive for a larger one or adding a second one is well within the abilities of most home users. Oh, and upgrading your OS will let you use the latest software.

More serious modifications, such as tweaking the CPU's clock speed or exchanging the CPU for a faster one, are not to be undertaken lightly. Be sure that your software will operate with the new board—you'd be surprised at how many applications get snippy when you mess with the processor speed. And whatever you do, back everything up before you start! I've swapped CPUs and lived to tell the tale, but there were many anxious moments along the way.

Before you sink a lot of time and money into your old machine, take a hard look at all of its components. If the system bus is slow, if it's got serial ports and an ancient drive controller, and if you're still backing things up to a floppy drive, maybe it's time to put the poor dear out to pasture.

That about covers it. I hope this chapter has given you a better understanding of what goes on under the hood of your trusty silicon pal. Be sure to check out the links in Appendix D if you'd like more information.

Of course, as computers are becoming both more powerful and less expensive, less and less of this stuff really matters. It won't be long until megafast computers are so cheap we buy and use them like we do toasters—who cares *how* they work, as long as they do?

In the next chapter, I'll talk about the software that makes it all possible.

4 } Choosing Your Software: What Do You Want to Do?

Now that we've looked at the components that compose your computer, let's take a quick glance at the stuff that makes it work—software. In this chapter, I've categorized software by function to help you get a handle on what you may need to follow your musical dream. Some programs, such as Ableton Live, transcend categories, so be sure to read the whole chapter in case the program you need is listed somewhere you don't expect! I have only scratched the surface; rather than attempting to give a comprehensive listing of each and every title, I've concentrated on widely available programs from the biggest companies. This means I've left out a lot of very good and inexpensive programs developed by individuals and distributed mainly on the Web. You can learn more about these programs by following some of the links in Appendix D, "Resources."

As I was putting this chapter together, I found myself amazed at the choices in every software category. Way back when I started in this field, you could choose any digital audio editor you wanted, as long as it was Pro Tools. The choice for MIDI sequencers was slightly better—there were maybe three titles for the Mac and zero for the PC. Plug-in effects? You could count 'em on one hand. And this wasn't very long ago, people. My late-model, low-mileage pickup is older than my first DAW program! All of this is to say that we live in a very exciting time for music.

By the time you read this, most of these products will have gone through one or more upgrades, with added features, more power, and greater flexibility. Some familiar warhorses may have vanished, while new titles may have cropped up that do things I can't even imagine. While I'm in disclaimer mode, let me apologize in advance for all the fine products I have had to leave out due to space and time constraints. As I said, this is a highly subjective grouping and in no way is meant to imply that any product is superior to any other. So take this chapter as a teaser—a sampler plate to whet your appetite and give you a taste of what's out there. If something piques your interest, go to the manufacturer's Web site to learn more. (See Appendix C, "Manufacturers.") Or download a demo to really get your feet wet!

In the short descriptions that follow, I'll give you an idea of the intended user where appropriate: beginner, intermediate, or pro. At the end of each blurb, I'll note the manufacturer, whether the program runs on Windows (W), Mac (M), or both, and some idea of the price: $ = under $100; $$ = $101–$299; $$$ = $300–$599, $$$$ = $600–$2,000, $$$$$ = sell the farm.

Educational Software

As I wrote in Chapter 1, "Music Making on the Computer," your computer may be the best music teacher you'll ever find. Musical-education software runs the gamut from basic children's music appreciation and activity programs to instrument lessons to full-fledged college-level music theory classes. And it's a very popular field. A quick Google query of "music+education+software" yielded in excess of 24 million results!

Here's a healthy sampling of software titles to get you started on your path to musical mastery.

Ear Training and Theory

As any secondary music student knows, music theory classes involve lots and lots of repetitive listening and writing drills. What better teacher is there than your tireless computer? Even better, thanks to snappy graphics and innovative gaming modules, the software makes it fun.

Auralia

Comprehensive ear training and aural testing. Graded lessons and activities. Designed primarily for teachers to use with their students. Prints reports, monitors progress. All levels. Sibelius. W, M $$.

MiBAC Music Lessons 1 and 2

MiBAC (Music Instruction by a Computer) offers two graded theory and ear-training programs. Music Lessons 1: Fundamentals teaches basic sight reading, pitch recognition, notational skills, circle of fifths, major and minor scales, basic piano skills, and much, much more. Music Lessons 2: Chords and Harmony, expands on the knowledge gained in the first level to include a comprehensive understanding of tonal harmony. Includes interval training, piano and/or guitar drills, visual recognition, ear training, triads, and seventh chords. All levels. MiBAC Software. W, M $ (Music Lessons 1), $$ (Music Lessons 2).

Practica Musica

A comprehensive ear-training and music theory tutor. Offers 80-plus customizable activities, games, and lessons to make learning fun. Pitch and rhythm matching, reading, scales and chords, harmony recognition, sight-reading, and more. Move at your own pace. For both beginners and experienced musicians wishing to expand their knowledge. Ars Nova. W, M $.

Composition

Here are a couple of interesting choices to help you learn the basics of music composition.

Counterpointer
Software for the study of counterpoint, as used by Bach and other composers. Writing and evaluation aides; work alone or with counterpoint textbooks. For music students and anyone studying counterpoint. Ars Nova. W, M $.

Sibelius Instruments
"The complete guide to orchestral and band instruments." Teaches proper compositional skills for band and orchestral instruments and historic and modern instruments and offers tips on playing techniques, recordings of ensembles and individual instruments, lesson plans, and student assignments. For educators and compositional students. Sibelius. W, M $$.

Instrument Instruction
Basically, if somebody plays it, chances are there's software available to teach it. That includes vocal techniques, too. Due to space limitations, I'm going to mention only a few titles for guitar and keyboard. The best way to find your instrument is to do an Internet search; I've found software for instruments as diverse as recorder, bagpipes, and 'ud, a type of lute.

Guitar and Bass
Judging from the sheer number of instructional resources available, the world is divided into two kinds of people: the ones learning guitar, and maybe a dozen poor souls who aren't.

GUITAR METHOD V3.0
Get started the right way with 165 lessons. Learn songs, strumming, and finger-picking. Video and MIDI backing tracks, tuner. Beginner. eMedia. W, M $. (Intermediate Guitar Method also available.)

ROCK GUITAR METHOD
More than 100 songs from such groups as Black Sabbath, Blue Oyster Cult, and Silverchair. Riffs, licks, soloing, power chords, gear tips, and more. Beginner. eMedia. W, M $. (Legends of Blues Guitar also available.)

BASS METHOD
One hundred and fourteen lessons that cover all the basses, so to speak. Beginner. eMedia. W, M $.

✷ **TRUEFIRE.COM WANTS TO TEACH YOU GUITAR**

An online company dedicated to teaching guitar, TrueFire.com was originally founded to publish lessons from major magazines such as *Guitar Player*. It offers everything from free downloadable lessons to full courses in jazz, country blues, rock (in all its forms), acoustic finger-style guitar, country, bass, and more. Lessons come in a variety of formats, including CD-ROM and DVD; most have interactive TAB, video and audio examples, and other techniques designed to get you playing quickly.

Piano and Keyboard

Thanks to MIDI (see Chapter 5, "Track One: MIDI"), learning the piano on your computer is truly a joy. Interactive tutorials abound for every age and skill level. Here's a couple, but there are many more.

PIANO AND KEYBOARD METHOD

More than 300 lessons, beginning with basics, hand position, and rhythm and moving into notation, scales, sight reading, and more. Features video, interactive lessons (with optional MIDI keyboard), ear training, MIDI accompaniment, and more. Beginner. eMedia. W, M $.

PIANIST PERFORMANCE SERIES

An amazing series of "direct-to-MIDI" performances by first-rate studio musicians. Styles include modern jazz, Latin, blues, and New Age. Suitable for listening, but great for study. (Also available: Oscar Peterson Multimedia Performances and note-for-note transcriptions.) Intermediate to advanced. PG Music. W, M $.

SmartMusic

Billed as "The Complete Music Practice System," SmartMusic melds auto-accompaniment and backing tracks with practice tools such as tempo following, a tuner for reference pitches, practice loops, and recording. For classroom and home use, based on a monthly subscription fee. Make-Music. W, M $–$$.

These programs are just a fraction of the instructional software available. And don't overlook the vast numbers of MIDI files dedicated to various musical forms. Want to learn Irish penny whistle? Download some song files and play along.

Scoring Programs

Scoring programs help you write down your musical ideas. They range from simple entry-level programs that let you place notes on a single line staff to full-featured suites suitable for symphonic and soundtrack work.

Features

Here's a quick rundown of some of the features you may look for. Not all will appear in every product.

- ❋ **Note entry.** Scoring programs often let you enter notation in a variety of ways. Tool bar/palette entry is where you choose the elements one at a time with a mouse or combination of keystrokes. MIDI entry captures a part you play on a keyboard or another MIDI controller. Pitch recognition converts monophonic musical lines sung or played into a microphone into notation.

❋ **Playback.** All programs let you hear your score; the best have full-featured polyphonic sequencers that follow your articulation and dynamics markings for more realistic playback. Some support General MIDI (see Chapter 5); others come bundled with virtual orchestras. Swing playback lets you hear your music played with a more "human" feel.

❋ **Number of staves.** Entry-level programs limit the number of staves per page; full-featured ones are up to the demands of orchestrators and band directors.

❋ **Part extraction.** Lets you "pull out" just the parts you need—just the brass section, say—from a larger score and transpose to the correct key.

❋ **Tablature.** TAB for short. Writes and, in some cases, reads tablature for guitar and other fretted instruments. May have support for alternate tunings, unusually fretted instruments (such as the Appalachian dulcimer), and alternate TAB styles.

❋ **OCR.** Short for optical character recognition. The program will "read" a printed page from a scanner and convert it into an editable score.

❋ **File support.** Will read and sometimes write files in formats used by other scoring programs.

❋ **Publishing options.** Saves the score to PDF, TIFF, PICT, or some other universally recognized graphics format for desktop publishing.

The Software

Although there are literally hundreds of freeware and shareware scoring programs for both Windows and Mac, much of the action centers around a handful of product "families": Finale from MakeMusic; GenieSoft's ScoreWriter and Overture; and the Sibelius products. Before we look at these, here are a couple of interesting offerings.

NoteWorthy Composer

Entry-level program to create, notate, play back, and print scores. NoteWorthy Software. W $.

Songworks II

A simple-to-use polyphonic scoring program. From lead sheets to full multipart scores, tool bar notation entry, MDI entry and playback, pitch-recognition (microphone optional), intelligent harmonization, part extraction. All levels. Ars Nova. W, M $.

The Finale Family from MakeMusic!

In the publishing world, there really are only two choices when it comes to scoring: Finale 2005 and Sibelius 4. MakeMusic! offers well-put-together programs for a variety of users. Some, such as Finale Guitar, are showing their age; all are excellent choices.

PrintMusic

Easy to use for lead sheets and scores. Up to 24 staves, setup wizards, OCR, MIDI, and pitch-recognition input, and multiple undo. Beginner. W, M $.

SONGWRITER

A scoring program optimized for songwriters. Up to eight staves, MIDI import/export, up to six verses, save MIDI files as digital audio files, drum grooves, and intelligent harmonization. Intermediate to pro. W, M $.

FINALEALLEGRO

Designed for educators, performing musicians, band leaders, and others who need powerful MIDI and notation tools without the detailed engraving options of the top-of-the-line Finale. MIDI and pitch-recognition input, intelligent harmonization, OCR, drum grooves, and more. Intermediate to pro. W, M $$.

FINALE GUITAR

Optimized for guitar and other fretted instruments. Supports multiple stringed instruments, including guitar, mandolin, banjo, ukulele, and bass, with customizable tunings. Can enter TAB and create standard notation or enter notation and convert to TAB. Multiple staves. Customizable chord fret board diagrams. Intermediate to pro. M (OS X in Classic only) $.

FINALE 2005

Full-featured, professional-level scoring program with all the bells and whistles. MIDI, pitch recognition, OCR, TAB, graphics export, "Instant Orchestration," part extraction, and professional-quality engraving. Pro. W, M $$$.

GenieSoft

GenieSoft makes two scoring programs: ScoreWriter 2 and Overture 3. The programs fit nicely between truly entry-level fare and the massive pro-level scoring suites such as Sibelius 4 and Finale 2005.

SCOREWRITER 2

Easy-to-use program for lead sheets and modest ensemble scoring needs. Guitar chords, up to 16 staves, and MIDI import/export. Beginner to intermediate. W, M $.

OVERTURE 3

Professional-level scoring program for up to 64 instruments. MIDI import/export, smart TAB, multiple notehead types, support for third-party fonts. Reads most file formats. Harp pedal markings, PICT and EPS export (Mac only), and more. Intermediate to pro. W, M $$$.

Sibelius Software

This European software company is giving MakeMusic! a good run for its money in the world of high-end scoring programs.

G7

Scoring program optimized for guitarists. TAB, notation, guitar expression marks, chords, lyrics, OCR, playback with Kontakt sample library, output as audio file. Intermediate to pro. W, M $$.

Sɪʙᴇʟɪᴜs 4
Professional-level scoring program—if you can think of it, Sibelius 4 can do it. Fully customizable to speed workflow. Professional-quality engraving. Pro. W, M $$$.

Auto-Accompaniment and Jam Tracks

Auto-accompaniment software has come a long way from those cheesy drum machines built into your grandmother's electronic keyboard. Today's programs can create stunningly realistic backing tracks for practice or inspiration.

Features

The programs generally work like this: Choose from a number of styles, such as medium rock, jazz combo, bossa nova, and others, select a tempo, and enter a series of chords. The program creates backing tracks complete with stylistically appropriate keyboard and guitar parts, bass, drums and percussion, and perhaps string and horn sections. You can loop the song as many times as you'd like and play over the changes or export the tracks to another program for further tweaking. Some styles work better than others, and each program has other strengths and weaknesses. Band-in-a-Box and MiBAC's Jazz excel at jazz; Jammer does a great job with rock.

Here are some features to look for:

❊ **Band styles.** No need to play along to the same bar-band shuffle again and again. Band styles include the instruments, harmonies, and beats you'd expect. Styles may range from bluegrass to salsa, and everything in between.

❊ **Style editor.** Customize existing styles or create your own.

❊ **Drum editor.** As with the style editor feature, you can build on stock patterns or create your own.

❊ **Export options.** Save your creation as a Standard MIDI File or as an audio file.

❊ **Audio/MIDI recording.** Record your vocal or lead part.

❊ **Printable lead sheets.** Handy for teaching the band your new arrangement.

❊ **Smart harmonizer.** Adds chords to your melody based on the style you select.

❊ **Tempo tracking.** Adjusts the timing of the accompaniment tracks to your playing.

The Software

Auto-accompaniment software is handy for creating instant backing tracks for practice. Many composers and producers use it to flesh out ideas or as an inspirational tool. Sometimes the only way to unlock a new melody is to noodle on your guitar while the band chugs away. Many people also use looping software to create backing tracks; I'll talk about these in a minute.

MiBAC Jazz

Learn to understand, write, and play America's classical music, jazz. Lessons in the blues, song form, harmony, and improvisation. Interactive lessons, play-along software, auto-accompaniment. Beginner to advanced. MiBAC Software. W, M $.

Band-in-a-Box

One of the best-selling programs, Band-in-a-Box (BiaB to its many fans) has an ever-expanding library of finely tuned styles—everything from simple rock and country to bluegrass to fusion and piano jazz. (See Figure 4.1.) Naturally, some styles are better than others, but the jazz styles in particular are stunningly realistic. It also features a sensational bit of programming wizardry that creates solos in the styles of well-known artists. Many extra styles, song libraries, and soloists are available. Beginner to pro. PG Music. W, M $–$$.

Figure 4.1

Band-in-a-Box creates fully realized backing tracks in a variety of styles.

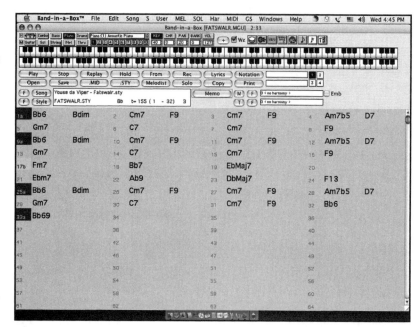

Jammer SongMaker 5 and Jammer Pro 5

Creates intelligent backing tracks for auto-accompaniment, practice, and composition in a variety of styles. Add-ons and additional styles are available. Jammer SongMaker 5 has fewer styles and features than Jammer Pro (116 band styles and 53 drum styles for SongMaker 5 versus 390 song band styles and 200 drum styles for Pro 5). Beginner to advanced. SoundTrek. W $–$$.

Looping

Looping programs are among the most popular musical software sold. Talk about instant gratification—drag and drop a couple of prerecorded elements and you've got a fully produced song in seconds. Why, even a child could do it!

About

Dance music relies on repetitive beats and rhythmic grooves—so why bother to play a drum pattern for 10 minutes when you can simply repeat the same couple of measures endlessly? In the old days engineers created endless tape loops. The earliest analog synthesizers featured sequencers and arpeggiators to play repetitive musical lines. Drum machines and beat boxes made it easy to string together short rhythmic patterns. Then someone realized you could use a sampler to play back a chunk of rhythm and trigger it via a MIDI sequencer.

These days it's all done inside the computer. Looping software often combines one or more of these approaches—MIDI, prerecorded audio beats, drum machine- or beat box–style pattern play, analog synth–style arpeggiators, and sequencers.

Features

Even the most basic looping software lets you mix and match short audio and/or MIDI clips together to create a finished song. The best programs are complete music-production suites capable of professional-quality song construction. Some, such as Ableton's Live 5, are optimized for real-time performance and creation; some are virtual instruments working as plug-ins in your DAW program; others, notably Propellerhead's Reason 3, take a kitchen-sink approach.

Here's a list to get you started. Not every program will have everything, and some will have many more features.

- ❈ **Loops library.** A loop is a short segment of audio or MIDI. It goes without saying that you'll need a lot of 'em if your style tends toward working with prerecorded loops. Most programs come with a goodly supply, and refills are available from the company Web site or third-party venders.

- ❈ **File compatibility.** Can you read loops made by or for other programs? Can you export your songs to another program for further recording, editing, or mixing?

- ❈ **Peer support and sharing.** Many programs attract a loyal online community that helps peers solve problems, posts clips and tips, and shares creations.

- ❈ **Software instruments.** At the very least, you'll need General MIDI instruments or SoundFonts (see Chapter 5) to play back MIDI files.

- ❈ **Audio recording.** To record your own loops or to add vocals or instrumental parts to the mix.

☀ **Time stretching.** Adjusts the length of an audio loop to fit the song without changing the pitch (also called time compression/expansion).

☀ **Tempo matching.** Adjusts the tempo of audio loops without changing the pitch. Harder than it sounds.

☀ **Transposition.** Changes the pitch without changing the tempo. Easy with MIDI; not so easy with digital audio.

☀ **MIDI.** Support for MIDI recording and playback. Sony's Acid, long the standard audio looping tool, only recently added MIDI support.

☀ **Plug-ins.** Plug-ins are small helper applications that add functionality to the host. Commonly used for effects or software instruments.

☀ **Mixing.** Lets you combine the multiple tracks of your song to a stereo audio file that can be burned to CD or shared on the Web.

The Software

The listing that follows is by no means exhaustive. I'm going to list only a few of the major players to pique your interest. Any sampler can function as a looping tool; see the discussion of software instruments below for more information. Also, most DAWs, MIDI sequencers, and audio editors have extensive looping capabilities.

In no particular order, here are some tools to drive you loopy.

Kinetic

A loop- and pattern-based sequencer with Roland drum sounds—including the legendary 606 and TR-808—Acid loops, audio and MIDI recording, point-and-click operation, and ReWire (a protocol for transferring audio data between applications) compatibility. Cakewalk. W $.

GarageBand

Included with every new Mac—and available as part of the inexpensive iLife family of applications—GarageBand is a remarkably powerful music-production machine. Acid loops, MIDI instruments, real-time control, and audio and MIDI recording. Outputs to various digital audio formats, including iTunes. Apple. M $.

Live 5

Designed specifically for the demands of stage use, Live has become the program of choice for legions of musicians, producers, and composers. Record, import, edit, arrange, and process audio loops while the music keeps playing. Live takes care of changing the loop's tempo and matching the pitch on the fly. Edit and add effects. Or rearrange the parts, record, and mix. You never have to stop the music. Ableton. W, M $$$.

Acid Pro 5

Sony's Acid began the whole looping phenomenon. It was the first program to automate the tedium of trying to force disparate digital loops to play with the same groove. Acid 5 now handles MIDI and supports VST plug-ins for greater flexibility. An industry standard. W $$. (The entry-level Acid Music Studio 5 is also available: $.)

FL Studio 5

Pattern-based sequencer, loop player, and production suite. Various "flavors," ranging from entry level to professional. Producer Edition features a huge track count, 64-channel mixer, audio recording, MP3 support, and waveform editor. The XXL Edition adds software instruments, video playback, larger sample library, and more. Image-One. W $–$$.

Traktor DJ Studio 2

Traktor DJ Studio uses the power of the computer to simplify the lives of DJs. Independent time stretching and pitch shifting, up to 10 cue points, tempo matching, up to 10 tempo-matched loops per track, waveform editor, track database with search, MIDI clock synch, and more. Native Instruments. W, M $$.

GrooveMaker

Remixers of the world, unite! GrooveMaker lets you remix hundreds of loops in real time to create hours of nonstop dance tracks. (See Figure 4.2.) Imports and matches grooves in any audio file format; exports to WAV, AIFF, and MP3. Comes with 500 loops of drum grooves, pads, effects, and ambient sounds. Three versions: LE, Standard, and DJ. IK Multimedia. W, M $.

Recycle

A digital-audio loop-editing tool. Handles many time-consuming looping chores, such as time compression/expansion, tempo matching, and transposition. Facilitates using sampled loops with songs created in DAWs. Propellerhead. W, M $$.

Reason 3

Reason really is in a class by itself. It's not exactly a looping program, although it excels at looping, and it's not really a software instrument, although it includes some of the most kickin' software instruments you'll find this side of the Synth Museum. Instead, Reason is a suite of software modules—synthesizers, beat boxes, effects units, samplers, romplers, mixers, and more—that you patch together in any order you choose. Reason is a self-contained, infinitely expandable music-production suite; however, Reason is not an audio-recording application. A protocol called ReWire links Reason to compatible DAW and looping programs. Propellerhead. W, M $$$.

Figure 4.2
GrooveMaker's hip user interface opens the door to powerful remixing.

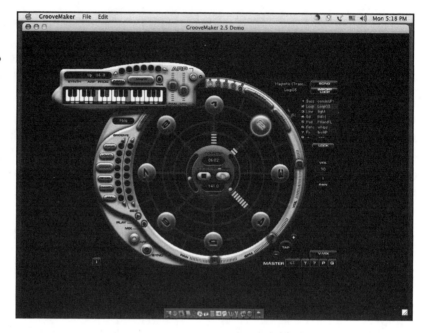

Project5 Version 2

Aimed squarely at the DJ and remix crowd. Combines powerful sequencing and audio recording with a full complement of loops, beats, and samples, plus software synths, samplers, and beat boxes. ReWire host or client, Acid loop support, VST and DirectX plug-ins. Cakewalk. W, M $$$.

DAW Programs

DAWs (digital audio workstations) are the big guns of the music software world. They combine the flexibility and functionality of a MIDI sequencer with the power of a digital audio recording studio. Even if you intend to do all of your work in the MIDI realm, you'd be better off buying a DAW than a MIDI-only sequencer—*if* you could still find one these days. DAWs have such a huge feature set and so many users that you'll be more likely to get the features and support you need. Besides, you may want to slip in a vocal or drum loop sometime.

About

Most DAWs started their lives as MIDI sequencers, and many still show their heritage. In fact, as they race to stay competitive, manufacturers keep adding more and more features, to the point that sometimes you need to dig back through the interface to uncover those you need!

As a result, DAWs have a reputation for being hard to learn. I suppose that's true to some extent, but why would anyone expect to learn everything about a program before he started to use it? After all, my car is a highly tuned, complex piece of technology, but I don't need to know how the fuel injection operates to drive to the store.

Even the most basic DAWs let you take a song from conception to completion. Many use a familiar tape-transport and recording studio metaphor. (See Chapter 2, "Understanding the Gear.") Entry-level DAWs may sacrifice track count or audio resolution to keep the price down and make them easier to use. The professional-grade programs are used every day in studios around the world, creating the hits, dance tracks, and soundtracks that flavor our world.

As you look through the software, keep in mind that the best tool in the world is worthless if you don't use it. Take a hard look at what you want to accomplish, and don't buy more than you need. Most home users can get by with 16 or fewer audio tracks. If you'll be mixing all your songs down to MP3, do you really need to record at 96kHz?

This is one area where price does equal power. And power has a cost—high-definition professional programs such as Pro Tools, SONAR, and Digital Performer demand fast computers with tons of memory.

MIDI Features

MIDI is a great tool for producing music. It's flexible, the files are tiny, and it's easily edited. Here's a quick list of a few MIDI features you may encounter in a typical DAW and what they mean.

✻ **Resolution.** MIDI timing is determined by the position of the note-on message relative to a very slow-moving clock. As such, early sequencers lacked the ability to replay music with the same timing as it was recorded. Programmers got around "MIDI slop" by cutting a quarter note into increasingly small chunks of data. Resolutions in excess of 990 parts per quarter note are pretty much standard now.

✻ **Patch librarian.** A memory location to store the names of the sounds found in your keyboard. Makes it a heck of a lot easier to select a patch for a track.

✻ **Step-entry.** Key in parts one note at a time. Handy for entering passages too difficult to actually play.

✻ **Piano Roll.** An edit screen that displays MIDI information horizontally. It looks like an old-fashioned player piano roll. Pitch is indicated relative to a vertical keyboard.

✻ **Quantize.** The ability to line up notes to precise locations, such as moving all of the snare hits to fall exactly on beats two and four.

✻ **Randomize/humanize.** The opposite of quantization. Moves notes slightly (and sometimes changes the velocity as well) to simulate the "feel" of a real person playing.

✻ **Arpeggiator.** Creates single-note passages from chords. Like the intro in the Who's "Baba O'Reilly."

✳ **Drum machine grid.** Create drum parts as you would on a drum machine. Don't know how to do that? Click a few times, and listen to what happens.

✳ **MIDI machine control.** Handy to control another device, such as a desktop recorder, from your computer. Or to control your DAW program from a remote device.

✳ **ReWire.** An interapplication protocol developed by Propellerhead that syncs compatible applications, such as a DAW and a virtual sampler.

Audio Features

Now let's take a quick look at some important audio features.

✳ **Resolution.** The sample rate refers to how many times a second the analog waveform is plotted; the bit rate (or bit depth) is the length of the digital word used to describe the sample. Audio CDs use a sample rate of 44,100 times per second at 16 bits. Higher rates yield greater detail, but at the price of greatly increased processor and storage demands.

✳ **Track count.** How many simultaneous audio tracks you can record and play back. Limited by CPU speed and RAM.

✳ **Virtual tracks.** Audio tracks that have been recorded but not assigned to playback.

✳ **Waveform editor.** Lets you zoom in and redraw flaws in the audio at the sample level. Not for the timid!

✳ **Nondestructive editing.** Edits that do not change the original audio file, such as cutting, pasting, moving, and deleting.

✳ **Destructive editing.** Edits that permanently alter the original, such as noise reduction and gain normalization.

✳ **Plug-ins.** Small helper applications, such as effects and software instruments. Most DAWs support one or more of the common plug-in formats. (See "Effects," later in this chapter.) DAWs often come bundled with a healthy set to get you started.

✳ **Mix automation.** The ability to write and edit mix parameters. At its best, automation extends to effects and soft instrument parameters as well.

✳ **Synchronization.** The ability to lock to another software program or hardware device, such as a video editor, second computer, or modular recorder.

✳ **Video playback.** A window that plays and locks to imported video files. For spotting dialog, effects, and music. If you want to be the next Danny Elfman, you want this.

❉ **Surround.** Most high-end DAWs support the major surround sound formats. Be aware that surround sound requires specialized effects, a DVD burner, and hardware capable of handling multichannel playback.

❉ **Freeze.** A relatively new function. Temporarily writes a new track incorporating all of your real-time edits, effects, and automation to cut down on the processor load.

The Software

There are many programs that combine MIDI sequencers with digital audio recording features. Rather than attempt to describe all of them, I'll highlight a few so you can get an idea of what's out there. Please note that many manufacturers have multiple titles or editions of their flagship programs. Some may be "lite" versions aimed at entry-level users; others will have specific features for guitarists, DJs, or other specialized users.

As I noted in the introduction to this section, I decided to concentrate on sequencers with digital audio capabilities. Legions of wonderful MIDI-only sequencers are available on the Internet. See Appendix D for some sources.

In no particular order, here are the programs that will turn your computer into a recording studio. To some extent, price is an indication of the intended user. Entry-level programs tend to have a street price under $100. Software designed for professional and high-end project recording studios starts around $500 and goes up from there. DAW programs aimed at the mid-level home-studio user who wants pro-quality results without the extensive features or complexity of the high-end offerings fall in between.

More and more, programs designed for one task are taking on new features. Many of the loop-based tools I mentioned have extensive digital audio and MIDI sequencing functions. And most of these DAWs have features that any looper would love. One product that totally blurs the lines is Ableton's Live 5; accordingly, I've included it in both sections. But check out the feature set of other looping tools as well if your song-producing style includes both prerecorded loops and digital audio.

Be aware that hardware and software compatibility is a sometimes thing; a given DAW might not work with a particular interface. Although most products support the most recent Windows or Mac OS, some might not. Be sure to visit the manufacturer's Web site or speak with a knowledgeable salesperson before you buy.

Storm 3

Storm combines a DAW, software instruments, loops, and effects with an intelligent Composition Wizard to help you get your dreams happening fast. Arturia. W, M $$.

PowerTracks ProAudio 10

An inexpensive Audio+MIDI sequencer with notation, Piano Roll editor window, time stretch, and pitch change for audio tracks. Includes three DirectX plug-ins (Real Time Analyzer, Vinyl Restoration, and Vocal Remover) and ASIO support. PG Music. W, M $.

Tracktion

Mackie practically created the project studio with its high-quality, low-cost mixers, monitor speakers, and control surfaces, so it's only natural that the company would focus its attention on the audio interfaces and software. Tracktion 2 packs a tremendous number of features into an inexpensive package: 64-bit mixing, 192kHz recording, ReWire support, video playback, and VST. Includes 70 plug-ins. Mackie. W, M $$.

Logic Pro 7

Apple Computer's own DAW software is designed to fully integrate with the Mac OS. Full-featured, professional-level program. 24 bits/192kHz, 70 bundled plug-ins, GarageBand instruments, video, intelligent tempo, and transposition. Allows networking of DAWs via Ethernet. Apple. M $$$$. (Also available in an entry-level version, Logic Express 7: $$.)

Live 5

Version 5 of this popular looping and live-performance tool adds many DAW features, such as plug-in delay compensation and freeze. Live's ease of use and powerful arranging and real-time recording features make it the DAW of choice for many producers and musicians. Ableton. W, M $$$.

Digital Performer 4.6

DP started out as Performer, a full-featured MIDI sequencer that quickly became the professional's choice. That legacy remains; DP is a first-class MIDI sequencer. It was also one of the first to add digital audio features, and it remains among the best. It's a huge program, capable of just about any music-production task you can name. Twenty-four bits/192kHz, TDM-compatible to integrate with Pro Tools, powerful quantize and humanize functions, beat and groove extraction, scoring, ReWire, pro-level bundled plug-ins, and MAS and AU support. Edit MIDI and audio in a single operation, Mark of the Unicorn. M $$$.

The Cakewalk Family

Cakewalk makes some of the most popular DAW software available for the Windows OS. Its products are well known for ease of use and innovative user interfaces.

SONAR HomeStudio

The title says it all. Aimed squarely at the musician setting up his first home studio, the program gives you everything you need to begin recording at home. Twenty-four-bit/96kHz audio, MIDI, Acid and ReWire support, point-and-click drum tracks, and VST support with bundled plug-ins.

Reads most audio formats. W $. (XL version adds DirectX, software sampler, and CD of audio samples: $$.)

Guitar Tracks Pro

This is a 32-track recording solution optimized for guitarists. Twenty-four-bit/96kHz audio, Acid support, Amplitude LE and GE-FX multieffects, VST and DirectX support, and many guitar-specific features. Reads most audio formats. W $$.

SONAR 4 Producer Edition

Arguably the most popular professional DAW for Windows. Supports all major surround formats and has sampling rates up to 348kHz (!) and extensive looping tools, including Acid support, VST and DirectX, ReWire, video, and extensive MIDI features. W $$$. (Also available in Studio Edition with the same features minus surround mix-down: $$.)

Project5 Version 2

I mentioned this under looping programs, but it fits in this category, too. Audio/MIDI recording and editing, Rewire host/client. Supports most sampler formats. VST, DirectX. W. $$$.

Steinberg Software

Steinberg's flagship home-studio program, Cubase, has legions of devoted fans. But Steinberg also makes high-end audio workstations used everyday in professional recording and film-scoring studios. And Steinberg invented VST, so you can be sure its products take full advantage of this cool plug-in protocol.

Cubase SE Hybrid

An entry-level program with professional-grade features. Forty-eight audio tracks, 24-bit/96kHz audio, complete MIDI recording and editing, looping, effects, and more. W, M $. (The Steinberg Studio Case bundles Cubase SE with several of its virtual instruments, including the Virtual Guitarist, Groove Agent, and HALion SE soft synth: $$.)

Cubase SX3

A complete audio and MIDI recording solution for home studios. Hi-res audio, MIDI device groups, real-time time stretching and pitch shifting, customizable user interface, and more. External FX plug-ins integrate hardware effects. The SL edition has fewer features for a slightly lower price. W, M $$$.

Nuendo

Nuendo has the features and flexibility professionals demand. These include 32-bit/192kHz audio, extensive sync options to external video gear, and more. Reads and writes just about any audio format. W, M $$$$.

Pro Tools

Pro Tools was the first digital audio editor to gain wide acceptance in the pro market. Although there are many more choices now, it has retained its edge with an uncompromising commitment to quality. Fully tricked-out pro-studio installations can cost as much as a new house; home-studio users have a couple of compelling options.

Pro Tools|HD

The *only* choice for many audio professionals. More than just DAW software—it's a complete system. Pro Tools|HD uses a system called TDM (time domain multiplexing) to allocate digital signal processing. TDM systems rely on processors welded to PCI cards for all of the audio and effects, freeing up the host computer for the chores it does best: file management and graphics. To build a Pro Tools system, select from a variety of audio interfaces, DSP cards for effects processing, control surfaces, sync boxes, and more. (See Figure 4.3.) W, M $$$$–$$$$$.

Pro Tools LE

Unlike Pro Tools TDM, LE is host based. That means it uses your computer's CPU for DSP processing, just like the other DAWs mentioned above. It provides 24-bit/96kHz audio, 32 audio tracks, up to 128 virtual tracks, MIDI, ReWire, and cross-platform support for Pro Tools TDM systems. W, M $$.

Figure 4.3

Pro Tools|HD is the audio editor of choice for many professionals. Home users can access the same features in native versions such as Pro Tools LE and Pro Tools M-Powered.

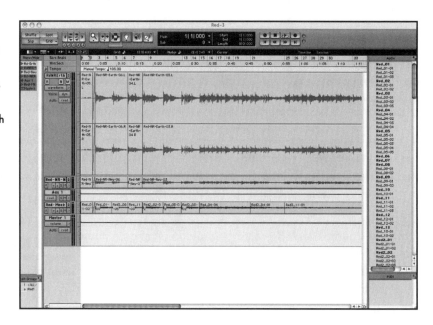

Pro Tools M-Powered

Brings the power of Pro Tools LE to any a M-Audio FireWire interface, including the Ozonic hybrid keyboard/audio interfaces. W, M $$.

HARDWARE and SOFTWARE BUNDLES

The best way to ensure compatibility among your computer, audio hardware, and DAW software is to purchase a bundle. Software such as Pro Tools, Cubase, and Mackie's Tracktion is often bundled with an audio interface, plug-ins, and other software. And you may save hundreds of dollars over assembling the pieces yourself!

Check with your favorite vendor to see if it has deals, or visit the manufacturer's Web sites.

Effects

Effects are tools that change the way an audio file sounds. They range from devices that simply adjust how loud a signal appears in the mix to guitar-style distortion and amplifier modeling to wonderfully indescribable audio contortionists that can change a simple vocal line into a spacey dance beat.

No matter what kind of music you'll be making, the right effects will make it sound better.

Once upon a time, professional effects were expensive and hard to come by. The only way for a home recordist to get a certain effect was to book time at Studio BigBucks. Thanks to legions of canny programs, anyone can amass an effects collection that would be the envy of yesterday's pro studio.

There is absolutely no way I could list, let alone describe, all of the software effects you can add to your computer. It's probably the fastest-growing segment of the music software biz. Every day brings new effects and revisions of the old warhorse.

Instead, I'll give you some guidelines for the different kinds of effects you'll encounter and mention a few examples in each category. As with the other sections in this chapter, be sure to check out the Web sites for product updates and system compatibility information.

Plug-Ins

Though some effects, particularly those for mastering, audio restoration, or vocal processing, exist as stand-alone programs, most are plug-ins. Plug-ins are small applications that work inside a host application. Each program handles plug-ins a little differently; generally they must all reside in a special folder to be recognized. Be sure to consult your software manual before installing.

Unless you are using a Pro Tools TDM system or one of the powered plug-in systems from UAD or TC, your effects will share the CPU with the rest of your programs. And effects can quickly run up a huge processor load, so check your CPU's performance regularly. (See Figure 4.4.) And don't forget to add the memory requirements of each plug-in to the amount needed for your host software. In other words, you need to install more RAM.

Standards being what they are, there are a number of them. The following list covers the most popular plug-in formats used for audio effects and software instruments:

Figure 4.4
Digital audio and effects processing quickly eat up processor overhead. Monitoring the CPU load and making adjustments as necessary can prevent crashes!

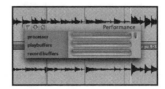

* **DirectX.** Microsoft's format for Windows-based audio and multimedia applications. Widely supported.
* **VST.** Virtual studio technology. Developed by Steinberg, the most widely supported plug-in format for Windows and Mac. In spite of the cross-platform nature of VST, Windows and Mac versions are not interchangeable.
* **AU.** Audio units. Apple's plug-in protocol; built into the Mac OS beginning with OS 10.2
* **MAS.** MOTU audio system. Mark of the Unicorn's proprietary plug-in format for Digital Performer. Digital Performer now supports AU, which widens the choices a bit.
* **TDM.** Time domain (or division) multiplexing. Digidesign's hardware-based plug-in format. Since TDM plug-ins do not rely on the host's CPU, they generally have far more processing power than host-based systems such as VST or MAS.
* **RTAS.** Real-time audio suite. Digidesign's host-based plug-in format.

Plug-In Adaptors

There's an old joke: "The great thing about standards is that there are so many of them." It sure is true in the computer audio world—why can't we all use the same format so everyone can have access to all of the fine plug-ins? I can't answer that, but I can offer some relief.

VST is by far the best-supported format. Thanks to a product called VST-AU adaptor (from FXpansion software), users of Digital Performer and other AU-compatible products now can use hundreds of VST effects and software instruments. The company also makes a VST-to-RTAS adaptor for Pro Tools users.

Similarly, Audio Ease offers VST Wrapper 4 so that users of MOTU's Digital Performer can use VST plug-ins, too.

Isn't it better when we all get along?

DSP Hardware Plug-Ins

I have already touched on Digidesign's TDM card-based plug-in format. In the past few years, a couple of companies have brought the power and flexibility of powered plug-ins to a number of

DAW platforms. Some use PCI cards, and some take advantage of the speed of FireWire 800 to move the DSP chips away from the host computer.

UAD-1

Universal Audio is dedicated to producing both hardware and software re-creations of classic studio hardware. Its UAD-1 system is a PCI-based, floating-point DSP processor that takes the load off of your CPU. (See Figure 4.5.) You may use up to four UAD-1 cards. The UAD-1 is bundled with UA's prizewinning effects software, including re-creations of 1176, LA 2A, and Pultec dynamics processors, plus reverbs, guitar effects, channel strips, and more. Various configurations. W, M $$$–$$$$$.

Figure 4.5
The UAD-1 plug-in places the DSP power on a PCI card to cut down on the CPU load. Used with permission of Universal Audio, 2005.

TC Electronics

Like UA, TC makes both hardware and software for project and professional studios. Its Power-CoreFW and Compact products connect to the host computer via FireWire; PowerCore PCI mkII uses a PCI card. But you could figure that out.

POWERCORE PCI MKII

Uses PCI-based digital signal processing for real-time processing with low latency. Comes with many TC effects and a growing list of third-party effects, including Sony Oxford plug-ins. VST, AU, and MAS. W, M $$$–$$$$.

TC POWERCORE FW AND TC POWERCORE COMPACT

TC brings powered plug-ins to computers without PCI slots! PowerCore FireWire packs all of the punch of the PCI mkII card in a rack-mountable unit. Lightweight, bus-powered DSP for the road! Two 150MHz Motorola DSPs and one 266 PowerPC chip. Compatible with VST-, RTAS-, and AU-compliant applications. W, M $$$–$$$$.

Receptor

Receptor is an entirely new kind of product. Billed as "a portable hardware VST plug-in player," it's a rack-mountable multitimbral sound module that runs software synthesizers, samplers, loop playback modules, effects—any Windows-compatible VST plug-in! Supports up to 16 simultaneous instruments and 57 effects. Receptor is a profoundly flexible tool for recording and performing musicians. Works in stand-alone operation or networked via Ethernet. Muse Research. W, M $$$$.

Software Effects

Here is a generous sampling of software effects broken down by category. As I have said, by mentioning a particular product, I am not implying that it is any better suited to your needs than any other product. It's just a sample to get you drooling.

Note that not every effect works with every plug-in format. Also, most DAWs come bundled with a healthy supply of effects. Some of these, such as MOTU's MasterWorks Compressor, are very good indeed.

Dynamics

Dynamics processors are used to change the relative level of an audio track in the mix. As such, they are generally inserted into a single mono- or stereo track when tracking or mixing.

UA LA-2A

A re-creation of the classic hardware unit. Universal Audio. TDM and UAD-1 $$$.

RENAISSANCE COMPRESSOR

The first software compressor to win the hearts and minds of professional audio engineers. Why? Because it sounds really, really good. Waves. VST, AU, MAS, TDM, RTAS $$.

QUAD COMP

Four-band compressor/expander for vocals, guitars and mastering. Akai. VST $.

❄ IS IT REAL, OR IS IT MODELING?

Certain vintage hardware effects units are second only to microphones in the passion they elicit among recording engineers. Various combinations of tubes, transistors, and electronic circuitry produced effects that went beyond mere specifications. Some gear has taken on legendary status, to the point that you can talk about the 1176 drum sound or debate the merits of the original TubeScreamer stomp box. The first software effects were designed to operate transparently. That is, a compressor may alter the mix dynamics, but it would not impart any of the characteristic colorization of the hardware boxes we engineers relied on. Like many, I hated the sound—or rather, the lack of sound—of early digital EQ. Modeling technology uses mathematics to re-create the various characteristics of real-world devices. As the technology improves, modeled effects are getting closer and closer to their hardware counterparts.

Can modeled software ever sound as good as a lovingly tended vintage effects processor? Personally, I doubt it.

But the current technology does sound very good indeed. The best modeled effects have many of the sonic quirks of the originals. Just as with the originals, used with care, they will improve your sound. And they cost a heck of a lot less, require nothing in the way of maintenance, and don't take up lots of space. What's not to like?

Channel Strips

Channel strips combine all of the processing needed to track vocals—dynamics, EQ, and sometimes de-essing—into a single module. (See Figure 4.6.)

Figure 4.6
The Waves Renaissance Channel combines a parametric EQ with a compressor and expander. Courtesy of Waves— www.waves.com.

Reverb and Time-Based Effects

Reverb is what happens when sound bounces around in a natural space. Or unnatural space, if that's your predilection. Mess around with the timing and tuning of the reflections and you get things like delays, chorusing, phasers, and flangers. You'll notice that the programs I listed aren't cheap. It takes a lot of processing power to get it right. Don't worry, every DAW, looper, and music production software suite known to man will include quite serviceable reverb, chorus, flange, and other effects. The programs here are for when you're ready to move beyond the basics.

ECHO FARM

Vintage tape-based echo and delay effects without the hassles of tape. Line 6. TDM $$$.

GIGAPULSE

A convolution reverb and microphone modeling plug-in. TASCAM VST $$$.

ALTIVERB

Altiverb features sampled acoustics of real halls such as Amsterdam's famed Concertgebouw, cathedrals, small rooms—even closets and bathrooms, plus the ability to sample your own space. Audio Ease. VST, AU, MAS, TDM $$$.

✳ WHAT'S CONVOLUTION REVERB?

Reverb effects have come a long way since the early days of running a signal through a tank full of metal springs. The latest incarnations are based on a mathematical process called "convolution," where one signal is modified by another. Convolution reverbs work by sampling an acoustic space to create an "impulse file"—essentially a mathematical description of how sound reacts to the space. The program then applies those characteristics to the desired signal.

The result is reverb with far greater detail and believability. The parameters may also include other tools to help place the audio and the listener in specific locations within the acoustic space. As you can imagine, convolution 'verbs require significant amounts of processing power.

Other Fun Stuff

Just about every studio processor you can imagine—and some you can't—is available as a plug-in. Need vacuum tube emulation, microphone modeling, pitch corrections, or time stretching? Not a problem. Here's a sampling.

ANALOG TUBE MODELING

Brings the warmth of analog to your cold digital recordings. Antares. DirectX, VST, MAS, RTAS $.

FILTER

Applies rhythmic multimode filters to audio files. Create dance tracks, animate audio, achieve synthesizer-like effects. Two drum machine–style rhythm generators. Antares. DirectX, VST, AU, MAS, TDM, RTAS $$$.

AUTOTUNE

This is the software that changed the way vocals are recorded. More than a few pop stars owe their careers to it. Used with care, AutoTune corrects even the most egregious tuning problems seamlessly and transparently. Antares. DirectX, VST, AU, MAS, TDM, RTAS $$$.

PITCHFIX

Easy-to-use vocal pitch-correction plug-in from Yamaha. MIDI input of guide pitch, basic formant (vocal characteristic) adjustments, creates multipart harmonies. Yamaha. VST, AU $$$.

Mastering Suites

Mastering is the last step in the recording process. It's where you polish your tracks until they shine. Mastering software generally includes two or more of the following tools: parametric EQ, multiband compression, a look-ahead peak limiter to get audio files as loud as they can possibly be, tube emulation, aural enhancer, spatial processor, and ultra-high-quality dithering and sample-rate conversion.

T-RackS

A stand-alone or plug-in master suite for Windows or Mac. Six-band parametric EQ, tube modeling, "tube" compressor, multiband limiter, and more. IK Multimedia. DirectX, VST, AU, TDM W, M $$–$$$.

MasterX

Puts TC Electronics's industry-standard Finalizer on your desktop. TC Electronic. TDM, PowerCore $$$.

Final Master

A three-band stereo-dynamics processor intended for mastering applications. Yamaha. VST, AU $$.

❄ **NOISE REDUCTION AND AUDIO RESTORATION**

As anyone with a turntable knows, phonograph records can get pretty noisy. Ditto analog recording tape; over time, the background noise hiss can overwhelm the music. Transfer your old recordings to digital files and the clicks, pops, hiss and surface noise will drive you crazy.

For anything but the most casual listening, the consumer de-hiss and de-click products don't really cut it. To do a professional job, you need specialized software. High-end noise-reduction software, such as the Waves Audio Restoration bundle or SoundSoap Pro, doesn't come cheap. But used carefully, restoration programs can make even the scratchiest 78 sound like it was recorded yesterday.

Bundles

Although it's possible to purchase individual effects, for most of us the best way to get the tools we need is to pick up a bundle. Just about every DAW and looping program comes bundled with enough effects to get you up and running. And the powered plug-in formats such as Universal Audio's UAD-1 and TC's PowerCore series are loaded with high-quality effects.

Here are a handful of plug-in bundles to consider.

Waves

Waves practically invented the concept of professional plug-ins. It offers a huge selection of bundles aimed at just about every kind of recording studio task you can imagine. Check out the popular Renaissance Maxx with classic and vintage effects or the inexpensive Musicians Bundle II. Waves. DirectX, VST, MAS, TDM, RTAS, W, M $$–$$$$$.

Oxford

From the makers of the legendary OXF-R3 recording console, Oxford plug-ins bring high-quality effects bundles for audio restoration, mixing, and mastering to Pro Tools and TC PowerCore users. Sony. TDM, TC PowerCore W. $$$$.

Rocket Science

Audio Ease offers three weirdly fun ways to mangle your audio. Roger applies human vowel sounds to any audio file. Sort of like a vocoder, but, well, stranger. Follow "dynamically adjusts the peak of a resonating bandpass filter according to the level of incoming audio." In English, that means it acts something like an auto-wah, only more, well, weird. Orbit lets you dynamically alter the position of a sound source in space. Audio Ease. VST, AU, TDM, RTAS, M $$.

Pluggo

Pluggo is massive—with more than 100 plug-ins, there is sure to be something for everyone. You geteverything from simple EQs and delays to software instruments, samplers, multi-effects, and some truly whacked processors. It's a tremendous bargain. Cycling 74. DirectX, VST, AU, RTAS, W, M $$.

Guitar Amp Modeling and Effects

Electric guitarists demand one thing: Tone with a capital T. And we're willing to spend a lot to achieve it. We try just about every new effects unit and stomp box on the market, fiddle with our amps and pickups, change strings, spend our hard-earned gig money on strange little doodads that promise to make us sound like our heroes. Is it any wonder that our friends the software companies are only too eager to help?

Guitar Rig

A nice combination of hardware and software dedicated to creating and producing great guitar tones, from classic to modern. Amp modeling, stomp box and rack-style effects, tuner, metronome, loop playback, and audio recording. Includes a dedicated foot controller with DI. (See Figure 4.7.) For live or studio use, stand-alone or plug-in operation. Native Instruments. DirectX, VST, AU, RTAS. W, M $$$.

Amplitube and Amplitube LE

Available in stand-alone and plug-in versions, these popular programs combine amplifier and cabinet modeling with multi-effects, stomp box emulations, and more. Less filling, sounds great. IK Multimedia. DirectX, VST, AU, RTAS $–$$$.

Amp Farm

The power of Line 6's legendary POD amp modeling in a plug-in. TDM $$$.

ChromeTone

Amp modeling, modulation effects, dynamics, and more. TDM, RTAS, McDSP $$$.

Figure 4.7

Turn your computer into a rack full of cool guitar effects with Native Instruments' Guitar Rig.

Software Musical Instruments

Software instruments range from simple General MIDI tone generators and SoundFonts built into most computers to hugely complex synthesizers and samplers. You find everything from finely modeled vintage analog synthesizers and electronic keyboards to acoustic basses to enormous re-creations of full orchestras.

As with the other sections in this chapter, there are simply too many choices to even attempt a complete listing. Once again, here's a sampling, intended to get you started. Don't forget that many music-production programs will be bundled with a number of software instruments.

Models of Hardware Instruments

This is a huge field; nearly every day brings another very cool re-creation of some vintage keyboard. Here I'll consider mostly those programs that model one or a handful of specific instruments. Be sure to check the headings below for many of the fine programs that combine extensive sample libraries and sample-playback engines.

Elektrik Piano

Why settle for one cool keyboard when you can own a roomful? Includes Fender Rhodes MK 1 and MKII, Hohner Clavinet E7, and Wurlitzer A200. Play that funky music! Native Instruments. W, M $$.

MiniMoog V

A digital re-creation of the classic analog synth, updated with MIDI, new arpeggiator, polyphony, and more. Arturia. DirectX, AU, W, M $$.

B4

The Hammond B3 organ captured in software from Native Instruments. Includes models of the Leslie rotating speaker, drawbar behavior, and tonewheel soundset. Add the hardware drawbar controller for the ultimate in realism. Native Instruments. Stand-alone, VST, AU, RTAS, W, M $$.

Legacy Collection

You know the re-creations of classic Korg analog and digital keyboards are authentic because the software comes from Korg itself. Relive the groovy sounds of the PolySix, MX-20, and Wavestation. Includes a dedicated hardware controller with knobs and patch cables based on the MS-20. Korg. W, M $$$.

Key Rig

All your basic keyboard needs in one virtual rack. Four modules: SP-1 stage piano for acoustic and electric pianos, MS-2 Polyphonic Synthesizer; MB-3 Electromagnetic Organ for Hammond sounds complete with Leslie, and the GM-4 General MIDI module. Designed for stage and studio use. M-Audio. W, M $.

Software Synthesizers

Here's a good collection of programs that combine one or more synthesis engines.

Sonik Synth

8GB packed with more than 5,000 sounds makes Sonik Synth a workstation powerhouse. Models of most synthesis forms: analog, FM, digital, wavetable, granular, and resynthesis. A veritable museum of vintage keyboards, search engine, multi-effects, and more. Compatible with Sample-Tank files. IK Multimedia. DirectX, VST, AU, RTAS, W, M $$$.

MX4

MOTU's software instrument with five different types of synthesis: subtractive, wavetable, FM, AM, and analog modeling. Mark of the Unicorn. AU, MAS, RTAS, M $$.

Ultra Analog

Not simply a re-creation of a particular vintage instrument, Ultra Analog brings the classic sounds of analog synthesis to the digital age. (See Figure 4.8.) Features include 32-voice polyphony, 32-bit internal processing, real-time sound generation, full MIDI implementation, and unlimited undo/redo. Applied Acoustics. VST, AU, RTAS. W, M $$.

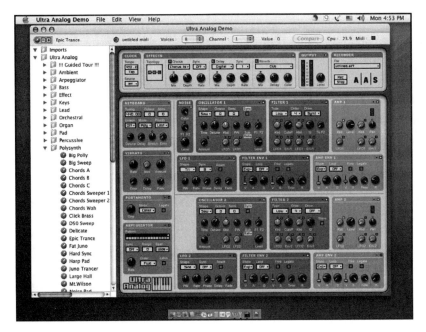

Figure 4.8
Ultra Analog, from Applied Acoustics, melds great-sounding analog synthesis with digital control.

Absynth 3
Combines synthesis and sampling for powerful sound design. Synthesis types include FM, subtractive, granular, and wavetable. Huge library of waveforms, envelopes, and oscillator channels. Native Instruments. DirectX, VST, AU, RTAS, W, M $$.

Samplers

Samplers are programs that use audio waveforms as the basis for sound creation. Samplers can record and play back complex beats, making them great loop-production tools. Most software listed here lets you record your own samples; all read multiple sample formats. Most come with large libraries of sounds to get you up and running quickly.

GigaStudio Solo
TASCAM's mighty GigaStudio sampler for the rest of us! Features include 96-voice polyphony, a lite version of GigaPiano sample, and GigaPulse reverb. TASCAM. W $$.

SampleTank 2
Full-featured sampling workstation. Supports AIFF, WAV, SDII, Akai, and SampleCell audio files. Time compression/expansion, resampling, looping, 30 DSP effects. IK Multimedia. DirectX, VST, AU, MAS, RTAS, W, M $$$.

HALion 3

32-bit/384kHz VST sampler. Akai, EMU, Roland, Kurzweil, and Giga sample formats. Effects and beat synchronization. Steinberg. VST, W, M $$.

Kompakt

Sample playback software. Eight-part multitimbral, 256-voice polyphony, imports Kontakt 2, GigaStudio,EX24, Akai and other sample formats, Streaming playback for large samples, large sample library. Native Instruments. Stand-alone, DirectX, VST, AU, MAS, RTAS, W, M $$.

Proteus X

E-MU's legendary Proteus modules live inside your computer. Reads samples in GigaStudio, HALion, and E-MU formats. Features include 24-bit audio, synthesis, powerful effects processing, sample editing, and streaming audio for huge sample sets. Includes PCI card with DSP. E-MU. Stand-alone, VST, W $$.

Virtual Instrument Collections

Imagine having a full orchestra at your beck and call. Now you can.

Miroslav Philharmonic

String and choral collections from the Miroslav Vitous sample library. Features include 5GB, more than 500 orchestral and choral sounds, 256-voice polyphony, and 16 multitimbral layers, plus effects. IK Multimedia. DirectX, VST, AU, RTAS, W, M $$$.

Personal Orchestra

The name says it all. Lush samples of every orchestral instrument, plus Steinway piano and pipe organ. Unlike most orchestra samples, build ensembles one instrument at a time. Sample library with Kontakt sample player plus Windows sequencer, reverb, Overture SE notation program, and more. Gary Garritan. Stand-alone, VST, W $$.

Ivory

Not one but three stunning acoustic pianos! Rich samples of a German Steinway D nine-foot concert grand, Bosendorfer Imperial Grand, and a Yamaha C7. Includes extensive editing options. Synthogy. VST, AU, RTAS, M $$$.

Symphonic Choirs

Library of five choirs recorded with close, stage, and hall mics. Boys, soprano, alto, tenor, bass, solo, and section voices. Includes Wordbuilder utility: Type in words, and the choirs will sing them! East West. W, M $$$$.

Drums, Percussion, and Beats

Why kill yourself trying to record a full drum kit when you can grab a sample from some of the world's best drummers? One of these programs is bound to soothe your inner groove.

Culture

Includes 9GB of percussion instruments from around the world, plus industrial and orchestral instruments. Add excitement and colors to your music with cool instruments and authentic performance samples. Includes custom audio engine for playback. Yellow Tools. Stand-alone, DirectX, VST, TDM, RTAS, W, M $$$.

BFD

Great-sounding sample library of drums and beats recorded in a top California studio. Includes grooves, beats, MIDI files, groove librarian. FXpansion. VST, AU, RTAS, W, M $$$.

Sounds of the '70s

Soul, disco, funk, and punk licks and riffs, powered by NI Intakt interface. Get down with your bad self. Zero-G. W, M $$.

Drum and Bass Rig

Combines sampled drum-sound modules with bass sounds, loop creator, and bass-line sequencer. Think of it as your own personal rhythm section. M-Audio. W, M $.

Intakt

Loop-based sample playback. Easy-to-use interface, powerful sound shaping with two LFOs, effects, loop library, time compression/expansion, and more. Native Instruments. Stand-alone, DirectX, VST, AU, RTAS, W, M $$.

Stylus RMX

Groove-based virtual instrument plug-in eight-part multitimbral, MIDI and REX loops, auto-synch, huge library of beats and grooves. Spectrasonics VST, RTAS, AU, W, M $$$.

If there is one thing to be learned from this quick tour of music software, it's this: Boy howdy, are we lucky! I have to admit, I am overwhelmed by the options we have at our disposal. Don't be put off by the choices—take some time to define what you want to do, and start small. If you want to record at home or get into dance music, start with a software/hardware bundle. As you become more familiar with the software, add a virtual instrument or two. Check out what an auto-accompaniment program can do.

By all means, take the time to visit the manufacturers' Web sites—you'll find a list in Appendix C. Download demos to get an idea of what the different programs do. Read what other people are doing on online forums and newsgroups. But above all, fire up the old computer and make some music.

That's what we'll be doing in the next chapter, when we learn about MIDI and sequencing.

5 } Track One: MIDI

In the last few chapters, you've learned how to buy and outfit your computer hardware and peripherals. And you've gotten up to speed with the recording terms and general practices that you'll need no matter what kind of music you'll be making. Until now, you've been assembling your tool kit—in these next four chapters you'll put the tools to use.

This chapter deals with MIDI—Musical Instrument Digital Interface. MIDI is without a doubt the most powerful musical tool to come along since written music. "But wait a minute," you say. "I don't play a keyboard, and I can't stand synthesized music. Why do I need MIDI?"

The short answer is that just about every single musical task you do on a computer involves MIDI in some way. Recording software uses MIDI to communicate with other programs and devices. Software mixers rely on MIDI for automating fader moves. Effects use MIDI for dynamic control. Notation programs create MIDI files so you can audition your work. Games rely on MIDI and downloadable sounds for music, sound effects, and even dialog. And that's just scratching the surface. With you or without you, MIDI is quietly going about its job in a million ways.

MIDI Defined

It's a safe bet to say that the desktop music revolution wouldn't have gotten off the ground without MIDI. The MIDI protocol was established to facilitate communication between electronic keyboards back in the dark ages of 1983. It didn't take long for enterprising programmers to realize that MIDI and the Personal Computer were an ideal match.

But what exactly is it? MIDI is a language. By itself, it doesn't do a thing. If you could listen to the raw MIDI stream, it would sound like noise. Ah, but connect two devices that speak the same language, and magic happens.

Here's how the MIDI Manufacturers Association puts it: "The MIDI data stream is a unidirectional asynchronous bit stream at 31.25 Kbits/sec. with 10 bits transmitted per byte (a start bit, 8 data bits, and one stop bit)." Got that? There'll be a test....

Okay, since I promised I'd lay off the math, here's the skinny: MIDI is very similar to computer language. It simply lets one device tell another device what to do. So, if I play middle C on my keyboard, the MIDI message says, in effect, "Hey! Wake up! The dude just pressed key number 64." Depending on what's receiving the message and how it is configured, it could mean, "Play the sound associated with that note," "Trigger the sample of the galloping horse," "Start playback of the new song and mute the vocals," or even, "Open the pod bay door, Hal." So you see, a little knowledge is a powerful thing.

Remember, MIDI isn't audio. MIDI only tells the device what to do. If you play your keyboard and record the MIDI data into a *sequencer*—a fancy word for a program that records and plays back MIDI—what is stored is a series of messages about which keys you played, how hard you played them, and when you lifted your fingers. Replay the sequence, and the sound module inside your keyboard will re-create the performance. Change the sound on your keyboard from an acoustic piano to a bird tweet, and the performance will continue. It may sound weird, but the sequencer won't know that.

That's the power of MIDI. As a language, it is profoundly easy to manipulate. If you want to change a note after you've recorded it, grab it with a mouse and yank it somewhere else. (See Figure 5.1.) Don't like the way the keyboard sound blends with the bass? Choose a different sound. Can't perform a tricky part that's crucial to the song? Slow down the recording to a crawl, or enter the part one note at a time. Need to change the key? Piece of cake with MIDI. (See Figure 5.2.)

Figure 5.1

MIDI notes appear as colored bars. The pitch is shown relative to the vertical keyboard on the left, timing by where the note starts, and duration by the length of the bar. To change the pitch, simply select a note and move it. In this example, the intended placement of the selected note is indicated with a dotted line.

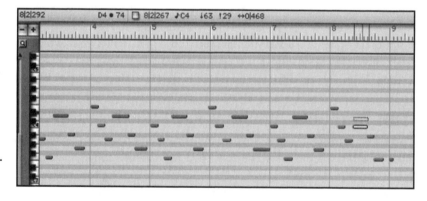

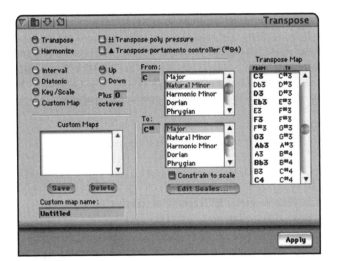

Figure 5.2
Since MIDI is just data, transposing notes is very easy. Many sequencers have very sophisticated transposition and harmonization functions. Shown here is MOTU's Digital Performer.

A (Very) Little History

Prior to 1983, if a keyboardist wanted to play two different sounds at the same time, he'd lug two keyboards to the gig. Or three. Or four or more. In the movie *This Is Spinal Tap*, a keyboardist stands surrounded by stacks of equipment, with his arms spread as wide as possible to reach two keyboards, while frantically grabbing knobs and sliders to modulate the tones. The movie's a farce, but the keyboard rig is dead on.

Sure, there were ways around the limitations. Analog synthesizers often included primitive sequencers to play back control information in a set order, freeing the operator to rush to another keyboard and play a monophonic melody over the repetitive pattern. That is, when she didn't need both hands in the endless struggle to keep the beasts from drifting out of tune. Numerous schemes surfaced to enable machines to interface, but most came up short. In an example of teamwork that is noble for its vision as much as its rarity, a group of electronic instrument manufacturers banded together to develop a set of standards so that any device could communicate with any other device, regardless of race, creed, or country of commercial origin.

The first MIDI devices were electronic keyboards, like the legendary Yamaha DX7, but it didn't take long for software designers to realize that MIDI data could be stored and manipulated on the new home computers that were just beginning to appear. Compared with digital audio, MIDI data is tiny; the MIDI instructions for an entire album's worth of songs could be stored on a floppy disk, with plenty of room to spare. And it wasn't long before MIDI began to show up in ways never envisioned by the originators. Who knew that the extraordinarily complex lighting and special-effects cues for a Las Vegas extravaganza would be handled by MIDI show control? Or that professional studios would use MIDI to write fader data on their mammoth mixing consoles and use MIDI machine control to interface computers with analog recording equipment? Or that cell phones would use MIDI and tiny onboard synthesizers to play a song complete with drums, bass, and screaming electric guitar to announce each incoming call—and annoy the heck out of anyone within earshot?

But, surprisingly, the original MIDI specifications are still very much in effect. Not bad for a 20-year-old technology developed to extend the reach of a performing keyboardist.

Connectivity: In, Out, Thru

MIDI devices communicate using special data ports. Since MIDI is essentially a one-way transfer, you'll usually see three MIDI jacks, labeled "in," "out," and "thru." (Sometimes a single jack handles both "out" and "thru" chores.) As a binary language, MIDI is well suited for both USB and FireWire, so more and more devices support these connections as well.

Although a MIDI cable uses five-pin DIN (Deuttsche Industire fur Normung) connectors, it's wired differently from the standard DIN cables used in the electronics industry. So be sure to buy high-quality cable designed for MIDI. Keep your cable runs as short as possible—not only does the signal degrade at cable lengths over 15 feet, but cheap MIDI cables make excellent radio antennae. In other words, they are noisy.

The trick with MIDI connections is to picture the flow of information: Data leaves a device via the "out" and enters via the "in" port. (See Figure 5.3.)

Figure 5.3
Basic MIDI connections from a controller (a device that sends MIDI) to a MIDI sound module.

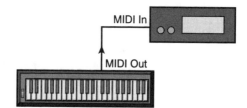

It takes two cables to establish two-way communication. (See Figure 5.4.)

Figure 5.4
In this case, the keyboard is acting both as a MIDI controller sending data to the sequencer via a USB interface and as a sound module playing back prerecorded data.

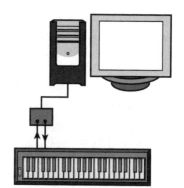

MIDI "thru" ports simply pass on any message received at the "in" port, without adding new data. Why would you want to do that? One reason would be to use a separate tone module for drum sounds. By setting each device to respond to a different channel (more on channels in a moment) you can chain multiple sound modules together. (See Figure 5.5.)

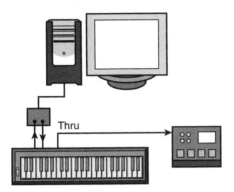

Thru

Figure 5.5
Use the "thru" port to daisy-chain several sound modules. In this case, a keyboard is playing a piano sound on channel 1 and a bass patch on channel 2 while the drum module responds to channel 10.

❋ **WHAT'S A CHANNEL?**

The original MIDI specification was designed to facilitate transmission between multiple keyboards and sound modules. To keep the data flowing in the proper direction, the spec called for 16 channels. The first part of any MIDI message specifies the channel; devices not set to receive on that channel blithely ignore the rest of the message. The easiest way to think of MIDI channels is to use a TV analogy: Your set may receive hundreds of cable channels, but you're likely to watch only one at a time.

To get around the 16-channel limitation, multiport MIDI patchers and interfaces allow 16 channels per port. So an 8-in, 8-out patcher allows a whopping 128 individual MIDI channels (8 ports × 16 channels.)

As I mentioned, MIDI data flows easily to and from your computer. Though you'll still find some older systems using serial or parallel ports, most computer-MIDI interfaces now use either USB or FireWire. In fact, many audio interfaces, including PCI and PCMCIA interfaces and most FireWire and USB audio cards, also include MIDI ports. What's more, many keyboards now feature either USB or FireWire connectivity—and some even include audio interfaces!

Be sure to analyze your needs before you purchase a combination audio/MIDI interface. If you have a large system or expect to use a MIDI control surface for mixing audio, it may be best to use a multiport interface.

Components of a MIDI Message
So far I've used the terms "MIDI message" and "MIDI data" pretty freely. Let's take a look under the hood and see exactly what's going on. Although you may never have the need to edit raw MIDI data, it's still a good idea to know what the different messages do.

A MIDI message is composed of three 8-bit "words." At their most basic, MIDI messages may be divided into *channel messages* and *system messages*. As you can guess, system messages refer to the entire system, while channel messages are specific to one of the 16 MIDI channels.

> ### ❊ WHAT ARE BITS AND BYTES?
>
> Bits, or "binary digits," are the building blocks of computer language. At its simplest, a computer is nothing more than a huge pile of electrical switches. Each switch can be in only one of two "states"—either it's on or it's off. To express these in numbers, computer wizards use two numbers: 0 for "off" and 1 for "on." Since a single bit doesn't convey a heck of a lot of information, multiple bits are chained together to form longer words. The number of bits in a word is called the "bit depth." Each increase in bit depth represents an exponential increase in the amount of information. So, while 2 bits convey twice as much information as a single bit, 4 bits convey 16 times as much (2 + 2 + 2 + 2).
>
> A byte is a binary word that is 8 bits long. A byte conveys a significant amount of information: As long as we're on the subject, a kilobyte contains 1,024 bytes—not the 1,000 you'd expect. That's because 1,024 is based on multiplying two, the original binary digit, by itself a number of times.

Channel messages are further divided into "channel voice messages," which contain most of the information about the musical performance, such as the notes, keyboard velocity, and aftertouch. "Channel mode messages," on the other hand, affect how the receiving device will respond to the incoming message. Likewise, system messages are divided into "system common," "system real time," and "system exclusive."

This will become clear when we take a look at the specifics next.

Channel Voice Messages

Here's where the data stream flows strongest. Channel voice messages convey essential performance data—which notes you played, when you played them, and how quickly you depressed the keys.

* ❊ **Note on/note off.** The keyboard on an electronic musical instrument is actually a row of switches. Touch a key, and you send a MIDI message that says, "On channel XX, note number YY was switched on." Remove your finger, and a "note off" message is sent.

* ❊ **Velocity.** Velocity refers to how hard you played the note, in a range from 0 to 127. The higher the velocity, the louder the note, just like on a piano. Surprisingly, note off messages also register a velocity value, but it is almost universally ignored by most software.

* ❊ **Aftertouch.** Many keyboards have a pressure-sensitive membrane running underneath the keys to register the amount of pressure applied after a key is depressed. Aftertouch information is commonly used to add vibrato or some other kind of modulation to the sound.

"Polyphonic aftertouch" registers the pressure of each individual note; "channel aftertouch" applies a single value for all of the keys.

❄ **Pitch bend.** Guitarists and wind players add expression to their playing by "bending" notes up or down, just like the human voice. Thanks to the pitch-bend message, a billion keyboardists can pretend they're shredding a solo.

❄ **Program change.** These messages select the sounds (called a *patch*) that the receiving instrument will play. Since every manufacturer—indeed, every individual model—has its own unique patch-numbering system, a specialized set of MIDI parameters called General MIDI was developed to standardize patch changes. To get around this limitation, sounds are usually stored in banks of 128 patches. (See below.)

❄ **Control change.** The MIDI spec contains a large number of control change messages. Some, such as #7 (volume), #33 (modulation), and #64 (hold pedal), affect how the sound is modulated. The "bank select message" (#0) increases the number of available sounds by choosing between internal sound banks. Control #120, the popular and useful "all notes off" command, is sometimes called the panic button. A number of controllers are considered "general purpose" or "unregistered," allowing for both future expandability and current flexibility.

MIDI control change messages work in real time to modulate and affect the sound. This added control brings a great deal of expressiveness to your performance. Some control messages simply toggle on and off, but most have a range of values between 0 and 127 (or, if you prefer, 1 to 128). You record, edit, and play back controller information just like note data.

Since MIDI control change messages are so powerful, check out Table 5.1 to get to know a few of the more commonly used controllers and what they do.

Table 5.1 MIDI Controllers and What They Do

Controller Number	Name	Notes
1	Modulation wheel	Mostly used to add vibrato to a sound, but different sounds may respond in unique ways. For example, the mod wheel may increase the amount of distortion on a fuzz guitar sound or create an expressive filter sweep.
2	Breath controller	Simulates the expressiveness of varying air pressure in wind instruments. Handy for adding realism to wind instrument sounds played on a keyboard.
5	Portamento time	Affects how notes slide into each other (aka "glissando"). Used in conjunction with #65

Controller Number	Name	Notes
7	Volume	Adjust the volume of the patch from 0 (off) to 127 (really loud). If you can't hear any sound coming from a particular patch, this is the first thing to check.
10	Pan position	Sets the left/right position of the sound in a stereo field. The range is 0 (hard left) to 127 (hard right). If you noticed that #7 and #10 have applications for automating audio mixer functions, you may go to the head of the class.
64	Damper or sustain pedal	Simulates the effect of the sustain pedal on a piano. It's either on, during which time the notes you play will hold, or sustain; or it's off, where they decay naturally.
65	Portamento	Turns the portamento effect on or off. Used in conjunction with #5.
92	Chorus depth	Controls the chorus effect on patches that support it.

As I said, there are 128 MIDI controllers. Not all are defined, so manufacturers may choose to implement them in various ways. Also, some continuous controllers—CC for short—come in two flavors: coarse and fine. For instance, #2, the mod wheel, is a coarse parameter with only 128 possible values, while the #33 mod wheel offers a much greater range of values. Why have two? For most purposes, the coarse parameter is just fine. And the coarse adjustments use far less processing power. But for some things, such as fine-tuning volume and panning adjustments, you really need the added resolution.

Channel Mode Messages

Like channel voice messages, channel mode messages specify the channel they will affect. Local control (controller # 122) sets the way your keyboard will operate; turn local control off, and no matter how much pounding you do, you won't hear a sound coming out of it. Believe it or not, there are times when that's useful, such as when you're using your keyboard to send data to a sequencer while playing back sounds stored in memory.

The other four messages can be a tad confusing. Omni on/off mode operates in tandem with poly on/off to set up four different ways the device will respond to incoming MIDI channel messages. Here's the skinny:

❋ **Omni on/poly on.** The device will play note messages received on any incoming MIDI channel and will play notes *polyphonically*, that is, a bunch of notes at the same time.

❋ **Omni on/poly off.** The device will play note messages received on any incoming MIDI channel and will play notes *monophonically*, or one note at a time. It makes sense if you're trying to emulate the sound of a wind instrument, since you wouldn't expect to hear chords coming out of a saxophone.

❄ **Omni off/poly on.** The device will play note messages received only on the specified channel and will play notes polyphonically. This is the basic setup when daisy-chaining several devices via the thru ports and you want each one to play a specific part.

❄ **Omni off/poly off.** The device will play note messages received on the specified MIDI channel and will play notes monophonically. Since only one note may be played at a time, omni off/poly off is useful for monophonic instruments such as wind synthesizers. A multichannel module set this way is ideal for guitar-to-MIDI controllers where each string transmits on a different channel.

System Common

System common messages are used to communicate with every device in the data chain. Typical usage would be to tell a sequencer or drum machine to select a song stored in memory (song select) or to start a song at a point other than the beginning (song position pointer). One system common message, called MTC 1/4 frame, is used in conjunction with MIDI time code (MTC) to synchronize MIDI devices with video or audio recording equipment. The tune request message tells an analog synthesizer to retune its oscillators. Unfortunately, this message has no effect on guitar players!

System Real Time

MIDI is handy for synchronizing several devices that need to play back together, such as an external drum machine and a sequencing program. A MIDI timing clock sends out a pulse 24 times for each quarter note, based on the playback tempo. Although that may not seem like a particularly fine resolution, at 4/4 time set to 144 BPM (the disco standard, in case you were wondering), that translates to just over 230 pulses per second. In contrast, SMPTE time code is based on the frame rate of motion picture film, which hovers around 24 frames per second.

❄ **WHAT'S TIME CODE?**

SMPTE time code was developed as a way to lock audio recorders to film so soundtracks and dialogue would line up correctly. In a process called *striping*, an analog audio signal containing the time code is recorded directly onto tape from a SMPTE generator. MIDI time code (MTC) is essentially SMPTE translated to a language digital devices can understand. Both SMPTE—Society of Motion Picture and Television Engineers—and MTC measure time in hours, minutes, seconds, and frames, like this: 00:07:11:01. That number refers to a point at 0 hours, 7 minutes, 11 seconds, and 1 frame.

Why do you need to know the frame number? Well, for one thing, it helps spot effects, say the sound of an explosion, to a particular point in the picture. For music, it just gives us a greater degree of timing accuracy than if we used only minutes and seconds.

Standards being what they are, there's no agreement on how many frames roll by in a second. Rates vary from 24 fps (frames per second), the basic rate of film, to 25 fps (for video in Europe), 29.97 for US video (in two flavors, drop-frame and non-drop—don't ask), and 30 fps, more or less the standard for music projects.

Other real-time messages include start, continue, and stop—handy for controlling the transport functions on a tape, er, digital recorder. You'll notice that most software recorders retain the look and feel of tape transport controls.

System Exclusive

Finally, system exclusive—sysex for the hip—involves messages that are specific to a particular make and model of device. Each manufacturer has its own sysex ID, as does each one of its products. Sysex messages vary from manufacturer to manufacturer and may be used for updating software, editing patches, off-loading the contents of a device's memory to another location for storage, and a host of other applications.

Thanks to sysex, patch editor and library programs abound. Take a look at MOTU's popular Unisyn in Figure 5.6. It is far easier to edit the sounds on a rack-mounted synth module or effects device with a computer than it is using the tiny knobs and scroll wheels on the unit's surface.

Figure 5.6

Patch librarians are handy for organizing sounds.

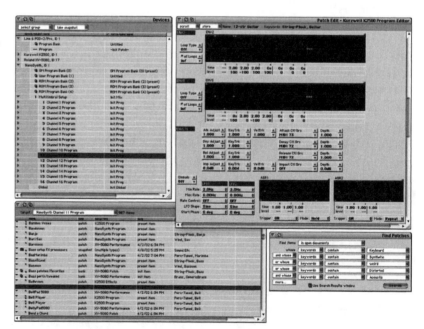

Thankfully, most of this happens behind the scenes, so all you have to do is cable up and run the program.

If you are interested in learning more about MIDI messages and how they work—and believe me, there is a *lot* more to learn—check out some of the sites in Appendix D, "Resources." And be sure to pick up a copy of *MIDI Power! Second Edition: The Comprehensive Guide* by Robert Guerin, published by Course Technology.

General MIDI

In the early days of MIDI, each manufacturer had its own way of organizing sounds and channels. Some gear used a single bank of 128 patches, and some cut things into multiple smaller chunks. You may find all of the piano and keyboard sounds clustered together, or they may be spread randomly through the device's memory. So a song you wrote using, say, an electronic drum kit, fretless bass, and organ sounds on the Electro-Key-O-Matic may play back on a new age pad, glockenspiel, and clarinet on the Zapsonic-X15. Needless to say, this caused no end of confusion. Composers writing for games and other applications that used the sounds generated on the primitive computer sound cards of the day had to write variations for every system.

General MIDI (GM for short) brings order to this chaotic world by creating a patch numbering system that everyone can agree with. Regardless of who made your synthesizer or sound card, patch number 1 is an acoustic grand piano, and number 128 is the ever-popular gunshot. GM also specifies how certain controllers will operate. Thanks to General MIDI, you'll never have to worry that your composition won't play back properly. Just about every synthesizer, sound card, and sample playback device made—both hardware and software—supports GM. So do both the Apple OS and Windows, so you don't even need an external sound module to take advantage of MIDI music. In fact, you probably have been using General MIDI all along and just never knew it.

The GM Programs

General MIDI uses channels 1 through 9 and 11 through 16 for pitched instruments, such as keyboards, guitars, and winds. (Channel 10 is reserved for drum sounds.) For these pitched instruments, the tuning is standardized so that playing key number 60 sounds a middle C. (Some of the odder effects residing at the end of the patches, such as "bird tweet" (number 124) and "fret noise" (number 121) do not follow the pitches you play.) Incidentally, most people use the words "patches," "programs," and even "instruments" pretty much interchangeably when talking about the sounds stored in an electronic instrument.

The sounds are arranged in a more or less logical order, with pianos grouped together in patches 1–9, followed by chromatic percussion sounds, such as vibes and marimba, filling slots 9–16. Basses are found in numbers 33–40. See Table 5.2 for a complete list of patches and some notes to help you choose your sounds.

Though GM specifies what sound will be called up for each patch change message, it says nothing about how that sound must be produced. Consequently, the quality and character of an individual sound varies wildly from one brand to another, or even between different devices within a given brand. Some GM sounds, such as Acoustic Piano, are notoriously difficult to render well—getting a good acoustic piano sound is the holy grail of electronic music. Others, like recorder (number 75) are fairly easy to re-create on even the cheapest sound card.

Although the programs are more or less standardized, names vary from brand to brand. So electric piano number 2 may be called Soft Tines, Digi Piano, FM piano, or something else on your General MIDI instrument. As you look at the table, you'll notice that GM covers a lot of ground, from rock and jazz instruments to orchestral instruments complete with string and horn sections, synthesizer sounds, and folk instruments from around the world. Even sound effects for game developers. This great flexibility is what makes GM so powerful.

One quick note: Some manufacturers number their programs from 0–127 instead of 1–128. Either way, the GM sounds will be compatible.

Table 5.2 GM Instruments

Program Number	Name	Notes
1	Acoustic piano	A grand piano sound.
2	Bright acoustic piano	Usually a more aggressive piano sound than number 1.
3	Electric grand piano	Like the ones used on rock stages.
4	Honky-tonk piano	A bright, funky upright piano sound.
5	Electric piano 1	A "hard-edged" electric piano.
6	Electric piano 2	A softer electric piano.
7	Harpsichord	A plucked keyboard. Think Bach.
8	Clavinet	A funk staple.
9	Celesta	Also known as a "bell piano."
10	Glockenspiel	Those big melodic bell trees you see in marching bands.
11	Music box	Another bell-piano sound.
12	Vibraphone	"Vibes" for short. The real thing uses electric fans to add vibrato; use the mod wheel for the same effect.
13	Marimba	Like a wooden vibraphone, without the tremolo.
14	Xylophone	Like a metal marimba. Found in orchestras.
15	Tubular bells	Like wind chimes, only huge.

Program Number	Name	Notes
16	Dulcimer	A folk instrument with lots of strings, played with small wooden hammers. Also called a santur, yang chin, or hammered dulcimer.
17	Drawbar organ	An electronic simulation of a church pipe organ. The drawbars open and close different lengths of pipes, called "stops," which alter the tone. The most famous electronic version is the Hammond B3.
18	Percussive organ	A mellow jazz organ sound.
19	Rock organ	Adds some fuzz and attitude.
20	Church organ	A familiar electronic organ sound. "Dearly beloved, we are gathered here ..."
21	Reed organ	Like an old-fashioned pump organ.
22	Accordion	Think Parisian café.
23	Harmonica	Yep, spent three grand on a keyboard so you can play the harmonica.
24	Tango accordion	Also called "bandeon." A large-button accordion from Argentina.
25	Nylon-string guitar	"Classical" guitar.
26	Acoustic steel-string guitar	Your basic folk guitar.
27	Jazz guitar	A mellow electric guitar sound.
28	Clean guitar	The sound of an electric guitar with no effects.
29	Mute guitar	Simulates the sound of palm muting on an electric.
30	Overdrive guitar	Turn it up!
31	Distortion guitar	A heavier version of number 30.
32	Harmonics	A guitar pick striking the string 12 frets above the note you play with the left hand adding a second tone one octave higher. Add a lot of distortion, and you get an arena-rock staple.
33	Acoustic bass	Also called jazz bass. A plucked upright bass.
34	Finger bass	An electric bass played with the fingers.
35	Picked bass	The same played with a flat-pick for a sharper attack.
36	Fretless electric bass	Use the pitch wheel and/or portamento to simulate the sound of sliding from note to note.

Program Number	Name	Notes
37	Slap bass 1	Two variations on the sound of a slapped electric bass.
38	Slap bass 2	
39	Synth bass 1	Variations on the synthesizer bass sounds popular in the 1970s.
40	Synth bass 2	
41	Violin	The next four are solo orchestral stringed instruments.
42	Viola	
43	Cello	
44	Contra bass	A bowed upright bass.
45	Tremolo strings	A string section playing with rapid bow movements.
46	Pizzicato strings	A string section playing with finger plucks instead of bowing.
47	Harp	The stringed instrument played by angels, not a blues harmonica.
48	Timpani	A big, tunable drum.
49	String ensemble 1	Sometimes called "marcato strings," after the string technique of playing each new note with a new bow attack.
50	String ensemble 2	Also called "slow strings." Simulates a string section playing legato—using a continuous motion of the bow from one note to the next.
51	Synth strings 1	Two variations on the synthesizer "string pad." A pad is a lush sound that fills acoustic space.
52	Synth strings 2	
53	Choir	The sound of a vocal choir singing "ahhs."
54	Voice oohs	Same idea, different syllable.
55	Synth voice	Same idea again, only this time it's *supposed* to sound like a synthesizer created the sound.
56	Orchestra hit	The sound of the entire orchestra playing one sharp note.
57	Trumpet	The next group includes solo orchestral brass instruments.
58	Trombone	
59	Tuba	
60	Muted trumpet	
61	French horn	
62	Brass section	Lots of horns.

Program Number	Name	Notes
63	Synth brass 1	Two versions of the classic '80s electronic horn section sound.
64	Synth brass 2	
65	Soprano sax	And now the winds ...
66	Alto sax	
67	Tenor sax	
68	Baritone sax	
69	Oboe	
70	English horn	
71	Bassoon	
72	Clarinet	
73	Piccolo	
74	Flute	
75	Recorder	A wooden wind instrument common in the Renaissance.
76	Pan-flute	A wind instrument made up of numerous small tubes. By blowing across the top of each tube, you sound a note. Just like blowing on a bottle. (See number 77.)
77	Bottle blow	Yep. What it sounds like when you blow across the top of a soda bottle.
78	Shakuhachi	A Japanese end-blown flute made from bamboo.
79	Whistle	"You know how to whistle, don't you, Steve? Just put your lips together and blow."
80	Ocarina	A little ceramic flute that looks a bit like a sweet potato.
81	Lead 1 square	The next eight programs are all synth leads suitable for solo work. This one is based on the characteristic sound of a square wave. Sounds a bit like a clarinet on steroids.
82	Lead 2 saw	Based on a sawtooth wave. Buzzier than the square wave.
83	Lead 3 calliope	A re-creation of the horse-drawn steam organ from old-time circuses.
84	Lead 4 chiff	Adds breath sound to the mix, like an overblown flute.
85	Lead 5 charang	Often sounds like a combination stringed instrument and a buzz saw. Try as I may, I cannot find a definition for "charang." (See also numbers 103 and 104.)

Program Number	Name	Notes
86	Lead 6 voice	A vocal synth sound good for melody playing.
87	Lead 7 5ths	Adds a tone a perfect fifth higher (or sometimes a tone a fourth lower—same difference). Two notes for the price of one!
88	Lead 7 bass and lead	A versatile patch that sounds good for both bass and lead lines.
89	Pad 1 new age	The next eight programs are intended as pads, lush washes of slow-moving sounds mixed underneath the arrangement. This one's sometimes called bell pad, fantasy, or something similar.
90	Pad 2 warm	A rich pad with a very slow attack. (That means the sound swells in volume after you press the key.)
91	Pad 3 polysynth	Based on the legendary Korg poly-6 sound. A string pad with a fast attack.
92	Pad 4 choir	More synthesized voices for fun and profit.
93	Pad 5 bowed	Usually called something like bowed glass, a more descriptive term.
94	Pad 6 metallic	Another variation on the pad theme.
95	Pad 7 halo	A lot of programmers make this one sound like a cross between a choir and a string section. As you can guess, there's a lot of leeway in interpreting what some of these names mean.
96	Pad 8 sweep	A rapidly rising pad with a very slow attack. Re-creates the characteristic "filter sweep" sound of analog synthesizers.
97	Effects 1 rain	The next eight programs really get into zoom-zoom land. Although you'd expect this one to sound like falling rain, it's often a weird little keyboard sound with sci-fi echoes trailing off after each note. Remember, each manufacturer is free to interpret what these names mean.
98	Effects 2 soundtrack	You've heard this one a million times at the local movie theater—the boy and girl fall into a final embrace as the music swells under the closing credits. A huge, cinematic pad with a very slow attack.

Program Number	Name	Notes
99	Effects 3 crystal	Imagine a piano made out of ice, and you'll get the idea.
100	Effects 4 atmosphere	Usually a combination of a hard-edged keyboard sound plus a pad.
101	Effects 5 brightness	Bright it is. Often a variation on an orchestral hit with a very metallic edge.
102	Effects 6 goblins	I have no idea what goblins are supposed to sound like. From what I've heard, there's not much agreement among sound designers either. Depending on your synth, this one can be anything from a nice, spooky vocal pad to a weird, effect-laden electronic burble.
103	Effects 7 echoes	Another twofer. Sometimes the sound is triggered both by the note-on and the note-off messages. So you get an echo effect when you lift your hands off the keys. Other designers simply program a sound that seems to echo itself.
104	Effects 8 Sci-fi	Another one that's all over the map. It's often another cinematic pad.
105	Sitar	A re-creation of the stringed instrument from India.
106	Banjo	Yep, a banjo.
107	Shamisen	A Japanese stringed instrument.
108	Koto	Another Japanese stringed instrument.
109	Kalimba	An African instrument. Sometimes called a thumb piano.
110	Bagpipe	The national instrument of Scotland.
111	Fiddle	What's the difference between a fiddle and a violin? Use this as a variation of number 41.
112	Shanai	The shanai is a raucous Indian oboe.
113	Tinkle bell	The sound of bells, not the character from *Peter Pan*.
114	Agogo	Cast-metal bells played with a stick in Africa and Brazil. Note that some of these next eight percussion sounds also appear as part of the GM drum kit on channel 10.
115	Steel drums	A melodic instrument made out of 50-gallon oil drums. The national instrument of Trinidad.
116	Wood block	A block of wood used as a percussion instrument.
117	Taiko drum	Huge drums played in Japan.

Program Number	Name	Notes
118	Melodic tom	No, this is not a guy named Thomas who whistles really well. Sounds like a tunable tom from a drummer's kit.
119	Synth drum	The ubiquitous syn-drum sound famous from a million drum machines.
120	Reverse cymbal	What it would sound like if you recorded a cymbal strike and then played the tape backwards.
121	Guitar fret noise	The sound of finger squeaks on a guitar string. Sprinkle some of these into your MIDI guitar and bass parts for added realism.
122	Breath noise	The sound of breath blowing into a wind instrument. Also called chiff. Add some to your MIDI flute and recorder parts.
123	Seashore	Waves breaking at the beach.
124	Bird tweet	I guess whoever thought up the GM programs just ran out of ideas. If you need bird tweets for your song or video game soundtrack, here's where you'll find 'em.
125	Telephone ring	The ring tone from an old-fashioned rotary telephone. I imagine most kids have never heard this sound.
126	Helicopter	A gamer's staple.
127	Applause	Give yourself a hand ...
128	Gunshot	Another staple sound for games.

The great thing about GM is that you never have to worry that your music will play on the wrong instruments. Just about any music program you use supports it, so all you have to do is select an instrument from a drop-down menu. For instance, the popular auto-accompaniment program Band-in-a-Box makes it easy to set up anything from a virtual jazz combo to a full-bore Latin band without having to enter program change numbers. (See Figure 5.7.)

Figure 5.7

Most music programs support GM patch lists. With Band-in-a-Box, you can choose instruments by their GM names.

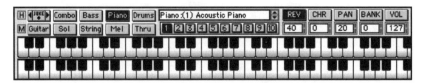

One drawback of GM sounds is that they often won't have the depth and character of the other patches in your keyboard or sample collection. So I'll use GM sounds to quickly sketch out arranging ideas in my sequencer. Once I have the song shaped the way I want it, I'll go back and begin the long task of auditioning sounds from the many hundreds stored in my collection.

GM Drums

Channel 10 is reserved for percussion sounds, such as drum kits and many of the hand percussion instruments found in Latin music. Unlike the chromatic sounds on the other channels, channel 10 sounds use the key numbers to select the particular percussion instrument. (See Table 5.3.) This key mapping lets you play a drum part right on your keyboard. For instance, use note numbers 60 and 61 (middle C and the D above it) to lay down a snappy high and low bongo rhythm.

Some GM keyboards and modules expand on the single drum kit idea. Using Bank Select messages, you can choose between kits designed for jazz, hard rock, electronic music, and more. To help you get oriented as you look at this chart, MIDI note number 36 is two octaves below middle C.

Table 5.3 GM Drum Assignments

MIDI Key Number	Drum Sound
35	Acoustic bass drum
36	Bass drum
37	Side stick snare
38	Acoustic snare
39	Hand clap
40	Electric snare
41	Low floor tom
42	Closed hi-hat
43	High floor tom
44	Half-open hi-hat
45	Low tom
46	Open hi-hat
47	Ride cymbal 1
48	Low-mid tom
49	Crash cymbal 1
50	High tom
51	Ride cymbal 1
52	Chinese cymbal

MIDI Key Number	Drum Sound
53	Ride cymbal bell
54	Tambourine
55	Splash cymbal
56	Cowbell
57	Crash cymbal 2
58	Vibraslap
59	Ride cymbal 2
60	High bongo
61	Low bongo
62	Muted high conga
63	Open high conga
64	Low conga
65	High timbale
66	Low timbale
67	High agogo
68	Low agogo
69	Cabasa
70	Maracas
71	Short whistle
72	Long whistle
73	Short guiro
74	Long guiro
75	Claves
76	High wood block
77	Low wood block
78	Muted cuica
79	Open cuica
80	Muted triangle
81	Open triangle

If GM makes selecting sounds so easy, why would you need to know the individual key assignments for the drum sounds? For one thing, it beats hunting around on your keyboard for the sound you need. Also, many programs generate MIDI note-on messages alongside the internal sounds for clicks and count-offs. This lets you easily route the click track to your headphones. Usually the default is MIDI note number 39 (handclap)—a nice bright sound that's easy to hear. But sometimes it works better to change the note assignment so you hear a different sound in the 'phones. For instance, I like to set my metronome so the downbeat is played on a bass drum (key number 36) and the other beats on a side stick snare (#37). (See Figure 5.8.)

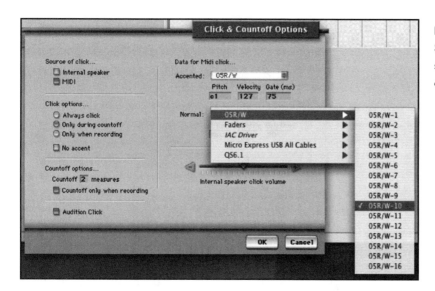

Figure 5.8
Select your favorite drum sounds for click tracks and count-offs.

The Rest of the Story

General MIDI is more than just a list of standardized program changes and drum assignments. The specification also requires that compatible sound modules (both hardware and software) recognize all 16 MIDI channels and use a minimum of either 24 dynamically allocated voices playing simultaneously for both percussion and melodic sounds—sometimes divided further into 8 voices for percussion and 16 for melodic sounds.

✼ **WHAT'S DYNAMIC ALLOCATION?**

Early MIDI devices had to cram a huge amount of processing into pretty tight quarters, electronically speaking. Although GM-compliant modules have to be able to play polyphonically (poly = many, phonic = sound) on all 16 channels, in truth they rarely can handle the sheer processing power to render all of the notes played on all of the instruments you'd expect in a huge ensemble.

To make the most of scarce electronic resources, dynamic allocation gives priority to the most recently played note. That means held notes played earlier in the sequence may disappear. For most of us, this isn't a huge problem. But if you're going to be working with orchestral scores or complex music with lots of chords, be aware that you will need multiple sound modules to cover all the bases.

GM also specifies how modules will respond to certain controller messages and other handy stuff. The bottom line is that you can create a song on your system and know that it will play back properly on any GM system. Since MIDI files are so small compared with digital audio files, MIDI is ideally suited for Web use.

❄ **STANDARD MIDI FILES**

Standard MIDI Files (SMFs) are files that can play back on any MIDI sequencer, regardless of platform. The MMA (MIDI Manufacturers Association, the group that oversees the MIDI standards) originally defined three flavors, or types, of SMFs, though only two are in use. Type 0 stores all of the sequence data in a single track; type 1 SMFs are true multitrack files.

Since they are tiny and truly universal, SMFs and the Internet are the greatest match since sliced bread and peanut butter. A quick search will yield millions of SMFs covering just about every musical genre you can imagine. Want to learn a difficult Irish reel? Load an SMF into your notation program and print it out, or loop it in your sequencer and learn it by ear. Like to sing karaoke? Choose from thousands of song files. Working with a writing partner on another continent? Zap her an SMF of your work. She can load it into her sequencer, add new parts, and e-mail it back.

General MIDI has been around for a long time, and it is beginning to show its age. For instance, the original specs limited the number of patches that could be stored. Fortunately, extensions to the GM specs, such as Roland's GS and Yamaha's XG, have greatly increased their power. I've already mentioned how you can use Bank Select messages to choose different drum kits; look for more development in the future. I should also point out that the overall sound quality of GM sets has improved quite a bit.

Downloadable Sounds and SoundFonts

Downloadable sounds (DLS) were added to the MIDI specs way back in 1997. The basic idea was to let sound designers and composers for games and Internet entertainment add custom sounds to the GM sound set. A DLS file contains both the MIDI file data and the parameters needed to create an instrument to play it back on, including a small WAV audio file.

Although you still may encounter it, the DLS format has been superseded by E-Mu's SoundFont format. SoundFonts work with any SoundFont-compatible device, including nearly 100 percent of SoundBlaster-compatible cards and Apple's QuickTime 5.0 and up. SoundFonts contain both small audio samples and the necessary information for the compatible hardware or software to render the desired sound. That means you can specify exactly how you want your sequence to be heard. SoundFonts, while larger than SMFs, are still far smaller than MP3s, making them the file format of choice for game developers.

As of this writing, SoundFonts are still a tad difficult to create and manage. That doesn't mean they aren't everywhere; the chances are pretty good that the computer you are using right now uses SoundFonts for its GM sound bank. However, most GM banks bundled with your card allocate only a tiny amount of memory for the sounds—as little as 2MB to handle 128 samples! Upgrading to a third-party GM SoundFont bank is one of the quickest, and cheapest, improvements you can make. (See Appendix C, "Manufacturers," for a list of sources.)

To create your own SoundFonts requires some basic sample recording and editing techniques that are well beyond the scope of this book. But watch this space; within a very short time, SoundFonts will be as pervasive—and user friendly—as General MIDI.

Gear Up

Before you can work with MIDI, you'll need something that will transmit data, an interface to funnel the information into and from the computer, and something to play it back on so you can hear it. Remember that MIDI by itself doesn't make any sound, so your MIDI instrument is vital. Although some MIDI keyboards handle all three of these tasks, let's take a look at each piece of the chain separately first so you'll understand how they are related. (I won't mention your computer system needs other than to say that they ain't much. Basically, if it'll boot up, it'll handle most MIDI sequencers.)

MIDI Instruments: Keyboards, Racks, and Software

Electronic musical instruments come in two basic varieties: *synthesizers,* which create tones purely by electronic means, and *samplers,* which play back short bits of recorded musical data called *samples.* Of course, life is never so cut and dried, so many instruments have features of both.

Hardware synthesizers and samplers may have keyboards that let them double as MIDI controllers (more on this in a second), or they may be housed in rack-mounted or desktop units called sound modules. More and more classic synths and samplers, as well as excellent general-purpose instruments, are showing up as software instruments. (See Figure 5.9.)

Most electronic instruments now can store many times the original 128 sounds specified by the GM standard. With a few notable exceptions, all are multitimbral: that is, capable of playing sounds on more than one channel at a time and polyphonically so you can play chords. Even sophisticated synths generally support the GM sound set, as do some sample-playback devices. But many do not; if GM compatibility is important to you, make sure your system offers it before you buy.

Keyboards come in a variety of sizes and styles as well. While piano players may prefer a full 88-note keyboard with weighted hammer-action keys, most consumer-level electronic keyboards have 61 or fewer unweighted keys. If you're going to use the keyboard only to tap in lead lines and bass and drum parts, you can get away with an octave or two as long as you can transpose the keyboard up or down to cover the full range.

Figure 5.9
Applied Acoustics' Ultra-Analog software synth has both the look and sound of a vintage modular analog synthesizer with all the benefits of MIDI.

Synthesizers

At its most basic, a synthesizer is an electronic tone-producing and tone-modifying device. Without going into detail, let's just say you can simulate natural sounds by first creating some basic sound, a buzzing reed-like sound, say, and then running it through additional electronic filters and other circuitry to modify the output—sort of like how you modify the basic sound of your vocal chords by changing the shape of your mouth, lips, and tongue. On a synthesizer, filters and modifiers work to build up the basic sound, and you use continuous controllers to change the shape of the sound in real time.

Of course, simulating natural sounds isn't all that synthesizers do, or even what they do well. They excel at creating brand new sounds. Early analog and digital synthesizers are prized for the unique tones and textures they created, from the sweeping outer space sounds of the Moog and the huge string pads of the Prophet 5 to the signature glassy keyboard textures of the Yamaha DX 7 and the now-ubiquitous Roland electronic drum sounds. All of these instruments are now available as software and for a fraction of the cost of buying and maintaining vintage gear. Re-creations of older analog synthesizers have another huge advantage over the originals—they now speak MIDI. Analog synths and their digital simulations really come alive when the parameters are tweaked as the music is playing.

Samplers

True samplers differ from synthesizers in that the basic building block of the final sound is a short digital recording that is created, or sampled, by the operator. Of course, it isn't always practical to record the hundreds of samples you may need, so sample libraries can be found, covering everything from orchestral instruments to short, rhythmic drums and bass patterns.

Samplers use all of the tone-shaping tools and effects found in a synthesizer to create the final sounds. Like synthesizers, samplers can make getting decent results a tedious process, which is where the sample-playback instrument comes in. Sometimes called romplers (a contraction of the acronym ROM, or Read-Only Memory, and sampler), these devices feature large banks of sampled musical instruments. As memory prices fall, software romplers and sample libraries such as the incredibly cool Sonik Synth (Sonic Reality) and MOTU's Symphonic Instrument (see Figure 5.10) have become the instruments of choice for many hard-working studios looking for maximum bang for the buck.

Figure 5.10
Mark of the Unicorn's Symphonic Instrument puts an entire orchestra inside your computer.

Virtual Instruments

A virtual instrument is a software re-creation of an actual musical instrument. Virtual instruments can act as stand-alone programs or reside as plug-ins within another application. Thanks to sophisticated modeling technology, many vintage analog synthesizers and electronic organs have been re-created as virtual instruments. Take it from one who's been there, it's a heck of a lot easier to move a laptop loaded with Native Instruments' delightful B4 organ than it is to lug a Hammond B3 up the club's back stairs.

Software emulations of "real" instruments can be pretty darn convincing. Some, such as TASCAM's remarkable Giga-Studio, have found a home in professional recording and scoring studios across the world. But great power comes at a great price, and I'm not just talking about money here. The more powerful the software instrument, the more load it will place on your computer. Even though MIDI files are small, be sure your CPU is up to the task before spending your paycheck on a huge sample library. At the very least, plan on a 2GHz processor and at least 1GHz of RAM. You'll also need to upgrade your audio interface to take advantage of the superior sound found in high-end software such as Giga-Studio, Garitan's Personal Orchestra, Native Instruments' Kontakt 2, and East West's aptly named Collossus.

For the rest of us mortals, there are literally tons of choices for all of the standard plug-in formats, such as VSTi, Direct-X, TDM, MAS, RTAS, and Audio Units. You can grab just one or two specific instruments, pick up a huge library of sounds to augment the squinky GM programs bundled with your sound card, or delve into the wonderful of analog synthesis.

❊ WHAT'S A PLUG-IN?

Plug-ins are small programs that add functionality to another program, called the host. In the world of computer music, plug-ins can be recording tools, such as reverb or EQ, or they can be virtual instruments. For example, a VST-compatible instrument such as Native Instruments' B4 Organ will appear as a window inside any VST-compliant sequencer.

Plug-ins let you add new instruments and effects as you need them. They're cheaper than buying a bunch of vintage gear, too.

Some software instruments, notably Propellerhead's Reason (more about this in the next chapter), operate as stand-alone programs. Many have built-in sequencers and interface with other programs via helper applications, such as Reason's ReWire technology.

Hardware instruments have one advantage over their software counterparts: They don't take up any of your computer's processing power. If you already have a keyboard or sound module, hook it up and wail away. Thanks to sysex, library programs make storing your sounds a snap—and many sequencers come bundled with patch lists from all of the common keyboards and sound modules. So you don't have to remember whether program number 64 was a bass/piano split or a nose flute.

LIBRARIANS AND EDITORS

Librarians are programs that store and organize patch list data. For instance, my ancient keyboard has four banks of 128 sounds, plus another bank of "user" programs to hold my edits, combinations, and splits. (FYI: A combination is a sound made up of two or more single sounds, such as piano and strings. A split is also made of two or more sounds, arranged to separate areas of the keyboard. A bass/piano split would have a bass sound for the left hand and a piano on the higher keys.) By using a librarian, I can create many more user programs than I can store in the keyboard's limited RAM and can recall them as needed. Universal librarians, such as MOTU's Unisyn, let you bundle patch lists from a number of devices into folders based on whatever criteria you wish. So you can collect all of the patches you need for an album project in one location.

Editors are programs that let you edit the sounds on an external device. Because you're working on a computer monitor and can use a QWERTY (standard) keyboard and mouse, editors make tweaking sounds far easier than on the unit itself.

Control the Input

A device that transmits MIDI data is called a *controller*. Many people use the term controller exclusively to mean a keyboard that transmits MIDI data but does not make any sound of its own, such as the Korg microKONTROL or Yamaha CBXK1. However, except for some vintage analog synthesizers and their modern re-creations, just about any electronic keyboard you can think of will do the job. Properly configured, a multitimbral keyboard (one that can play many sounds simultaneously) can act both as the input and a sound-playback device.

Many players prefer dedicated keyboard controllers with semiweighted action or even fully piano-like hammer-action, such as the elegant Studio Logic VMK-188. You can even opt for a MIDI rig grafted onto a full concert grand piano if you have the space and the budget.

MIDI GUITARS

Guitarists haven't been left out of the electronic music world. In fact, guitar-to-synthesizer interfaces have been around even longer than MIDI. Although the heyday of MIDI guitar seems to have peaked in the early '90s, you can still use your guitar chops in a keyboard universe.

Pitch-to-MIDI converters sense the vibrations of a plucked string and output MIDI note and velocity messages. Both Roland and Yamaha make special pickups and interfaces to turn most popular electric guitars into MIDI controllers. Or grab a ready-to-go guitar from Fender, Brian Moore, or Godin. Acoustic players haven't been left out. Godin makes a nylon-string guitar with a built-in MIDI pickup, or you can install a custom pickup system from RMC in your existing guitar.

One drawback to pitch-to-MIDI conversion is a slight pause equal to about 2 or 3 cycles of the waveform while the software figures out what note you played. Different brands handle the problem in slightly different ways. For example, the Roland GR-20 and GR-33 interfaces track well when playing live using the onboard sounds, but the latency is quite noticeable when sequencing via the MIDI out ports. There are easy workarounds, of course, such as recording each string to a different track and then shifting all the notes forward a few milliseconds until they line up.

Some guitarists can never get used to it; for others, MIDI guitar opens up a whole new world. The bottom line is to treat your MIDI guitar as a new instrument that requires new techniques.

For the ultimate in control, pick up a dedicated guitarlike MIDI controller, such as the Starr Labs Ztar, shown in Figure 5.11.

Figure 5.11

The Ztar MIDI guitar uses pads and switches to transmit MIDI data, eliminating the latency problems of pitch-to-MIDI conversion.

Drummers have long used MIDI triggers and electronic drum pads to play samples. These same controllers may be used to send data to your computer. And wind players using the Yamaha WX5 or other MIDI wind instruments can take advantage of the added expressiveness of breath-controller data.

As you see, basically anything that transmits MIDI will work as a controller. This opens up some exciting avenues for real-time control of effects and DJ applications. More and more controllers combine a small keyboard with numerous user-configurable knobs, wheels, and data sliders to handle everything from inputting notes to tweaking synth parameters to cueing prerecorded loops and even mixing. Taking things into the next dimension, the Alesis Photon X49 incorporates a revolutionary infrared "controller dome" for three-dimensional control over multiple MIDI parameters with the wave of a hand! (See Figure 5.12.)

Interface Options

Although you may still encounter some older systems using serial, parallel, or even joystick port interfaces, these days USB is the way to go. Options range from the truly Spartan—the Yamaha UX16 is essentially a USB cable grafted onto two MIDI cables, with a little lump of circuitry in between—to fully featured multiport switchers with time-code generators, extensive MIDI merging and filtering, and up to 160 MIDI channels!

More and more audio interfaces also have MIDI in and out ports—handy if you'll be adding digital audio to your sequences.

Before you decide to buy, think about your present and future needs. A simple one-in/one-out unit is fine if you're using a single controller and/or multitimbral keyboard and routing 16 channels

Figure 5.12
The "AXYZ controller dome" on the Photon series keyboards senses the position of your hand in space to control multiple filters, modulators, and other MIDI parameters.

in and out of the computer. If you'll be using more than one controller or have a couple of sound modules, consider a multiport interface such as the Edirol UM-880, MOTU MicroExpress, or similar system. Your data will be a lot happier if each device has its own clear pathway. MIDI data can get quite dense, particularly if you're using a lot of aftertouch or breath controller data. Figure 5.13 shows one way to configure a larger MIDI system.

Of course, the simplest interface would be a controller or multitimbral keyboard with a built-in USB port. In that case, all you have to do is run a USB cable between the keyboard and computer, and you are good to go.

Making Music with MIDI

As you have gathered, MIDI is a powerful tool. But tools by themselves are worthless unless you use them to do something. I've sprinkled some hints and tips around in the first half of this chapter. Now let's get down to the nitty-gritty of using MIDI to make music on your computer.

Sequencing

A sequencer is a recorder for MIDI data. The term comes from the analog days: Certain electronic control information could be stored and played back in sequence. Sequencing programs often have the look and feel of analog tape recorders, complete with transport controls such as "play," "fast forward," and "rewind." (See Figure 5.14.)

Sequencers often carry the analog tape analogy even further. You record data to tracks and mix using a software mixer complete with virtual faders, inserts, and pan knobs. See Figure 5.15 for an example from a shareware program called Sweet Sixteen.

Figure 5.13

Complex MIDI systems work best when each device has its own MIDI port. In this example, the keyboards, MIDI Faders, and BeatBox can both input and play back data. The synth module and effects device only receive data.

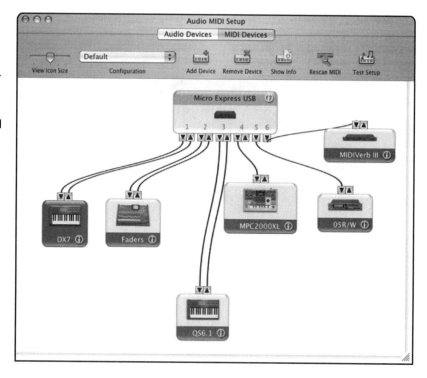

Figure 5.14

Even though digital information is random access, many sequencers still use tape-style transport controls.

Any number of stand-alone MIDI sequencer programs can be found for both the Windows and Mac operating systems—including some excellent shareware. What's more, most scoring, looping, and auto-accompaniment programs include sequencing functions. SoundTrek's Jammer Professional 5 retains the look and feel of a traditional sequencer while including powerful auto-accompaniment features such as style editors and virtual musicians. (See Figure 5.16.)

Linux users have jumped on MIDI in a big way. (See Figure 5.17.)

These days you're likely to find sequencer functions as part of a DAW (digital audio workstation) program such as Cubase, Digital Performer, or Logic for the Mac or the Cubase and Cakewalk family of products on Windows. DAWs have the advantage of flexibility—if at some later date you want to add vocals or other "real" instruments to the mix, no problemo.

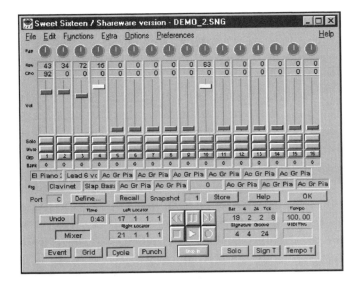

Figure 5.15
Sequencer programs use familiar tape transport controls and mixer interfaces. MIDI data is recorded to "tracks," just like on an analog tape.

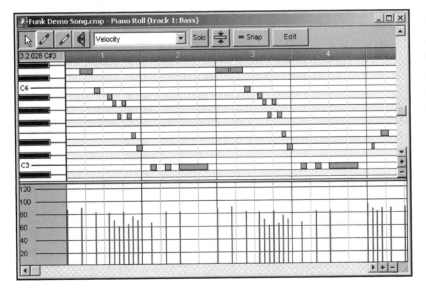

Figure 5.16
Jammer Professional's piano roll editor displays MIDI notes (grey rectangles) and velocity data (the vertical lines at the bottom). Each note's pitch is indicated by its position relative to the piano keyboard on the right side.

Sounds Like ...

MIDI doesn't really care what you play it back on. The exact same sequence of notes and controller data will trigger an elegant multigigabyte grand piano sample or cheesy little keyboard patch inside your GameBoy. This is important, so I'll say it again: MIDI does not make any sound.

I discussed software musical instruments earlier; don't forget that these are MIDI devices. Even the sound sets bundled with your OS or sound card act as MIDI instruments. This is great news

Figure 5.17

MIDI Mountain is a Linux-based sequencer. This is the main window overview, showing MIDI data as colored chunks lined up in tracks.

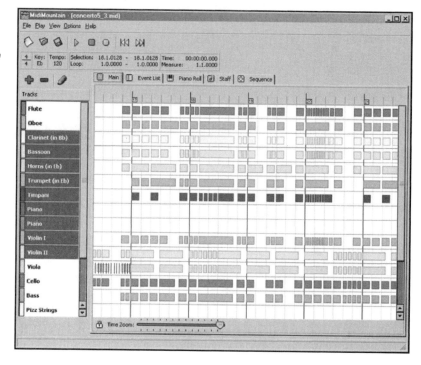

because software instruments take up a lot less real estate than their real-world counterparts. Except for the most basic freeware, chances are you'll have access to a number of sound sources bundled with your main musical sequencer program.

What Gets Recorded

Although many sequencers look and even feel like digital audio recorders, they operate very differently. Remember, MIDI is a digital language to transmit performance information, so a MIDI sequencer actually tells your sound modules what to play. As you learned earlier in the chapter, pressing a key on your MIDI keyboard—or playing a note on a MIDI guitar or MIDI wind instrument—sends a whole raft of information down the pipe. A sequencer stores all of the data, along with time reference information to keep everything in the proper order. Since we're talking about binary data here, not only are the files tiny, but they also can be edited and modified just like the text in a word processor.

Before I get into what you can do with your MIDI data, take a look at Figure 5.18. This is the familiar Event List window common to all sequencers since the Dark Ages. It shows all of the MIDI messages that were captured when you hit record.

Sequencers record all of the MIDI data, not just the note-on and note-off messages. That means all of your velocity and aftertouch info and pedal presses, as well as any pitch-bend or mod wheel

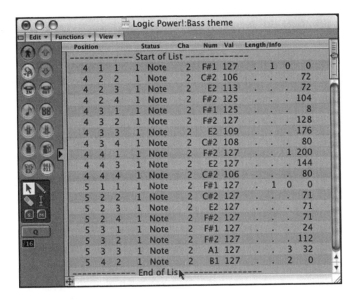

Figure 5.18
MIDI sequencers store data in the order it was received. Note-on and note-off messages, note velocity, program change, and continuous controller data is also displayed.

moves, are stored right alongside the note info. Yes, that can be a huge amount of info—so much so that it is sometimes necessary to filter out any continuous controller data you don't really need.

❊ **A CONTROLLER IS A CONTROLLER, ISN'T IT?**

If you're a little confused about MIDI controllers, you aren't alone. The MIDI specification allows for a number of ways to modulate the sound of an electronic instrument. These MIDI controllers range from simple on/off switches such as the sustain pedal to complex parameters that vary dynamically over time, such as pitch bend, aftertouch, and the modulation wheel. This last group is generally called continuous controllers, or CC for short. And MIDI messages pertaining to the various MIDI controllers are called either controller data or control-change data.

At some point, people started referring to a MIDI keyboard, MIDI wind instrument, or MIDI guitar that made no sound of its own as a controller, too. To make matters worse, you may call any MIDI keyboard, regardless of whether it produces sounds, a controller if it is being used to transmit MIDI data to a sequencer or another MIDI device. Confusing? You bet.

I'm sorry to say that you'll just have to get used to it. For the most part, you can figure out what kind of MIDI controller someone is talking about from the context. So it's perfectly okay to say, "Hey, wiggle the controller on the controller so I can check if the computer is getting any controller data...."

Building Your Sequence
The best way to explain MIDI sequencing is to take you step by step through the process of creating a simple song. For this example, I'll be using just the MIDI functions of Mark of the

Unicorn's Digital Performer software, but you'll find the steps are much the same with any platform.

My setup consists of a multitimbral keyboard that will serve as both controller and sound module and an inexpensive sound module—both of which I picked up used, by the way—connected to a simple four-in/six-out USB MIDI interface. I'll also use software instruments.

Before I do anything else, I make sure that all of my MIDI cables are running in the right direction—MIDI outs connected to MIDI ins—and are securely fastened. I next make sure that the keyboard is set with local control off and configured to receive on all 16 MIDI channels. I then open the software, create the tracks I need, and test to see whether MIDI info is moving through the system by looking at the status lights on my interface. (Every system has a different way of doing this; you may have to record some data and play it back. If you don't hear anything, go back and check your cables and input/output assignments on the software. See Figure 5.19.)

Figure 5.19

MIDI information is recorded in tracks, just like on an analog recorder. Be sure to match up the input and output channels with your external gear, or simply use software instruments.

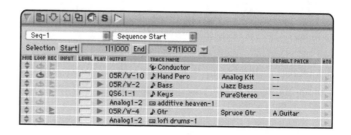

GET THE BEAT

To show you some of the techniques involved in creating a MIDI sequence, I've decided to record a simple salsa-style jam using hand percussion, bass, piano, and flute. Let's start with the percussion track.

Rather than play an entire song's worth of percussion, I open a drum-machine-style window and create a four-bar loop in 4/4 time at 120 BPM. (It really doesn't matter what tempo I choose, since I'll be changing it later.) I set the metronome to give me a nice solid MIDI click and a two-bar count-off so that I'll have time to reach the keyboard after I press record.

❋ **WHAT'S A LOOP?**

You have probably noticed certain kinds of music have lots of short musical patterns that repeat over and over. This is particularly true in the rhythm section—drums, hand percussion, and bass. For highly repetitive parts, it's become fairly standard to record a short section of music and "loop it"—play it over and over as many times as needed.

The term comes from the old days of analog tape, where an engineer would splice a bit of tape to itself, creating an endless tape loop.

Nowadays a loop refers both to a musical section—four bars, say—that is repeated over and over *and* to a little bit of MIDI data or short audio segment that's used as the building block for an arrangement. We'll cover looping in greater detail in the next chapter.

With my left hand, I play in a simple conga and bell pattern. (See Figure 5.20.) I could have simply "drawn in" the notes by clicking with the mouse, but I wanted the part's timing and velocity to vary slightly. Subtle changes like this help create a human "feel."

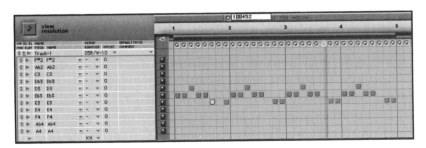

Figure 5.20

A drum pattern sequencer makes creating drum parts as simple as pointing and clicking. Make a mistake? Use your mouse to drag the offending note where it needs to go.

❋ WHAT'S QUANTIZING?

MIDI notes are referenced to a specific time location given in measures, beats, and tics (fractions of a beat). In spite of our best efforts, sometimes we play a note ahead of or behind the intended beat. Sure, we could grab each individual note and move it, but what if you need to fix the timing on a whole passage? Enter quantization. Simply put, quantizing lines up all of the notes to lay right on top of the beat.

Since heavily quantized parts take on a cold, robotic feel—nobody plays that precisely—quantizing often includes "humanizing" options to inject a bit of randomness, simulating the minute timing fluctuations of a real player. "Groove quantizing" rearranges a group of notes to fall into a predetermined "groove." For example, a passage of straight-eighth ride-cymbal hits can be made to swing like crazy simply by applying a shuffle-type groove. (See Figure 5.21.)

Quantizing is a hugely powerful tool that can completely transform a track. What's more, quantizing has migrated to the world of digital audio, as we'll see in the next few chapters.

BASS REFLEX

Once I'm satisfied with the percussion part, I move on to the bass. By the way, the old-school way to build a song starts with the drums and bass and then adds chordal instruments such as keyboard and guitar before moving on to horns and leads. I still prefer to work that way, but you can record your parts in any order you want.

Figure 5.21

Transform a boring group of straight-eighth-note ride-cymbal hits into a lounge-approved swing with groove quantizing faster than you can say "bada bing."

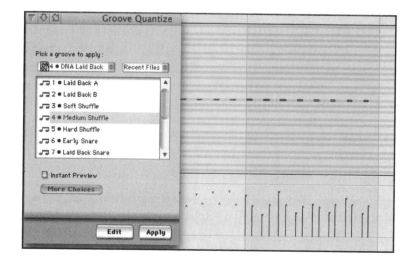

I select the GM instrument "jazz bass" as the output for the bass track, turn off the metronome so I'll match the timing of my drum parts, and play away. At this point, all I need is a few bars of the basic pattern and another bit for the bridge. As I arrange the song, I'll copy and paste the parts as many times as needed for each section. (See Figure 5.22.) Try doing that with analog tape!

This modular approach to song creation works great for many kinds of music. MIDI data is so easy to copy, paste, cut, and transpose that it makes writing a song almost too easy. Of course, there's no reason you can't play your parts all the way through.

ADDING THE KEYBOARD

Confession time: I'm a guitar player; I cannot play the keyboard to save my life. Up until now, I've entered all of the parts using a couple of fingers on one hand. So how in the heck can I record the intricate two-handed montuno-style piano part I want?

Simple—I cheat. Here's how.

* **Slow down.** MIDI doesn't care how fast or how slow you play it back, so set the tempo where you can play the part. In my case, it's an embarrassing 60 BPM. Once I have a part, I put the tempo back where it was, and no one's the wiser.

* **Step record.** The *ultimate* slowdown. Enter the part one note a time in stop motion.

* **Overdub record.** Play in the part one hand at a time. If your sequencer supports overdub recording (and most do), simply superimpose the second part on the first one. Otherwise, record each hand on a separate track. If you want, go back and merge the two tracks into one.

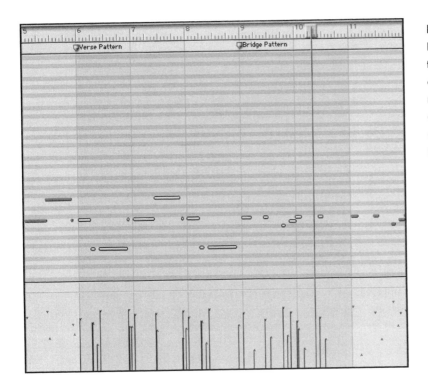

Figure 5.22
It's easy to reuse MIDI data to create the different parts of an arrangement. I've recorded two short sections of bass patterns, which I'll copy and paste as many times as needed.

❋ **Transpose.** Here's another MIDI shortcut: Instead of struggling to play in an unfamiliar key, temporarily transpose the song. (Be sure you leave any percussion tracks where they were; transposing GM drum parts will change the percussion instruments, so your cowbell part may end up played on a vibraslap.) Once you play the part, shift everything back where you started. (See Figure 5.23.)

❋ **Notate it.** Many sequencers support standard musical notation. For many people, it's far easier to enter a part by writing it down.

❋ **Something borrowed.** You can find literally millions of MIDI song files, loops, and style clips on the Internet. And many sequencers come bundled with a full complement of parts to use as building blocks in your creations. Don't overlook the auto-accompaniment software. More than one hit record features parts that were originally generated in Band-in-a-Box, Jammer, or similar programs. All you have to do is save the file as an SMF and import it into your sequencer.

FLUTE THING

Now that I've got a basic arrangement going, I'm going to add a simple flute melody. The first trick is to think like a flute, so chordal playing is out. And I have to take care to stay in the basic

Figure 5.23

Transposing with MIDI is as simple as pie. I entered the chords in the people's key of C. With a mouse click they'll be in the decidedly unfriendly key of C sharp.

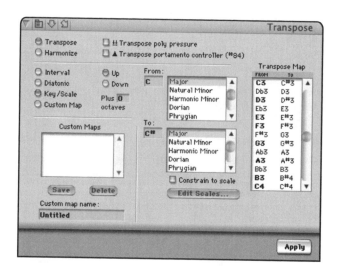

range of the instrument I'm emulating if I want it to sound realistic. Of course, that's just a taste thing—the whole point of your music may be to sound like something that's never been heard before. So, if you want to meld a flute sound with heavy power chords, be my guest.

As I play in the part, I add some pitch bend data so the notes swoop up or down. Then, to add even more expression, I go back and overdub a pass with just modulation wheel data, adding vibrato on certain notes. This is where a breath controller would really come in handy! You can see the continuous controller data in Figure 5.24.

PUTTING IT ALL TOGETHER

At this point I have a very simple song consisting of a repetitive section with a simple melody and a short bridge. From here, I could copy the various sections and stack them up in different orders until I find something I like. Then I may record an ending, or maybe I'll stick with the time-honored recording trick called a "fade-out." If I save the song as an SMF, I can post it on my Web site. But first I may want to add other instruments and new parts to each section, or maybe I'll send this off to a buddy who plays a wind controller and let him come up with a better melody.

Or I could add audio loops and record vocals to the sequence using my digital audio workstation. But that's a matter for a later chapter.

As you can see, this little tutorial just scratched the surface of what's possible with MIDI sequencing. Stayed tune for more on MIDI in the next chapter, where we cover looping for recording and live performance.

I'll round out the chapter by mentioning a couple of other dandy things you can do with MIDI.

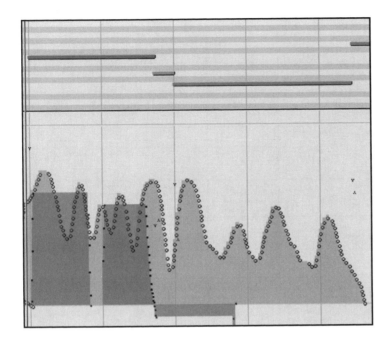

Figure 5.24
Pitch bend and mod wheel continuous controller data shows up as curves below the MIDI notes. As with every other kind of MIDI information, CC data is easily edited.

Notation Programs

Not many people realize that scoring programs incorporate powerful MIDI features. High-end programs such as MakeMusic's flagship Finale make it possible to audition your opus played by a virtual symphony orchestra. Even more modest programs such as Sibelius's G7 let you hear your work played back through a SoundFont, or software or hardware instrument.

Don't want the tedious task of entering your score one note at a time with a mouse? Hook up a MIDI instrument and play the part, then sit back and watch it take shape as notation or tablature. I've used an ancient MIDI guitar to write numerous instruction books and lessons.

Most notation programs both import and export SMFs and will extract and print out multipart scores from the track data. Here's a cool idea: Scan a piece of music and use your scoring program to play the part back to you! It's a great way to learn unfamiliar music or to add a difficult part to a sequence.

Automating Effects

MIDI is not just for making music—many electronic effects devices sport MIDI jacks. I've seen them on everything from guitar multi-effect floorboards to inexpensive rack-mounted reverbs to full-featured studio processors. Open the manual for gear of this sort and you'll find something called a *MIDI implementation chart* (Figure 5.25) buried in the back. The chart lists how the device

Figure 5.25

The MIDI implementation chart maps out how you can use MIDI controllers to control effects units, synthesizer parameters, or, as here, a software mixer using a MIDI control surface.

Baby HUI MIDI Implementation Chart		Version: 1.0.0		Date: 7/01/02
Function		**Transmitted**	**Recognized**	**Remarks**
Channel	Default	O	O	Channel 1 only
	Changed			
Mode	Default	X	X	Not Applicable
	Messages	X	X	
	Altered	X	X	
Note		O	X	90 00 00 Sent
Number	True Voice	X	O	90 00 7F Received
				Used for Compatibility with HUI
				"Active Sense"
Velocity	Note ON	X	X	
	Note OFF			
Aftertouch	Keys	X	O	Used for Signal Present LEDs
	Channels	X	X	
Pitch Bend		X	X	
Control Change		00-07 Faders MSB	00-07 Faders MSB	Fixed Specification
		20-27 Faders LSB	20-27 Faders LSB	Fader Resolution:
		40-4C V-Pots	0C, 2C LEDs	(00-07 MSB)
		0F, 2F Switches		(20-27 LSB)
Program				
Change	True Number	X	X	
System Exclusive		X	O	7-Segment Display
System Common	Song Pos	X	X	
	Song Sel	X	X	
	Tune	X	X	
System	Clock	X	X	
Real-Time	Messages	X	X	
Aux	Local Control	X	X	
Messages	All Notes Off	X	X	
	Active Sense	X	X	
	System Reset	X	X	
Notes:		A full description of System Exclusive and command architecture is available to developers through Mackie Designs Inc. Software Engineering Department.		

Mode 1: Omni On, Poly	Mode 2: Omni On, Mono		O: Yes
Mode 3: Omni Off, Poly	Mode 4: Omni Off, Mono		X: No

responds to incoming MIDI messages. Most people ignore this, but you aren't "most people," are you? Because MIDI control of effects parameters is beyond cool.

At the very least, most effects units respond to program change commands. That means you can use a sequencer on your laptop to alter the effects used on your vocals from a mild plate on the verse to a wild adenoidal scream for the ride-out—in real time while playing a gig. When recording and mixing, this is a great way to make the most out of limited effects resources. So, if you have only a single high-quality processor, use program change and CC messages to reconfigure it as the song plays. It'll sound as if you used a whole raft of studio gear.

For even more fun, map the knobs, sliders, and wheels on your controller to parameters such as effects level, chorus depth, or Leslie rotor speed (a simulation of an old-fashioned rotary speaker used for organs) and write the changes to your sequencer. Or modify the sounds in real time for live performance. Or sync tempo-based effects such as delay and tremolo to MIDI time code. The possibilities are truly endless.

Don't forget that all of your software effects plug-ins speak MIDI, too.

MIDI Mixing

Automated mixing used to be the domain of big-budget studios. The rest of us had to call in reinforcements. I can vividly remember lining up an entire band at the console, assigning each member a couple of faders, and rehearsing moves for a particularly complex mix. What with the giggling, spilt beer, numerous botched takes, and eventual recriminations, it was not a pretty sight.

As with software effects, software mixers sport extensive MIDI implementation. Just about any digital audio DAW software or hardware will benefit from MIDI-controlled mixing. (I'll go into MIDI-automated mixing in detail in Chapter 8, "Track Four: All Together Now: The Desktop DAW.") You don't even need a dedicated MIDI mixer; any continuous controller will do the trick. More and more multifunction controllers bristling with knobs, buttons, and sliders appear on the market every day. (See Figure 5.26.) Most come bundled with presets and templates for all of the major software applications.

Figure 5.26
Multifunction MIDI keyboard controllers, such as the M-Audio Ozonic, feature easily configurable MIDI faders, switches, and knobs for automating mix functions.

After 20 years, MIDI remains an extremely powerful tool. No matter what type of music you make on your computer, MIDI will be at work behind the scenes. If you want to learn more, be sure to check out the Internet resources in Appendix D.

Next, we delve into the loopy world of looping.

Track Two: Looping Tools

For many people, making music on your computer means one thing: looping. What's that? Looping involves creating grooves and entire songs from bits and pieces of repetitive musical data. As even the most casual look at any pop chart in the past 20 years reveals, looping has profoundly changed the way music is produced.

In this chapter will look at looping and loop-based music production on your computer. I'll discuss basic concepts, such as where to find loops, and talk about how you can create and modify your own loops, as well as the software you'll need. And I'll reintroduce some of the software you read about in Chapter 4, "Choosing Your Software: What Do You Want to Do?," focusing on the functions and tools you need to achieve your musical goals.

As my old woodshop teacher used to say, the only way to understand what a tool does is to use it. So the bulk of the chapter is devoted to getting our hands dirty.

First, I'll guide you through the creation of a dance groove using Reason 3, a popular software-music production suite from Propellerhead. Reason combines a number of software musical instruments—beat boxes, sample players, and synthesizers—with effects, mixers, and other studio tools into one self-contained program. Although I'm using Reason, you can apply the same techniques to any similar collection of software instruments and plug-ins.

Next, I'll discuss where loops come from and offer some tips and techniques for creating your own. Finally, I'll discuss some of the features of looping digital audio workstations (DAWs). In this section I'll be using Ableton's Live workstation. Again, the techniques may be used with any loop-based production environment or DAW.

But first let's get a good handle on exactly what we'll be talking about.

What Is Looping?

In one form or another, looping has been around a very long time. The term itself—a legacy of tape-based audio recording—predates digital audio and computers by many years. But you may not know that the concept of creating musical compositions by repeating short bits of rhythmic musical material is as old as humans.

Loops Versus Samples

A lot of people use the terms "sample" and "loop" interchangeably, but they don't mean exactly the same thing. All samplers can record and play loops, but not all loops are samples. Broadly speaking, a "sample" is a snippet of audio intended for playback on a keyboard, drum machine, or beat box. Unlike a synthesizer, which creates musical sounds electronically, a sampler plays back these digital recordings, which we call "samples." That means each key on a sampler or each pad on a drum machine can play back a completely different musical sample. A sample can be anything from a recording of a bodhran playing a jig to the individual notes of a piano or acoustic harp to a complete performance of "Stella by Starlight."

In the early days of rap and hip-hop, producers routinely "sampled" (recorded) a few bars from iconic funk and soul hits of the 1960s and 1970s. Then they'd add short vocal lines, electronic hits, and other one-shot sounds and effects. Mapped across the keys on a sampling keyboard or the pads on a beat box, the producer could instantly rearrange the song simply by hitting different keys. These days we are more apt to call these audio bits "loops" and use special looping hardware and software rather than a keyboard to pull them together into a song. Why the name change? Fashion, as much as anything. Since the audio samples are repeated over and over, just as they would be in an endless tape loop, producers started calling them "loops."

Likewise, a short bit of MIDI data that is intended as a musical building block can be called a "loop." I'm going to define "looping" as the process of creating music from prerecorded pieces of musical data—both digital audio and MIDI files. Looping, then, covers finding and creating loops, recording new loops, manipulating and editing them, and arranging them into a finished composition.

History of Looping

Believe it or not, the first people to create new musical compositions out of prerecorded musical chunks were modernist classical composers. Starting in the 1920s, such composers as Stefan Wolpe, Paul Hindemuth, and John Cage experimented with phonographs, radios, and other sources of prerecorded sounds in their compositions.

In the 1940s, experimental composer Pierre Schaeffer anticipated many of the techniques we use today: sampling and creating new musical sounds by manipulating the recorded waveform, musical composition via a mechanical process, and the rearranging of prerecorded musical elements into a new composition. The musical form he created and called *musique concrete*—music based on recorded "natural" or concrete sounds instead of music composed on a score to be played in the usual way—is very much the forerunner of techno and industrial music.

The advent of recording tape following World War II brought the technique into the hands of the masses—or at least the masses with access to tape recorders and splicing blocks. And it went from the experimental to the mundane: When I was a kid, radio DJs would routinely air funny little interviews, the answers spliced together from odd bits of popular songs. Tape loops became a staple of sci-fi movie soundtracks, while tape-based effects bred a million stupid records, such as Sheb Wooley's immortal "Purple People Eater."

Maybe the most famous use of looping in a pop context can be heard on the Beatles' masterpiece *Sgt Pepper's Lonely Hearts Club Band*. But by the time that epic album was released, Jamaican producers such as Lee "Scratch" Perry had already realized the primal power of a good groove, constructing song after song on the same drum and bass tracks, often recorded years earlier.

Early analog synthesizers had electronic sequencers, circuitry to play back short musical sections. What was more, by fooling around with the oscillators and filters, synth operators could create huge electronic beats, such as the one Pete Townsend used as the rhythm for "Baba O'Reilly." About this same time, small electronic drum sequencers appeared on the market.

Things really took off with the advent of the digital sampler. The original samplers were designed to overcome the limitations of analog and digital synthesizers by letting the keyboardist play actual recordings of, say, a grand piano or trumpet. But musicians and producers quickly noted that you could record and map entire performances, rearranging them as easily as playing the keys.

No longer did you need to find a drummer, bass player, and guitarist. All you had to do was sample a few bars of a James Brown record, throw in some extra sounds, add your own vocal, and sell a couple million units.

And so it goes. More and more, our music is made from prerecorded loops, beats, breaks, grooves, hits, pads, chunks—the list of terms goes on. As the tools have improved, so has the reach. These days, looping has found its way into live performance, film scoring, TV production, dance clubs, and beyond.

❄ **OUR BODIES, OUR MUSIC**

Music means many things to many people, but at its core, music is made up of very simple elements. A musical scale is nothing more than a group of pitched sounds—air molecules vibrating at certain frequencies—that we recognize as pleasing. If the pitches move around within a small compass and repeat in certain more or less predictable ways, we call it a melody.

The other major element is beat, sometimes called rhythm or pulse. The beat is a repeating cycle that defines and supports the music.

So where do beats come from? Our bodies, actually. Simply by walking, our footsteps create a repetitive pattern in duple meter. (Meter means "musical time," and "duple" is a fancy term for "can be divided by two.") It should come as no surprise that most American popular music is based on a common form of duple meter called 4/4 time.

Musical meter is described with a symbol that looks like a fraction. The first number represents the pulse—how many beats you'll hear in each repetitive unit, or measure. The second number represents the kind of note that gets the beat. So 4/4 means there are four beats per measure, and each beat is a quarter note. Say "ONE two three four/ONE two three four ... " over and over, and you'll get the idea. The other source of rhythm is our heartbeat. You can vocalize your heart's internal rhythm as "lub-DUB ... lub-DUB ... " That's a triple meter, with the stress on beats one and three: "Three/ONE two Three/ONE two Three/ONE two Three/ONE ... " Notice that the pattern starts before the first beat of the measure (called the downbeat).

So what? If you combine groupings of duple meter together, you get 2/4 time, 4/4 time, and other variations—the basic building blocks of military marches, folk dances such as square dances, and just about every single rock, R&B, hip-hop, disco, rap, techno, you-name-it pop music of the last 100 years. Triple meters use 3/4 (waltz time), as well as fun ones such as 6/8. Ah, but that's not all. Things really start to get interesting when you combine duple walking rhythms with triple heartbeat rhythms. In some parts of the world, complex meters such as 5/4 (3/4 + 2/4: "ONE two three One two/ONE two three One two"), 7/4 (3/4 + 2/4 + 2/4: "ONE two three One two One two/ONE two three One two One two ... "), and others are common.

On the great continent of Africa, ancient musicians developed complex, interweaving polyrhythmic patterns that combined duple and triple meter played at the same time. The two different pulses interrelate in highly complex ways that cannot help but get your body rocking.

This intensely swinging musical feel was carried to the New World with African slaves and forms the basis of all of the great New World musical traditions, from Brazilian bossa nova to Jamaican reggae to Puerto Rican salsa to American blues, rock, and jazz—and all of their musical progeny.

Looping in the Material World

Just to hammer home the point that looping is about music first and technology second, take a look at Figure 6.1, a basic Brazilian samba rhythm. Throughout the world, many kinds of percussion ensembles and rhythm sections work much the same way. Musicians playing a set group of instruments work together to execute short, repeated patterns that define a style of music. Interestingly, these patterns are often two bars long in many of the New World traditions based on African music. Standard combinations include the clave, congas, maracas, and cowbell of Cuban *son* and the surdo, tamborim, and agogo of Brazilian *samba*.

Most everyone is familiar with the drum set—in reality, a group of individualized instruments, each with its own rhythmic role, that's played by a single individual. And let's not overlook the bass. In many forms of music, the bass takes on a rhythmic role much like that of a drum, playing short phrases that repeat throughout the song.

Figure 6.1
The samba rhythm is a two-bar pattern of interlocking beats. Many other African-derived patterns, such as salsa, son, and even the Bo Diddley guitar groove, are based on two-bar patterns. The surdo is like a large floor tom, the tamborim is a tiny hand drum played with a single stick, and the agogo is a set of two metal bells with slightly different pitches.

So what's this got to do with anything? Simply this: The reason that music built from looped grooves is so powerful is that it says something very primal about who we are. Every culture has drums, every culture dances. The more we learn about how these rhythms are created and how they work, the better musicians we will become.

Why Looping Is Cool

Before we talk about looping software and techniques, I want to list some of the reasons loops and looping have changed the way music is made.

It's Easy

Face it, there is nothing quite as simple, or as fun, as remixing a song using a program such as GrooveMaker from IK Multimedia. Load the software, punch a few buttons with your mouse, and instant Ibiza. Even a gray-haired old geezer like me has fun punching up the groove, or whatever it is you kids call it today.

This is a two-edged sword. Sure, parents and educators wring their hands and lament the fact the children aren't learning to play "real" music anymore. Maybe yes, maybe no. (See the sidebar "Why Looping Is Uncool," later in the chapter, for more on this argument.) Yet even a casual listen will convince anyone that remixing is an art in itself. Besides, as you mess around with remixing software, you learn to listen to how the beats interact, how songs are structured, and how music can affect emotions differently, depending on how it's arranged. Even if you never play a note, you are starting to think like a musician.

All in all, I'd say programs such as GarageBand, GrooveMaker, Traktor, and all the rest have it right. Sometimes, music should just be fun. Even beginning musicians can quickly assemble complex musical compositions from prerecorded loops and grooves.

Aside from the instant gratification bit, looping software such as Ableton's Live and Cakewalk's Project 5 make the nuts and bolts of serious production accessible to advancing musicians. Maybe you'll start by changing some of the parameters on a synthesizer of effects devices; maybe you'll try programming your own beats into a MIDI beat box. Or maybe you'll start recording your own audio loops.

Whatever path you take, looping software makes it easy. And easy is very good.

It's Powerful

Easy doesn't mean stupid. These are tremendously powerful tools, capable of giving even the most experienced studio dog a serious case of the happies.

For example, at the dawn of the digital age, I once spent the better part of two days fixing drum parts because the client wanted to use a particular drummer who was long on charisma but short on skill. This entailed manually cutting each and every offending kick, snare, and high hat hit and pasting it on the beat. Thanks to beat detection and manipulation tools built into DAWs such as Digital Performer, Live, and Cubase, the same job takes seconds. (See Figure 6.2.) And I can do it in real time, listening to the changes as they happen.

Figure 6.2
The drummer didn't always hit right on the beat. Thanks to Ableton Live, now he does.

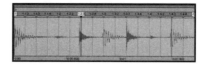

Many of the most difficult audio engineering tasks—beat matching, pitch changing, automated recording, and sample editing—are routine in looping programs.

Wouldn't it be great if you could hear what your song sounded like with the chorus repeated a second time before the solo? You can, and you can hear it without stopping the music. Wish you had a drummer and a bass player on hand to try out your new song? Grab a couple loops. Want to come up with a soundtrack for your next sales meeting? Dazzle 'em with a smooth jazz groove assembled in Cakewalk's Project 5.

It's Creative

Looping software does a lot more than make dance music. Here's a short list of some creative uses I've uncovered.

- **Librarian.** In an interview printed in *Ableton Live 4 Power!* (Chad Carrier and Dave Hill, Jr., Thomson Course Technology), Charlie Clouser (Nine Inch Nails, TV and film scores) detailed how he uses the software as a gigantic musical instrument and sample library rather than in the "traditional" way. He slaves Live to his main DAW and auditions samples at the correct pitch and tempo. Any looping platform that supports digital audio can do this.

- **Sound design.** If your processor is fast enough, you can wire together rack after rack of samplers, synthesizers, drum machines, and effects modules in a Reason 3 Combinator—more gear than you could possibly cram into your basic home studio. You can program complex soundscapes that evolve and change over time using nothing more than a mouse.

- **Audio editing.** I already mentioned how looping DAWs facilitate the formerly tedious task of fixing out-of-time drum tracks. Those same tools will work on any audio file. That's right, with a little deft tweaking, the guitar player's boyfriend can finally sing in time.

- **Real-time arranger 1.** Here's an interesting trick: Use a looping program to rearrange music that doesn't contain loops. How? Cut a mixed song into short audio files: one for the intro, one for each verse, and so on. Load the files as if they were loops and trigger as needed. It's a great way to lengthen or shorten a song for a video soundtrack.

- **Video.** Speaking of soundtracks, one of the hardest things is to get your music to match up with the length of a scene change. Looping software makes it easy to lengthen or shorten a bit of music without losing the feel.

- **Real-time arranger 2.** Use the powerful time-compression/stretching capabilities of the software to fit the music without changing the pitch.

- **Rhythm trainer.** Take a difficult piece or scale study and play it along with a groove you've created in GarageBand or similar software. Gradually speed up the tempo until you can execute it flawlessly. Way more satisfying than working out with a metronome.

- **Songwriting.** Songwriters often need to spin endless variations of lyrics and melodies. Why not record each line as a loop and use the software to spin out new verses?

And that's just the tip of a very big iceberg.

It Doesn't Require a Ton of Gear

Since you'll be working with very small audio and/or MIDI files, looping doesn't require monstrously fast processors and huge hard drives. Even inexpensive home computers have the juice to run basic programs. Software instruments and real-time audio effects processing add a lot of overhead; plan on a 1- to 2GHz processor with at least a gig of RAM if you'll be running lots of these.

For most software, a USB MIDI controller that combines a basic keyboard with lots of sliders and knobs is essential. Check out inexpensive offerings such as the Korg microKONTROL, M-Audio Ozone, and the Edirol PCR-M30.

Unless you'll be recording your own audio, you can get by with a basic sound card. Even Sound-Blaster and other cards designed for games often have a rudimentary line-in that will accept a high-impedance mic. In fact, I have a buddy who recorded a very cool fiddle funk CD using nothing more than GarageBand and the tiny mic built into his iBook.

Although I briefly discuss recording your own audio loops in this chapter, see Chapter 7, "Track Three: Digital Recording for the Solo Musician," for details on audio interfaces, how to set up and use microphones, basic recording techniques, and more.

Some other things you may want include a second hard disk to store and organize your loop library, a CD or DVD burner to archive and share your music, a good set of multimedia speakers, and some decent headphones so you can work into the night without disturbing your neighbors.

❄ WHY LOOPING IS UNCOOL

There is a very real difference between playing music yourself and rearranging music from bits and pieces someone else has created. Some musicians and music educators feel that looping is on the same basic creative level as scrapbooking or paint-by-numbers kits.

I used to write for a well-known dance and DJ magazine; each month I heard track after track (after track, after track ...) made from little more than a couple measures lifted from an iconic 1970s funk record, sprinkled with sampled African and Latin-American percussion, and filled out with one-note analog synth pads. No matter how good the music was—and some of it was very good—it often left me feeling empty.

Rock, jazz, and funk musicians know that there is no feeling like hitting that space when the group locks in to something bigger than any single player. It's that animal energy that drives dancers wild, not the robot precision of an electronic kick drum hitting downbeats at 144 beats per minute. You can hear it in James Brown, or Funkadelic, or the Meters, or any of the bands whose records have been sampled repeatedly.

New mixes based on samples work as dance tracks for the same reason the original beats did: Musicians played a funky groove that made it onto a record. The extra stuff is just window dressing.

All this musical recycling begs the question: Who's going to play the music today that inspires the next generation?

Before we return to our regularly scheduled programming, I must mention one more thing. Without the express permission of the original copyright holder, releasing a song containing a loop sampled from another song is morally wrong. It's also illegal. Better to use some of the great royalty-free loops available.

Now let's take a longer look at how the software works before we start making music.

Looping Software

Loosely speaking, looping software falls into a few broad categories. I say "loosely speaking" because nothing is ever completely as it seems in the world of computer music. Software never seems to stay neatly within its niche. Entry-level programs such as GarageBand and Mixman Studio hide powerful features beneath the hood; looping software with digital audio recording features such as Live 5 or Cakewalk's Project 5 is simple enough for even a complete newbie to use.

With that in mind, here's a rundown of features you should look for.

Remixing and DJing

Remixing is the process in which you build a new song from elements of an existing song. Remixers strip the tracks down to the essential vocal lines and hook, add new beats and sometimes new instruments, rearrange the parts, and add new vocals and a thousand other tricks. Remix software comes with a number of songs already cut into the components—and huge libraries are available for your remixing pleasure—that you then load into tracks and remix in real time as the music plays.

Mixman Studio (Mixman Software) and GrooveMaker (IK Multimedia) feature cool graphical interfaces and great songs that make it easy to get up and going. (See Figure 6.3.) As you move up the food chain, you'll find features that let you record and edit your own loops, add vocals, and even create complete songs from scratch.

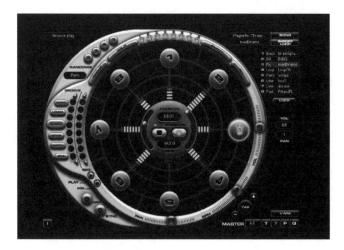

Figure 6.3
Combining innovative graphics with an intuitive interface, GrooveMaker unleashes your inner DJ.

Software for the semi-pro or pro DJ includes more features aimed at the dance market, such as the ability to select and beat-match songs from a library of CDs or MP3s, cueing and audition channels, and special effects such as turntable-style scratching. DJ software runs the gamut from freeware MP3 mixers such as MixVibe to full-featured software such as Native Instruments'

Traktor DJ Studio 2.6 to professional tools such as Evolution's X-Session that combine a USB DJ mixer with special editions of Ableton's Live and Arturia's Storm software. Stanton's Final Scratch 2 takes the process one step further, melding MP3 file playback with innovative time-coded vinyl records and an audio interface designed to work with a traditional DJ setup of mixer and turntables.

Loop Arranging and Playback

These programs let you create new compositions by adding together various prerecorded audio and/or MIDI loops. (See Figure 6.4.) Offering easy entry into music making, these programs may hide some fairly sophisticated features just below the surface.

Loop arrangers will automatically adjust the tempo of loops to fit the song, so you can confidently slide a Bach chorale on top of a drum 'n' bass groove. Then speed things up or slow them down, and the entire band responds. Changing the pitch is a snap. So is making multiple versions of a song. Most come with a goodly supply of raw material with refills available both from the manufacturer and third-party sources. Almost all will import loops from formats such as Sony's Acid and Propellerhead's REX or basic WAV or AIFF audio files. Some programs even let you record your own audio loops.

Figure 6.4
GarageBand—one of the easiest loop arrangers to use—is included free with every new Mac.

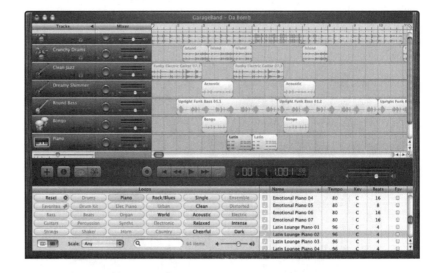

MIDI Software: Beat Boxes, Samplers, Synths, and Romplers

This is a huge category, ranging from plug-in and stand-alone virtual instruments that generate patterns and/or playback loops all the way to massive production environments such as Arturia's Storm 3, Propellerhead's Reason 3, and Cakewalk's Project 5.

To make sense out of it all, I'll break them down into their parts.

- ❈ **Beat boxes** are software instruments, or modules within a sequencer, that emulate hardware drum machines of the past few decades. Basically pattern sequencers, they include sampled or GM drum sounds, which you program by clicking squares on a grid or punching virtual buttons as the pattern loops. The beats are quantized as you enter them.

- ❈ **Pattern sequencers** are modules for programming short, repetitive bursts of notes or other control data. Usually used in conjunction with a sampler, rompler, or synth to create rhythmic effects, pads, and beats.

- ❈ **Bass sequencers** are specialized pattern sequencers for writing simple bass lines. You choose a bass sound and enter notes while the pattern plays, either with a MIDI keyboard or by clicking on an on-screen keyboard.

- ❈ **Romplers** are sample-playback devices. You can use them as software instruments to create pads or to play back complete loops and beats. (See Figure 6.5.)

Figure 6.5
Romplers like Reason's
Dr. Rex may be used to
play back drum loops.

- ❈ **Samplers** are similar to romplers, with the addition of extensive editing, key mapping, and resynthesis features for applying synthesizer-like tone-shaping to the sampled waveform.

- ❈ **Synthesizers** are musical instruments that create, shape, and manipulate tones electronically.

- ❈ **Arpeggiators**, usually a component of a synth or sampler but sometimes a separate module, create a repeating series of pitches that step up or down (or both) a user-defined scale from a single note. One of the defining sounds of '80s synth-rock.

- ❈ **Effects** are special audio techniques such as reverb, distortion, and chorus that change the way something sounds. Some effects, such as ping-pong delays, auto-panning, and flanging, can have profound effects on the timing of a groove.

Although you won't find every one of these functions in every program, the big dogs have all of these and more. In many case, these functions will appear as modules that interact in various ways, depending on where you place them in the signal chain.

Reason 3, in particular, allows users to combine its various modules in a huge variety of ways. That's why it's such a powerful program: No two users will stack things up the same way.

Loop-Based DAWs

These are programs that combine the ease of looped audio playback with extensive digital audio and MIDI recording and editing capabilities. It's a huge category, too, for the simple reason that every single DAW made can be turned into a loop tool. For instance, although it's designed more for traditional recording tasks, MOTU's Digital Performer contains a module called Polar that makes recording audio loops a breeze.

Truly full-featured, loop-based DAWs such as Acid Pro, Ableton Live 5, FL Studio XXL (see Figure 6.6), and others have most, if not all, of the features already mentioned. In addition, here's a look at some more advanced features you may expect:

* **Beat detection.** Automatically senses the beat division and creates "slices"—small sections of editable audio.

* **Real-time beat matching.** Automatically adjusts the timing of audio loops to fit the song's tempo as the song is playing.

* **Time compression/expansion.** Lengthens or shortens an audio file without changing its pitch.

* **Real-time transposition.** Changes the pitch of an audio clip without changing the timing.

* **Software synchronization.** The ability to interface with other programs running simultaneously. Propellerhead's ReWire is the most common software protocol.

* **Acid or REX compatibility.** Reads audio loops created or edited in Sony's Acid or Propellerhead's ReCycle. Acidized and REX files have coding and slices that allow the tempo and pitch manipulation found in looping programs. Most programs support one or the other; a few support both.

* **Loop browser.** Lets you audition audio or MIDI loops played back at the current selected tempo.

* **Audio recording.** Record one or more audio tracks while the loops play.

* **Audio editing.** Apply both nondestructive and destructive editing to digital audio clips.

* **MIDI sequencer.** Record and play back MIDI data.

* **MIDI editing.** Write, erase, move, lengthen, shorten, and otherwise mess around with your data.

* **Software instruments.** Most DAWs include a full complement of virtual instruments, samplers, romplers, beat boxes, and all the rest.

* **Built-in effects.** You need 'em. 'Nuff said.

* **Plug-ins.** Supports one or more plug-in formats for third-party software instruments and effects.

- ❄ **Automation.** The ability to write and edit mix, control change, and effects automation that plays back while mixing your finished song.
- ❄ **Song arranger.** Lets you create alternate arrangements of your song. If you can do it without stopping playback, so much the better.

Figure 6.6
Loop-based DAWs such as FL Studio offer a powerful alternative to traditional recording technologies.

That's a pretty good overview. But the best way to learn what these programs can do is to use them. And that's just what we'll be doing next.

Composing and Arranging with Loops

In this section, I'm going to take you through the process of creating music using two very different types of software. First, I'll show you how to use the software instruments found in Propellerhead's Reason 3 to come up with a smokin' little groove. Next, I'll talk about where loops come from and give you some insight into how you can create your own. Then I'll show you how the advanced features of DAWs such as Abelton's Live 5 make recording your own audio loops a groove, so to speak.

Don't worry if you don't have these exact programs. I'm using them to illustrate techniques common to a wide range of products. Of course, you can always go to Web sites listed in Appendix D, "Resources," to download demos so you can follow along.

Groovin' with Reason

Much can be made of Reason's unique self-contained design philosophy, but at its core it's a collection of software modules that can do very specific things. As such, the techniques I'll cover in this brief tutorial can be used with any MIDI sequencer, along with a software rompler, beat box, soft synth, and plug-in effects.

What You Need

As you learned in the last chapter, MIDI doesn't require much in the way of computer speed or RAM. Neither do simple romplers or other programs that play back short audio loops. The same goes for basic GM (General MIDI) virtual instruments. Software synths and samplers are another story. They literally create sound out of mathematics. If you'll be running a bunch of them—and you will—you'll need a solid, fast computer with at least 1GB of RAM.

If you've got Reason 3 on your hard drive, you are home free. Programs with similar features include Cakewalk's Project 5, FL Studio XXL, and Arturia's Storm 3. Otherwise, you'll need a DAW such as Cubase SE and several virtual instruments, including a loop-playback module such as NI's Kompakt sampler player, a beat box or drum pattern sequencer—most likely part of your DAW's interface—and a software virtual analog synth such as Rob Papen's Albino 2. Refer back to Chapter 4 if you need a refresher on software musical instruments.

Building a Drum Part

We'll start by creating the foundation—the drum part. Why? Because the drums are what defines the groove. Most "real" pop recordings are done the same way. The first thing you lay down is the drums and bass, then stack the rhythm and lead instruments on top, and finally add the vocals.

We're going to use two different modules: a rompler or sampler to select and play back a drum loop and a beat box–style pattern sequencer to add percussive spice to the mix.

Reason uses a *virtual rack* to connect the various components such as samplers, pattern sequencers, mixers, and effects devices. Other programs may use a different visual metaphor, but the effect is much the same. (See Figure 6.7.) Each virtual device acts like a separate piece of studio gear—by routing them to a sequencer track, we can construct our song.

In Reason, devices are automatically routed to the mixer as they are created, so all we have to do is call up the Dr. Rex loop player from the Create menu and get started.

Figure 6.7
Arturia's Storm 3 loop arranger places software instruments in virtual racks in the middle window, between the sequencer's edit window (top) and a virtual mixer.

LOOPS IN A LOOPS PLAYER

I'm afraid this is going to be a very boring section. Here's how you create a drum part in Dr. Rex: Select a drum loop. Play it. Done. And that, kids, is why looping software is so common. In the interest of science, let me discuss some of the fine points of working with drum loops inside a rompler. A little later on, I'll talk about creating your own loops.

First, *how do you select a drum loop?* It helps to know a little bit about different styles of music. Most loops libraries will be arranged in folders with names like Hip Hop, House, Techno, Ambient, and so on. The larger your loop library, the more you'll come to reply on descriptive names like "sidestick shuffle_102" or "Metal-verse." That's good up to a point, but what you really have to do is hear them. And unless your software has an audition function built into the browser (Reason does), you'll need to load each loop into a track and play it. Some find this sort of thing fun.

Here's a musician's secret you should know: Play exactly the same thing more than three times in a row and listeners get bored. So a real drummer will vary the pattern slightly every fourth time or so. Since much of our pop music can be broken up into four- and eight-bar sections, this means that the drummer will accentuate part of the verse or set up a change into a chorus with an extra snare hit or a variation of a cymbal pattern. Notice I'm not talking about a run-around-the-toms drum fill, but just a subtle shift to tickle the ears. In Reason, you do this in the sequencer, shown in Figure 6.8.

Figure 6.8
The MIDI event triggering each slice is represented by a thin bar. In this example I've subtly changed the loop by erasing a couple of MIDI events and drawing in new ones.

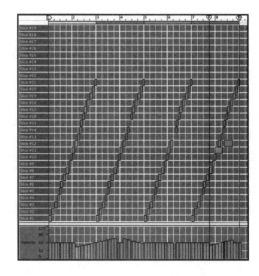

Often the most effective drum parts are the simplest. Yet the overwhelming majority of the drum loops I've auditioned—and I've auditioned a lot—are busy to the extreme. A drum part that fills every available rhythmic space may sound good all by itself, but add a bunch more instruments and your great groove will start to sound muddy and indistinct.

Here are some other simple things you can do to change the feel of a recorded drum loop.

* **Effects 1.** Run the loop through a guitar-distortion device. Sure, it's a common effect, but that's because it sounds so cool.

* **De-tune.** De-tune selected slices to alter the sound. Or change the tuning on the whole loop.

* **Swing.** What's swing? Lady, if you have to ask, you'll never know, to quote Louis Armstrong. Okay, I'll tell you: Swing is a subtle shift of the beat toward that three-against-four feel I described earlier. Most sequencers include swing as a quantization option.

* **Effects 2.** Set up a ping-pong delay, an effect with different delay times for each side of the stereo field. Set one side to an eighth or quarter note, the other to a triplet. Used with care, it can bring life to a sterile loop.

* **Offset.** Move the start point of the loop to some place other than the downbeat. This works particularly well when you're building a groove from a number of percussion loops.

* **Control change.** Record pitch-bend data to dynamically alter the sound of the loop as it's playing.

* **Filters and oscillators.** Run the loop through the sampler's various circuits. Expect the unexpected.

I'll talk more about how you can mess with audio files later on, in the section "Finding and Creating Loops." But first let's add some additional percussion sounds to customize our groove.

MIDI Beat Boxes and Drum Machines

Most everyone is familiar with beat boxes and drum machines, hardware devices combining sampled or electronic drum and percussion sounds with a basic pattern sequencer. Software instruments may model the look and feel of a hardware box (see Figure 6.9), or they may resemble more traditional MIDI sequencer tracks. All work pretty much the same way.

After selecting a drum kit, you trigger sounds one at a time by hitting pads or selecting spaces on a grid as the pattern plays. Input quantizing ensures that even the sloppiest mouse click or pad thump results in a dead-on-the-money beat. The higher the number of beat divisions, the greater the options for rhythmic subtlety. For instance, in 4/4 time, selecting a 16th-note grid lets you program realistic Latin shakers and disco-style hi-hats.

Figure 6.9

Like many beat boxes, Reason's Redrum combines a pattern sequencer with a sound module. You fill each of the 10 instrument slots with drum and percussion samples, then use the row of 16 buttons at lower right to program the pattern.

There are a million different ways to approach programming a beat box, but the time-honored method is simplicity itself. Start the sequencer and begin banging on things. If something sounds good, keep it. If not, unselect the offending note.

It's pretty common to combine the full drum kit on a beat box—kick, snare, cymbals, and all—with a drum loop from a sampler. That's great if you like really dense beats. But if you prefer rhythms that truly groove, take a hint from generations of percussionists and leave some holes in your tracks.

Try programming the two-bar pattern shown in Figure 6.10 for a swinging Afro-Cuban feel. Incidentally, you can find tons of great drum and percussion patterns at your local music store, inside books written for drummers.

Figure 6.10

Program this example into Redrum or any other beat box. Play it around 118 BPM and see if you can keep your feet still.

	1	2	3	4	5	6	7	8	9	10	11	12	13	14	15	16
Kick	X				X				X				X			
Side Stick			X		X				X			X				
Snare			X	X							X					
Closed Hat			X		X	X			X	X			X		X	X
Ride Bell	X		X		X	X		X	X		X	X		X		X

If you use two complete drum parts in your music, try panning the sets apart slightly. Or make one dominant in the mix and set the level of the other lower. Later, for another part of the song, swap the pan or volume settings to bring in some variation. Even tiny changes can make a big difference.

Adding the Bass

After a gig many years ago, a very beautiful woman approached me and said something that has stuck with me my whole life: "People may fall in love the singer, clap along with the drummer, and idolize the guitar player, but it's you bass players who make us dance." (We're still married, by the way.)

There is something vital about those low-frequency sounds. No matter how much the drummer sweats, how many notes the guitarist plays, how impassioned the singer's pleas are, or how many sounds the keyboardist can coax out of single note, the dance floor's deserted without the bass.

So how do you add a bass part if you can't play bass? Simple. You cheat.

The easiest way is to grab a bass sample and layer it in, just as we did with the drum loop. Or use a Standard MIDI File (SMF) bass loop, adjusting it as needed. But it's really not that hard to cob together an effective part using a software synthesizer and a MIDI keyboard, even if you can't play a lick.

Here's how to play a simple bass part that will work with the drum part you just programmed.

1. Call up a software synth, such as the Reason Subtractor, and select an electric bass patch. If necessary, audition the sounds while you hold down a key on your MIDI keyboard.

2. Arm a track in the sequencer window to prepare it for recording.

3. Turn on input quantizing and set it to eighth notes.

4. Slow the tempo way down so you have plenty of time to place each note.

5. The first note you need, F#, is the first one in the series of the three lowest black keys. Next comes G#, just to the right of F#. And the third is the lowest black key on your keyboard. Yep, C#. Don't worry, you can change the key later if you need to.

6. Begin playback, hit record, and play the keys one after another in time with the track. How do you do that? By listening. Play the first note (F#) on beat two and the next, G#, in between beats two and three. The pattern concludes with another F# on beat four and the last note (C#) on the "and" of four. For an even hipper pattern, add a pickup note, a 16th, before the first F#.

7. If you did it right, it should look something like Figure 6.10. If it doesn't, grab the notes using your mouse and move them where they belong.

8. Cut and paste as many times as you want.

9. Now let's add some control change data. Make sure Overdub Record is enabled and use the mod wheel to add vibrato, filter changes, or whatever else your heart desires.

10. Pick up the tempo and listen to your stunning bass part.

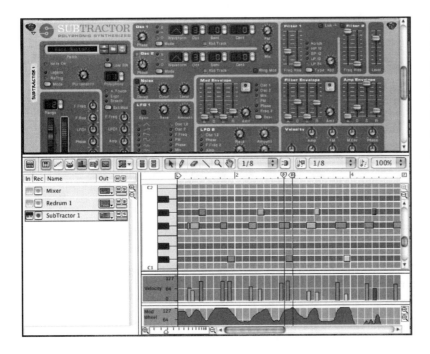

Figure 6.11

Here's a simple little bass part to go with your Latin groove. Can't play it? Use the pencil tool to draw it in, then add continuous controller data to bring the part alive.

Padding

A pad is a wash of sound. It can be anything from a string section swelling under the final kiss as the screen fades to black to an undulating synthesizer sound from outer space. Since we're dealing with Reason's software, let's do the latter. Again, you can do this with any software that supports virtual instruments. The key is to be sure that any rhythmic effects you create via the synth's oscillators or arpeggiators stay synched to the song's tempo.

I'm afraid a discussion of how synthesis works is beyond the scope of this book, so this will be brief. Dial up a patch. Mess around until you like the sound. Okay, here are some hints. In Reason's Malstrom synthesizer, the basic sound starts out as two small audio files that are sliced into grains—tiny component parts that form the basis of the sound acted upon by the two oscillators. (See Figure 6.12.) The sliders marked A, D, S, and R refer to the attack, decay, sustain, and release components of an audio waveform. For instance, raising the value of the attack slider creates a percussive sound; lower it, and the sound fades in like a bowed string.

The two mod sections apply various parameters to the waveform to modify the sound, add rhythmic effects, and so on. You can get an idea of what they do by looking at the waveform graphic in each section. This is where you set up complex rhythmic loops that swirl around when you hold down a key. If the synch button is lit, the patch plays in perfect time with the rest of the song. Believe me, this is a million times easier than it was in the old days.

Once you've arrived at a sound you like, record MIDI note data and control change data into the sequencer like you did for the bass part.

Figure 6.12

Reason's Malstrom synthesizer takes granular synthesis to a whole new level.

This has been a pretty quick run-through on how to set up a groove using the types of software modules you'll encounter in almost any loop-creation software. I've used Reason because it's a popular program that runs on both Windows and Mac. And you can download a free demo so that you can follow along. You'll find the link in Appendix C, "Manufacturers." But these same ideas will work no matter what software you use.

As you have seen, it is unbelievably easy to get going. Simply start plugging in loops and patches, stack up a few instruments, plug in a MIDI controller—or just use your mouse—and twist a few dials.

There's a lot more to Reason 3 than what you have seen. For a good introduction to the program, see *Reason 3 Ignite!* by Eric Grebler and Chris Hawkins or *Reason 3.0 Power* by Michael Prager and Matt Piper (both books published by Thomson Course Technology, naturally).

Next, let's look at where loops come from and how you can create your own.

Finding and Creating Loops

Before you can make music with loops, you need the loops themselves. Lots of them. Any looping software you buy—and that includes most romplers and samplers—will come preloaded with a good basic starter set to whet your appetite. But where do you go from there?

Loop Formats

Loops fall into two main categories. MIDI loops are usually SMFs (Standard MIDI Files), though more and more use SoundFonts. Any MIDI sequencer can play 'em.

Audio loops come in a couple basic flavors. WAV and AIFF are high-resolution file standards for Windows and the Apple OS, respectively. Most, but not all, Apple software can also read WAV files; some Windows software reads AIFF. (Another hi-res audio file format, SDII, is less widely supported.) MP3 files are ubiquitous and widely supported. They have the advantage of small size, which makes them quicker to download than WAV and AIFF loops. More and more, MP3 files are used in DJ programs.

Audio loops need additional processing before you can do all the cool stuff like time compression and pitch changing that makes loops so powerful. Ableton's Live creates its own tags (called "warp markers") for time compression/expansion. Most programs rely on either Sony's Acid or Propellerhead's REX format. Apple Computer introduced its own format, called Apple Loops. A few, such as MOTU's Digital Performer and Apple's Logic, support all three formats.

Acid and ReCycle (the program that creates REX files) take the tedium out of looping. Before Acid, the only way to change the timing of a recorded drum track or other clip was to manually slice the waveform into its component bits. This involved cutting out each and every drum beat, starting right on the attack portion and ending before the next time division. Once you had the files cut into little pieces, you could use your sequencer's quantize function to move them around or do it by hand. (See Figure 6.13.)

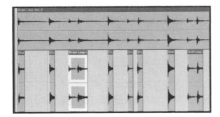

Figure 6.13
Without looping tools such as Acid and ReCycle, changing the groove on a recorded drum part means separating the original file (top) into individual beats (bottom).

Both Acid and ReCycle automate the process, detecting the beats and dicing the file into independently editable slices. That means Acidized and REX files can be loaded into your compatible loop player and twisted into shape, instantly synching to any tempo changes or anything else you throw at them.

I should mention that Acid, REX, and Apple Loops all work nondestructively, which means that altering tempo or pitch does not affect the original audio file. This is good.

I should also mention that pitch changes of more than a few half steps (the distance between a white key and a black key on a piano) may sound pretty funny, depending on the quality of the original sample and a few other factors. In other words, a single guitar E chord won't stand up to close scrutiny after being transposed up a fourth to A and fifth to B. Which may be why "Louie Louie" isn't showing up on too many dance floors these days.

Most loop composers hide the sonic degradation by adding distortion or other effects. In fact, lo fi is *the* characteristic sound of looped music. You can even buy effects plug-ins to make your pristine digital audio sound like it was sampled from a scratchy old phonograph record.

Buying Loops

Loops and samples—often called *soundware*—have long been a staple of music marketers. A number of companies, such as Big Fish Audio, retailer Sweetwater Music, Ilio, and many more, specialize in sample libraries for a number of formats. Likewise, the companies that made the looping software you use may have extensive sets of samples and loops already formatted for seamless integration into their platforms. Check out the manufacturers' Web sites listed in Appendix C.

Sample libraries range from lovingly detailed recordings of a handful of instruments playing in a single style, such as IK Multimedia's Axé collection of Brazillian percussion, to volumes dedicated to synthesizer textures to huge collections of beats and grooves in a variety of styles, replete with drums, bass, guitars, keyboards, horns, and even vocals!

No matter what style of music you play—and that includes quite a number of exotic musical styles from the far-flung corners of our planet—you can find the raw materials for your composition. You don't think those guys who write movie soundtracks really go to India to record the tablas, do you?

Downloads

Sometimes it appears as if the entire purpose of the Internet is to store and disseminate dance music. Literally millions of free loops, in every style and format imaginable, are out there waiting for your browser.

Harmony-Central.com and SynthZone.com are good places to start searching, or check into some of the user groups dedicated to specific software.

Repurposing Existing Tracks

Converting existing digital audio tracks into usable loops isn't a huge deal. As I said earlier, Sony's Acid and Propellerhead's ReCycle are the tools you need if you'll be doing a lot of this sort of thing. But you can get by with an audio editor such as Bias Peak LE and some prerecorded WAV or AIFF audio, say ripped from an old band demo or sample CD.

The best raw materials are files with strong rhythmic content, like drums and percussion. It's usually pretty obvious to tell where the beats are just by looking at the waveform display, which makes the job a lot easier. Dense band mixes, especially if they've been heavily compressed, can be harder to work with.

The first step in turning your raw tracks into loops is to cut out any extraneous noise at the beginning and end of the file. Next, select and cut out a good representative section, say two bars. Begin your cut right on a downbeat. You may need to zoom in to get it right, as in Figure 6.14.

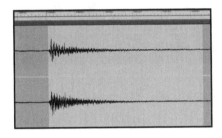

Figure 6.14
Slice directly on the down-beat. Even a tiny bit of extra space will seriously mess up the groove.

Do the same thing to find the downbeat of the third measure. Cut just in front of it and *voilà!* A two-measure loop.

If you know the tempo—or if you are using Live, Acid, or ReCycle—you can simply import the file into your looping program and get to work. Otherwise, you'll need to figure out how fast the drummer was playing.

Here's a trick I use to figure out the tempo of an unknown drum loop. First, I listen to determine the time signature and approximate tempo. After importing it into my DAW, I place the file so its downbeat exactly matches that of the sequence. Finally I move the tempo slider until the beat divisions in the edit window line up with the drum hits visible in the waveform, as you can see in Figure 6.15.

Figure 6.15

By noting how the recorded beats match up with the sequencer's barlines and beat divisions, I can determine the tempo of the original recording.

Recording Your Own Loops

This is by far the best way to create a sound that no one else has. Again, I'll leave the details about microphone placement, sound isolation, and other considerations for the next chapter, but it is surprisingly easy.

The easiest way may be the most overlooked. Reason Live and similar programs have the option of rendering your songs into audio files. Well, why not use that feature to create short loops for your library? Come up with a cool beat box pattern in Redrum? Save it as an audio file. Any combination of software synths, drum modules, and loops is a powerful loop-creation tool.

Incidentally, although Reason 3 does not record audio, you can import your own samples and loops to use in the various modules.

Recording your own audio file loops in DAWs such as Sony's Acid Pro and Ableton's Live is sublimely simple. I'll take you through the process of adding some kitchen-sink percussion tracks in Live. To follow along, you'll need a sound card and a basic microphone. I'll be using nothing more than the tiny built-in mic in my obsolete iMac computer. Sticking with the low-tech approach, I've chosen a half-empty can of Macadamia nuts and a CD jewel case as my instruments. Again, although the specifics will be different, all looping DAWs work much the same way.

1. Fire up the software and slide a basic percussion loop into any open track. This will be our guide track.

2. Set your preferences so that the program accepts input from the mic plugged into your sound card. In my case, I selected Built-in.

3. Create and arm (record-enable) a new audio track. Clap your hands a few times and watch the meters. If you don't see any signal, check again to see that the preferences are set properly.

4. Use headphones so the sound of the prerecorded loops won't get into your new tracks. Mute or turn off the audio output on the new track so you won't be bothered by latency, a slight delay in the sound reaching your headphones. (See Figure 6.16.)

5. Play the improvised shaker along with the percussion loop until it feels right, then hit record. After a couple bars, disable recording. You'll hear your new part playing alongside the original groove. Add some effects to the new track for sonic and rhythmic variety. (See Figure 6.17.)

6. Repeat steps 3–5 to lay down a funky box part.

7. Trim the start and end times of the new clips and use the warp markers to slide any errant beats into place.

8. Repeat as often as necessary.

Figure 6.16
Recording in Ableton Live is as simple as pressing a button. Notice that track 2 is muted so I won't be disturbed by latency.

Figure 6.17

Here's Live's Arrangement
View, showing the two new
tracks I've just recorded
and the effects I'm using to
mess 'em up.

What Now?

In this section we've looked at some of the features and uses of looping software, but there is much, much more to be learned. What's the best path? Only you know. But I'd suggest digging in and making some music. The deeper you dig, the more you'll learn.

Loops and looping software truly offer something for everybody. Even the most musically inexperienced among us can jump in and make real music right away using remix programs such as GrooveMaker and Mixman Studio. Apple's GarageBand may be the simplest loop player to use, but it hides some very sophisticated functions under the hood.

No matter what your skill level, budget, or musical taste, you'll find programs that combine ease of use with tricked-out features to get you up and running with a minimum of fuss. Powerful programs such as Reason 3, Acid, and Ableton Live 5 have forever changed the way music is composed and recorded.

In the next chapter I'll talk about desktop audio recording and answer that familiar question, "How do I record a song on my computer?" Chapter 7 is all about recording acoustic guitar and voice. Why did I choose those two? Because 10 million singer-songwriters can't be wrong, for one thing. But more important, the techniques I'll discuss are the same that you'd use to record any combination of instruments. Even if you just want to add some rhymes over a beat box, check it out.

In the final chapter, I'll discuss hooking everything together—MIDI, loops, samplers, multitrack recording, the whole schmeer, and take you through the process of creating and mixing a finished recording. Here's where your computer studio really *does* become a musical instrument.

7 } Track Three: Digital Recording for the Solo Musician

Pete Townsend of the Who said it all: "Never sell your guitar or your pen!" There's a very special bond between us songwriters and our instruments that can only be described as magical.

Acoustic music—that is, music made primarily on instruments that do not require electricity to be heard—has gone in and out of fashion over the years. Certain genres, primarily folk music, such as bluegrass, Celtic, and old-time, tenaciously hold onto their acoustic roots. As I write this, the pop, country, and alternative music worlds are in the middle of an acoustic boom that shows no signs of letting up. And the phrase *singer-songwriter* is practically synonymous with a lone voice and an acoustic guitar. Even if your main musical love is speedcore–death metal, the chances are that you will use an acoustic guitar at some point.

In the past few chapters, we've discussed recording and music creation using MIDI and prerecorded loops. This chapter will teach you how to record acoustic music at home. I have chosen the example of the solo singer-songwriter with an acoustic guitar because it lets me talk about a number of important recording tasks that may be generalized for other instruments or genres. Recording an acoustic guitar involves learning to hear how sound is produced, discovering how to capture the sound with a microphone, and, finally, learning what you can do to the sound once you've captured it on disc. It's the same process you'd use to record piano, cello, mountain dulcimer—or drums and an electric guitar played through a screaming amp.

There is one feature common to almost every type of music heard in the world today: the human voice. Whether you rap, mumble, sing, screech, scat, hum, whisper, or wail, you're using that most marvelous of wind instruments. Until vocal synthesis matures, the only way to get your voice into the mix is to record it yourself.

No matter what type of recording you wish to do, this chapter will give you the essential tools to record voice and/or a musical instrument. I'll discuss exactly what gear you'll need; how to set up your system and microphones and how to use them; how to listen to your recordings; and how to make sure your recordings sound as good as they possibly can. You'll get step-by-step guidance on setting up and laying down tracks, editing, and mixing.

If you haven't done so already, be sure to read Chapter 2, "Understanding the Gear," so you will be familiar with many of the basic recording terms and concepts I'll be using. If you get stuck on a word, chances are it's defined in Appendix A, "Glossary."

Gear Up

It takes surprisingly little to record acoustic music at home. Sure, you can spend the big bucks on a dedicated computer system with high-end professional software and hardware, dedicate a room for your home studio with state-of-the-art soundproofing, and invest in exotic microphones and vintage rack gear—or you can use an inexpensive PC with a basic sound card and a single all-purpose mic. Which approach is going to give you the best results? Read on. You may be surprised.

Unlike MIDI, digital audio puts a formidable processor load on the CPU. And digital audio files are huge, so storage becomes a real issue. So does memory. Data transfer is another area where digital audio requires greater speed. If you are looking to use your existing computer, you'll need to take a hard look at each of these areas and then make an informed decision whether to upgrade your system or replace it.

Your Computer

I have said it before, but it bears repeating: You can record at home on just about any computer made in the past few years. So if you have a relatively new machine and a limited budget, you can still get in the game. And be sure to check out Appendix B, "Buying Used Gear," where I discuss buying used gear. Pro studios have to upgrade to the latest and greatest regularly, often selling off perfectly serviceable gear for pennies on the dollar.

Of course, some systems work better than others, and you'll avoid a lot of potential headaches by getting exactly the system you need.

I've already discussed various systems in a general way in Chapter 3, "Choosing Your Computer." Here I'll look at what you need to record two or more tracks of uncompressed, CD-quality digital audio at home. And I'll give you some tips on how to make it all work. If you are planning to buy a new computer for digital audio, consider choosing your software first and then build around it.

CPU Speed and Type

Faster is better, right? Actually, yes... and no. Speed is only one piece of the puzzle, as you will see. It doesn't matter how quickly your central processing unit is crunching data if the hard drive can't keep up. One other thing: For some reason, Macs and PCs appear to exist in different numerical universes. So a 1.5GHz G5 Mac and a 3.7GHz Pentium PC may perform very much the same when handling real-world tasks such as rendering audio in benchmark speed tests. In case you missed my disclaimer about the Mac and Windows operating systems earlier, here it is again: It doesn't matter. Use whichever system you are comfortable with. Both have huge user bases of professional engineers and amateur recording enthusiasts. Both are well supported with software and hardware. Increasingly, files and projects made on one platform may be imported and read on the other. It is beginning to look like we can stop arguing and get down to work.

As I said in the introduction, I have experienced both platforms, but I do most of my work on the Mac. So don't be alarmed if you see lots of Mac screenshots, okay?

Regardless of which platform you decide on, get the fastest machine you can afford. For new machines, 1 to 2GHz is a practical minimum. No need to mortgage the house to get the fastest computer made: My original system boasted a whopping 33MHz processor, and I recorded dozens of CDs on it!

Newer-model processor chips by Intel, such as the Celeron or Pentium, are all capable of handling the loads of digital audio with nary a whinny. A short while back, savvy users avoided computers with AMD processors, but I'm happy to say they, too, can cut the mustard with aplomb.

Unless you know your way around, stick with established brands such as Gateway, Dell, Hewlett-Packard, and Sony. Super-bargain brands may not have the ports for connecting hard drives, sound interfaces, etc., or expandable memory you'll need.

On the Mac side, for basic home recording you'll be safe with pretty much anything they make, including the tiny Mac Mini and the elegant new iMac. (See Figure 7.1.) Kind of takes the pressure off, doesn't it?

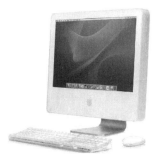

Figure 7.1
The G5 iMac boasts power to spare and looks great on your desk.

Memory

Nothing will affect your computer's performance more than RAM, or Random Access Memory. Buy and install as much as you can: 512MB would be a bare minimum, particularly if your computer's main memory is shared with the video system. (Budget models do this to avoid the expense of a video card.) For practical purposes, install at least one gigabyte.

Avoid off-brand discount memory cards; for slightly more money, you get security and performance. And be sure to carefully match the card to your computer's specifications.

Hard Drives

Audio files take up an enormous amount of space. A 44.1kHz, 16-bit stereo file—the CD standard—uses 10MB per minute of audio. If you record three or four takes of each track for each of a dozen songs, your simple little voice and guitar CD can quickly balloon to 5 or 10GB of data! Record at higher sample and bit rates, and the file size grows exponentially.

Go for at least a 60 to 80GB internal hard drive. It really doesn't matter all that much what the internal bussing architecture is: Both ATA and SCSI are more than able to handle digital audio. That means you can safely use your older computer.

Your CPU has a thousand and one chores it must perform every second: everything from checking things in and out of memory to spinning the hard drive and moving the read/write head to monitoring data coming in from the various ports to drawing and redrawing the monitor, and many, many more. It does this by breaking up data into chunks and dealing with things on a "need-to-do" basis.

Much of the information it needs to perform these essential tasks is stored on the internal drive. If you record audio to your system drive, you run the risk of over-tasking the system, which could lead to crashes and data loss. If you are working with lots of tracks or making critical recordings with long audio files, consider recording directly to an external drive.

❋ **KEEPING YOUR DRIVES HEALTHY**

Data stored on a hard drive is constantly being read and rewritten as it is needed by the CPU. As this happens, the data gets fragmented—split up into chunks written to different parts of the platter. Fragmented files slow down data acquisition; the read/write head has to roam over ever-greater distances. In extreme cases, a heavily fragmented drive will cause the computer to crash. That is very, very bad. To keep your drives healthy, run a defragging or optimization routine regularly. Use the hard disk utility built into your OS, or choose a popular third-party program such as Symantec's Norton Speed Disk. Although defragging is a routine chore, always back up your data first.

In certain cases, as when you don't have an external drive for recording, it's best to set up an internal drive with two or more partitions. As far as the CPU is concerned, each partition is a separate hard drive. This speeds up the defragging tasks quite a bit and helps keep your audio data separate. Be aware that partitioning a drive will erase everything on it, so don't take this step unless you have reliable backups of all of your programs and files.

External hard drives come in an array of flavors and sizes. Like memory, you get what you pay for. If all you will use it for is data storage and backups, go ahead and save a few shekels. But for recording and playing back digital audio, invest in a drive rated for AV use with a minimum spin of 7200 RPM.

USB 1 is too slow for serious work, so make sure your system supports USB 2.0. SCSI and ATA-100 devices, if you can find them, have proven track records and are still used in some dedicated recorders such as the TASCAM MX2424. They have largely been supplanted by the high-speed data protocol IEEE 1394, also called FireWire.

FireWire drives are the hands-down best choice for digital audio and video. If you'll be doing a lot of recording, consider picking up a drive built and tested for exactly that task.

External Storage

A CD burner is useful both for burning audio CDs of your finished masterpieces and for making frequent backups of all the files and folders used in recording it. A time-tested adage among pros puts it this way: Digital data does not exist until it is backed up. Twice! Recordable DVDs, capable of storing huge amounts of data, are an even better choice. Be sure you buy the right kind. Macs use DVD-R, while PCs favor DVD+R.

YOU CAN TAKE IT WITH YOU

Portable storage devices, such as USB flash drives, are great for moving files from place to place. And don't overlook your portable music player: I once carried all of the mixes for a new CD from the studio in Hawaii to the mastering house in LA on an iPod.

In/Out Ports and Card Slots

You'll need multiple USB 1 or 2.0 and/or FireWire slots to connect external drives and certain audio interfaces. USB is also handy for printers, scanners, digital cameras, and a host of input devices, including a QWERTY keyboard and mouse. Due to its superior speed, camcorders often rely on FireWire (IEEE 1394) for connectivity.

Audio inputs and headphone outs indicate a computer with some kind of internal sound card. Most of these bundled cards are not suitable for the kind of recording we're concerned with; use these for playing games.

Internal PCI expansion slots (PCMCIA for laptops) are useful for adding sound cards (see below), video cards to support a second monitor, FireWire ports, and other functional enhancements. Be sure you've got some way to connect to the Internet, too.

Choosing an Audio Interface

Your audio interface is a vital part of the signal chain, so don't be tempted to skimp. No matter how good your microphone, voice, or instrument, it won't sound anything like the real deal if you try to run it through a junky sound card designed for game playing.

Your audio interface is designed to get sound into and out of the computer. On the input side, it will have one or more channels to connect line ins or microphones and an Analog to Digital Converter (ADC) for each. The other half of the equation includes Digital to Analog Converters (DACs) and either a headphone out, stereo monitor outs, individual line outs, or some combination of all three. Some audio interfaces include MIDI in and out, which is handy if you use a keyboard or MIDI control surface. (See Chapter 8, "Track Four: All Together Now: The Desktop DAW.") Digital in/out is useful for transferring music to and from a CD recorder or DAT or interfacing with a digital mixer or modular digital recorder.

A basic stereo card, with two channels of input/output, will get the job done; however, I strongly recommend going for at least four input channels. Nothing is more frustrating than running out of channels in the heat of a recording session. With four inputs, you can simultaneously record your voice and mic the guitar in stereo, leaving an open channel for your friend the bass player.

Unless you have a mixer or outboard microphone preamp (a mic-pre), be sure your interface has real mic-pres and not simply XLR jacks. You'll also need to be able to tailor the input gain to your mic and the sound level. Look for an interface with a peak or clipping indicator light; better yet, find one with meters. If you plan to use condenser microphones, be sure your interface generates phantom power. These days just about every interface supports 24-bit depth, with sampling frequencies up to 96kHz increasingly common. (See Chapter 2 for more about bit depth and sample rates.) Balanced in/outs, while not a necessity for most home studios, do help a bit with noise and allow you to use professional gear.

No matter what interface you choose, be sure your software supports it. Or pick up a package with hardware and software bundled together to avoid the headache.

Internal Sound Cards

PCI cards pack a ton of functionality into a small space, effectively becoming part of the computer itself. (See Figure 7.2.) PCI card interfaces have been around since the early days of computer audio, so you know they're proven technology. A PCI card is also a must if your computer doesn't support USB or FireWire.

Most have a short cable with a multi-pin connector on one end and various short cables for hooking up line ins, mics, and other gear, though a few put the jacks on the card itself. Either situation practically begs for an outboard mixer or mic-preamplifier; otherwise you'll be spending a lot of time crawling behind your desk to reach the inputs. Without external gear, you'll be forced to do all your level adjustments using software—a dubious proposition.

Where PCI cards shine is in the details: very low-latency operation and extra DSP for effects processing without taxing the CPU. Some, like E-MU's Emulator X series, are full-blown samplers that also handle recording chores. In an interesting twist, E-MU's 1820M and 1220M cards sport FireWire interfaces.

Figure 7.2
M-Audio's Audiophile 192
is a versatile PCI interface.

Choices range from Spartan to deluxe. On the no-frills side, check out the M-Audio 2496 with four unbalanced in/outs using RCA connectors, or E-MU's budget 0404 with an equal number of tip-ring-sleeve–balanced in/outs. One serious drawback: You'll need a mixer or mic-preamplifier to record acoustic guitar and voice, so be sure to figure that into your cost.

As you move up the price ladder, look for more channels, greater connectivity, better converters, and added features, such as digital in/outs and synchronization. Higher-end cards, designed to interface with professional recording gear such as dedicated ADCs and DCAs, digital mixers, etc., offer stellar performance.

Laptops with PCMCIA slots can get in on the action, too. The Echo Indigo, EMU 1616m, and Digigram's VX pocket interfaces let you bring low-latency monitoring and professional-grade converters on the road.

PCI Cards with Breakout Boxes
PCI cards with breakout boxes combine the best of both worlds. You get all the benefits of an internal card—extra DSP power for effects and low latency—plus real microphone preamps, multiple ins and outs, and hands-on level control. In addition, you can put the breakout box on your desk or in a rack for easy access. With enough ins and outs, you can leave all your gear wired up permanently and eliminate the need for an external mixer or patchbay. Options range from basic two-in/two-out devices by E-MU and others by M-Audio and Edirol all the way up to high-end gear such as Digidesign's flagship Pro Tools|HD systems.

USB
The first USB audio interfaces barely wheezed along; thankfully, USB 2 makes real multichannel desktop recording a reality. As with the PCI breakout boxes described above, a USB interface lets you record and play back audio without the need for an external mixer. Choices range from rugged, bus-powered two-channel units designed for remote recording (great for laptops!) all the way up to feature-laden rack-mount gear.

This is where the action is: It seems like a new USB desktop recording system appears every other day. Companies are scrambling to make their products easier to use and to buy. Guess who wins in this race? You do.

Some of the best choices for the solo musician combine solid mic-pres and line-level in/outs with first-class software. Mackie, justly renowned for its small-format mixers, entered the fray with its Spike system. The desktop interface has two of Mackie's best mic-pres, as well as hardware dynamics processing. Not to be outdone, Lexicon's Omega Studio™ (Figure 7.3), with eight ins and four outs, is bundled with a VST version of its famous reverb and Steinberg's popular Cubase LE software. Digidesign's Pro Tools hardware and software are industry benchmarks; find out why with the new M-Powered software, designed to work with M-Audio's inexpensive audio interfaces.

Figure 7.3
Lexicon's Omega Studio.
USB interface features
award-winning reverb and
low latency.

For greater flexibility, TASCAM's US-428 combines an audio/MIDI interface with a control surface. Both Edirol and Behringer have USB interfaces welded to mixers with varying amounts of processing.

FireWire

FireWire wins the speed wars hands down. Unlike USB, FireWire can easily handle the huge amounts of data needed for professional multitrack recording. That's why you'll find lots of high-end, multichannel FireWire recording interfaces, such as Mark of the Unicorn's 896HD, Digidesign's 002, and the Fireface 800.

But don't think FireWire's out of your range. A fair number of excellent smaller interfaces from M-Audio, Edirol, and Presonus are aimed squarely at the solo musician. Prices are generally in line with comparable USB gear. Or consider a multichannel interface, such as the MOTU 828 or Presonus Firepod, that can grow with your needs.

> ### ❋ GUITAR-SPECIFIC INTERFACES
>
> Most of the interfaces I've mentioned will handle both microphone and line-level inputs. But what if you want to plug in your electric guitar? Simply inserting a 1/4-inch jack to a line-level input won't cut it: The high-impedance output of your guitar or bass will overload the circuit and ruin your sound. Fear not: Guitar-friendly devices can be found for every taste and budget. Some feature a dedicated Hi-Z instrument input with amplifier and microphone modeling and effects, so it will sound like you're playing through you favorite rig. Others let you switch between line level and instrument level. Make sure yours does before you plug in!
>
> TASCAM's inexpensive US-122 features two line/instrument inputs plus MIDI I/O in a bus-powered USB device. Grab your axe and a laptop, and you can record anywhere!
>
> Digitech's innovative GNFX4 combines all features of a high-end floor-mounted effects processor with a drum machine, a mic-pre, and built-in 8-track recorder with USB for streaming audio directly to your computer.

Software: Features to Look For

I discussed software at some length in Chapter 4, "Choosing Your Software: What Do You Want to Do?" Here, I want to give you an overview of the essential features you'll need. I'll also talk about some extras you may consider.

Obviously, you'll need software designed for recording audio. But should you go with a bare-bones two-track recorder, guitar-specific software with amp modeling and effects, or a full-bore multitrack DAW with looping, MIDI, and unlimited recording and editing capabilities? As you read through this list, try to define your recording goals. Are you simply trying to document your playing or share a new song? Do you plan to use the recording as a demo that will guide a professional recording session? Or do you intend to produce a polished, professional-sounding recording? Knowing what you want to do will go a long way in helping you decide how to get there.

❋ **Audio tracks.** It goes without saying that you'll need at least two tracks for stereo recording. Two-track editors, such as Bias Peak LE and Sony Sound Forge, can handle most basic recording chores. However, if your audio interface supports it, consider software that lets you track four or more channels simultaneously. It's not uncommon to run two or three mics on an acoustic guitar, plus a signal from the pickup. Add in a mic for your voice, and you're already talking serious tracks. Lucky for you, today's faster processors mean increased track counts, so even entry-level software gives you more than enough. I'd say 12 is a practical minimum.

❊ **Virtual tracks.** Virtual tracks are audio tracks that haven't been assigned to a mixer channel. Virtual tracks let you keep multiple takes so you can choose the best one. Most software supports virtual tracks, though they may be called something else.

❊ **Low-latency monitoring.** Digital recording involves huge amounts of data. All that number crunching takes time, with the result that tracks you've already recorded may not sound exactly in sync with the sound of your live playing that's coming back in your headphones. This short delay is called latency, and it will drive you crazy. Some software lets you bypass much of the processing for near-zero latency; some hardware does the same thing by keeping the processing away from the CPU. Either way, insist on this feature.

❊ **Input metering.** Digital audio is finicky. Try to record at too low a level, and the sound won't have the full range of detail and may even get lost in a bed of digital noise. Hit the ceiling, and it distorts horribly. Meters are essential, period. I'll discuss how to use them shortly.

❊ **Software mixer.** Mixing is the process of blending all of your tracks and effects into a harmonious whole. Even if you are only recording live in stereo, you'll still need some way to adjust the final output.

❊ **EQ.** Here's a professional secret: Microphones don't hear things the way a human ear does. EQ (short for equalization) lets you make tonal adjustments to the sound after it's been recorded.

❊ **Dynamics.** Certain sounds, like the snap of a fingernail when it hits a guitar string, are much louder than they appear to our ears. These high-intensity sounds, called *transients* because they last just a split second, appear as brief spikes that tower above the rest of the waveform. This limits how loud your recording can be; if you boost the whole signal, these peaks will clip and distort. *Compression*, a type of dynamics processing, alters the relative height of the peaks so you can safely boost the overall levels.

❊ **Effects.** When you hear your voice, you hear the resonance inside your head as well as the sound of your voice bouncing around the room and back to your ears. A mic hears only what comes out of your lips. Effects such as reverb and delay restore that natural sound the microphone missed, or they can paint an aural picture. The choice is yours.

❊ **Mastering tools.** Mastering is the final stage of the recording process. It's where a collection of songs is polished so they all sound like they belong together. At the very least, you'll need to be able to adjust the overall level, cut unwanted sounds from the beginning and ending of each song, and prepare the songs for burning to a CD.

❊ **Support for multiple sample rates and bit depths.** What do all these different bit rates and sampling frequencies mean? The short answer is, the higher the number, the more detail. Of course, there's absolutely no point in recording a cheap guitar through a junky mic at

24 bits and 192kHz. But 24-bit recording, even at 44.1kHz, can sound dramatically better than 16 bits.

✳ **Support for multiple file formats.** If you are going to record, mix, and listen to only your own music, it doesn't matter what file format your software uses. At the very least, you'll need to be able to save files as WAV (PC) or AIFF files (Mac) for burning to CDs. The ability to read and write MP3 files is great for Internet distribution and portable music players.

✳ **Plug-ins.** Software plug-ins let you customize your recording experience with third-party effects, virtual instruments, and much more. Standards are still evolving, but at this writing Steinberg's VST has the edge for flexibility and compatibility. If you have your eyes on a particular plug-in, be sure your software supports it!

✳ **MIDI.** Why do you need MIDI if you're recording only digital audio? Well, for one thing, sending a MIDI click track to a keyboard or drum machine gives you far greater control over the sound. For another, you can assign the data wheels and sliders on your keyboard to control the levels and panning of your audio tracks when it's time to mix. Take it from me, mixing with a mouse is a pain.

As I said earlier, you'll be ahead of the game if you choose your software before you pick out an audio interface and computer. So much of your recording experience depends on the fit between your needs, goals and experience, and software tools. The fastest computer in the world matched to a high-end interface won't do you a bit of good if you aren't comfortable working with the software. Take some time reading product descriptions. Browse online discussion groups to learn what successes and failures real people are having. Read product reviews. Talk to other musicians. Download demos of popular programs such as Cubase or Logic and try them on for size. When you find software that seems to be a good fit, check for compatibility with interfaces, plug-ins, and operating systems.

Do this even if you are contemplating purchasing a bundle. You'll be able to work better, work faster, and get better results when you build a system around your way of working.

More Essential Gear

Aside from your computer, audio interface, and software, you need surprisingly little gear to make great recordings at home.

If you've been performing for a while, chances are you've already collected some of the gear you need.

Microphones

Your microphone is the biggest factor in making the difference between a so-so recording and a great recording. Pro studios are well known for extensive microphone collections; we should be so lucky. I discussed the basic kinds of microphones and what they are used for in Chapter 2; go back and brush up if you need to. Here I'm going to give you some tried-and-true recommendations for home studios; as with any opinion, you have the right to disagree. Microphone prices have dropped dramatically in recent years, offering a huge range of affordable options. Aside from some truly awful bargain-basement mics, it's pretty hard to go wrong.

Pick up any basic recording book or magazine article, and they'll all say the same thing: "For recording an acoustic guitar, you can't go wrong with a Shure SM57." Well, maybe that was true 20 years ago, but you can do a lot better. These days most pros choose a small-diaphragm condenser mic—or two—to capture the transparency and airiness of a finger-picked or strummed acoustic. The AKG C1000S small-diaphragm condenser operates with battery power, making it an ideal choice for studios without phantom power. For slightly more money, both the Shure SM81 and Audio-Technica AT4041 are proven winners.

If you want to go with a dynamic, the Sennheiser MD 421 shown in Figure 7.4 is a terrific choice. Plus the large-diaphragm dynamic element, cardioid pattern, and five-position bass switch make it a versatile vocal mic as well.

Figure 7.4
The Sennheiser MD 421 is a studio favorite for recording guitar. Courtesy of RØDE Microphones, LLC, 2005.

Large-diaphragm condensers are the hands-down best choice for recording vocals. And many engineers, including me, favor them for acoustic guitars as well. Choosing a vocal mic is like choosing shoes; there's no substitute for trying it on. Every voice is different, and a mic that sounds great on one could leave the other sounding nasally and thin. Fortunately, you no longer have to pay thousands of dollars for a great mic. Excellent choices abound from such makers as AKG, Audio-Technica, Shure, and RØDE. (See Figure 7.5.)

Do not be tempted to buy microphones designed for stage use. For the most part, these mics lack the clarity and response you'll need to capture the nuances of your voice and guitar. Of course, sometimes that's just the ticket, particularly for a rude, aggressive track. One other thing: With microphones, more money does generally buy better quality. The mics I've listed retail for between $179 and $499. They represent solid choices that will give great results. And yes, there is a huge difference between a $99 mic and a $1,999 mic.

Direct Injection

If you plan on plugging in, a DI is a must. A DI, short for Direct Injection, takes the Hi-Z output from your guitar or bass and transforms it to a nice, friendly mic-level signal. Why would you want to do that? For one thing, low-impedance mic cables are far better at rejecting noise than your standard guitar cable, particularly over long distances.

For another, unless your audio interface has an input specifically designed for guitar, you can't plug a guitar directly into the ¼-inch line ins on your interface: The difference in levels will rob tone.

DIs come in several flavors. Passive models, such as the ART Zdirect, Whirlwind IMP 2, or Pro Co DB 1, do nothing more than match the impedances, so they are great choices for capturing exactly what goes in. Active models, such as the SansAmp Acoustic DI, Bss AR-133, and Stewart ADB-1, may have tone shaping or other controls. A tube DI can add a bit of warmth to the sound. Many under-saddle pickups used on acoustic guitars require preamplification and/or other tonal modifications; be sure to match the DI to your pickup.

As a bonus, owning your own DI gives you better control of your sound on stage, too.

Cable

As with microphones, better cable makes better recordings, right? Well, yes and no. The jury is still out on whether super-premium cable really brings a discernable improvement over good, solid pro-grade wire and connectors. But this much is true: Leave the cheap cable for the do-it-yourself hobby crowd. Junk is junk, and no amount of fiddling will help your recordings if the quality isn't there in the first place. Stick with mid-priced cables from a reputable music store or online dealer. Look for hefty, flexible wire firmly soldered to metal connectors. Heat shrink tubing and strain relief are often the hallmarks of professional-grade cables.

Keep your cables as short as you can get away with. Nothing's worse than a tangle of spaghetti lying all over your studio floor, and extra-long cables can act as antennae, picking up noise and even radio interference.

Figure 7.5
A large-diaphragm condenser, such as the inexpensive RØDE NT1-A, is a must for vocals. Courtesy of RØDE Microphones, LLC, 2005.

> ### ❅ WATCH YER IMPEDANCE
>
> Generally speaking, microphones operate at *low impedance* (under 1,000 ohms) while *high-impedance* (Hi-Z for short) equipment—keyboards, outboard gear, and electric guitars and basses—runs from 20,000 ohms on up.
>
> Low-impedance connections are far less prone to signal degradation or noise over long distances (say, more than 20 feet) than high-impedance connections.
>
> Microphone connections have three pins connected to thick cable containing two wires and a shield (to help cut down noise). Hi-Z cable may have a single wire wrapped in a shield (for unbalanced connection via RCA or tip-sleeve phone plug) or two wires and a shield for balanced operation, terminating in a tip-ring-sleeve plug. (See Figure 7.6.)

Figure 7.6

Connector diagram: XLR mic, ¼-inch tip-sleeve and ¼-inch tip-ring-sleeve plugs and jacks.

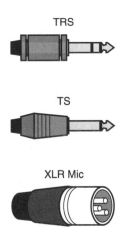

TRS

TS

XLR Mic

Stands and Stuff

Mic stands do more than just raise a microphone off the floor. Since moving a microphone even a fraction of an inch can change the character of a recording, the stand must be able to adjust easily and hold the position against the weight of the microphone. You don't want the frustration of getting the perfect recording position only to see the stand droop and swivel away. An adjustable boom extension is useful for moving in close to an instrument. Booms are also great for guitarists who sing when they play.

Shock or suspension mounts are specialized microphone adaptors that prevent sounds from traveling from the floor up through the stand and into the mic. A stereo bar is handy for quickly setting up a pair of mics on a single stand.

Certain vocal sounds, particularly p's and b's, explode with tremendous force into a microphone. A pop filter placed between the singer and mic is the only way to tame these plosives. Professional pop filters usually come with a short adjustable gooseneck boom that clips on to the mic stand. Some budget-minded folks fabricate their own from pantyhose stretched over a coat hanger or embroidery hoop plus some duct tape. Save the foam windscreens that attach over the microphone for playing outdoors.

Don't forget cable ties to keep everything neat, a nice comfortable—and non-squeaky!—chair to work in, and some place to store everything when you need the spare bedroom for guests! You may also consider a music stand, hooks or a "cable claw" to stow extra cables, tags to label everything in case you have to pull some gear, and a guitar stand.

Power conditioning is a must for computers and sensitive electronic gear. If you live in an area with frequent power outages, consider an uninterrupted power supply. It will supply enough juice via an internal battery to save all your work and power down.

And a lava lamp, while not essential, is always a nice touch.

Headphones and Monitors

So far we've talked about what you need to get sound into your computer. But how are you going to hear it? And, more important, how are you going to know if what you're hearing is the Truth?

Professional studios invest huge amounts of money in stellar-quality playback speakers and tuning the listening environment so that nothing colors the sound. Unless you are among the select few who will build a home studio from scratch, chances are you're recording and listening in a less-than-perfect environment. No worries; we can deal with that. First things first: Pick up a good set of pro-quality headphones.

Save the earbuds for your Walkman and don't be seduced by hotshot home stereo headphones with heavy presence (treble) and bass boosts. Professional headphones are designed to faithfully reproduce what's on the recording—nothing more, nothing less. For tracking, closed-ear designs keep the headphone mix from leaking back into your mic. Look for a good comfortable fit and high-quality parts that can be repaired easily.

Since headphones play directly into your ears, they don't really tell you how your mix will sound in the real world. For that, you need monitor speakers. Which brings us to another pro secret: Home stereo and multimedia speakers are designed to lie to you. Like consumer headphones, they usually accentuate the high and low ends to make up for the deficiencies in most rooms. What's so bad about that? Your mix will have too little treble and too light a bottom for one thing. Which means it will suck.

Do you need to rush out and buy a pair of studio monitors today? Not necessarily. *If* you have a good set of professional headphones, *if* you spend some time getting to know what your existing speakers sound like, and *if* you check your mixes on a variety of systems, you can get away with recording and mixing on home speakers. Whether you use your home speakers or purchase dedicated studio monitors, be sure they are set up properly. Refer back to Chapter 2 if you need a refresher.

Hook It Up!

Okay, the time has come to assemble all of your stuff and get down to work. By now you should have a pretty good idea how to set up your monitor speakers, how to tame your room, and what software and hardware you need. Refer to the hookup diagram in Figure 7.7 for help putting it all together.

Figure 7.7

Hookup diagram for a basic, small studio.

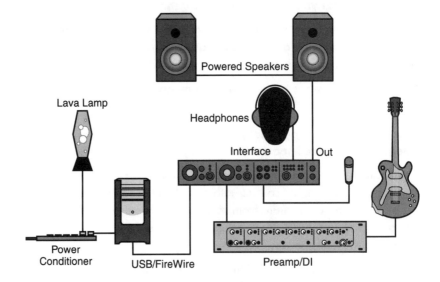

Dedicated studios always have clean power with clear paths to ground. You may not be able to do this, but do make sure everything is grounded properly. Ground loops cause an annoying hum that will seep into your recordings. If it's at all possible, avoid sharing electrical circuits with heavy appliances such as refrigerators or washers and dryers that run periodically. If worse comes to worst, you'll have to turn off the offending devices while you record. Don't forget to turn 'em back on. Nothing's worse than emerging from a marathon session to find your kitchen awash in melted ice cream!

One more thing before we start to record: Do not simply run everything to a power strip and flip the switch! To avoid damaging your hearing and your gear, you must power up in a certain order and power down in reverse!

Here's the correct order for powering up your studio:

1. Any FireWire or USB devices

2. Computer

3. Any external devices, effects, preamps, and so on

4. Amplifier or powered speakers

Winning Microphone Techniques

I'm going to guide you step by step through the process of choosing and setting up your microphones. For this tutorial we'll be working with an acoustic guitar and vocal, but you can use these same techniques for many other instrument-and-vocal combinations. I'll also discuss recording electric guitars and touch on live recording setups.

Recording Guitar

Considering how many classic songs feature the acoustic guitar—hits by Buddy Holly, the Beatles, and (insert your favorite singer-songwriter here) leap to mind—you'd think that there would be a consensus on how to record the dang thing. So all we should have to do is follow the formula, stick a mic just so, and get a perfect recording every time, right?

The truth is that every guitar is different, and every player unique. Professional engineers know that when it comes to placing microphones, there is no substitute for careful listening, adjusting, listening again, adjusting again… you get the idea. With that in mind, I'm going to walk you through the process of setting up one or two microphones to get the best sound you can out of your acoustic guitar. Don't fret: I'll mention recording your electric, too.

Know Your Axe

True or false: Great guitar tracks begin with great guitars. Well, the truth is great guitar tracks start with the right combination of guitar, microphone, and performance. A good guitar helps, of course, but sometimes a mediocre axe can outshine the best handmade creation.

The body of an acoustic guitar is designed to do one very important thing: amplify the vibrational energy of the strings and direct the sound outward to the listener. Most of the action takes place as the guitar's top flexes in harmony with the energy passed down through the bridge. Solid woods vibrate more uniformly than laminated composites, which is why most guitars have a solid top. The size, depth, and shape of the body affect the volume of air inside and so will modify the tone by selectively increasing or decreasing certain harmonic components of the fundamental tone. As with the top, solid-wood backs and sides contribute to the purity of the tone.

The best way to get to know the sound of your guitar is to have a friend play it while sitting or standing where you'll be recording. Notice how the sound focuses several feet in front of the guitar's body. Now pretend you're a microphone: Cover one ear with your hand, cock your head to the side, and stick your uncovered ear about six inches away from the guitar. This simulates the monaural pickup pattern of a microphone. Notice how the sound changes as you move around: thin and trebly near the bridge, fuller and rounder as you move up toward the fingerboard. Be sure to move up and down as well as closer and farther, too, comparing the sound right in front of the top to what you hear listening a foot in front and six inches higher. Make a mental note of anywhere the guitar sounds particularly good to you—that's a good place to stick a mic.

What you have just done is followed exactly the process experienced recording engineers use. Sure, there are some standard mic placements, and I'll get to them in a moment. But the best way is still the simplest: use your ears.

Here are a few other questions to ask yourself:

- ❉ Is the guitar well balanced so that each string sounds equally loud, or is it tipped to the bass or treble side?
- ❉ Do certain notes or chords jump out at you?
- ❉ Can you hear any buzzes or rattles from loose tuning knobs or untrimmed string ends?
- ❉ If you have internal batteries or preamps, are the wires and fittings securely fastened?
- ❉ Do any of the strings buzz at certain frets?
- ❉ Is the pick guard loose?
- ❉ Is the guitar in tune as you move up the fingerboard?
- ❉ Is the action set properly?
- ❉ Do you need to change the strings?

> ❉ **STRING THING**
>
> Many guitarists prefer to record with brand-new strings in order to get the most treble response. Steel strings made from a phosphor bronze alloy are the brightest. Likewise, new nylon strings are noticeably brighter than a set that has been played. New strings also do a much better job of reproducing all of the harmonic overtones. The downside is that brand-new strings tend to go out of tune quickly. Nylon strings are the worst; sometimes it takes days for my classical to hold its tune.
>
> By sure to match the string gauge to your guitar and your playing style. All things being equal, moving to a slightly heavier gauge will make your guitar louder and bring out more bass. Lighter strings are easier on the fingers and tend not to squeak as much.
>
> New strings, both nylon and steel, are much more prone to squeaks as you slide your fingers up and down the neck than a set that's been played in. Coated strings, such as those sold under the Elixer brand, sacrifice a little brightness for greatly reduced finger squeaks, making them very popular in recording studios.

Finding a Space

The best place to record an acoustic guitar is where it sounds the best. Okay, so that's kind of obvious. Ideally, you want to capture both the sound of the guitar and just a bit of the sound that's bouncing around the room. Set up at least three feet from any walls. If you are lucky enough to have a hardwood floor in your studio, try setting up on a small area rug so that several square feet of floor is exposed directly under the guitar.

Avoid aiming your guitar directly at a corner. It doesn't matter whether you sit or stand, but make sure you're comfortable. Unless you have a friend who'll be running the computer for you, you'll need to be able to move quickly between it and your recording position.

CHECK THE CHAIR, CHET

I can't tell you how many takes have been ruined by chair noises. Before you get too comfortable, check your chair for squeaks, creaks, fabric noises, whoopie cushions, and any other unpleasant noises. You may not notice them when you are practicing, but believe me, they'll jump out on the recording.

Taming Room Noise

The best way to deal with unwanted noise on your tracks is never let it get there in the first place. Take a moment and listen to what's going on in the room: Can you hear any fans, electrical appliances, traffic noises, or other distractions? Clap your hands loudly and check to see if anything on the wall or windows rattles or buzzes. Heavy drapes help tame sounds creeping in through the windows or doors. Turn off any appliances you don't absolutely need, and set your thermostat so the fan won't come on in the middle of a take.

Computers make a dreadful racket, with noisy fans and clicking and whirring hard drives. If you can, place your CPU away from where you record, say, under your desk or in a special enclosure. Don't be tempted to disconnect the fan: Your machine will melt down before you've played the second chorus. Or buy extension cables for the monitor, keyboard, and mouse and move the CPU to another room.

Some computers—particularly those built expressly for music, such as the MusicXPC—are downright quiet. Laptops in particular are noteworthy in this regard, making them great choices for home studios. Some computers rely on sensors to turn on the fans only when necessary, giving you a fairly long window of quiet in which to record.

If you can't do away with the computer noise, take advantage of your microphone's pickup pattern to minimize the damage. As I discussed in Chapter 2, cardioid and hypercardioid mics are designed to pick up sound directly in front of the capsule. Sounds coming in from the sides are greatly reduced. Directly behind the mic is a virtual dead spot. Set up your mics several feet away and make sure the backs of the mics point toward the computer. Some sound will still leak in, but it should be quiet enough that whatever's on the track will totally mask it.

It almost goes without saying that you've turned your phone off, right?

Monaural Mic Placement

Using just a single mic to capture the big sound of an acoustic guitar makes sense in a number of scenarios. For one thing, it's easy. And it gives you the opportunity to place the guitar in the mix with more focus. And, sometimes, all you've got is one mic.

Here's a good, all-around position that will give excellent results whether you use a dynamic or condenser microphone. Aim a directional (cardioid or hypercardioid pattern) mic at the point where the neck joins the body (usually the fourteenth fret) about six to eight inches away from the guitar. Angle it in slightly toward the sound hole. You may need to move it slightly closer or farther away, and be sure to listen to the effect of changing the angle. This position tends to give a well-balanced picture of the guitar. It works equally well for steel strings, arch-tops, and classical guitars.

To emphasize percussive strumming, try placing the mic closer to the bridge. A good starting place would be about four to six inches in front of bridge and between the sound hole and the lower edge of the top. To avoid excessive boominess, be careful not to point the mic directly at the sound hole. Some engineers even aim the mic at the top a couple of inches behind the bridge!

Stereo Mic Placement

Stereo is an attempt to simulate the experience of sound in three-dimensional space. We have two ears, so why not use two microphones? Stereo miking yields the most realistic picture of your guitar. It takes a bit more to achieve good results, but it's worth trying.

Stereo recording usually involves two nearly identical microphones; in fact, pros spend extra money to buy matched pairs of microphones with consecutive serial numbers! That's beyond the reach of most of us, though some companies are offering inexpensive matched pairs and specialty stereo mics. But for practical purposes, you'll get excellent results with two mics of the same make and model. Again, you can use dynamics, but stereo recording is truly the domain of both small- and large-diaphragm condensers.

I should warn you that stereo mic placement is a huge subject. I'm only going to give you the basics; if you want to learn more, check out some of the resources in Appendix D, "Resources."

One classic technique is called the coincident-pair, or X-Y, method. Place two directional microphones so that the grills are stacked one above the other and the capsules are almost touching. Angle the capsules inward between 45 and 60 degrees—the exact angle will depend on the pickup pattern and the width of the stereo field you want. (See Figure 7.8.)

Coincident-pair miking can really open up the sound of your guitar. A good place to start is to set the pair about a foot back from the sound hole, with one mic pointing toward the fourteenth fret and the other toward the bridge. If you hear too much bass, move the pair to one side of the hole or the other. Experiment with placement until you hear something you like.

Figure 7.8
Coincident pair, or X-Y, miking technique for stereo.

❋ STEREO MIKING AND PHASE CANCELLATION

Sound waves are funny things. Not only can they bounce off of solid objects, but they can interact with other sound waves. The waves radiating out from your guitar will arrive at the two microphones at slightly different times. If one mic picks up the peak of the wave while the other hears the trough, the two signals are said to be "out of phase" (Figure 7.9). When you mix the signals back, the addition of the wave's peaks and troughs results in "phase cancellation." In a nutshell, that means that a big part of the sound will disappear!

The best way to avoid phase cancellation is to use two small-diaphragm mics placed very close together, as with the coincident-pair technique described above. Even then, some phase problems can creep in. To hear if you've got problems, listen to the mics panned full left and right and then in mono (panned straight up, if you don't have a mono switch). If it sounds like some part of the sound went missing, go back and change the angle of the mics slightly. Severe phase problems may be fixed by flipping the phase switch on your software mixer.

But aren't all songs mixed in stereo? So what's the problem? It's a little-known fact that stereo FM broadcasts become mono at the edge of the broadcasting range. A buddy of mine once had the wonderful experience of hearing his new single playing on the radio as he cruised out in the country. You can imagine his horror when his amazing guitar solo completely disappeared because the engineer forgot to check the phase.

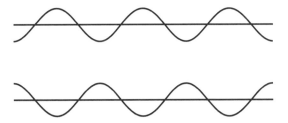

Figure 7.9
The two waves are 180 degrees out of phase. Added together, they will cancel each other out.

A variation on the coincident technique places the two directional mics with the capsules spread apart, as illustrated in Figure 7.10. Again, the angle can vary quite a bit, depending on the stereo spread you want. This mic technique is called near-coincident, and it's handy for getting a slightly wider and more realistic stereo image. It works particularly well for capturing the sound of a guitar played in the room. Set up the pair several feet back from the guitar. Naturally, a good, quiet performance space is a necessity.

Be careful, though, as near-coincident pairs are very prone to phase problems.

Figure 7.10
Near-coincident miking
yields a wider stereo field.

I'll mention just one more stereo miking technique. Called, ahem, the spaced pair, this one uses two mics spaced some distance from each other. Spaced-pair miking works best with two similar omnidirectional mics, but many engineers employ mics with two completely different characters for special effects. For instance, you may aim a small-diameter condenser at the bridge to grab the sound of the pick on the strings and place a large-diaphragm mic in front of the sound hole for the bass. Once again, be sure to check for phasing problems before you start recording.

Unlike coincident and near-coincident miking, the idea of spaced-pair miking isn't always to re-create a true stereo image. Rather, it involves using a recording to paint pictures with sound. If you record this way, be sure to try out different panning and levels for the two tracks. Maybe the 12-foot-wide guitar is the sound you were looking for!

Pro Recording Tip: Use a DI... Sparingly

As I mentioned earlier in this chapter, a Direct Injection is essential if you want to plug in your acoustic electric. If you are lucky enough to have an exceptionally accurate internal pickup coupled with a terrific DI, you may even get away with eliminating the microphones altogether. More likely you have the kind of rig that I have: It sounds okay on stage through the PA, but yuck, what an ugly noise it makes when you record it!

Even so, I always run a DI and record the pickup right along with the mics. Why? Because the very thing that makes acoustic pickups sound so funky can really help a track leap out of the mix.

One thing: It takes a short time for the sound to travel out of your guitar to a microphone, while the pickup responds almost instantaneously. As with stereo miking, this can cause phase problems that will degrade the sound. (See Figure 7.11.) The usual fix is to slide the DI track back by a few milliseconds until the waveforms line up again. Science is a beautiful thing.

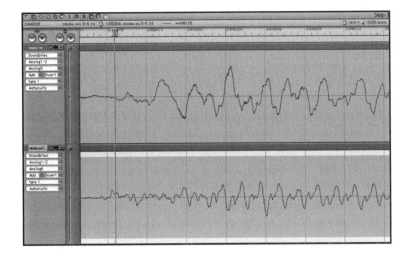

Figure 7.11

Waveform display showing phase problems between tracks recorded with a mic (top) and a DI (bottom). To avoid phase problems, nudge the DI track back until the peaks match up.

❊ **PICTURE THIS**

Okay, you've set up your mics and you've got a great guitar sound. As you've discovered, moving the capsule even a fraction of an inch makes a big difference. Everything's great now, but tomorrow you need the room for something else. How do you find the same sound the next time?

Two words: digital camera. Take a bunch of pictures showing the distance and angles of the mic relative to the guitar. Be sure to take some that will help you place yourself, too. If you've got a patterned rug or floor, note where you stand or sit. Load the pix onto your computer and save them in the same folder as all of your recording files.

Recording Your Electric

Ever since Line 6 unveiled the first POD a few years back, recording an electric guitar has been a breeze. These days, just about every bit of recording software has some kind of built-in amp modeling and guitar-effects generator built in. And many interfaces include Hi-Z inputs, so you can dispense with the DI. If your music is built around an electric instead of an acoustic guitar, consider a dedicated guitar interface and software bundle such as Line 6's GuitarPort RiffTracker. If you already have an interface, Cakewalk's Guitar Tracks Pro 3 has many features to make your tracks shine, including a free version of the Amplitude LE amp modeling plug-in.

Mic Techniques for Voice

The human voice is the most expressive instrument we have. It can whisper or wail, caress your ears with soothing melody or fry your brain with a piercing screech. Some voices emanate deep in the chest, some sound like singing noses. Basses rattle the windows with profound low-frequency tones; some celebrated mezzosopranos sing with such purity and intensity the high-frequency energy *breaks* the windows. Transforming all of that amazing range and color into electrical impulses is no simple matter.

Know Your Voice

Maybe you've experienced the shock of hearing a recording of your voice for the first time. Why doesn't it sound like you? The short answer is that we hear our own voices differently from how we hear anything else. The voice begins with air passing through your vocal chords. Folds of skin deep in our throats vibrate much like the reeds on a saxophone. The sound is amplified by the air cavities in your throat and shaped by your lips and tongue, undergoing still more tone shaping and resonance as it rattles around inside your nasal passages and sinuses. All of that vibration also sets the bones of your skull to vibrating. Since bone is an excellent tone conductor—yes, there are cultures who have made sacred flutes from human bone—it shouldn't surprise you that much of the quality of your own voice is the result of picking up the direct vibrations inside your skull.

There's an old African proverb that says, "If you can talk, you can sing; and if you can walk, you can dance." Ah, but *how* you sing makes all the difference. Just as you did with your guitar, take the time to get to know your voice. Although there is no substitute for consulting a professional vocal coach, a few minutes thinking about the basics will make the difference between a wimpy vocal track and one you can be proud of.

* Do you run out of air easily? Chances are you aren't breathing properly. Take deep breaths that completely fill your lungs. If your belly moves out while your diaphragm moves downward, you're on the right track. Then support your voice with a steady, gentle pressure from your diaphragm.

* Do you have trouble staying on pitch? Although pitch-correction software can help, an out-of-tune track is an ugly track. Trying to sing above or below your range often leads to pitch problems. So does forcing too much air, or not giving your voice enough support.

* Do you sing through your nose? Nasal vocal tones are great for some types of music— everybody do their Dylan impersonation now—but inappropriate for others. Sometimes all it takes is relaxing to move your voice out of your nose and into a more natural place.

* Are you straining to reach certain notes in the song? Perhaps the song is in the wrong key for you. Try knocking it down to a lower key.

* Does your voice sound completely different at the top and bottom of your range? It's not uncommon for singers to have a "head voice" and a "chest voice." With training, you can learn how to smooth out the differences, but why not use them to your advantage? I once worked with a singer who had always performed as a high tenor, sounding just like a million other screaming rock star wannabes. While working on a ballad, we discovered that he had one of the most beautiful, soulful baritone voices I'd ever heard. He had no idea he could sing like that. It made the track.

✳ This may be obvious, but always record your vocals standing up. Unless you have a physical condition that prevents it, standing up is the only way to get the support you need. Good posture makes a difference, too. Your mother was right: Stand up straight!

Choosing the Right Microphone

Pretty much any mid-priced large-diaphragm condenser microphone on the market today will give you great vocal tracks. Before you bust a gut, by mid-priced I mean *inexpensive*. That doesn't mean you should rush out and buy the $49 bargain advertised in the local Guitar-O-Rama catalog. Cheap is still cheap. But there are a surprising number of outstanding mics costing well under five bills, and some that don't hit $200.

I'll mention a couple personal favorites; of course, your ears may disagree. The RØDE NT1-A is a great-sounding vocal mic with very low shelf noise—that means the microphone is very quiet. The AKG C3000B features a tight cardioid pattern, 1.0 dB pad and bass roll-off, and a smooth presence boost that makes vocals stand out. I've also been impressed with mid-priced mics by Audio-Technica, Shure, and Blue.

Spend just a few bucks more and you start getting into some seriously great microphones. Neumann brings its legendary performance and sound to the masses with the new BCM 104 and the amazingly quiet TLM103. Blue has a number of interesting microphones tailored for specific recording tasks; both the Blueberry and Bluebird work exceedingly well in the home studio. The Audio-Technica AT4047 shown in Figure 7.12 offers the versatility of multiple pickup patterns in a very affordable package.

Figure 7.12
Vocal mics often use suspension mounts to keep the mic from picking up vibrations through the stand (shown here on an Audio-Technica AT4047).

The best way to choose a vocal mic is to hear it in action. If you know anyone with a personal studio, set up a listening session. Pro-audio retailers often have demo models you can audition.

Even better, most catalog and online retailers have extended trial periods of a month or more so you may thoroughly test your purchase. If the mic doesn't cut it, you're only out the postage.

So how do you know if you've got the right mic for you? Basically, you want to hear a clear vocal image, with lots of detail and what engineers call "air"—that sparkly, high-frequency crispness that adds sheen to the sound. Beware of excessive upper mid-range frequencies that sound harsh or brittle. A mic that emphasizes the lower mid-tones will make your voice sound tubby or muddy.

Vocal Mic Placement

Proper mic placement is as important as selection in determining the end result. Simply raising a mic off the floor and aiming it toward your mouth ain't going to cut it. Since it is pretty hard to listen to your own voice the way you did to your guitar, here are some tips to help you decide.

Do you move around a lot when you sing? If so, you'll need a microphone with an omnidirectional pattern. The good news is that an omni will pick up your vocal no matter how far you move from side to side. The bad news is it will pick up every other noise in your studio, too.

Do you shout or whisper? If you sing exceptionally loud, be sure you've got a microphone that can handle the high SPL (Sound Pressure Level). Loud singers can get away with standing farther away from the mic—say up to 14 inches. Move in closer for a more intimate sound.

❋ THE PROXIMITY EFFECT, OR, ELVIS IS IN THE BUILDING

Cardioid and hypercardioid microphones have a curious property: As the source of the sound gets very close to the capsule, the bass response becomes much more pronounced. Stage singers and vocal percussionists use this proximity effect to dramatically boost the bass on their voices for certain effects. When you're recording, be aware of how close you are to the mic so you don't suddenly start sounding like Elvis.

Set up where you will feel comfortable. Avoid standing too close to walls or corners to minimize reflections and unwanted resonances. Although it's tempting to record in a naturally reverberant space, it is far better to record the vocals with little or no room sound. You can always add reverb in the mix, but once it's on the track, you're stuck with it.

Place your large-diaphragm condenser mic on a straight stand or boom with the element a bit higher than your mouth and angled down slightly. Many engineers prefer to set up so the body of the microphone hangs below the boom. If you opt for this, be sure your mic clip or suspension mount holds the microphone securely. To avoid tripping over loose cables, secure the cord by wrapping it around the stand or use clips or Velcro ties. A tidy studio is a productive studio.

To prevent problems with plosives, place a pop filter between your mouth and the capsule. (See Figure 7.13.)

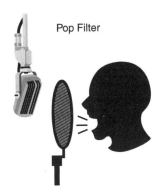

Pop Filter

Figure 7.13
Use a pop filter in front of the vocal mic to tame plosives.

Unless you're using an omni pattern, be sure that you stay *on axis*, that is, directly in front of the microphone. The sound will change dramatically if you move even a few inches to one side or the other! For a good starting point, stand about 6 to 8 inches away. When you've got a good sound, stick a bit of tape on the floor to mark where to put your feet in case you have to walk away for any reason.

✳ USING PHANTOM POWER

Unlike dynamic mics, condensers need a power supply to charge the diaphragm. (See Chapter 2 if you need to bone up on the different types of microphones.) The juice comes from a DC voltage source— either a battery or 48-volt "phantom power" supplied from a preamp or audio interface. Phantom power runs up the wires in the mic cord; you don't need a special cable.

To avoid damaging the mic, always turn on phantom power after you've connected the mic to the cable. Likewise turn off the phantom power before you disconnect the mic and wait a couple of seconds before shutting down the preamp or interface. Some devices have an LED that slowly dims to indicate a "soft power-down" of phantom power. Don't be alarmed if you see a peak level light flash momentarily when you turn the phantom power on or off.

Dynamic microphones are unaffected by phantom power. That's a good thing, because some audio gear supplies phantom power to all of its mic inputs globally. However, be very careful when using a ribbon microphone; accidentally applying phantom power will shred the delicate element.

Live Recording

Okay, so now you know how to set up mics for your guitar, and you know how to set up mics for you voice. What if you want to sing and play at the same time?

I'll risk sounding snide: You combine the two.

Here are some things to consider:

❋ Do you normally sing and play standing up or seated? While standing is the only way to get a great vocal, many people find their guitar playing suffers when they stand up.

❋ You will not have as much control over your sound once it's committed to tape, er, disc. Your vocal mic can't avoid picking up the guitar, just as your guitar tracks will have off-axis vocals all over them. Take extra care that everything is perfectly balanced before you hit record.

❋ Adding effects in the mix can be problematic. Maybe a little bit of chorus is just what the guitar needs, but watch out for what it does to your vocal! And adding delay on your voice will destroy the timing of the guitar part.

❋ Fixing mistakes is a lot harder than overdubbing guitar and vocal parts separately. If you flub a word on the chorus, you'll pretty much have to go back and start over. Ditto if you clam on the guitar underneath a flawless vocal.

So why record live? Because it sounds good and it feels good, that's why. Sure, it takes more effort to set up, but who ever said life was easy?

❋ **DOIN' IT LIKE BOB**

Some of the greatest acoustic recordings ever made featured a lone singer/guitarist performing live in front of a single microphone. If you want to capture the immediacy of your performance with minimal fuss, try this: Set up a large-diaphragm condenser mic with an omni pattern midway between the top of you guitar and your mouth. Move back at least a foot or two to let the sound of your voice and guitar have a chance to fill out and mingle. Experiment with moving the microphone up or down slightly to change the balance between your voice and instrument. Record in glorious mono. Denim cap and squeaky harmonica optional.

I promise that setting up your microphones will take a lot less time in real life than it has to read about it.

Now that we have the mics up and ready to go, it's time to make some tracks.

Recording Your Song

Okay, you've acquired the gear, hooked it all up, and learned how to choose and place you microphones—so all that's left is to hit the record button, right? Not so fast. We're almost there, but first follow along as I show you how to plan your session and set up your software so you don't lose any time or data.

Once again, I'll be working with a basic song consisting of two guitar tracks (mic and DI) and a vocal. But the techniques are the same no matter what you record. I'll be illustrating the process with screenshots from Mark of the Unicorn's Digital Performer software. Although some of the specifics may vary in your software, the general steps will be the same.

Before we get started, be sure to install your software and any drivers you need for your audio interface. Refer to your manuals if you need help; I'm afraid I can't cover all of the different combinations in this book.

The Recording Session

The key to successful recording is in the preparation. Sure, attitude and a great performance are vital. That's why you want to be ready to go when inspiration strikes. Take it from me, nothing squashes the moment faster than having to search around for all of your cables and gear, not to mention the agony of trying to find files stashed randomly around a 60-gig hard drive.

So get in the habit of beginning each and every recording session the same way. I generally do all of my planning and setup a day or more before I plan to record. That way when the time comes, all I have to think about is playing.

Setting Up the Song

Depending on your software, your first task is to set up and create a song file to hold all of your tracks, tempo maps, editing, and mix data. (Don't worry if you don't know what all these terms mean yet; you will by the end of this chapter.) If you haven't already, power up your gear and turn on the computer. Leave your monitor speakers off for now; we'll be using headphones until we finish recording the basic tracks. Why? Two reasons: We don't want the sound from the speakers to bleed into the mics; and we don't want to create a feedback loop that can destroy your ears and ruin your equipment.

Open your recording software and create a new song file (sometimes called a "project"). Give it a name, and save it somewhere you can find it easily. I keep all of my songs in individual folders organized by the name of the CD or project I'm working on. All of these folders are stored inside a folder named Recording Files. That makes finding and backing up songs a snap.

We'll be using two tracks for the guitar plus one for the vocal; if you need to add some tracks, do so now.

Setting the Tempo Map

Tempo maps are extremely handy in all phases of recording and mixing. Recording software uses the tempo map to keep all of the tracks playing together, to set starting and ending times for edits based on useful musical terms like bars and beats, and for handling sophisticated processes, such as adjusting the timing of a prerecorded drum loop. You may set a tempo map to follow the "feel" of a live player by tapping in timing information on a MIDI keyboard or mouse or by manually entering time signatures and BPM (beats per minute) for different parts of your song. At the very least, setting a time signature and tempo for your song lets you play to a click track generated by the software. But many other day-to-day tasks, such as loop recording, automating punches, setting markers, synchronizing effects, and editing tracks, are much, much easier if you take a few minutes to figure out the tempo and time signature.

If you don't like to play to a click track, you can still use a tempo map to set a one- or two-bar count-off. To determine your song's tempo, turn on the click track—and make sure it's routed to your interface's headphone output if that's different from the stereo left and right outs. Play along while you listen to the click in your headphones and adjust the tempo until the click falls on the strong beats. It may take a few tries to get it right. If you have a MIDI keyboard or drum pads, select Tap Tempo and enter the tempo manually.

> ### ❄ SCRATCH TRACKS
>
> If you are used to singing and playing at the same time, recording a guitar part by itself can be difficult. Many musicians first record a rough version of the song as a guide. Since it won't be part of the final mix, this "scratch track" doesn't have to be great quality or even well played. I usually do my scratch parts with just a DI on the guitar and a vocal mic so that there's a minimum of setup time. I can then take my time to record the keeper guitar tracks while listening to the scratch vocal so I won't get lost. Scratch tracks are also handy as guides for any other musicians you may bring into the project.

Setting Up Sample Rate and Bit Depth

The sample rate refers to how many times per second analog audio waves are measured in order to turn them into digital audio data. Although you can make changes to the sample rate after the fact, the process of sample rate conversion is extremely processor intensive, and not all software is truly up to the task. Unless you have a very good reason to record at a higher sample rate—you'll be transferring tracks to a modular digital recorder, for instance—set your software and interface to record at 44.1kHz per second, the CD standard.

Bit depth refers to the length of the "digital word" used to describe each snippet of audio. While the sample rate determines the maximum frequency that can be recorded—44.1kHz can reproduce tones up to 20,000 cycles per second, the upper limit of human hearing—bit depth has to do with the dynamic range of the recording. Sixteen bits yields a signal-to-noise ratio of 96 dB, a pretty impressive number.

Even though the CD standard calls for 16-bit recording, most interfaces now support 24 bits or higher. Recording at 24 bits has a number of clear advantages, chief among them the ability to better capture dynamic material, such as the jangly sound of an acoustic guitar. The files will take up quite a bit more space than they would at 16 bits, though. Changing bit rates after the fact is not a huge deal, so I'd suggest setting your software at 24 bits.

Setting Up Your Tracks

Professional studios meticulously document every inch of the session. More to the point, professional studios have interns write out track sheets listing what's recorded on each track, along with information about mics, panning, timing, and anything else that may come in handy in later sessions. Lucky for you, your software handles all of that for you.

First, be sure you name each track. For instance, for our basic song, I'd label the two guitar tracks "guit mic" and "guit D/I" and the voice track "vox." You can call them anything you want, of course.

If you don't name your tracks, each audio file you create while recording your song will have the same name except for a number appended to the file name. (See Figure 7.14.) The problem will compound with each new song. Maybe you can tell the difference between "WAVfile 23" and "WAVfile 32," but I sure can't. That's why I give each track a unique name and make sure all of the audio files are safely stored inside the proper project folder.

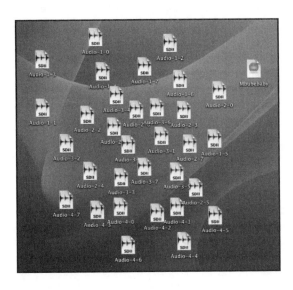

Figure 7.14
Don't let this happen to you! Give your tracks clear, distinctive names before you record.

The next task is to select the input and output source for each track (Figure 7.15). The input source is where your microphone and DI are connected; the output refers to the outputs on your interface. In most cases, this will be called either the Main or Monitor outs, or simply outs 1 and 2.

Make sure the track is play enabled. If you want, pan the guitar tracks hard left and hard right and leave the vocal straight up. Otherwise we'll deal with the pan later.

If you haven't already, save your work. In fact, get in the habit of saving every time you change *anything*, no matter how minor. My rule of thumb is never to go longer than five minutes without pressing Save. You do not want to see a couple hours' work evaporate with a system crash.

Figure 7.15

Set input and output assignments for each track.

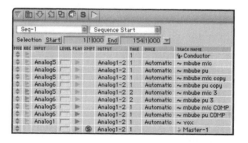

STEREO TRACKS VERSUS DUAL MONO

Although most software supports recording and playing back stereo tracks, sometimes it's better to record a stereo-miked instrument to two mono tracks. Here's why: Dual mono tracks can be manipulated independently of each other. So it's easy to boost one side or the other or selectively change the tone to make up for deficiencies in microphone placement. Also, you may find the mix sounds better if you alter the pan of the guitar. Stereo tracks are usually panned hard left and right. With two mono tracks, you can make the guitar as wide or narrow as you need.

If you'll be recording a number of songs with the same basic track layout, save your project as a template that you can reuse. If your software doesn't support templates, just save it under a different name: "Basic GTR/VOICE," for instance. Next time you want to use the "template," open it up and save it under the new name.

Okay, time to dim the lights, turn off the phone, and record something.

First Pass: Recording the Guitar Track

If you are using a condenser microphone, make sure you've turned on phantom power. Pick up your axe and get in position in front of the mics. While you play, adjust the input gain on your preamp or interface so the peak-level light starts to flash on the loudest notes, then back it down a hair. If you have to move away from the mic to make the adjustments, be sure you set up exactly the same way each time.

Now's the time to record-enable the guitar tracks. Some programs call this "arming" the tracks. Check your input meters (see Figure 7.16) to see how much signal is reaching the software. Adjust the channel output gain (if it has one) on the interface, or fine-tune the input gain so that the peaks hit somewhere around –4 to –10 dB. Be very careful to keep from clipping: If anything on the software meters lights up red, back off until you're safe. Since we're recording at 24 bits, we can get away with recording a quieter signal.

Some software and hardware combinations have a feature called input monitoring, which allows you to hear what's coming into the recorder. Input monitoring has much lower latency than monitoring after the sound has passed through the software. Check that you can hear your guitar in your headphones, and adjust the headphone level up or down as needed.

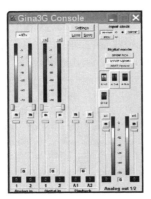

Figure 7.16
Input meters give you the information you need to record a hot signal without clipping.

❄ WHY CAN'T I HEAR THE GUITAR?

Don't panic if you can't hear your guitar; the problem is usually something simple. Work backwards to isolate the problem.

If you don't see anything on the software's input meters, check to see that you've set the input correctly and record-enabled the track. Check the connections between your guitar and the audio interface and between the interface and the computer. Make sure you've turned on phantom power if you are using a condenser mic. Don't forget to check the battery in your DI or internal preamp.

If you see signal present LEDs or clip lights, you know the signal is reaching the interface. In that case, the problem lies between the computer and your headphones. Check that the output is set correctly. Make sure the track isn't muted and that no other track is soloed. Be sure you've turned up the master and headphones volume on your interface.

And you did plug in the headphones, didn't you?

Set the click track to give you two measures of count-off, punch record, and you're good to go. Make a mistake? No worries. Just go back to the beginning and try again. Depending on your software, each new recording pass may overwrite the previous one, or it may be saved as a new virtual track. Virtual tracks are useful because you can record numerous takes and then go back and choose the best one.

Be sure to stay absolutely still for several moments after you finish recording a take while the guitar fades away. I can't tell you how many perfectly good takes have been ruined when the guitarist abruptly shifts in her chair, or sniffs, or even slaps a hand over the strings immediately after playing the final chord.

Here's a handy tip: I usually set up three sets of tracks with identical input and output assignments for my guitar. Then I record three quick passes, muting each as soon as it's done. This way I can quickly listen to and compare all three takes without taking the time to assign a virtual track.

> ❋ **TRACKS VERSUS TAKES**
>
> Keep in mind that a track refers to a linear chunk of recorded audio that is assigned to a mixer channel. The term comes from analog recorders, where the record and playback heads were divided into a number of smaller pieces, each of which left a "track" of magnetized particles on the tape. Even though digitized audio is stored in a different way on a hard disc, the concept is still used.
>
> A "take" is what you call the process of recording. It's also the name for a particular recording pass, so you can have multiple takes for each track of audio. With tape, each new take replaced anything already recorded. Random-access digital audio eliminated that requirement, so you can keep as many takes as you have room for in memory. Depending on your software, these may be called virtual tracks, takes, or something similar. Some software holds all of your takes in RAM until you decide to assign one to a track.

After you have laid down one or more good takes, spend a few moments listening to each one. Pay particular attention to your timing and intonation. It's pretty hard to fix these problems later on, so get them right now. Also, check to make sure your levels never exceeded digital zero. Clipping—what happens when the audio is so loud the waveform is cut off—creates ugly distortion that can damage your speakers. And don't neglect to check the takes for "feel."

Once you're satisfied with your guitar part, it's time to add the lead vocal.

Second Pass: Recording the Vocal

Get ready to record your vocal track just as you did for the guitar.

1. Set up the microphone and make all the proper connections. Use a pop filter if necessary.

2. Turn on your preamp and phantom power, if needed.

3. Set the input gain on preamp or audio interface.

4. If you haven't already done so, create and name a track for the vocal.

5. Assign the input and output on the vocal track to match your setup.

6. Check input levels and adjust so the peaks fall between −6 and −12 dB. If you'll be singing louder as the song progresses, back down the settings to give yourself more headroom.

7. Arm the vocal track so you're ready to record.

8. Make sure the guitar tracks are play enabled so you can hear them in your headphones.

9. Turn off the phone, dim the lights, and do whatever you need to do to set the mood.

Before you start recording, take a few minutes to get a good headphone mix. You may notice that your voice sounds delayed coming back to you. This latency is the result of the time it takes the software to process audio. Latency varies from slightly annoying to unbelievably annoying. Fortunately, many audio interfaces support very-low-latency monitoring. If you can't deal with the latency, try this: Turn off playback on the vocal channel. Set your headphones so they cover only one ear, with the other cup sitting flush against the side of your head so the sound won't leak into your mic.

Many singers like to hear their vocals with some reverb or other effects. Be sure you add the effects to the output side, as illustrated in Figure 7.17. Don't be tempted to record your vocals "wet"; there's no way to make changes to the reverb once it's recorded. Also, punching in and editing tracks laden with reverb is a dodgy proposition.

Figure 7.17
I've inserted a reverb into the master channel so I'll hear effects on the play-back while recording "dry."

There's no reason to roll all the way back to the beginning of the song each time to record your vocals. Set a marker a couple of measures before each verse and chorus. Use these to pinpoint your location. Not only will this save time when you're recording, but it also keeps unwanted noise from getting into the tracks in the spaces between the vocal sections.

Markers are also handy for automating recording tasks. Set the software to begin recording just before and to stop just after the verse, and you can concentrate totally on nailing the vocal. Even better, by carefully setting up automated punch-in and punch-out points, you can replace a single line, or even a word, in a previously recorded track.

Few arts are as personal as singing. Great vocal recordings are the result of a combination of many factors—a first-class mic, a great-sounding preamp, meticulous attention to detail, careful use of dynamics, tone shaping and effects—but nothing is as important as the performance. Simply put, the world's best engineer equipped with the world's best technical tools can't do a thing if the singer ain't cuttin' it.

So what makes a good vocal performance? Attitude, more than anything. Vocal chops help. Intonation helps—though software like Antares AutoTune has practically eliminated the problem of singing out of tune.

But, like the old song says, "It's the singer, not the song." The way you tell the story is more important than how well you sing. It doesn't matter if you have a great voice or a frog-toned three-note yawp; what's important is that you put the song across to your listeners.

So how do you get to that special place? Some things to consider:

* Sing when you are comfortable. If you need to record the vocal at 4:00 AM, do it.

* Have lots of water around and keep your voice hydrated. Some singers use spray bottles; some like lemon juice. Beer will make your voice raspy in no time at all. Of course, maybe that's what you are looking for.

* Be yourself. All those famous singers are famous because they don't sound like anyone else. You are unique, too.

* Automate the recording process so you can concentrate on singing.

* Learn to listen critically and know when to do another take.

* Don't push yourself. If you're tired, it'll show in your voice.

* Never record when you have a cold. It sounds obvious, but you wouldn't believe what I've heard people try to get away with in the studio.

* Make the effort to set up your space so you're comfortable. Invest in some mood lighting, put up an inspiring picture. Move the microphones to another room. Close your eyes. Do whatever it takes.

Now that you've recorded a vocal, we'll move on to mixing our song. But first, I want to talk a little bit about editing.

Editing Basics

Back in the Dark Ages, recording engineers edited songs by slicing the recording tape with a razor blade and splicing it back together. As you can imagine, it was tedious in the extreme. Thanks to the miracle of digital audio, editing on your computer is as quick and easy as cutting and pasting text in a word processor. The best news is that most editing is nondestructive, which means it leaves your original audio tracks untouched.

But why would you want to edit? For a lot of reasons:

- ❊ To remove unwanted noise before the song's downbeat and after the fade-out.

- ❊ To change the order of your song's parts. Think the second bridge doesn't really belong? Cut it out. Need to repeat the chorus? Copy and paste as needed.

- ❊ To fix problems within a track. Say you find you flubbed a chord one measure into the first verse, but you played it perfectly the next time. It's a simple matter to replace the flubbed chord with a copy of the good one.

- ❊ To speed up the recording process. Why record an identical chorus six times? Track it once and use clones for the others.

- ❊ Comping tracks. Assemble the best parts of multiple takes into a single composite track.

- ❊ Cloning tracks. Make a copy of an entire track. Pan and process the clone differently from the original using equalization, dynamics, or other effects. Handy for creating quick-and-dirty vocal doubling or thickening instrumental parts.

Editing takes two basic forms. Nondestructive editing does not change the source file. Destructive editing, as its name implies, does. Most of the basic editing operations, such as copy and paste, move, trim, replace, etc., are nondestructive. You can perform nondestructive edits on a single track, a group of tracks, a region, or the entire song. It's a tremendously powerful tool, allowing you to quickly reshape your project with just a few mouse clicks. We'll talk a lot more about editing in the next chapter.

Destructive edits usually involve some kind of basic change, such as changing the sample rate of a sound file. For that reason, it's always best to work with a copy of the original file. As processor speeds increase, many operations that used to require changing the original file, such as time expansion/contraction and pitch shifting, are now safely handled nondestructively.

❊ WHAT'S A CROSS-FADE?

Splice two bits of audio together, and the matchup is rarely perfect. Sometimes you'll hear a pop or click right at the slice, or perhaps the transition just sounds abrupt. A cross-fade simultaneously raises the volume of one side of the edit while lowering the volume of the other, as illustrated in Figure 7.18. Used well, cross-fades smooth the transitions between edits. Short-duration cross-fades are handy for eliminating clicks and pops; longer-duration fades create the impression of one sound blending into another.

Editing is so much a part of digital audio that it is difficult to separate it from recording and mixing. Depending on how you work, you may find yourself editing as you record. Many classical musicians record one or two complete passes of a piece along with numerous "patches" consisting of a few difficult passages with the intent of editing together a complete track.

Figure 7.18
Cross-fades ease the transition between edits.

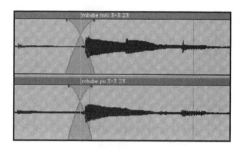

For others, editing is part of mixing. As you fine-tune your song, you may discover bits and pieces that need to be replaced or tracks that could be cloned.

Or you could mix your song and bounce it down to stereo and then go back and edit it to the final form.

Speaking of mixing, let's get on with it.

Mixing Down to Stereo

Mixing takes numerous individual audio tracks, polishes them to a fine sheen, and blends them into a finished song. There's a lot more to mixing than simply setting the levels. In this section I'll cover the basics of monitoring, setting pan and EQ, and using effects, and I'll show you some tips for making your mixes stand out from the crowd.

Monitoring Basics

Up until now, we've relied on headphones for all of our recording and spot listening. Now's the time to fire up your monitor speakers, settle down in the "sweet spot," and get down to the serious fun of mixing. If you followed the directions for setting up your monitor speakers in Chapter 2, they will focus at a point that is the same distance from each speaker as the speakers are from each other. This way, you are hearing the playback directly from the speakers, with minimal coloration from the room.

Adjust the left and right balance on your amp or power speakers so a track panned straight up appears to come from a point exactly between the two speakers. While you're at it, check to see that you've got the left and right speakers properly wired; otherwise your mixes may sound funny on someone else's speakers.

It's best to monitor at a medium volume. If it's too loud, your ears will get tired very quickly; if it's too soft, you won't be able to hear all the low-frequency tones. I like to keep a set of 'phones handy to spot-check problem areas that sometimes get masked by fan noises and other distractions in the room. While you can mix entirely on headphones, it takes a lot of practice to know how your mix will translate. If you choose to go this route, make sure you burn CDs with test mixes at various stages of the process and listen to them on a variety of speakers and systems.

The Software Mixer

Open up the mixer window in your software. Each track will have a pan control to set its left/right balance and a fader to control the relative level. Mute any extra tracks you don't need.

> ❄ **MUTING AND SOLOING**
>
> Why would you mute tracks when you could simply leave the fader down? Lots of reasons. If you need a track to appear suddenly, say a vocal line that shows up just for the chorus, set the pan and levels but keep the track muted. When you need it, you can unmute that track with just a mouse click. Muting a track also ensures you don't accidentally leave the fader open enough for the track to leak into the mix. Like everything else, mutes are easily automated.
>
> The solo button mutes everything but the selected track. The feature allows you to quickly check a single track or group of tracks without the distraction of all the other tracks. You can set the solo function to listen to the track pre-fader, handy for setting levels when recording, or post-fader (sometimes called "After Fader Listen" or "Solo in Place") to spot-check EQ settings and panning.

When you change the pan and fader positions, you are actually writing MIDI controller data. Your recording program can record and play back this information in real time. Mix automation like this used to be the domain of the select few; now anybody with basic software can take advantage of this powerful tool.

Thanks to automation, you can use your mouse to handle one track at a time. Automation data can be edited just like anything else on a computer. For instance, create a fade-out for one of the two guitar tracks, and then paste it to the other. A real timesaver!

Before we commit to our fader moves, let's work on equalizing the tracks and add some basic effects. For right now, set the pan of the two guitar tracks more or less halfway left and right, and keep the vocal straight up.

EQ Basics

EQ is short for equalization. EQ works like the tone controls on a boom box; you can tweak certain frequencies to emphasize the bass or treble. Recording EQ is far more precise, enabling pinpoint control of multiple parts of the audio spectrum. If you recall, the human ear hears sounds ranging from 20Hz (cycles per second) all the way up to 20,000Hz (or 20kHz). Sounds at the low end are heard as bass tones; higher notes vibrate faster and faster until they disappear into the range only dogs hear.

The most practical type of EQ for recording is called parametric EQ. Parametric EQ allows precise adjustments over very small segments of the frequency spectrum, letting you simultaneously boost the bass strings on your guitar while you cut out the sound of your nails hitting the strings. EQ can make the difference between a muddy, unfocused track and one that jumps out of the mix.

Typically parametrics consist of three, four, or six bands, each acting on a desired frequency range. (See Figure 7.19.) The highest and lowest bands are often set as band pass filters, which allow tones only above or below a set frequency to be heard. Each band has controls to determine the center frequency, as well as the "Q," or width of the spectrum affected. For instance, a band set at 440Hz with a three-octave Q will affect everything from around 220 to 880Hz, with most of the boost or cut noticeable at 440. The same band with a 1/12-octave Q and an infinite cut will simply remove the A note above middle C from the mix!

Figure 7.19

Four-band parametric EQ. Note the different curves for the high, mid, and low bands.

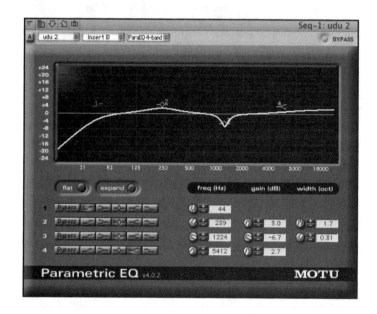

Although every instrument is different, a typical setting for an acoustic guitar would be to boost about +2 dB around 250Hz to bring out the bass strings with a 1.5 to 2 dB cut at 2.0kHz to attenuate the mid-range. Some guitars do well with a slight boost above 4.5kHz. I usually set one band of the EQ to block anything below 75Hz. This helps tighten up the sound.

For the DI track, the trick is to eliminate the overall upper-mid-range honk. Cutting between 1.5 and 3kHz usually does the trick.

Vocals have their own set of particulars. But you can almost always bring a vocal into sharper focus with a slight boost around 4.5kHz. Boosting above 12kHz adds "air," while cutting around 1.5kHz can help tame nasal tones in a vocal a bit.

Here are some tips to help you get the most out of EQ:

* Solo your tracks to spotlight problems and make broad EQ settings.

❈ Don't be seduced by how great your voice or instrument sounds by itself; everything will change when they are mixed together.

❈ Guitar and voice cover a lot of the same frequencies, so sometimes you have to alter the sound of the guitar to make the voice stand out.

❈ It's always better to cut than to boost. If it sounds like the high end needs to come out more, try cutting a little of the mid-range. If you do need to boost something, pay careful attention to the output meters so that you don't clip the signal.

❈ There is no point in boosting anything that's not there. For instance, trying to pump up the bass on a female singer will only amplify any noise on the track.

❈ Be careful where you place the EQ in relationship to other effects. If you are using compression, it's better to have the EQ module in line after the compressor.

❈ Pay attention to your overall levels when you EQ so you don't accidentally clip the signal.

❈ Know that something's wrong but can't find the offending frequency? Try this: Set one band to a very narrow Q and boost it as much as +10 dB. Play back the track while you sweep the band's frequency up and down. When the bad spot leaps out at you, you've found the correct frequency. Simply change the boost to a cut, and it's gone.

❈ Any time you make a change to a track, go back and check all the other tracks. Chances are the new EQ has affected another track. Tedious? Yep. But that's what makes a great mix.

❈ Be sure to check the EQ while listening at different volumes. EQing at low volumes will make you overemphasize the bass. Believe it or not, so will adjusting the EQ at high volumes. The only sure way to get it right is to listen at different volumes.

❈ Sometimes the best EQ is achieved via the pan knob. If two tracks are getting in each other's way, separate them. Panning the acoustic guitar slightly off to the left and the vocal off-center to the right may be just the ticket.

FX Basics: Reverb Is Your Friend

Reverb simulates the effect of sound bouncing around in space. Some of the earliest studio reverbs routed audio through springs or metal plates. Although the sound of the mechanical devices is anything but natural, spring reverbs are still desirable on guitar amps. And digital simulations of plate reverbs are still the first choice for vocals.

We'll get much deeper into effects in the following chapter. For now, we want to dial up some basic ambience to make our vocal and guitar tracks stand out.

Reverbs are typically assigned to an aux channel (sometimes called an effects bus or effects channel). Using the aux sends routes various amounts of each individual track to the effect. This saves processing power—reverbs are notorious processor hogs—as well as letting you place all of your tracks in the same acoustic "space." Here's how to do it. (See Figure 7.20.)

1. Create a new aux track.

2. If necessary, assign the aux's output to the stereo master out. In most cases, this will be analog outs 1 and 2.

3. If necessary, assign the aux's inputs to a bus. Busses are signal paths for audio. Depending on your software, the busses may be called "aux sends," "effects sends," or simply "busses."

4. Insert a reverb and choose a preset. We'll audition and tweak the presets in a moment. For now, choose a "large hall" setting. Since this track is devoted solely to the reverb, set the mix to "100% wet."

5. While listening to playback, raise the level of the aux send on the vocal channel. You should hear the voice start to sound like it is reverberating inside a huge concert hall. Now send a little bit of each guitar to the 'verb. Notice that the guitar is affected differently from the voice: As you add more reverb, the guitar starts to sound unfocused. The usual trick is to keep the guitar relatively dry compared with the vocal.

6. Try out various presets until you find one you like. And don't be afraid to tweak the parameters. Changing the pre-delay affects how soon the reverb effect "blooms" behind the source; diffusion alters the reverberation's "thickness," while hi-frequency damping makes the room sound "darker."

If you prefer, you may also insert reverb effects directly into each channel or even insert the 'verb across the main stereo outs. Each has its advantages and disadvantages—if you've read this far, you'll know that there is no single "right" way to record!

Experiment with other effects. Chorus is a well-loved effect on acoustic guitar. A quick delay thickens a vocal; longer delays create drama and tension. Flanging is a "whooshing" sound often heard on electric guitars and synths. The only way to know which one works for your song is to hear them, so have fun.

The Mix

By now, you should have your tracks sounding pretty darn good. You've removed excess noise from the beginnings and ends and fixed any clams (bad notes). You've checked your edits and adjusted cross-fades so the transitions are absolutely smooth. You've set your panning so the guitar and voice complement each other, adjusted and readjusted the EQ, and placed everything in a nice acoustic space.

So now all that's left is to take three individual tracks and bounce them down to a single 44.1kHz, 16-bit stereo audio file.

Figure 7.20
Mixer view with reverb inserted in an aux channel. The sends on the guitar and vocal tracks adjust the amount of signal feeding the reverb.

Again, each program handles these chores in a slightly different way. But here's a checklist of steps to help you get the best possible result.

1. Set the master fader to 0 dB (also known as *unity*).

2. Insert a stereo compressor into the master channel. (See Figure 7.21.) Grab a mastering preset or set a modest ratio, say 2.5:1, with a quick attack and release. Adjust the input as desired—the lower the threshold, the more compression. If you want the total AM effect, go ahead and squish it; otherwise just tame the peaks and keep the dynamic range intact. Set the output so the peaks fall between –1 and –2 dB. For a visual example of what compression can do, see Figure 7.22.

3. Mute any tracks you don't want in the mix.

4. Play back the song and write in mix automation for level changes for each track as needed. For example, you may want the guitar to be louder for the introduction and then duck down for the verses. Watch the output meters for clipping!

5. To create a fade-out at the end of the song, jump to a point just before where you want the fade to start, then play back the song and fade as desired, writing automation data to the

master fader. Avoid super-long, linear fades; as the volume dips below a certain threshold, any noise in the room will mask the audio, and all your listener will hear is a long space before the next song on the CD starts up.

6. Bounce the song down to stereo. Bouncing combines all of the tracks, along with the effects, EQ, and automation moves, as a new stereo audio file (or, in some cases, as two mono files labeled "left" and "right"). If it isn't turned on by default, set the software to *dither* the bounced file from 24 to 16 bits. Be sure the file is saved as a 44.1kHz stereo WAV or AIFF file.

7. Congratulations! You have just mixed your first song!

Figure 7. 21
MOTU's MasterWorks Mutiband Compressor is a powerful mastering tool that gives you precise control over three different frequency ranges.

✻ WHAT'S DITHERING?

Dithering is the process of adding a tiny amount of noise to the audio file when changing the bit depth. Why would you want to *add* noise? The short answer is to mask an even worse problem, called quantization noise, that occurs when digital converters try to figure out what to do with very quiet signals. When down-converting bit depths, it's always better to dither; otherwise the extra bits will simply be cut off in a process called "truncation," and you'll lose some of your hard-earned audio fidelity.

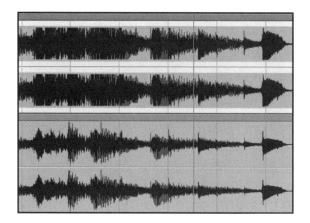

Figure 7.22
"Before" and "after" waveform displays showing the effects of compression. No prizes for guessing which is which.

Your new song is now ready to be burned onto a CD or converted to MP3 for distribution over the Web. Even if I'm going to distribute a song on MP3 or some other Internet-friendly format, I still save a high-fidelity copy to CD. While I'm at it, I also burn a CD with all of the raw tracks and program files and store it in a safe place. You never know when it could come in handy.

✳ TAKING YOUR PROJECT TO A PRO

As you have seen, it is not all that difficult to record a song, mix it down, and burn a CD on a very modest home studio. But there are times when you may consider taking the project to a professional for mixing and *mastering*—the final preparations for producing a finished CD. For one thing, pro studios will likely have far better collections of EQ, effects, and dynamics processors at their disposal. And there is no substitute for experience. If you want your CD to sound as good as a professional product, get a pro involved.

When you make your appointment, be sure to ask what kind of audio formats the studio can read. It is unlikely the studio will have the same software as you, so be prepared to give them your tracks as WAV or AIFF files. The easiest way to ensure compatibility is to bounce each of your tracks, complete with any edits and cross-fades, down to a single contiguous track. Always start the bounce from the absolute beginning of the song, even if you'll be bouncing nothing but silence until the music comes in. That way, all the studio has to do is line up the beginnings of all of the audio files and they will play back in sync.

In previous chapters we've looked at various ways to record and produce music: MIDI, loops, and digital audio. In reality, life is rarely so segmented. Most of us will use all three of these approaches at various times. In the next chapter I'll talk about getting the most out of your DAW—your digital audio workstation. Just like we did here, we'll take a song from start to finish. We'll dive deeper into effects, learn how to dial in the best EQ for drums, bass, electric guitar, keyboards, and voice, and fathom the mysteries of dynamics.

8 Track Four: All Together Now: The Desktop DAW

"Project studios" are defined as small home-based recording studios capable of professional-quality work. Although no two are the same, a project studio might combine computer-based MIDI sequencing, sampling and synthesis, sound design, and looping with a small live room for basic recording. Often the big recording tasks, such as recording drums and live bands, take place at larger professional studios. The tracks can then be brought back to the project studio for editing, arranging, and vocal recording. More and more, record producers use project studios for mixing or remixing before sending the song off to the mastering house and then on to the record label and the "Under-Assistant West Coast Promo Man" who makes you famous.

That's what we're talking about here. Congrats! You've made the big time!

All kidding aside, let's turn our attention to the gear you'll need to integrate the different kinds of music production we've discussed in the previous three chapters. I've already described some of the gear as they relate to those tasks, but here I'll be emphasizing how you build a system. Once we get wired up, I'll talk about how to set up your recording space. Then we'll put it all to good use when we discuss recording later in this chapter. Since I'll be building on concepts discussed earlier, I strongly suggest you read Chapter 7, "Track Three: Digital Recording for the Solo Musician" before you tackle this one.

In the real world, few projects go from start to finish in just one format or using just a single program. I've touched briefly on this in Chapter 6, "Track Two: Looping Tools," when I showed you how to add your own audio loops using a funky built-in mic and Abelton's Live software. In this chapter, I'll take you through a multitrack recording session using everything we've learned so far. I'll discuss what kind of hardware and software you'll need and how to get them to work together. And I'll talk about some of the studio "extras," such as hardware mixers, control surfaces, headphone amps, and outboard effects, that make your tasks much easier.

As with the other chapters in this book, the goal isn't to turn you into an instant power user. Instead, I want to give you a basic understanding of what's involved and a good grounding in the basic techniques so you can get the most out of your computer music experience.

Gear Up

As your skills improve and your understanding of music technology changes, you may find yourself thumbing through recording magazines and drooling at the gleaming racks of gear stacked alongside limo-sized consoles gleaming with more lights and dials than a 747. Well, now you get to indulge some of those fantasies.

Once you move beyond simple MIDI sequencing, looping, and basic recording, your gear needs start to grow. Here's some idea of the hardware and software you'll need to record and mix a multitrack song. Later on I'll discuss setting up your recording environment.

System Needs

I discussed computer needs for basic digital recording pretty thoroughly in the previous chapter. Basically, all the same stuff applies here as you move into more complex recording tasks, only more so.

The Computer

Creating a truly flexible computer DAW is not the budget-wrecking proposition it was once. Computers are so fast—and memory so cheap—that a smokin' machine capable of handling 48 tracks of uncompressed 24-bit, 96kHz audio plus a full complement of software instruments and high-end plug-in effects is well within your reach. That is, if your reach extends to the biggest, fastest, most tricked-out Windows or Mac computer you can buy. These days, that means spending anywhere from $1,000 to $3,500. Not bad, considering.

On the Windows side, start with a 2GHz or better Pentium or Athlon processor and as much memory as you can cram on board. One to two gigabytes of RAM is the bare minimum here. Dual core processors offer significant speed advantages, but not all current music software can fully take advantage of the technology.

On the Mac side, even the current flat-panel G5 iMac has plenty of muscle, but for serious audio wrangling get the desktop G5. Fast is good, faster is better. Again, load the puppy up with all the RAM you can squeeze in.

As I write this, any program running on Mac OS X can use both processors of a dual CPU Macintosh, and a number of Windows-based music programs take advantage of dual-processor Windows machines (providing you are running Windows XP Professional). This will change in a hurry as more and more of these machines hit the street. If you are in the market for a new machine, buying one with two processors won't hurt, and it will put you ahead of the game as the programmers catch up.

Although more expensive than desktop computers, high-end laptops make excellent remote recording rigs. If you want to use a PC laptop at home, consider picking up a dock—a hardware interface to connect peripherals such as an external monitor, keyboard, mouse, and hard drive. Saves unplugging a lot of cables when you need to grab the laptop and run to the gig. Many manufacturers, including Toshiba and Dell, make docks for their products, and third-party sources abound.

Monitors, Interface, and Peripherals

A pair of decent-sized video monitors—assuming your computer can handle two—will serve you far better than one mammoth screen. With two separate displays, you can use one to keep track of all the basic recording tasks, such as input and output metering, and leave the other free for detailed audio editing or synth-patch tweaking. Flat-panel monitors save a lot of real estate on your desk, and prices are steadily dropping.

Many people like the convenience of wireless QWERTY keyboards and mice. But for true convenience, you'll want a dedicated control surface, such as the Mackie Control. Don't know what a control surface is? Don't worry, I'll talk about it later in this chapter.

Be sure you've got multiple FireWire inputs for your audio interface and external hard drives, as well as a couple of USB 2 ports for MIDI, printing, and other tasks.

Hard Drives

We covered this in the previous chapter, but it bears repeating: As long as your track counts are low, you *may* get away with recording to your system drive. But as soon as you start moving tons of data around, you absolutely need at least one, and preferably two, external drives. Multimedia-friendly drives from LaCie, Maxtor, and EZQuest (to name but a few) make excellent choices. But many pros insist on a drive designed from the ground up for digital audio and video use, such as the Glyph GT 050.

How big a drive do you need? Depends on what you'll be doing. Huge drives can hold a lot of data, but they can take a long time to make backups or to reformat. Plus, if they fail, you can lose everything. I'd suggest getting several smaller drives, say 80 to 120GB each, and dedicating each one to a different project.

Hot-swappable drives—drives that plug in and out of a fixed chassis without the need to power down—are a great way to keep the creative flow going as you work on multiple projects. While I'm on the subject, portable flash or mini–hard drives such as Kanguru's 1 gigabyte Fire Flash or Seagate's ST1 Series of mini-USB drives are great for moving projects between studios or for temporary backups.

One more thing before we move into audio hardware: If you'll be doing serious audio work, such as recording, editing, and mixing a complete CD for your band, think about dedicating a computer to the task. Keep a second machine on hand for e-mail, games, and school and Internet stuff. Go through your files on the music computer and strip out anything you don't need to run your software—you can generally find lists of necessary drivers and resources, as well as known conflicts, in the manuals or on the manufacturer's Web site. Be particularly wary of programs that load at startup or run at predetermined times, such as automated updaters. Running a lean system means your computer can concentrate on helping you make music.

Software

We've already touched on most of the software you'll need in previous chapters, so I'll make this section brief. I'll discuss some of the high-end digital audio workstations and how they differ from their mid-level brethren, focusing on what features to expect and how you might make use of them.

DAW = Digital Audio Workstation

Serious audio professionals demand serious professional tools. That's why the heavy hitters such as Pro Tools TDM, Apple's Logic Pro, MOTU's Digital Performer, Nuendo from Steinberg, and Cakewalk's SONAR 4 Producer's Edition offer so many more features than more modest programs. That's not to say you can't do professional work with programs like Cakewalk's HomeStudio 9, Cubase SE, or any other product aimed squarely at the home studio market. The truth is, with a decent signal path and a bit of care, you can produce a great-sounding recording on an entry-level platform. So why do they make the more expensive stuff?

What sets these flagship products apart is their flexibility. Not only do they do some things well, they do *everything* well. Although different programs attract fanatically loyal followings, the truth is that they aren't all that different from each other in what they can do. A company may come out with a new feature in June; by the following December everyone will have some version of it. The main differences lie in the user interface. The best way to find the right DAW for you is to download demos and work with them for a while.

Even if you'll never need a full-featured studio suite such as Pro Tools|HD, learning about what these programs are capable of may help you decide where you want to go with your computer-music journey.

DAW FEATURES

Just to set the record straight, here's my working definition of a digital audio workstation. A DAW combines MIDI sequencing with multitrack digital audio recording, editing, and mixing. DAWs can synchronize with external gear, such as video editors or outboard digital recorders and analog recorders. They are flexible, powerful, and customizable. In short, a DAW is a recording studio that lives inside your computer.

Here's a rundown of some of the features you might expect to find in DAWs aimed at the project studio and professional market. I've mentioned some of these in a general way in Chapter 4, "Choosing Your Software: What Do You Want to Do?" Refer back to that list if you need a refresher. Remember, not every DAW has every one. Generally the "light," or less expensive, versions of the flagship software have fewer features, but they may be just what you need. And there is no sense paying for a bunch of features you won't use.

- ❄ **Multitrack audio recording.** The number of tracks is often limited only by your processor speed and/or RAM. Entry-level programs tend to limit the track counts.

- ❄ **Multitrack audio editing.** The ability to edit multiple audio tracks at once. Handy for instantly cutting out a verse that really didn't work out.

- ❄ **Waveform editing.** Digital audio editing at the single-sample level. Yes, there are times when you need this detail.

- ❄ **Sample accurate synchronization.** Refers to the ability to lock to an external digital recorder at the resolution of a single audio sample, say, 96kHz. Vital if you are going to be using the DAW for editing tracks that will then be dumped back to the digital recorder for mixing elsewhere.

- ❄ **Surround mixing.** Surround uses a number of speaker configurations, with or without sub-woofers, to simulate a 360-degree aural experience. Common formats include LCRS (left, center, right, surround), 5.1 (five speakers: left, right, center, and two rear speakers; the ".1" refers to a subwoofer), 6.1, 7.1, and many more. The more formats your software supports, the greater your flexibility. I'll talk more about surround mixing later in this chapter.

- ❄ **Hi-res MIDI sequencer.** The MIDI standard falls short when it comes to timing. High-end sequencers offer huge improvements in resolution so your grooves groove and the fader moves that are in your mixes sound natural.

- ❄ **Support for multiple multichannel interfaces.** There is nothing worse than running out of inputs or outputs.

- ❄ **Video scoring features.** Aside from the ability to synch to video, DAWs often include a small window to play QuickTime or Windows Media Player video within the program. Other video features might include streamers (visual markers to help place music and effects), markers, multiple time-code formats, or the ability to extract audio from video.

- ❄ **Mix and effects automation.** Mix automation means that you can record all of your fader moves, pan settings, and channel mutes and play them back in real time. Handy for mixing a large number of tracks. Effects automation adds the same functionality to software effects.

- ❄ **Flexible mixer routing.** Just like professional mixing consoles, the software mixers in DAWs have tons of routing options. Not only do you want numerous internal busses, sends, and insert points, but you may find that you need to bring signals in and out of outboard effects processors, recording devices, and samplers.

- ❄ **Control surfaces support.** Control surfaces (more on that later) come in all shapes and sizes. The more your software supports, the more you can customize your workspace.

❊ **Customizable views and windows.** No, I'm not talking about "skins" to dress up the look. Rather, you want the ability to customize how information is presented to you. For instance, you might want to see a large input meter when recording but not when editing.

❊ **Data import/export options.** Pro studios need to be ready for whatever comes in the door. Same goes for software. At the very least, DAWs will be able to read both AIFF and WAV audio files. SDII files are used by Digital Performer. The ability to read OMF (Open Media Framework, a.k.a. OMFI) files means your work can be transferred between audio and video editing applications.

❊ **Stability.** Believe me, you do not want your computer to crash in the middle of a huge 64-track, 6.1 mix at 2:30 AM the day before the producer's flying the tracks to a banker in Bangkok. Okay, maybe that's a bit of a stretch. But crashes still suck. And products that crash die out very quickly, because people who experience crashes tell their friends. That's why they build stability into the high-end DAWs.

❊ **Tech support.** All things being equal, the more expensive the product, the better the support. That's a good thing, because you will need it sooner or later.

ARE THEY WORTH THE PRICE?

Considering that you can pick up a very good product with MIDI and audio recording, plus third-party plug-in support, for under $500 that will let you take your song from concept to completion, why should you spend the big bucks for a full-bore DAW such as Logic Pro 7 or Nuendo? The answer depends entirely on what you want to do *now* and what you want to do down the line.

Examine your present and future needs carefully. Maybe you are just starting out as a professional musician, but you know in your heart that you won't quit until you've given it your best shot. Maybe you've been around and you have a good idea of how you might make and distribute an independent CD. Maybe you're a composer who wants to work with a lot of real and virtual instruments, and you demand absolute freedom in organizing your workflow.

For people like you, there is simply no choice but the professional choice. If you'll be recording and producing music intended for commercial release with national or worldwide distribution; if you'll be creating soundtracks, music beds, and scores for TV or film; if you plan on becoming creatively involved with a number of different bands and singers as a producer/engineer; if your work demands perfect timing and absolute sonic integrity; if you want to be sure your recordings meet or exceed the demands of CD, DVD, and whatever format comes down the pike; yes, you need the best software and hardware you can buy.

If you are curious but not sure you want to spend the extra money, consider a "light" version of the DAW software such as Cakewalk's Sonar 4 Studio Edition, Cubase SL, Logic Express, or the native versions of Pro Tools until such time as you find you need all the advanced features. Most companies offer an upgrade path when you are ready to move up. What's more, projects begun on one version of the software, say Pro Tools M Powered, are fully compatible with the professional-level programs. That means you can do much of your work at home and still take advantage of commercial recording studios for difficult recording tasks or mixing.

So how much do they cost? That's a hard question, actually. The software itself may only cost a few hundred bucks, though Logic Pro weighs in at just under a grand, and Nuendo has a street price of twice that. It's the rest of the package that can add up. For example, Digidesign's Pro Tools LE software bundled with the Digi 002 FireWire audio/MIDI interface/control surface tips the scales at just under $2,500. Likewise, MOTU's HD192 12 in/12 out hi-res audio interface coupled with Digital Performer 4.5 will set you back about $2,300. Pro Tools TDM systems start around $8,000. Don't forget to budget for pro-level plug-ins, software instruments, sample libraries, and more. And we haven't even started to talk about the rest of your hardware needs, such as microphones, channel strips, hardware mixers, monitors, and ... you get the picture.

If professional tools are your goal, it is not at all difficult to sink upwards of $6,000 to $10,000 into a home studio, and you can easily spend much more. Start saving.

Audio Editors

If you can accomplish every music-production task within a single DAW program, why would you need a dedicated program for audio editing? There are several good reasons, actually.

For one thing, not every DAW lets you edit at the waveform level. Believe it or not, there are times when it is necessary to go in and physically redraw the waveform, such as when a clocking error caused a few samples to be dropped. Dedicated audio editors, such as Sony's Sound Forge 8, Wavelab 5 from Steinberg, and Bias Peak 5, are handy for mastering your stereo files. These comprehensive programs include waveform editing, plug-in support, powerful file format conversion, and CD burning.

Audio editors are great when you need to make permanent changes to audio files, such as when you need to trim the silence before and after the finished mix or convert your mix to MP3 or some other delivery format. In most cases, they will work right alongside your DAW, so you can switch back and forth between the two programs as needed.

Hardware

I've already covered your basic hardware needs in the previous chapter. Here I'm going to talk about some of the gear you will use as you move into multitrack projects.

Multichannel Audio Interfaces

Although you can get by with a stereo or four-channel interface for many simple home recording tasks, when it comes to building a project studio, an eight-in/eight-out interface is the practical minimum. Even a simple live recording with two singer-guitarists can easily use all eight channels—two vocals, two stereo-miked guitars, and two DIs. As you'll learn later in this chapter, adding a drum set can push the channel count way up.

Not too long ago you had to have open PCI slots to use an interface with eight or more channels; thanks to the increased throughput of USB 2 and FireWire, you have many more choices. Bus-powered interfaces such as the MOTU Traveler (see Figure 8.1) make it possible for anyone with a laptop to do serious multichannel field recordings without electricity.

Figure 8.1

MOTU's Traveler FireWire interface's 20 input channels and 4 mic-pres put the remote in remote recording.

MULTICHANNEL AUDIO INTERFACE FEATURES

Here's a rundown of some of the features you'll find in a multichannel audio interface. Again, not every product will have all of the features mentioned, so make your choice based on your needs.

* **Mic-pres.** The more you have, the more mics you can set up without resorting to an external mixer or preamp. I'd consider four to be the practical minimum; eight is better.
* **Analog I/O.** Eight channels of line-level ins and outs is pretty much standard. Many interfaces use TRS jacks for +4 dBu levels to save real estate.
* **S/PDIF (Sony/Phillips Digital Interface) I/O.** For interfacing gear such as CD recorders and digital mixers. Maybe use RCA co-ax jacks or optical cables via TOSlink (Toshiba link).
* **Lightpipe I/O.** Lightpipe is a multichannel digital I/O developed by Alesis for its ADAT Modular Digital Recorders. Used by many manufacturers for multichannel I/O. Lightpipe I/O looks just like TOSlink, and some interfaces have a switch for choosing the format of the port. TASCAM uses a different format for its digital gear called TDIF (TASCAM Digital Interface). TDIF uses a 25-pin connector and shielded cable.
* **Onboard mixing.** Some interfaces double as stand-alone mixers.
* **Low-latency monitoring.** Allows you to monitor through the interface instead of passing the signal through the software. Cuts down on the time it takes the signal to return to your headphones.
* **Word clock I/O.** Word clock is a digital timing standard for synchronizing digital devices.
* **Multiple FireWire/USB ports.** Allows daisy-chaining of multiple interfaces, hard drives, and other gear.
* **Headphone/control-room out.** Eliminates the need for a separate mixer.

- ❋ **Hi-Z instrument input.** Eliminates the need for a direct box when recording electric guitars, basses, and other instruments.

- ❋ **Metering.** Lets you see what's happening on the input and output sides. Most interfaces make do with simple peak LEDs.

- ❋ **MIDI.** More and more interfaces include MIDI I/O. Handy for basic needs such as a single keyboard or control surface, though consider a dedicated multichannel MIDI interface if you have a complex MIDI rig.

- ❋ **Multiple bit depths and sample rates.** Most contemporary interfaces support 24-bit audio at 96kHz or higher.

- ❋ **Daisy-chaining.** Lets you add multiple interfaces for 16 channels, 24 channels, or more of simultaneous recording and playback. Not all interfaces with multiple ports can handle daisy-chaining, and it's not universally supported by your software, so do your homework before you buy.

INTERFACING WITH OUTBOARD RECORDERS

Many engineers like the stability and convenience of recording on hardware digital recorders such as the Alesis HD 24 or TASCAM MX2424. Likewise, legions of home recordists prefer desktop DAWs such as the Roland VS series and the Yamaha AW2816. But there are times when you need to get those tracks into you computer for editing or mixing.

That's where the Lightpipe and/or TDIF interfaces come in. (See Figure 8.2.) Both protocols can transfer up to eight channels of digital audio at a time. As long as you've got the synch worked out (see the next section, "Digital Clocking"), you can blithely move tracks back and forth between devices with nary a whimper.

Figure 8.2
The MOTU 2408mk3 combines eight channels of analog I/O with three banks of Lightpipe TDIF digital I/O and S/PDIF.

DIGITAL CLOCKING

So how does an ADC (Analog to Digital Converter) or DAC (I'll let you figure it out) keep track of the sampling frequency? Remember, even the lowly CD requires 44,100 samples per second—that takes a pretty accurate timing reference. Meet the digital clock. Every single digital device has a small bit of quartz crystal that vibrates at a set frequency when excited. All the device has to do is keep track of the vibrations and apply a little simple math. These digital clocks are all over the map in terms of stability, by the way. But as long as you keep to a single digital device, everything works fine.

However, problems arise when you try to interface two or more digital devices, as when you are transferring signals from your modular recorder or digital mixer to your audio interface or vice versa. If each device uses its own clock as the reference, you'll hear ugly clicks and pops in your audio. The solution is to make one device the master clock source and slave all the rest to it. (See Figure 8.3.) This is true whether you are using S/PDIF or TOSlink to transfer stereo tracks or Lightpipe or TDIF for multichannel transfer. The clock signal is passed along the cable, or you can use a separate path (usually called "word clock") to keep the clocking signal separate from the digital data. If your device supports it, word clock is usually the better choice. Word clock usually requires coaxial cables with BNC connectors, similar to the ones you use for connecting your TV to the cable box, though some gear uses RCA plugs. (BNC refers to a bayonet-type connector invented by Neill Concelman, if you must know.)

Figure 8.3

When interfacing two digital devices, select one as the master clocking source and the other as the slave. Here I've chosen S/PDIF as my clocking source to lock to a digital mixer.

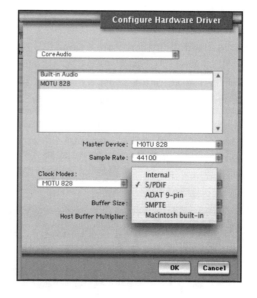

Unfortunately, there is no hard-and-fast rule to help you decide which device should be the master and which the slave. Sometimes it's easy, as with some older digital mixers that operate only as the master clock source. But more often it's a matter of trial and error. For instance, I know that in most cases I use my venerable FireWire audio interface as the master clocking source because it has a very robust clock, but I recently came across a situation where I was transferring a mix made on an inexpensive desktop recorder. The only way I could get a stable signal was to make the DAW the master and slave my interface to it.

Things start to get even messier when you add a third digital device into the mix. Simply daisy-chaining the devices together can introduce clocking errors, so it's preferable to use a distributed signal from a stable source. Pro studios, particularly those that do a lot of audio-to-video, use a dedicated device to send clocking signals to every piece of digital gear. Smaller studios on a budget may be able to get by with a simple T-connector to distribute the clocking signal, as in Figure 8.4.

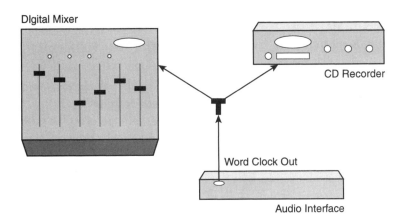

Figure 8.4

Synchronizing more than two digital devices can be tricky. Here I used a simple T-connector, available in most electronic supply stores, to send the word clock signal to a digital mixer and a CD recorder. The clock source on the interface is set to "master"; those on the slaves are set to "word clock."

※ What's Jitter?

Spend any time reading manufacturers' blurbs about their digital audio gear and you'll encounter some variation of the phrase, "Our product reduces jitter." So what are they talking about, and should you care?

Simply put, jitter is an audible distortion that creeps into digital audio when it's played back on a device with a less-than-stable clock source or has other timing imperfections along the signal path. Jitter is the bane of audio professionals because it's device dependent. In other words, you can produce a perfectly recorded CD that plays with nary a hint of jitter on your equipment, but listen to it at your buddy's house and it sounds like the music is covered with a thin layer of dust.

The good news is that you really don't have to be all that concerned. Even if your equipment's DACs induce a slight amount of jitter on playback, it won't be transmitted to the CDs you burn inside your computer. Nor will it show up on any cloned CDs.

Inexpensive internal audio cards are notoriously prone to jitter, by the way. That means you won't be able to really hear your music properly, which translates into a substandard mix—yet another reason to use the best-quality components you can afford.

Hardware Mixer

This one's a big head-scratcher for many people. If you've got a multichannel interface, why would you need a hardware mixer? The short answer is, it depends on your situation.

Interfacing outboard gear such as dynamics processors, microphone preamps, and effects units with your audio interface can be tricky since most don't have insert or aux sends and returns. (See Chapter 2, "Understanding the Gear," if you need a refresher.) With a mixer, it's a simple matter. Plug in a couple of wires and away you go. The same goes for those of us with a lot of keyboards, sound modules, and guitar effects. My eight-in/eight-out interface requires that I repatch every time I want to change instruments. It's easier to keep everything wired up permanently and simply send the ones I need to the computer via the mixer's sub outs.

I also prefer the convenience of setting the level going to tape, errr, disc, on my mixer instead of fumbling with the rotary pots (short for "potentiometer"—engineer-speak for gain knobs) on my audio interface, which is mounted in a rack some distance from my desk. Same goes for setting playback levels. If the phone rings while I'm editing audio, I can dim the playback in a fraction of the time it takes to navigate to the mixer screen.

Of course, I can accomplish a lot of that with a control surface, as you'll learn in the next section. But I just plain like having a hardware mixer around. And in spite of the glories of software mix automation, I truly prefer mixing the old-fashioned way when I can get away with it. Besides, there are times when I want to fool around with stuff without turning on the computer.

❄ Analog or Digital?

A digital mixer affords the hands-on control and convenience of a "real" mixer while keeping the signal entirely in the digital domain.

As long as you've got your clocking issues under control (see "Digital Clocking" in the previous section), integrating a digital mixer into your studio is fairly straightforward. Digital mixers, such as Yamaha's 02R96V2 or TASCAM's DM3200, offer a wealth of professional features in relatively small footprints. Be aware that this power comes at a significant price, and I'm not just talking about the moolah. Yes, digital mixers are quite a bit more expensive than their analog counterparts, but they more than make up for it in the sheer number of features they have, such as dedicated dynamics processing on every channel, flexible routing, and first-class digital effects.

The price I'm referring to is the learning curve. That's because digital mixers are essentially computers, with all of the complexity that implies. Scrolling through windows and trying to figure out which layer is currently active may not be your idea of a good time. Unlike an analog mixer, mixing on a digital desk is rarely a "grab and go" proposition.

The best way to know if a digital mixer is right for you is to use one. For some the feel is all wrong; for others, a digital mixer is the ticket to sonic nirvana.

Hardware mixers come in every size and configuration imaginable, from simple little deals, such as the Spirit Notepad, that fit in a backpack to rack-mount mixers for keyboards and other line-level sources, to multichannel mixers of every flavor and stripe. Many small-format mixers in the 8- to 16-channel range, such as the Mackie Onyx series, the Alesis MultiMix series, and the various Spirit mixers from Soundcraft, are designed to do double-duty onstage and in the studio.

Numerous hardware mixers from companies such as Behringer, Alesis, and Mackie now sport USB or FireWire ports, essentially eliminating the need for a dedicated audio interface altogether.

Powered mixers, such as those used for small coffeehouse PA systems, generally do not make good choices for recording. Thanks to the proximity of the power supply and amplifier, they tend to be fairly noisy. What's more, they generally have very limited bussing and output options.

Control Surfaces

As long as you are working with one or two tracks, you can get by with using you mouse or the data sliders on your keyboard for mixing. But wouldn't it be great if there were some way to grab a handful of faders and knobs and tweak them all at once? Well, Bunky, there is, and it's called a control surface.

How They Work

Control surfaces come in a variety of sizes, shapes, and configurations, but basically they all do the same thing. They let you use hardware faders, knobs, switches, and buttons to move corresponding faders, knobs, and buttons in your software. You'll notice that I am being very vague here. I didn't specify "in your DAW software"—that's because control surfaces are the ultimate chameleons. Most will work with any supported software. The same device that helps you automate a 24-channel mix can tweak the parameters on a software sampler or program an analog synth.

One common communication protocol for control surfaces is MIDI, yet another reason for insisting on MIDI I/O in your audio interface. FireWire and USB surfaces are increasingly solid choices.

Depending on your software and the control surface you choose, interfacing the two can be as simple as powering up and choosing your device from a menu.

Some, such as the Mackie Control Universal, Digidesign Command8, and TASCAM US-2400, are designed to emulate all of the features of a recording console, while others, such as the tiny CS-32 from JL Cooper or the Evolution UC33e, take a "less-is-more" approach. All enable you to get your hands inside the software, so to speak. There's even a dedicated controller for Apple's GarageBand software! (See Figure 8.5.)

And don't overlook the many keyboard controllers and all-in-one interfaces such as the Korg Kontrol 49, Novation X-Station, and M-Audio Pro-88 or Ozonic that sport a full complement of easily configured sliders and knobs.

Figure 8.5

M-Audio's iControl brings hands-on convenience to Apple's GarageBand software.

CONTROL SURFACE FEATURES

As I said, control surfaces vary widely in configuration and intended use. Here's a list of some of the features you may expect to find; remember that not every control surface is likely to have every single feature.

* **Motorized faders.** Motorized faders move in response to the on-screen moves of the faders in your software. Aside from looking really cool, they help you find your way when punching in mix automation.

* **Soft knobs.** Also known as "rotary encoders," these knobs take on whatever function they are assigned to. For instance, the same knob might be used to set a channel's pan one moment, then adjust the bandwidth of an EQ or select the waveform in a software synth's oscillator.

* **Virtual channel strip.** Mimics the look and feel of an analog mixer. Instead of a single soft knob to handle pan, aux sends, and other tasks, a virtual channel strip would have knobs and switches corresponding to those on your mixer. Handy for old guys like me who'd rather just grab something than scroll through a bunch of menus.

* **Scribble strips.** Displays the track name or other information you've entered into your software's virtual scribble strips. You do name your tracks, don't you?

* **Channel select.** Selects the channel that you'll be manipulating. It sounds obvious, but I guarantee you'll forget to do it sometime.

* **Channel mute/solo.** Mutes or solos the selected channel. Sometimes doubles as the channel select button.

* **Transport controls.** Tape-style rewind, play, record, and fast forward controls. Great for recording yourself at a distance from your computer.

- ✳ **Master section.** Controls for master level, aux sends, returns, control room level, and so on.

- ✳ **Channel banks.** Most controllers save real estate and cost by having a single bank of eight channels. The bank-select parameter allows you to access a group of channels, such as 9–16 and 17–24.

- ✳ **Jog/shuttle wheel.** A honking big knob handy for scrolling through edits, selecting a section of audio for editing, and other tasks.

- ✳ **Templates.** Allows the device to be quickly reconfigured for different applications.

ALL-IN-ONE INTERFACES

If you like the convenience of a hardware control surface and don't need a separate hardware mixer, consider a control surface with an audio interface built in. This might be the hottest new category of home-recording gear; new choices keep popping up almost daily. They range from very simple USB units such as the TASCAM US-428 and Edirol UR-80 all the way up to the TASCAM FW-1884 FireWire interface with 18 channels of up to 48kHz I/O (14 channels at 96kHz), eight mic-pres, S/PDIF and Lightpipe digital I/O, MIDI I/O X 4, and eight motorized faders. (See Figure 8.6.) If Pro Tools is your bag, check out the Digi 002.

Is this a great time to build a home studio, or what?

Figure 8.6
TASCAM's FW-1884 combines all of the features of a dedicated DAW control surface with a high-resolution audio and MIDI interface.

Gear, Gear, and More Gear

Wait, don't put away your checkbook yet! Here's a healthy list of some of the gear you may want to pick up as you make the jump into the wonderful world of project studios and integrated DAWs. Don't forget that this is in addition to your instruments, synth and sampler modules, DIs, software, hard drives, and all the rest that I've discussed in earlier chapters. I told you it could get expensive!

No, I don't expect you to run out and buy everything on the list. In fact, you'll only need what you need. Rather, my intention is to give you an overview of what's out there so you can make intelligent decisions about where you want to go with your computers and music adventure.

- **Microphones for each need.** Great studios are known for their mic collections. To get yours started, pick up a large-diaphragm multipattern condenser for vocals, a pair of small-diaphragm condensers for acoustic guitar and drum overheads, and a dynamic mic for kick drum, guitar amps, and other high-SPL instruments.

- **Hardware mic-pres.** Microphone preamplifiers are among the most critical component of the recording chain. The world's best voice through the world's best microphone will sound like it's in a cardboard box with a lousy mic-pre. They are so important that professional engineers take their favorite gear with them wherever they go. And yes, a great mic-pre can make a cheap microphone sound better.

- **Channel strip.** A channel strip combines a microphone preamplifier with tone-shaping tools such as EQ and/or dynamics. This gives you much greater control over the sound before it gets to the computer. Some include a tube stage to "warm up" the sound; others boast "straight wire with gain" transparency. In many cases, the microphone preamplifiers found in rack-mounted channel strips far surpass those in all but the very best audio interfaces. Channel strips often double as DIs, so you can take advantage of their superior performance and tone-shaping qualities for your acoustic-electric guitar or bass.

- **Headphones for everyone.** If you'll be recording the whole band, they all need to hear. Inexpensive cans (the studio term for 'phones) are fine, but be sure to choose closed-ear designs to prevent to sound from leaking into the mic.

- **Headphone amp.** Provides amplification and individual level control for each set of cans. You feed it a signal via the aux sends.

- **Rack FX.** Although plug-in effects are getting better all the time, many people prefer the sound of hardware reverb, delays, and dynamics processors.

- **Patch bay.** One of the most important, and most often overlooked, studio tools you can buy, a patch bay lets you keep everything in your studio permanently connected and instantly accessible.

- **Another set of monitors.** Pros know that a mix needs to sound good on a variety of speakers. Some monitors, such as the Alesis ProLinear 820DSP, use digital signal processing to mimic the characteristics of different monitor configurations.

- **Surround speaker system.** It goes without saying that you'll need a full complement of speakers and amps for surround mixing. Check out the Alesis Proactive 5.1 for an all-in-one solution. M-Audio's inexpensive LX4, which ships with a powered sub and two active near fields, offers an easy upgrade path when you are ready to make the jump.

- **Mic stands of all sizes.** Vocal mics can be heavy, so invest in a heavy-duty stand and boom. Short stands are handy for kick drums and amp cabinets.

- ❋ **Dedicated converters.** Worried that the inexpensive ADCs on your sound card might not be doing a good job? Want to really hear your mix? Pick up a good set of converters, such as the M-Audio SuperDAC2496 or Apogee MiniDAC.

- ❋ **Power conditioner.** Essential. Power spikes and voltage irregularities can damage your gear. Buy a good one, such as the Furman PL-8 II or Monster Pro 2500, and plug everything into it. If you live in areas with frequent blackouts, consider an uninterrupted power supply for your computer.

- ❋ **Drum pads controller.** Handy for setting tap tempo, as well as quickly roughing out MIDI drum parts.

- ❋ **Roll-around rack.** Handy if you've got a bunch of rack gear.

- ❋ **Studio furniture.** Nothing speeds your workflow like having a place to put everything.

- ❋ **A really good chair.** Do your back a favor.

As I said, this is just a sampling. Not every project studio will have every item, and many will have much more.

❋ **Don't Mourn, Organize!**

Take it from me, there's nothing that kills inspiration faster than tearing apart your room looking for some vital cable or connectors you've misplaced.

Organize your growing collection of mic cables, MIDI cables, guitar cords, and power chords, err, cords by hanging them on coat hooks or wooden knobs. Keep all of your program discs together in case you need to reinstall some software. I keep a notebook with all my serial numbers and software authorization codes, too. I keep all of my backup CDs in wooden CD crates, labeled by project and date. Manuals, sample CDs, and music for whatever I'm currently on gets moved to a standing file on my desk, in between the computer monitor and my equipment rack. That way I can find something quickly without leaving my chair. When I'm done with the project, everything goes back where it belongs.

One of the handiest items in my home studio is a large metal office cabinet with two big doors. It's where I keep my microphones, mic clips, extra connectors, soldering iron, DI boxes, software and gear manuals, miscellaneous hand percussion instruments, and all the rest that I've accumulated over the years.

Before I get into the nuts and bolts of recording and mixing, I'd like to revisit a topic I talked about in Chapter 7.

Setting Up Your Room

Your room isn't all that important as long as long as you are doing all of your music making inside your computer. And, as I discussed in Chapter 7, you can make some very slight modifications to a basic spare bedroom and record great-sounding acoustic guitar and vocal tracks.

When you start recording multiple instruments simultaneously or work with loud instruments such as drums and electric guitar, you'll need to take a hard look at your recording space. A full discussion of room acoustics and studio construction techniques is well beyond the scope of this book, so I'd suggest picking up a basic recording book such as *Home Recording Power!* by Ben Milstead (from Course PTR, of course) if you want to learn more. But I do want to let you know a little of what's involved, so you can decide if it's a path you want to pursue.

Soundproofing

Sound waves travel faster through solid materials, such as wood, than they do through air. That's why guitars and pianos are made out of wood. That's also why your neighbors won't appreciate your late-night recording sessions. That's also why it is almost impossible to eliminate traffic noise in your studio. The sound travels directly through the building's structure.

❄ Isolating the Computer

Desktop computers are notoriously noisy brutes. The CPU generates tons of heat as it goes about its business. I mentioned in Chapter 2 that the only way to keep the beast from overheating—and dying—is to move the heat away quickly with a combination of fans and heat sinks. The more powerful they get, the more active cooling they need.

Some brands and models are quieter than others, and computers designed specifically for recording can be very quiet indeed. If you're stuck with one of the noisy ones, and you're not comfortable with getting inside your machine to install a low-noise fan, there are only a couple of things you can do to keep the fans and other computer noise from getting into your mics.

In the previous chapter, I mentioned how you can take advantage of the dead spot in a cardioid-pattern mic to minimize the leakage. If your room is big enough, it may be enough to set the mics as far away from the computer as you can.

If your computer is sitting directly on a hard surface, such as your desk or a hardwood floor, the fan vibrations will be transmitted and amplified. Decoupling the computer—placing it on hard rubber legs or some other surface that won't transmit vibrations—greatly reduces the problem. You can tame some of the reflected sound by sticking a small sound-absorption panel on the wall directly behind the beast.

But the best solution is simply to remove the source of the problem entirely. You've got three choices: record in another room, move the computer to another room, or place the computer in a sound-proof isolation box. Let's look at them one by one.

Recording in another room is easy, as long as you have space to spare and some long mic cables. Of course, you'll also need some way to run the computer if you're recording yourself. Unless you can train the cat, a control surface—or a MIDI keyboard and a little time setting up shortcuts in your software—is essential.

Another option involves moving the computer and hard drives outside of your studio. Several companies, including Geffen and Belkin (see Appendix C, "Manufacturers") make extender cables for your monitors, keyboards, and mice. Simply place the hardware in a closet or some other location and run the cables through the wall back to your desk. The downside is that you'll need to leave the room every time you need to change a DVD or CD-ROM, but that's a small price to pay for peace and quiet.

For many one-room home studios, the best solution may be the isolation box. Don't be tempted to simply stick your computer in a box in order to save a few bucks. Without proper ventilation, heat builds up very quickly. Sound-isolation boxes for computers, including Middle Atlantic Products' Side Bay Racks series and the Isoraxx from Raxxess, feature superior double-wall construction, hinged glass or plexiglass front doors for easy access, sound-proofed cable routing, and powerful fans coupled with filters to trim the noise.

If you choose to build your own, be sure that you vent it properly to an outside room or window.

Pro studios are built in such a way that they are structurally separate from the outside world. In other words, they use double-walled construction with little or no direct contact between the studio walls and the building. Any holes and passages—for cables or air conditioning ducts—are carefully routed and insulated to avoid sound transmission. For the same reason, studios use two sets of doors placed back to back, with an airspace between them, and doubled windows.

Unless you are willing to spend some serious bucks, building a totally soundproofed studio in your home is probably not an option. Still, the situation comes down to two main problems—keeping outside noise out and keeping the music from leaking out and bothering your neighbors.

In Chapters 2 and 7, I gave you some advice on how to deal with these problems (see "Basic Room Issues" in Chapter 2 and "Taming Room Noise" in Chapter 7), so I'll only touch on the subject here.

One of the easiest ways to keep traffic noise and other sounds from leaking into your mics is to isolate the mic from the floor. Suspension mounts work great if you have one. Here's another tip: Set the whole stand on a small piece of foam to decouple the mic stand from the floor.

You can do the same thing for guitar amps and some hand drums. Big instruments, such as pianos and drums, are harder to deal with. The time-honored way of dealing with a drum kit in a one-room studio is to set up portable walls, called gobos (see Figure 8.7), around the kit to quell the racket and pad the windows and doors down with quilts and heavy blankets. (Stay tuned: I'll cover setting up and recording drums soon.)

Oh, I should also mention that recording studios usually have several "live" rooms for recording, a small vocal booth (sometimes used for drums), and a separate control room containing the mixers, effects, and monitors and where the engineer runs the session and all of the mixing takes place. Each room is tailored to its purpose.

So how much of your apartment are you willing to sacrifice to your muse, anyway?

Treating the Room
Taming unwanted echoes and reverberation is the second half of the equation. Studio designers go to great lengths to ensure that there are no reflective surfaces, down to building control rooms with no parallel walls and angling windows away from the perpendicular.

Figure 8.7

Gobos are wooden panels, often with one side covered with sound-absorbent material, used to isolate instruments in recording studios. Building one is well within the skills of most home wood-butchers.

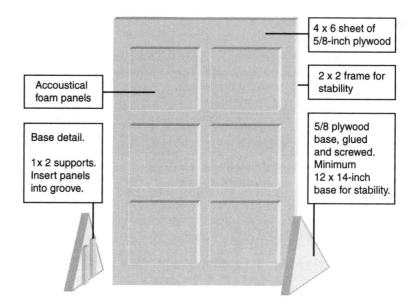

Accoustical foam panels

4 x 6 sheet of 5/8-inch plywood

2 x 2 frame for stability

Base detail.

1 x 2 supports. Insert panels into groove.

5/8 plywood base, glued and screwed. Minimum 12 x 14-inch base for stability.

While that may be out of your reach, room treatments such as the "studio in a box" Roominator series from Auralux will go a long way toward turning your spare bedroom into a real recording studio.

Okay, enough jabber. Let's make some noise.

The Recording Session

As promised, I'm going to talk you through recording and mixing a song using all of the tools you've read about so far. Although I'll mention MIDI and looping, I'll be concentrating on multitrack digital audio, as that's the one thing I haven't covered.

I'll mostly be using two programs: Reason 3 for the basic looped percussion parts and software synths, and MOTU's Digital Performer for everything else. Once again, you can use any combination of programs you wish; my intention is to give you an understanding of the process, not to teach you to use any specific tool.

Sounds Like ...

For your educational pleasure, I've chosen an original dance hit called "Do the Lizard." (Sample lyric: "Do the lizard, baby; do the lizard, unh!") I'll be using the Afro-Cuban groove I showed you in Chapter 6 (refer back to Figure 6.10) as the basis for the track. I'll bring in some ringers to overdub real drums, bass, and keyboard and then add my own rhythm and lead guitar and vocals. Finally I'll add some more bits in Reason to fill out the percussion and analog synth parts in the middle section.

> ### ❋ Have a Plan, Stan
>
> Great engineers know what the finished mix will sound like *before* they start tracking. You read that right: The mixing process starts before the first instrument is laid down.
>
> "But isn't recording a process of fooling around in the studio, trying out ideas and adding new stuff until you have a finished song?" While it's true that many people record that way, it often leads to self-indulgent recordings that have to be dissected bit by bit by a careful engineer to uncover the kernel of creativity. Save that process for songwriting. Once you have the puppy composed, plan out your recording sessions. If you know you'll be using live drums, record them first so everyone else will be able to play off of them. Lay down the harmonic structure—keyboards, bass, and rhythm guitar—at the same time if you want a "live" feel.
>
> Think about what instruments will ultimately appear in the song to avoid clashes. For instance, the low register of a grand piano, the bass strings of a big dreadnaught acoustic guitar, and a male baritone voice all occupy the same sonic "space." So I might record the piano to emphasize the upper strings slightly or use mono miking on the guitar so I can pan it out of the way of the vocalist when it comes time to mix.
>
> The same goes for vocals. Try to match the mic both to the vocalist and to what you want the finished mix to sound like. If it's a rocker, a honking dynamic mic such as the Shure SM58 may give you the fat sound you need, while the transparency of a high-end studio condenser would be totally wrong.

Preparing for the First Session

After I jammed along with my drum parts for a while to develop a chord structure for "Do the Lizard," I popped over to Band-in-a-Box to rough out the basic song. Even though the song is in a pretty simple form, I wanted to have a quick-and-dirty demo I could give my musicians, so I saved the song as an SMF (Standard MIDI File) and e-mailed it to each of them. Then I printed a lead sheet showing the chord changes for the bass and keyboard player and added some notes as to what kind of a feel I was looking for.

Then I opened my DAW, created a new song with all of the track assignments and markers that I'd need for the session, and saved it inside a folder on my second hard drive. I also created an alias ("shortcut" in Windows) on my desktop so I could find it easily.

Slaving Reason to Digital Performer via ReWire is a piece of cake. All I have to do is launch Digital Performer first and choose Reason from a list of ReWire devices in the track input pane (I named it "Reason Redrum" for clarity) and then launch Reason. When I hit play on the Digital Performer transport, the Redrum part plays along in perfect synch. Slick.

Each DAW and software instrument has its own unique procedure for implementing ReWire. Refer to your manual, or see *Reason 3 Power* by Michael Prager and Matt Piper (published by Course Technology).

Next I decide where I'll put everybody in my tiny room and check that I have enough mic stands, cables, music stands, headphones, and other gear, and that everything is in good working order. Since I'm a neat freak, I straighten up the clutter and run the vacuum, too.

The last thing I do before closing up the studio for the night prior to the big session is defrag my external drive. I want my machines to be in top form for the big day.

The *Riddim* Tracks

The day of the session dawns clear and bright. I've alerted my neighbors to expect more noise than usual for a few hours while I record the *riddim*—a reggae term for bass and drum tracks. (Of course, since I live way the hell out in the country, my neighbors couldn't care less, but it's always a good idea to be polite.)

Setting Up the Drums

Setting up and miking drums can be a time-consuming process, so I've asked the drummer to arrive at my studio about an hour before everyone else. As I'd requested, he brings a minimal kit—kick, snare, high hat, and a single ride cymbal. We'll be adding most of the percussion parts in Reason, so there's no need for more. I have him set up at the far end of my room where I know the drums will sound the best. Besides, it's the only place there's room. Since the keyboardist will lay down her part to MIDI and I'm using a DI for the bass, I'm not concerned about the drums leaking into the other tracks.

Rather than close-miking each individual drum and high hat cymbal and throwing up a stereo pair of overheads for the cymbals, as is common in recording pop music, I'm going to use a more minimal miking technique. While Tom's checking his tuning, I stick an SM 57 dynamic mic on a short stand in front of the kick drum. Like a lot of drummers, Tom favors the sound of a drum without a front head, so I can aim the mic directly at the point where the pedal hits the rear head. Using a stereo bar (a.k.a. a "spreader"), I attach two small-diaphragm condenser mics to a single tall boom stand and position them about 24 inches above the drummer's head and angled slightly towards the center of the kit. (See Figure 8.8.)

I set up a basic headphone mix and have Tom play along with the Redrum part while I fine-tune the microphone positions and set levels. I've noticed an annoying rattle from some loose hardware, so we spend a few minutes tightening and adjusting until it goes away. I also ask him to mute a ringing tone on his snare, which he does by sticking a panty liner to the drumhead. Quicker than masking tape, and much more effective. You learn something new every day! Just about then Uji and Newt walk in.

Bass and Keys

The time-honored way to record electric bass is straight into the board via a DI, so who am I to mess with tradition? It takes about a minute to have the bass dialed in. I decide to forgo compression at this stage, since I'm recording at 24-bits. (The higher bit depth translates to increased

Figure 8.8
Although there are many ways to mic a drum set, a basic three-mic setup is a great way to get a "live" sound. Place a dynamic in front of the kick and a pair of condensers above the drummer's head and angled in slightly. Adjust as needed for balance, and don't forget to check for phase cancellation. (See "Stereo Miking and Phase Cancellation" in the previous chapter if you need a refresher course.)

resolution at lower volume.) I can get away with backing off the input level a bit to leave Uji lots of room to groove.

Newt's got it easy. She's just going record a MIDI part, so all she needed to bring was a lightweight controller. I want to be able to choose different instrument sounds for the various sections of the song when I mix. We do need to hear what she's playing, though, so I set up a basic electric piano patch on one of my synth modules and route the audio output to the headphone amp via my mixer's aux sends.

Hearing Each Other

I've mentioned headphone mixes a couple of times now, so I guess I'd better tell you how to do it. Actually, since I have a hardware mixer, I have a couple of different options.

The easiest is to feed the headphone amp via two aux outs from the mixer. I can then adjust how much of each signal goes to the headphones before it reaches the computer via each channel's aux 1 and 2 send knobs. (See Chapter 2 if you need a refresher.) This is called "input monitoring," and it eliminates the latency problems caused when the signal has to pass into the audio interface, to the computer, through the software, and back out to the interface. (Of course, many interfaces now offer "low-latency monitoring," "zero-latency monitoring," or "direct hardware monitoring," which means that the input signal appears directly at the headphone out. In that case, you feed the headphone amp from the interface's headphone out and everybody hears the same mix.)

If you don't have an external mixer, you'll need to set up a couple of aux sends in your software, as I did in Figure 8.9. In this case, I'm feeding the headphone amp from outputs 7 and 8 on my interface.

Figure 8.9
I've set up a headphone mix by sending a portion of each track to outputs 7 and 8 using the aux sends in Digital Performer. When it comes time to mix, I'll reconfigure the sends to feed my effects. Flexible routing is one of the joys of using a DAW.

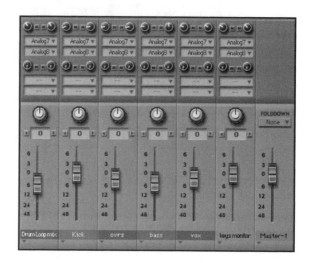

So why didn't I simply let everybody hear the same headphone mix that I'm using? Because I like to solo channels while I'm tracking, to check how things are sounding. If everybody heard the mix from the main headphone outs, they'd hear all the other channels drop out while I checked the bass level, then just the kick drum, and so on. As you can imagine, this wouldn't make a happy session.

Doin' It in the Red

Since everyone will be playing along with the drum loop in Reason, I can forget about setting up a click track.

After a few passes to get levels and fine-tune the headphone mix, the band announces that they are ready. Since I've prepared a *session sheet*—a page with track assignments and room to jot down notes about EQ, level, and take info—I'm ready, too. I place the software's position line two measures in front of the first verse, and away we go. Why didn't I start at the top of the song? Well, I only need the whole band for a couple of short sections that I'll be looping to flesh out the arrangement, so why waste time? Pros that they are, they nail it in three takes.

On listening to the playback, Uji hears a clam (a bad note) he'd like to fix. I grab a locate point a couple bars in front of the spot, place punch-in and punch-out markers on either side of the problem area, and hit record, and the software takes care of the rest while Uji plays along. The entire fix took just a few seconds.

We move on to the bridge and lay that down. While Tom takes a break, I ask Uji and Newt to see if they can come up with a better two-bar walk down from the bridge into the percussion section than the one I had in mind. After a couple of tries , they've got something, so we jump there and record it lickety-split.

At this point I'd planned on letting Newt go home, but she decides to hang around for the rest of the session. I promptly put her to work improvising a solo to fit over the intro section, so everybody takes it from the top. Just to be sure we don't record over anything we want to keep, I select new virtual tracks. The intro sounds so good I let them keep playing through the verse and bridge sections. Between this take and the original one, I've got what I need.

With the basic tracks done, I have enough material to construct the song. I get out the check book—you don't think I'd ask my friends to work for free, do you?— and everyone packs up. Elapsed time from load-in to load-out: a hair more than two and half hours. As I said, a little preparation pays big dividends.

❄ **Overdub Strategies: All for One Versus One at a Time**

There is a lot to be said for recording everybody at the same time. Nothing can match the push and pull of real musicians playing live. But there are some times when it's better to layer the tracks one at a time. In the example I just gave, there was no chance of leakage between any of the tracks. That meant I could easily go back and punch in the bass track. If I had recorded the bass part using a microphone in front of an amplifier in my small studio, any flubs would be clearly audible on the drum mics, so we'd have to record the whole thing again. (Punching in an entire drum kit can be problematic: cymbals ring, snares buzz, that sort of thing.)

How you choose to record your sessions depends on how well your musicians can play together live and how well you can isolate the various instruments.

ADDING ELECTRIC GUITAR

Next up: El Guit. No, this isn't Spanglish or a new superhero. El Guit is a common scribble strip shorthand for electric guitar.

Although the easiest way to record an electric is to go direct and use amp modeling and effects to tailor the sound, sometimes nothing else will do except the whump of a speaker pumping air. Time for another pro secret: Tiny amps sound huge in the studio. There's no need to set up your massive stage stack and blast out the neighbors. Believe it or not, oodles of classic snarlin' guitar leads were tracked using small, low-powered amplifiers with tiny speakers. Here's how to do it.

Set your amp in a large room or empty hallway so the sound has a chance to bloom. If the cabinet has multiple speakers, stick your ear next to each and find the one with the best tone. (Be very careful you don't hurt your ears; even a few seconds' exposure to extremely loud sounds can do irreparable damage.) Now place a dynamic mic—the Shure SM 57 is *the* standard—a few inches away from the edge of the speaker. Experiment with different placement until you get the tone you want. Place a second mic a couple of feet out in the room to capture the racket as it bounces off the walls. A large-diaphragm condenser such as the RØDE NT1 fits the bill nicely, though some engineers favor ribbon mics, while others opt for a stereo pair of condensers such as the AKG C451 B. (As you can see, choosing a microphone is seldom a cut-and-dried proposition.) Mix to taste.

Some engineers prefer to pack padding around the amp to eliminate the reflections and just go with the close-miked speaker. In this case, you might want to add some ambience from your effects plug-in to compensate for the lack of room sound.

Remember to check for phase if you're also using direct outs from the amplifier! Why? Because it takes the sound a short time to reach the microphone, even if it's only inches from the speaker. The tiny time difference between the miked and direct signals can seriously mess up your tone. The best way to fix it is to zoom down to the sample level and manually line up the tracks like I showed you in the previous chapter. Don't worry so much about the room mic. It's supposed to be delayed.

I recorded the rhythm guitar part using the miked-amp technique I just described. Just to make things interesting, I tracked the lead fills using a DI and used an amp-modeling plug-in. Rather than print (record) the effect, I placed it on the track's output for the same reason I recorded the MIDI stream from Newt's keyboard: I want to have the flexibility to change the sound later.

Obviously, it's time consuming to pick through myriad synth patches and choose suitable guitar tones when you are mixing. To be honest, it's not my preferred way of working, either. I'm a huge fan of throwing up some mics in front of a live band and capturing the moment, actually.

But I want to make the point to you that you have this option when you record. With a DAW, the lines between composition, recording, editing, and mixing are blurry to the extreme.

Vox ODs

I covered recording vocals pretty thoroughly in Chapter 7, so I won't go into details about microphones and techniques here. What I do want to do is talk about a couple of more advanced vocal recording techniques. Oh, in my continued effort to teach you recording engineer's slang, I had better define the section heading: "Vox" means "vocal" (actually, it's Latin for voice) and "ODs" (pronounced "oh-dees") are "overdubs," or recordings made after the original session.

Inserting Dynamics

The customary way to record vocals is to place a compressor, a form of dynamics processor, between the microphone preamp and the recorder's inputs. Dynamics processors change the relationship between the loudest and softest sounds. Since vocal parts often cover a huge dynamic range in the course of a typical song, they are prime candidates for compression. By keeping errant peaks from clipping and ruining your take, compression will make your life a lot easier.

There are several ways to do this. A few interfaces, such as the Edirol FA-66, have mic-pres and limiters built in. And many channel strips also include limiting. If you are using outboard mic-pres and either rack-mount hardware (inexpensive examples include the BlueTubeDP from Presonus, DMP3 from M-Audio, and tiny ART TubeMPSTV3) or a mixer such as the Mackie Onyx 1620, you may use the channel insert jacks to send the signal to and from an outboard compressor, such as the dbx 166XL or Art Pro VLA. (See Figure 8.10.)

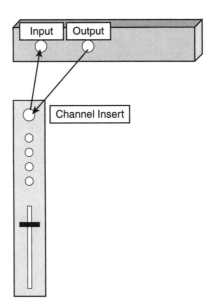

Figure 8.10
The insert jack on your mic-pre or mixer channel strip routes the signal to and from an outboard compressor. Insert cables have a ¼-inch TRS plug on one end of the Y and a pair of ¼-inch TS jacks on the other. Be sure to check the labeling on the cable: Insert the "send" plug into the "IN" jack on the compressor. The output from the compressor gets fed into the "receive" plug.

Sticking a compressor in front of the vocal in your software can be as simple as selecting the proper plug-in from a drop-down menu, or it may involve some routing gymnastics, depending on your DAW.

If your software doesn't make it easy, you can always use an auxiliary send/return channel setup. Keep in mind that not every application handles auxes the same way. Your software may use the name "bus," "send," "return," or some other name. Here's how to set it up:

Route the vocal mic to an aux track's input and insert the compressor. Set the recording track's input to accept the output from the aux. (See Figure 8.11.)

Set the compressor to a fairly small ratio, say 3:1 or less, with a moderate attack and release. (See Figure 8.12.) Adjust the threshold so only the loudest sounds are affected, and set the makeup gain so the peaks fall slightly below –2 dB. Many software compressors are stocked with presets to help you get up and running.

Figure 8.11
Input and output assignments for each mixer channel appear directly above the channel names in this mixer view from Digital Performer. I've inserted a compressor into an aux channel. The signal flows from the input ("TL Pre left") through the compressor, and then out via internal bus 3. The compressed signal is recorded on the vox track, which takes its input from bus 3.

Figure 8.12
Wave's Renaissance Compressor plug-in is a great choice for tracking vocals. Notice the relatively small compression ratio.

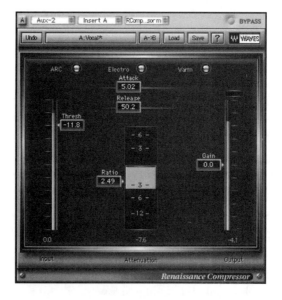

Vocal Doubling

One of the reasons that the vocals on professionally recorded songs sound huge is that they are huge. It's not at all uncommon for the vocalist to "double track," or record exactly the same part to different tracks. The minute fluctuations in pitch and timing create a subtle thickening of the sound. In fact, many pop vocalists are known for layering four, five, or more tracks!

If you don't want to take the time to overdub numerous identical tracks, you can fake a double-tracked vocal. Simply cloning the track won't cut it because it's the differences between doubled vocal tracks that make them work. Likewise, simply offsetting the cloned track, or using a slight delay, won't sound as convincing. Here's how to create a solid, realistic double-tracked vocal.

1. Make a copy of the vocal track you want to double.

2. Insert both a delay and a chorus effect into the cloned track.

3. Map a MIDI controller, such as a data slider or mod wheel, to the delay time parameter. Do the same for the delay time parameter on the chorus.

4. Now comes the fun part. While playing back the track, make very slight, random changes to the parameters. If your software supports it, record this automation data.

5. When it's time to mix, experiment with panning and levels between the real and "doubled" part until you find the balance you want.

This is a favorite producer's trick for guitars, by the way.

> ❋ **Fixing Pitch Problems**
>
> The easiest way to deal with vocal pitch problems is to re-record them. If your track is out of tune, go back and sing it over. However, sometimes a few errant notes slip by in the heat of the performance. A number of software and hardware solutions, including AutoTune from Antares, Melodyne from Cele-mony, and Pitch Fix from Yamaha, will help coax the ugly little tones back in line.
>
> Although you can insert pitch-correction software in between the mic and the track, it works best after the vocal has been recorded. Details vary, depending on the product you choose, but the process works like this: The software compares your vocal's pitch to a scale and key you've selected. The audio is pitch-shifted up or down as needed. Depending on the quality of the original vocal and amount of shift, the results may vary between stunning realism and Looney Tunes.

At this point I have everything I need to finish my opus. I can take the new tracks and copy and paste them to outline the arrangement. With Reason humming along in the background, I can add more percussion parts, analog synth pads, or anything else. I can send the MIDI data from Newt's keyboard part to one of Reason's virtual instruments or any other software instrument I choose.

Life is good.

Mixing

Before the world can fall in love with your new song, you have to take all of the elements—the virtual instruments, drum loops, MIDI tracks, and digital audio tracks—and blend them together into something your listener can play. Welcome to the wonderful world of mixing.

Mixing involves listening to what's been recorded, selecting which bits come to the foreground and which stay out of the way, placing the tracks in a harmonious spatial relationship with each other, using EQ to bring each instrument into (or out of) focus, adding effects for polish or punctuation, and much more.

If I can leave you with one piece of wisdom, it's this: Mixing is an art. You cannot simply apply a set of standardized EQ curves, preset compression settings, factory effects patches, scientific principles, and/or mathematical formulas to your tracks and come up with a great mix. Perhaps you were hoping I'd reveal the Secret Formula. There ain't one, sorry.

That being said, I'd like to share some mixing tips and techniques. Once again, the purpose isn't to teach you how to mix, but instead to give you some understanding of the process and highlight ways in which your computer DAW can assists you in your musical goals.

To keep it manageable, I'm only going to talk about mixing down to stereo. Surround mixing is a whole other ball of wax.

❋ Your Most Important Mixing Tool ...

...is stuck to the sides of your head. Yep, I'm talking about those funny little ears that your mother always thought were so cute. The best way to learn how to mix is to listen. So grab a bunch of recordings and listen to them. I mean, *really* listen. Play them on the same speakers that you'll be mixing on. Play them on headphones. Play them over and over. But *listen*.

Listen to the soundstage—the placement of the different elements across the stereo field. Pay attention to which instruments appear in the mix at different times, and then get out of the way so others can take the focus. See if you can figure out what kinds of effects are being used on which instruments. Notice how long it takes for the reverb to decay on the lead vocal and if there are any delays bouncing around after certain words.

Play recordings that are similar in style to the ones you make, and see if you can re-create the sound in your mixes. Play recordings you can't stand and try to find one new technique that you can use. Play poorly made recordings and see if you can figure out what's wrong with them.

That, my friend, is the secret to learning how to mix.

Making the Virtual Real

"Do the Lizard" is made up off a number of different types of computer files. At this point I've got tiny looped beat box tracks, a variety of MIDI files, and a variety of digital audio files. As long as I'm running the various software programs such as Reason and Digital Performer at the same time, I can mix the various tracks together and hear them on my monitors. But at some point I'm going to want to burn a CD. That means I have to turn the tracks that are being created in real time—all the MIDI tracks, all the short loops, all the beat box tracks—into digital audio files.

Relax, it's a no-brainer: I choose "bounce to disc" (or "mix" or whatever your software calls the process) and sit back while all of the Reason tracks and virtual instruments, along with the audio tracks, are rendered down to a CD-friendly stereo file. ("Bouncing" refers to the process of combining two or more tracks. In this case, it's the process where the DAW creates a new stereo audio file from the selected tracks.)

There are a number of alternate ways to mix to stereo, of course. If I want, I can set up and automate the mix in my DAW (hang on, I'll tell you how to do this in a minute), play it back, and record the result onto a second recorder fed via the audio interface's main outs. That's the way we did it in recording studios when I was coming up.

Or I could set up my mix the same way and route the output back to two tracks on the DAW and record the mix that way. Another time-honored practice.

But I prefer to do things the hard way. (Why weren't you surprised?) That involves recording the output of the Reason and MIDI instruments as new audio files in my DAW. I also will need to commit to a sound for the lead guitar and record that, too. Why do I like to work this way? Because I'm an old guy, that's why.

No, that's really not the answer. I like to have all of my tracks in the same format for two very important reasons. In the first place, it means I can see the waveforms of all of the tracks. This makes it much easier to fine-tune the timing between the live tracks and those created by loop players and software instruments. It also lets me pinpoint mix automation data, either visually or by scrubbing a section of the waveform, for example, to open and close an effects send feeding a delay at a precise location. I'm also a bit obsessive when it comes to drawing fadeouts, so I like to be able to tailor each track's fade individually. Again, this is far easier when I can zoom in and highlight a section of an audio file than it is when I'm listening to loops or software instruments playing in real time.

For me, working with all of the tracks in a single program speeds up the editing and mixing process. Instead of shuttling back and forth between applications, I can simply drag and drop tracks—or groups of tracks—to try out new ideas. This makes it very easy to create numerous variations of the mix.

My other reason for turning all the software instruments into audio files is archiving. Operating systems change rapidly, software comes and goes, revisions can make older files unreadable. I've got samples, sound effects, synth patches, written scores, songs—even a couple of complete books—stored all over my studio that are for all intents and purposes locked away in a secret vault without a key because I didn't take the time to archive them to a universal format.

AIFF and WAV files have been around for a long time, and it's likely they'll be with us for some time to come. It's unlikely that I won't be able to find an application to read my audio files in another five years.

EQ Essentials

EQ is the tool we use to place a fine polish on our audio tracks. Before I pass on some sage advice on how to use EQ effectively, I need to hip you to a bit of definition.

Engineers use terms such as "low-mids" and "highs" and "air" as if they had real, objective meanings. They don't. They are relative terms for a broad range of frequencies. For all practical purposes, low or bass frequencies are anything under 150–200Hz. Mid-range occupies the huge area where most musical stuff happens, say between the bass strings on your guitar and its highest note. Much of this would be called "low-mids" by most folks. The "upper-mids" seem to fall from around 1kHz up to maybe 3.5kHz. Then there's "breath" around 4.5, followed by "high-highs" up to maybe 8 or 12kHz, and finally, the rarified "air" range above that.

Here are some tips to start you on your way to EQ wizardhood. I'm assuming you have a good set of near field monitors and that they are properly set up. Otherwise, all bets are off.

Don't forget to refer back to the EQ section in Chapter 7, too. One more thing: Every list of suggested EQ ranges for specific instruments is wrong, including this one. There is simply no way to apply a general set of EQ ranges and get quality results. Use these as a starting point, but trust your ears. After all, it's your music.

* **EQ for the song, not the track.** A huge, full piano sound may be great on its own, but it could get in the way of the vocal, drums, or bass.

* **Start from the bottom.** In most pop music, the most important instruments are the kick drum and bass. Get them right, then build from there.

* **Kick drums are really hard.** Sorry, that's just the way it is. Try boosting a tad at 2kHz to bring out the snap of the beater. Cutting at 300Hz or thereabouts can help, too.

* **Cymbals can be hard.** Overhead mic tracks for cymbals can often use a bit of help above 10kHz, particularly if it's a dense mix. Pay attention to what's going on around 2.5–3kHz in the rest of the tracks and cut the cymbals a bit if they are in the way.

* **Snares and toms are hard, too.** I like to roll off everything below 80 on the snare to keep it distinct from the kick. A boost at 1–2kHz adds sizzle and pop to the snare. Listen to the toms carefully and cut out any ringiness. Beyond that, you're on your own, I'm afraid.

* **Basses are hard, likewise.** Don't be tempted to max out the super lows; unless your listeners have a subwoofer, they'll never hear them. You can tame finger squeaks with a de-esser (see below) or by setting up a deep cut around 4.5kHz. (Try the sweep technique I taught you in the previous chapter to pinpoint the offending frequency.)

- ❈ **El Guit.** Probably the most over-EQ'd instrument on the planet. I'm afraid I can't offer much more than to say, "Try something and see if you like it."

- ❈ **Keyboards.** The trick is to keep them out of the way of everything else that's going on. Sometimes that means cutting the bass frequencies; sometimes it means cutting the mids.

- ❈ **Lead vocal.** Depends on the singer, the song, the style of music. But, generally, a little presence boost (another very subjective term; try 4.5kHz) adds definition. If the voice is too much "in your face," try cutting around 1.5–2kHz. Or boosting, if you want to give the vocal a harder edge. Cutting both the lows and the upper mids gives you the "telephone" effect, a longtime rock staple.

- ❈ **Effects change everything.** Always revisit your vocal EQ settings after you've dialed in the reverb. Sibilance really stands out in certain reverbs, so it may be better to dull the voice by attenuating the highs and then adding EQ to the reverb.

- ❈ **Fill up the plate.** The best recordings are those where every frequency is covered, though not all at once. That's why there aren't too many successful bands with only bass drum, tuba, and Fender bass.

- ❈ **Leave holes.** Most home recordings suffer from the "more is better" philosophy. Leave room for individual instruments to shine through by thinning out the pianos, synth pads, acoustic guitars, fuzzed electric guitars, and all the rest of the mid-range hogs.

Pan It

I used to work in a recording studio where we calibrated our monitors by playing Nashville recordings. If the lead vocal wasn't dead center, we knew we had a problem.

Though it's still pretty common to pan the lead vocal, kick drum, and bass straight up, you can do anything you want. The trick is to use panning to draw your listener into the song and to keep the various instruments from clashing with each other. If you want to stick the whole band all the way in the right speaker and place the singers and a solitary tambourine in the left like the old Beatles recordings, be my guest.

Effective Effects

Effects are like seasonings—sometimes it's best to just use a dash and let the purity of the recording shine through, and sometimes ya want to pour on the hot sauce. It's all a matter of taste, to push the metaphor further. I've covered this subject pretty thoroughly in earlier chapters, so I'm only going to talk about a couple of things that relate directly to the quality of your mixes.

DYNAMICS

I've already discussed dynamics in reference to track vocals. Compressors, limiters, expanders, and gates all have their place in your mix.

The usual way to use dynamics processing is to insert the effect directly in a track. Here's a rundown on the different uses of dynamics processing. Again, this list is only to get you started; there is no right way to do it.

Generally speaking, use compression to change the apparent loudness of a track. For instance, insert a compressor into a bass track and choose a moderate ratio, say 6:1. That means that the dynamic range at the output will be one-sixth the level of the recorded track. In other words, the difference between the loudest spike and the quietest sound is one-sixth as much as it used to be. Which means you can raise the level of the whole track by means of the makeup gain (a.k.a. "output level") on the compressor, in effect making the entire track louder. Cool, huh?

Limiters work the same way, except that instead of lowering the ratio of the loudest to softest signals, limiters simply cut off everything above the threshold. So if you stick a limiter in a track and set the threshold at –2 dB, no matter how loud the track gets, the output won't exceed –2 dB. That's why limiters are usually placed in front of the inputs going to digital recorders. Bear in mind that simply cutting off the peaks may have unpleasant sonic consequences. "Soft knee" limiters gradually attenuate the signal as it approaches the threshold.

"Look ahead" limiters, such as the Waves L1 Ultramaximizer, are great for making your tracks louder during premastering, the last step in the recording process before a song is sent for duplication. (See Figure 8.13.)

Figure 8.13

The Waves L1 Ultramaximizer plug-in combines transparent limiting with dithering and noise shaping, making it a powerful tool for mixing and premastering your audio. Dithering adds a tiny bit of controlled noise to mask the evils of quantization noise when changing sample rates. Noise shaping places it in a part of the audio spectrum we can't hear.

Expanders are essentially the opposite of compressors. Instead of narrowing the dynamic range, they increase it.

Gates work by effectively shutting off the signal below a set threshold. Why would you want to do that? One common use is to tighten up drum and bass tracks. Another is to eliminate the noise certain guitar effects make when the guitar isn't playing. And fans of '80s rock have heard gates in conjunction with huge reverbs on drums: the Phil Collins snare sound.

DE-ESSING

Vocal sounds containing the consonants *s*, *th*, *ch*, or *z* can really jump out in the mix. The best way to tame this sibilance is never to record it. Some vocalists go to extraordinary lengths to avoid saying words that can cause sibilance, to the extent that they'll actually sing "eee" for "see" and "coogin'" for "chuggin'." You can also tame the problem by placing the mic above the vocalist's mouth and angled slightly down.

But once it's on the track, you'll need to get rid of it. The easiest way is to use a de-esser plug-in inserted directly in the vocal track. A de-esser is simply a compressor that is set to operate at a very narrow frequency range. As long as the vocal doesn't have any sibilance, it passes through with no change.

The moment the de-esser detects sibilance, the compressor kicks in. The result is a rapid attenuation of the signal at that particular frequency. In other words, just the sibilance is affected.

The trick to using a de-esser is to loop a selected area containing sibilance and sweep the effective frequency range until you find the frequency that works best. The actual frequencies of the sibilant sounds vary, depending on the singer, the style, the syllable, and the microphone. Sometimes, the range is right around 5.1kHz, but it could be lower or go as high as 7.5kHz. Particularly bad cases may take a couple of passes with the de-esser set differently each time. In that case, you'll need to bounce down to a new track after each pass.

BUSSED EFFECTS

While EQ and dynamics are usually inserted directly into a track, time-based effects such as reverbs and chorus work best when they are assigned to an auxiliary channel. That's because you may want to send portions of a number of tracks to be affected.

For instance, I recently did a mix where we used only three such effects: a bright "vocal plate" reverb, a modest chorus, and a longer "hall" reverb. I sent all of the vocals to the vocal plate to fatten them up. I used the chorus for the background vocals on the chorus, naturally. And I used the hall both as an effect on the lead vocal, by varying the amount I sent at different parts of the song, and as a way to place all of the various instruments in the same acoustic "space," by adding minute amounts. The result was a very human, very live-sounding recording.

Your Call

Some effects work equally well as insert or aux effects, and some lean one way or the other. For instance, it's common to use guitar distortion as an insert effect, but it can create wonderful sonic havoc to drums and other multitrack parts when used in an aux. Likewise, you may think of using, say, a delay as inserted into the vocal track. But using an aux allows you to better control the effect.

And in the End …

The tracks are all recorded, the EQ's set, dynamics and sibilance tamed, and effects chosen. So I get set to write the mix automation—level changes, pan setting, and mutes for each track and changes to the effects parameters—with my control surface. That's a simple matter. I select Write from the automation menu on each track in the DAW and start the mix. As the song plays, I use the faders, pan knobs, mute buttons, and other elements on the control surface just as I would do with a hardware mixer. The software mixer immediately registers the settings, and when I review the mix, the motorized faders on my control surface move in unison. If I don't like a fader or pan move, I can either go back and redo it in real time or make the change in the track's edit window.

All that's left to do is to pinpoint the song's start and end points and sit back while my DAW bounces the track down to stereo. I insert my favorite mastering compressor across the master outs, adjust it to pump up the beat, and set the output to 0 dB so I know my mix will be as hot as any commercially recorded product.

Even though I recorded everything at 24 bits, I know the mix will translate to CD because I choose 16-bit, 44.1kHz from the list of output options. (That's the CD standard, in case you've forgotten.) I know it will sound good because I chose dither instead of simply truncating the extra bits. (Need a refresher on dithering? Read "What's Dithering?" in Chapter 7.) I run off the mix and give it a listen. Sounds like a keeper. Just to be sure, I go back and make two more mixes: one with the vocal slightly hotter, and one with it slightly quieter. And just in case I ever want to sing my own karaoke, I bounce a dub sans vocal. It only takes a minute to burn them onto a CD. Just to be sure, I burn a second copy, label it, and stick it in a safe place.

Since I've kept all of my project files together, it's a snap to back everything up to a data CD. Naturally, I make a safety copy. Of course, "Do the Lizard" used only a few minutes of digital audio spread across a handful of tracks; a 24-track song can easily require a couple gigs of storage: one more reason to add that DVD burner to the shopping list.

And so the project is done. I flip off every light in the studio except the lava lamp, kick my feet up on the desk and call my wife to come up to listen.

Is this a great way to record, or what?

That's a Wrap

I hope you have enjoyed this quick trip through the world of computer music. I've covered a lot of ground in these eight short chapters, and yet there is so much more to learn. But don't let all of these details scare you off—you don't need to be a master before you begin. Take it slow; you'll find that your skills will progress rapidly once you get your feet wet. Or your hands dirty. Or whatever metaphor you prefer.

As you can see, no matter what your musical tastes, skills, or needs, your computer will be your willing partner in achieving your goals.

So put the book down and get out there and make some music.

Appendix A

Glossary

A

ADC/DAC—Analog to Digital Converter/Digital to Analog Converter. Circuitry to move audio into and out of the digital domain.

AFL—After fader listen. Soloing a channel at a point after the EQ, pan, and fader. Also called solo in place.

aftertouch—A type of MIDI continuous control. Some keyboards have pressure-sensitive pads running underneath the keys; pressing harder after the key is depressed sends aftertouch data. Monophonic aftertouch sends a single value for all the keys; polyphonic aftertouch senses the pressure of each individual key.

AIFF—Audio interchange file format. A digital audio format common to both PCs and Macs.

algorithm—A step-by-step problem-solving procedure. Often used as subroutines.

algorithmic composition—A type of computer musical composition done via algorithms. Often a feature of auto-accompaniment software.

aliasing—Distortion in digital audio that occurs when the frequency being digitized is greater than half of the sample rate. See *Nyquist frequency*.

ambience—The sonic "signature" of a particular space. In electronic music, ambience is a type of reverb processing that adds subtle cues to fool the ear into thinking the sound is playing in a physical space.

amplitude—Sometimes called *level*. The strength of an electrical signal.

analog—In audio, analog refers to a continuously variable "picture" of the sound. For instance, a microphone represents changes in sound pressure levels at fluctuating voltages.

analog synthesizer—An electronic musical instrument that uses voltage-controlled analog modules to synthesize sound. Compare to *digital synthesizer*.

analogue—British for *analog*. Looks hip in ads.

antialiasing filter—A component of ADC and DAC circuits to remove frequencies that cause aliasing (distortion).

arpeggiator—A device commonly found on electronic musical instruments that electronically creates an arpeggio—chord tones played in rapid succession rather than all at once.

arrange window—The window in a digital audio workstation, looping, or MIDI sequencer program where the various pieces of a song are put together.

arrangement—The setting of a piece of music, including the choice of instruments, harmonies, order of the various parts, and other elements.

ASIO—Audio Stream Input/Output. A software protocol for managing multichannel digital audio and interfacing with other multimedia components, such as MIDI and video. ASIO was developed by the audio and media equipment maker Steinberg.

assign—To route a signal to a particular path in a mixer.

ATA—Extended version of the IDE peripheral connection between computers and hard drives.

ATAPI—Advanced Technology Attachment Packet Interface. A form of control interface between computers and hard drives. Similar to IDE (Integrated Drive Electronics).

ATRAC—Adaptive Transform Acoustic Encoding. A "lossy" compression algorithm for digital audio developed by Sony.

attack—One of the components of a sound. All sound can be thought of having an attack (the initial impulse), sustain (the portion where the sound is continuous at constant volume), and decay (the fade out). The combination of these components is called the envelope.

attenuation—A decrease in the level of a signal. Sometimes used as a verb (attenuate).

Audio Suite—A host-based plug-in format unique to Digidesign hardware and software. See also *Audio Units, Direct X, MAS,* and *VST.*

Audio Units—A host-based plug-in format developed by Apple. Works in conjunction with Core-Audio, a feature of the Mac OS beginning with OS X 10.2.

auto-accompaniment—A program, keyboard, or hardware device that automatically creates dynamic musical parts. For example, auto-accompaniment can be used to provide a backing band for practice or composition-based parameters set by the operator, harmonize a melody in real time, or create drum and bass patterns based on what you play.

auto punch—Short for automated punch in. Most recording software will automatically flip into and out of recording mode at user-defined points. Auto punch makes re-recording a small bit of audio or MIDI far easier than doing it manually.

automation—MIDI control data for such elements as volume, pan, and modulation that is written to and read back from a software mixer, effect, or electronic instrument. It's used primarily for the mixing stage of the recording process, but automation data can also be effective for applying dynamic changes to effects and electronic instruments during live performances.

aux send/return—Short for auxiliary. A mixer bus (circuit pathway) for sending signal to and from auxiliary equipment or software, such as a headphone mixer or an effect. See *effects send/return*.

B

balanced—An electrical wiring scheme using two wires for the signal and a third for the ground. Balanced connections are much better at rejecting noise than unbalanced circuits.

band—1. A specific range of audio frequencies. A mixer with hi, mid, and lo EQ knobs has three bands of frequency adjustment. 2. A loosely organized group of hominids. Sometimes used to describe musicians.

band pass filter—An EQ filter that allows a certain range of frequencies to pass through unaffected, while attenuating all others. For example, a low cut switch will cut off all frequencies below a certain value, typically 60–70Hz.

bandwidth—The frequency span over which a piece of gear or circuit operates. See Q.

bank select—A MIDI message used to choose between memory locations.

bass—Low-frequency sounds and the instruments and voices that make them.

beat—The most basic timing element in music. BPM means "beats per minute." Sometimes used to mean a loop or sample with drums, bass, and other rhythm instruments used as a building block in composition.

beat-box—A device for playing short patterns of electronic and sampled percussion parts. May incorporate pitched instruments. Longer arrangements are made by chaining together multiple patterns.

binary—A numbering system using only two elements: 0 and 1.

bit—Short for binary digit. The smallest unit in a binary system.

bit rate—Also called bit depth. The number of bits used to describe a single sample of digital audio. For instance, CD audio uses a sample rate of 44.1kHz at a bit rate of 16 bits. The higher the bit rate, the greater the dynamic range of the recording. See *Sample rate*.

Bluetooth—A short-range wireless communication technology for transferring data between cell phones, PDAs, computers, and related equipment.

boot—The process a computer's CPU goes through when starting up. It involves a number of tests and other routines to load the operating instruments. Sometimes the only way to fix a problem with software or an electric device is to reboot.

bouncing—The act of combining several tracks and recording them to another track. Used to free up tracks on systems with a fixed number of tracks. Also used to create a new track that combines all the bits and pieces and automation moves of an edited track. With digital audio, bouncing tracks does not degrade quality.

boundary microphone—Sometimes called PZM, for pressure zone microphone. A microphone capsule is fitted to a large, flat plate.

breakout box—In the world of computer audio, a breakout box is a multichannel computer-to-audio (and/or MIDI) interface that connects to the computer either directly or via USB or FireWire and features numerous short audio and/or MIDI cables on the other end.

breath controller—A MIDI continuous controller command for modulating a sound based on the air pressure from a player's mouth. Mostly used with electronic wind instruments such as the Yamaha WX5.

buffer—A temporary storage area for data. Buffers are used to ensure the timely transfer of data between two devices, such as a computer and CD burner, that might not be able to maintain consistent synch.

bug—A serious problem with software or hardware that causes a malfunction. Not to be confused with a glitch, which is temporary, or a #@%!!-up, which is an operator error!

burn—To write data to a recordable CD or DVD. The term is descriptive: A laser actually burns tiny pits into the media's surface.

bus—A circuit where several other circuits are brought together. Mixers typically have a mix bus for the main left and right output and several aux busses for feeding auxiliary gear such as effects. Software mixers usually retain the look and feel of hardware mixers but offer much greater routing flexibility.

byte—In the digital world, bits are grouped together to form words. The byte, a binary word 8 bits long, is the basic building block of computer processing. A kilobyte (Kb) contains 1,024 bytes.

C

cache RAM—Also called static RAM. High-speed RAM (Random Access Memory) used for critical data needed by the CPU. Sometimes called L2 (level 2) cache. Up to a point, more is better. Contrast with dynamic RAM.

capsule—The part of a microphone that converts sound to electrical energy. Also called the element.

card bus—An advanced PC card specification for laptops using a 32-bit data transfer rate. See PCMCIA.

cardioid—A heart-shaped microphone pickup pattern. Cardioid patterns tend to minimize sounds coming from the rear, making them good choices for home recording. Hypercardioid patterns are narrower.

CD—Compact disc. Usually refers to an audio CD. A CD is a form of optical data storage that can hold up to 700MB of data, or 80 minutes of 16-bit, 44.1kHz stereo audio.

CD-R—A writable CD. CD-R discs have a thin layer of dye backed by a reflective layer. Writing data to a CD-R consists of burning tiny holes in the dye layer using a laser—hence the term "burning a CD."

CD-ROM—A data CD. Stands for compact disc—read only memory.

CD-RW—A rewritable CD.

channel—1. Refers to a signal path in a mixer. 2. MIDI channels are discrete transmission and reception paths for MIDI data.

channel strip—The signal path down one channel of a mixer. Also, a device or software that combines a mic preamp with EQ and/or dynamics processing.

chipset—The integrated circuit chips that handle the functions of the CPU on a Personal Computer.

chorus—An electronic effect that relies on numerous pitch-shifted delays. In small amounts, it simulates the slightly spread-out sound of a vocal chorus. In large doses, it sounds like an underwater nightmare.

click track—The sound of a metronome or other steady beat source used as a timing reference by recording musicians.

clipping—What happens when audio signals are too strong to record accurately. Digital clipping looks like a flat chunk was bitten out of peaks of the waveform. It will hurt your ears and damage your equipment.

codec—Software to compress and decompress audio. Different codecs are used for MP3, RealAudio, Windows Media, and other Web-friendly audio formats.

coincident pair—A stereo miking technique. Two mics are placed with the capsules very close together and spread apart between 45 and 90 degrees.

coloration—A completely subjective term to refer to how something changes the way something sounds. For instance, a slightly overdriven tube amp has a different color than the same amp at a clean setting.

comp track—Short for composite. An audio track made up of bits and pieces of several takes.

compact flash—A type of small, portable memory card used for digital cameras and some portable music devices.

compressor—A processor that reduces the dynamic range of a signal, usually expressed in terms of a ratio. At a setting of 3:1, the dynamics will be reduced by one-third. By lowering the peaks and adding make-up gain, compressors appear to make a track louder.

condenser—A microphone with a thin electrically charged membrane stretched near a charged backplate. Capable of reproducing fine detail, condenser mics require a power source via phantom power or a battery.

continuous controller—Part of the MIDI specification. Continuous controllers, such as the modulation wheel or aftertouch, change the way a note sounds by adding pan, volume changes, vibrato, or other effects.

control surface—Hardware intended to interface with software. Control surfaces often have numerous faders, knobs, and switches that afford hands-on control over software parameters.

controller—Anything that transmits MIDI data without making a sound of its own.

CoreAudio/CoreMIDI—Built-in audio and MIDI routines in the Apple OS 10.2 and higher.

CPU—Short for central processing unit. The chip on the motherboard that acts like the brains of your computer.

cross-fade—Simultaneously raising the level on one sound while reducing it on another. Quick cross-fades are used to mask transitions across edits.

cut—A computer operation where the user removes a section of data to the contents of a "clipboard." The cut data may be "pasted" in another part of the same document or even into a different program.

D

DAE—Digidesign Audio Engine. A software program that handles communication between Digidesign products such as Pro Tools and the CPU and computer hardware.

daisy chain—Connecting multiple devices one after another in series. For example, MIDI devices may be chained using the out and thru ports.

DAO—Disc at Once. The entire contents of a CD-R are written in one pass without turning off the laser. See *TAO*.

data—Information. As far as a computer is concerned, data is data, whether it represents digital audio, MIDI messages, or digital photos of your spring break.

DAW—digital audio workstation. Generally refers to a desktop or computer-based digital audio recorder. Also used for software that combines digital audio with MIDI.

dB—Short for decibel. A bel (named for Alexander Graham Bell) is a unit of measure for the power of an electrical or audio signal. A decibel equals one-tenth of a bel and represents the ratio of two values, such as power and voltage levels. Various types exist, such as dBu (used to measure signal levels in pro gear), dBV (used for consumer electronics), and dB SPL (for sound pressure level).

de-ess—To remove the sibilant sounds of certain syllables and sounds using the letter *s*. (Say that out loud to understand what it sounds like.) A de-esser is a frequency-dependent compressor used to cut down the sibilance.

decay—The portion of a sound envelope that fades away. See *attack*.

defragment—A hard disc maintenance routine that rewrites data in continuous blocks. See *fragmented, optimize*.

delay—An effect used to simulate an echo by playing back the audio later than the original signal.

DI—Short for Direct Injection. A device to change the level of musical instruments like electric basses and keyboards to something a mixer can handle.

diaphragm—A thin membrane inside a microphone that vibrates in response to changes in sound waves.

digital—Refers to binary information used in computers.

digital synthesizer—An electronic musical instrument that uses digital signal processing (DSP) to create and modify sounds.

DIMM—Dual Inline Memory Module. Memory chips for computers with 64-bit processing.

DirectX—A plug-in format developed by Microsoft. Similar to VST, MAS, and RTAS.

dither—A slight amount of controlled noise added to digital audio signals to mask the much larger problem of quantization noise. See *quantization noise*.

DJ—Short for disk jockey. Originally it meant someone who plays records. Now it means somebody who plays, um, records, although the recorded music is likely to be from CDs stored and mixed inside a laptop computer.

drum machine—A device to play back synthesized or sampled drum patterns.

dry—A term for audio without any added effects. The opposite of wet.

DSP—Digital Signal Processing.

dub—To make a copy of a recording. Also, what you call the copy. In reggae, a dub is a version of the song with the lead vocals removed.

DVD—Originally Digital Video Disc, the name was changed to mean Digital Versatile Disc. Apparently, now the initials don't stand for anything, sort of like KFC. A large-capacity optical storage medium.

dynamic allocation—Synthesizers can produce only so many notes at once. Dynamic allocation ensures that new notes will always be heard by turning off earlier notes. Sometimes called "voice stealing."

dynamic microphone—A rugged microphone that does not require an outside power source. Dynamics are great for recording loud sources like drums.

dynamics—Refers to the difference between the loudest and softest portions of a sound.

E

early reflections—The sounds that arrive at your ears after bouncing off the walls and ceiling. Early reflections arrive slightly later that the direct sounds but before the main body of the reverbera-tions. Since reverbs give clues to a room's size and shape, many include parameters to control early reflections.

edit—To manipulate audio after it is recorded. Nondestructive edits, which might include cutting, pasting, copying, and moving chunks of data, don't alter the original sound file. Destructive edits permanently change the file. For example, you might wish to shorten a track. If you choose to do the edit nondestructively, you can always go back and recover the original. However, if you choose a destructive edit, the orginal file will be overwritten by a new one.

effects—A term for different ways to alter the sound. Compressor, limiters, and noise gates affect the dynamics; time-based effects such as delay, reverb, and chorus alter the perception of the sound in space. Other effects include wah-wah, distortion, tube-emulation, and vocoding.

effects send/return—An aux bus dedicated to an effects processor or effects software.

EIDE—Enhanced Integrated Drive Electronics. A communication standard between computers and storage media.

envelope—Describes the way a sound varies over time.

EQ—Short for equalization, a device or software to boost or cut selected frequencies in order to change the tonal characteristic of a sound.

event list—A listing of all of the MIDI messages in the order they were written to a sequencer track. Event lists provide detailed editing of MIDI data.

F

fade—To gradually lower the volume over time.

fader—A straight-line volume control found on mixer channels.

feedback—What happens when some of the output signal gets sent back to the input. In audio, feedback happens when a microphone picks up the sound from a speaker, which gets amplified and fed to the speaker, where it is picked up by the microphone...and so on until it becomes an obnoxious squeal.

figure 8—A bi-directional pickup pattern where sounds directly in front of and behind a microphone are reproduced, while those to the side are rejected.

file—A bunch of data stored together on a computer under a name.

file sharing—Interfacing two or more computers so files move easily between them. Nice people use file sharing to share files they create themselves. Mean people use file sharing to steal files created by nice people.

filter—An electronic device (or its software equivalent) to reduce a signal's energy at a specific frequency.

filter sweep—One of the characteristic sounds of analog synthesis, achieved by dynamically varying the cutoff frequency of a filter.

FireWire—A high-speed data-exchange format developed by Apple. Also called IEEE 1394, FireWire handles speeds up to 400Mbs (megabits per second). It's well suited to the rigorous demands of high-definition audio and video. FireWire 800 operates twice as fast as standard FireWire. See *USB*.

flanger—A whooshing effect. The term comes from the days of reel-to-reel tape, when an engineer would apply pressure to the reel's flange to alter the speed, and hence the sound, of the playback.

floppy disk—A type of removable storage medium for computers, now mostly extinct. Storage was limited to a few megabytes at best. Originally, floppies really were made of floppy plastic.

FM synthesis—A form of digital synthesis used in Yamaha's famous DX7 keyboard and other synths. Excels at bell tones and electric piano sounds.

fold down—To consolidate several audio channels, such as down mixing a six-channel surround mix to stereo.

FPU—floating point unit. A processor found in many computers capable of handling extremely large numbers efficiently. The general availability of machines with FPUs made the digital audio and video revolution possible.

fragmented—Data is seldom written to a hard disk in neat blocks; instead, bits and piece of a file might be written at widely different locations. If a disk is highly fragmented, the read/write head has to travel all over the place to read it. At best, this can slow things down. At worst, it causes the drive to crash. See *defragment* and *optimize*.

freeze—A routine in some digital audio workstation (DAW) software to save processor resources by temporarily recording an audio track or software instruments and all effects of any plug-ins.

frequency—Literally, how many times something happens in a given time period. Engineers use frequency to describe the relative pitch of a sound, based on how many times the sound wave vibrates per second. Bass sounds have lower frequencies; high-pitched sounds have higher frequencies. The human ear can hear sounds between 20Hz (Hertz, the same as cycles per second) and 20kHz (20,000Hz.)

FX—Shorthand for "effects." Get it?

G

gain—Relates to how much an amplifier circuit boosts or cuts a signal. An amplification point along the signal path is called a gain stage.

gain staging—The process of setting all the gain stages along the signal path to the proper level.

gate—Sometimes called a noise gate. A dynamics device (or software) that blocks the transmission of an audio signal below a certain volume threshold. Generally used to cut off unwanted noise.

General MIDI—A MIDI standard that ensures a level of compatibility among devices.

GHz—Gigahertz. One thousand million hertz. Related to the clock speed of Personal Computers, and therefore a measure of their computational power. More is better.

gigabyte—One billion bytes. Refers to a computer's storage capacity. More is better.

gigaflop—Refers to computing speed. 1 gigaflop = 1 billion floating-point operations per second. That's a lot.

gooseneck—A flexible extension for microphone stands.

granular synthesis—A type of resynthesis that seriously warps the sound of the input by slicing it into "grains" and applying heavy-duty mathematical processing.

grid—A two-dimensional or sometimes three-dimensional screen overlaid on certain windows in software to help orient the placement of images, MIDI notes, or audio tracks. The command "snap to grid" automatically aligns the selected objects to the grid.

ground—The point of zero voltage in an electrical circuit. The ground serves as a safe path for excess electrical current from malfunctions and other problems. Proper grounding of electrical gear is vital to your safety and keeps noise from leaking in.

ground loop—What happens when several different devices in an audio system have multiple paths to ground. Ground loops sound like an audible hum with a frequency of 60Hz (in the United States). To fix a ground loop, make sure all the gear follows a single path to ground.

GUI—Short for graphical user interface. The common computer interface using windows, icons, and other graphical elements to represent specific functions.

H

hard drive—Refers both to the read/write mechanism on a computer's mass-storage hard disk and to the hard disk itself.

headroom—The difference between the nominal output level and the peak ceiling in an audio system.

Hi-Z—High Impedance. Hi-Z equipment, such as electric guitars, must be connected to a Hi-Z input to avoid compromising the sound.

host-based—Refers to DAW software and plug-ins that rely on the computer's CPU for processing power.

hum—What you do when you don't know the words. In the studio, hum is noise from improperly grounded gear or from interference from the electrical lines.

hypercardioid—A very narrow directional microphone pickup pattern.

Hz—Hertz, or cycles per second. A measurement of frequency. 1 kilohertz (kHz) = 1,000 Hz. Humans perceive sounds between 20Hz and 20kHz.

I

image file—A file that exactly mirrors the data on a selected drive or in RAM. Image files are sometimes used to prepare data that is to be written to a CD.

impedance—The resistance of a circuit to AC (alternating current), measured in ohms.

initialize—To bring back a hard disk to its original state. Initializing wipes all of the information stored on the drive and rewrites the drive software. Also known as formatting.

insert—A point in a mixer at which you can interrupt the signal flow of a single channel and send it to an external device for processing. The processed signal then flows back to the same point to continue its route through the channel strip.

intelligent arranger—Software or hardware that provides backing tracks, harmonization, and other features based on your input.

instrument—Something that makes sound and a tool for making music.

intellectual property—A term for the ownership of creative output. By law and custom in our society, artists and musicians have the exclusive right to decide what becomes of the songs, poetry, videos, and artwork they produce.

J

jack—The receptacle that you insert an electrical plug into.

jitter—Timing errors in digital audio caused by poor digital clocking.

K

kernel—The bottommost layer of a computer's operating system, responsible for low-level functions such as memory management. A kernel panic is what happens when the OS screws up at a really basic level.

keyboard—A catchall term used for electronic and acoustic instruments with keys, such as a piano or synthesizer, or the sounds made by such an instrument.

kilohertz—Abbreviated as kHz. A frequency of 1kHz is 1,000 cycles per second.

L

LAN—Local area network. A group of computers and/or other electronic devices connected together to communicate and share information.

large-diaphragm—A microphone with a diaphragm larger than ¾ of an inch. Large-diaphragm mics generally have a bigger, more "open" sound than small-diaphragm mics.

latency—The time it takes for a device to respond. In computer audio, latency is caused by the time it takes for audio to be routed through the software and back to the listener. Low-latency monitoring involves tapping the input signal before it is sent through the software.

lead sheet—A paper with the words and chords for a song.

LFO—Short for low-frequency oscillator, an LFO is an oscillator operating below 20Hz that's used to modify another signal. LFOs are used to create vibrato, chorus, and other effects, and in synthesizers as sonic building blocks.

librarian—A software program for organizing MIDI program names and patch parameters.

limiter—A dynamics processor (similar to a compressor) that sets the maximum gain and keeps signals from going past it. Useful to prevent clipping on a signal going to a Digital to Analog Converter (DAC).

line level—The electrical operating level of audio gear, as opposed to mic level. Audio gear uses two different scales for line-level gear. "Pro" gear operates at +4 dBu and generally uses either balanced TRS or balanced XLR connectors. "Consumer" gear operates at –10dBV and uses ¼-inch TS connectors. The key is not to connect +4 gear to a –10 input or vice versa.

local-control—A MIDI parameter that determines whether a device will respond to incoming messages from its own keyboard and controllers.

loop—A short section of audio or MIDI data that is repeated.

LP—Short for long-playing phonograph recording. A 12-inch vinyl disc with recorded music.

M

makeup gain—The point in a dynamics processor where the signal is amplified to "make up" for the gain reduction caused by compression.

MAS—Mark of the Unicorn brand's host-based plug-in format for Digital Performer.

mastering—The final stage of the recording process. Mastering involves preparing the song or collection of songs for the delivery medium, such as CD, DVD, or MP3. It generally involves setting levels, EQ, dynamics, and other subtle changes.

meters—Refers to dials, LEDs, or their software equivalents that give visual information about signal strength. In music, meter refers to "pulse" or timing.

mic level—The electrical output level (voltage) of a microphone. Mic level is considerably lower than line level, which is why microphones need preamplifiers to boost the signal.

MIDI—Musical Instrument Digital Interface. A computer language originally devised to let one keyboardist play several synthesizers simultaneously, MIDI is now used for everything from mixer automation to controlling stage lighting systems.

MIDI interface—A device to get MIDI information into and out of a computer.

mix—To blend several signals together. Mixing a song involves selecting the best tracks, placing each in the proper relationship, adding EQ and any effects, and generally making everything sound as good as possible. The rule of thumb is, "If it sounds good, it is good." As a noun, mix refers to the completed song.

mixer—A specialized piece of equipment or software to control and route multiple audio and/or MIDI sources. Software mixers may include (among other features) inserts for effect plug-ins, faders to control relative levels, pan controls to place a sound in a left-to-right stereo field, and sends to bus some of the channel to an effect.

modeling—Re-creating a physical object or process using mathematics. Thanks to modeling technology, digital re-creations of analog synthesizers, effects units—even acoustic instruments—can live happily on your hard disk.

modular synthesizer—An analog synth that used various components wired together with electronic patch cables. Modular synths had no memory, were fiendishly difficult to program, and tended to drift out of tune—but boy did they sound good. Modular synths were all the rage until MIDI and digital synthesizers replaced them in the early 1980s.

modulation—To modulate means to change something. The modulation wheel (mod wheel for short) on a MIDI keyboard adds expression to the sound, usually by triggering vibrato.

monitor—1. To listen, with the implication that you are listening critically. 2. A specialized audio speaker used in studios. 3. The CRT (cathode ray tube) or LCD (liquid crystal display) screen used with computers.

motherboard—The main circuit board in a computer or electronic device. The motherboard contains the CPU and has slots to plug in other subassemblies such as the video board and ADCs/DACs.

MP3—MPEG (Motion Picture Experts Group) audio layer 3. MP3 files use a "lossy" compression scheme that throws away much of the "superfluous" data in an audio file. MP3 files are therefore far smaller than CD audio files, which makes them handy for transmission via the Internet.

multi-pattern—A microphone with selectable pickup patterns.

multitimbral—A keyboard, sound module, or software instrument capable of producing more than one sound at a time.

mute—To shut off the output of an audio channel. As a noun, a control that "turns off" the signal flowing through a mixer channel. Mutes are handy for quickly bringing a channel in and out of a mix without having to reset levels.

N

native—Basically the same thing as host-based. Digital audio workstation (DAW) software and plug-ins that rely on the computer's CPU. Non-native applications, such as Pro Tools|HD and TC Electronics PowerCore, use cards or interfaces with dedicated Digital Signal Processing (DSP) chips.

near-coincident pair—A stereo microphone technique. Similar to coincident-pair miking, except that the capsules are placed some distance apart.

near field—Refers to the space very close to a sound source, where the sound has not begun to reflect back from the walls, floor, and other surrounding surfaces. Used to describe studio monitor speakers intended for close listening.

noise floor—The level of noise generated by an electrical device itself when no signal is present.

normalize—A process that raises the level of digital audio data to some set value. Unlike limiting or compression, normalizing does not change the dynamic range. It simply raises everything by a set amount.

Nyquist frequency—The highest audio frequency that can be accurately sampled based at a given sample rate. The Nyquist frequency is half of the sample rate, so at 44.1kHz the highest frequency that can be reproduced is 22.050kHz.

O

off-axis—Directional microphones pick up sounds best that are directly in front of, or in line with the axis of, the capsule. Sounds coming in off-axis may be distorted or colored in some way. Engineers note these changes and use them for effects when recording.

omnidirectional—A 360-degree pickup pattern. As there is no proximity effect, omni mics are useful for extremely close miking.

onboard/outboard—Refers to the physical placement of effects modules. For example, most recording studios have large mixing boards connected to racks of individual "outboard" microphone preamps, effects processors, compressors, and other equipment. In contrast, a desktop digital audio workstation (DAW) might include built-in (onboard) microphone preamps and effects.

optimize—To defragment a hard drive. Optimization software, such as Norton's Speed Disk, moves the data to a buffer before rewriting it to contiguous blocks.

OS—Short for operating system. The software instructions that make your computer work.

oscillator—In electronic instruments and effects devices, an oscillator is a circuit producing a signal of a specific frequency that varies with time. Analog synthesizers use LFOs (low-frequency oscillators) and VCOs (voltage-controlled oscillators) as two of the building blocks of synthesized sounds.

overdrive—Refers to the pleasant-sounding (to guitarists, anyway) distortion caused by pushing a guitar amp's tubes hard enough that the sound just begins to break up.

overdub—Adding additional tracks to a multitrack recording.

P

pad—1. In music, a pad is a lush, sustained wash of sound mixed below the main level of the song. 2. In electronics, a pad is a circuit that cuts the level of a signal by a specific amount. Many microphones feature pads so they can handle high sound-pressure levels from drums and similar instruments.

pan—In audio, pan refers to the placement of a signal relative to the left and right speakers.

parameter—Something that can be tweaked. Electronic devices and effects often have a bewildering number of parameters. The best way to learn what they do is to start fiddling with them.

parametric equalizer—A type of equalizer, often with precise control over the behavior of the filters applied to audio. Generally, parametrics let you select filer shapes, the frequency and gain, and the bandwidth (or Q).

partition—In the computer world, a hard drive might be partitioned (or divided) into two or more parts. As far as the OS is concerned, each is a separate drive. With large drives, partitioning makes it easier to keep related data together and speeds up data access.

passive—An audio device with no amplification circuits.

patch—A "sound" created by a synthesizer, such as a piano patch or a woodwinds patch. The term comes from the days of analog synths, when physical patch cords routed signals between modules.

PC—Short for Personal Computer. Generally refers to a machine running some version of Microsoft Windows.

PCI—Peripheral component interconnect. A type of computer expansion slot.

PCMCIA—A sort of mini-PCI expansion slot for laptop computers. Short for Personal Computer Memory Card International Association.

peak—The loudest part of an audio signal. Peaks show up as the highest points in a graphical waveform display.

phantom power—Voltage supplied via a microphone cable to power condenser mics. Usually 48 volts. Phantom power does not affect dynamic microphones, but it might destroy a ribbon mic.

pickup pattern—Refers to how a microphone "hears" sounds. Also called the polar pattern.

plug-in—Audio processing software that works inside a host application.

preamp—A specialized amplifier to boost a weak signal from a microphone or instrument to a usable level.

project studio—A small, usually home-based, recording studio capable of doing professional-quality work.

proximity effect—An artificial boost in lower frequencies heard when a source moves closer to a cardioid or hypercardioid mic. Many singers take advantage of this to boost thin vocals.

punch-in/punch-out—Recording over an existing portion of a track at a specific location.

PZM—Short for pressure zone microphone. Also known as a boundary mic, a PZM consists of a small condenser mic attached to a large, flat plate. PZMs are great for capturing live performances.

Q

Q—The bandwidth control, usually measured in octaves, on a parametric equalizer.

quantization noise—Digital noise that creeps in when analog audio falls in between the range of two digital sample points.

quantize—In audio, the process of cutting a sound wave into discrete steps. Also, moving MIDI data or audio regions to line up with a tempo grid.

R

RAM—Random Access Memory. Computer chips used to temporarily store information.

random access—Refers to the fact that computer data is not written sequentially, so it's possible to jump to any point at any time. Compare to analog tape that must be rewound or fast-forwarded between memory locations.

remix—Literally, to mix again. In the dance world, a remix usually is a complete reworking of a song with new rhythms, new instruments, and new beats.

return—In a mixer, the opposite of a send. Returns bring signals back to the mixer.

reverb—The sound created from a sound source reflecting off the walls, ceiling, and floor of a room or space. As an effect, reverb is an important component of the recording process.

ribbon mic—A microphone whose element consists of a thin ribbon. Though highly accurate, ribbon mics tend to be extremely delicate; even a stray breath may cause damage.

ROM—Read-only memory. A chip containing data that cannot be overwritten.

rompler—A new word that combines ROM with sampler. A sample-playback instrument.

S

S/PDIF—Sony/Phillips Digital Interface. A digital audio transfer protocol using either RCA or optical connectors. Handy to connect third-party audio converters to an internal sound card.

sample—To digitally record a small bit of audio into a sampler.

sample rate—Digital audio represents a sound wave as a series of discrete steps, or samples. At 44.1kHz the audio is sampled 44,100 times per second. As it takes at least two samples to represent a given frequency, 44.1kHz audio can reproduce sounds up to 20kHz.

sampler—A hardware or software device that records digital audio to be played back on a keyboard, drum pads, or some other kind of MIDI controller.

scratch—1. In recording, a scratch track is a disposable track recorded as a guide for overdubbing. 2. In the dance world, scratching is moving a vinyl record back and forth under the needle to create beats and sound effects.

scribble strip—A flat area on some mixers reserved for writing notes about track assignments and other details. Most software mixers and DAWs have virtual scribble strips.

SDII—A common audio file format for the Mac, SDII (Sound Designer II) was created by Digidesign, makers of Pro Tools.

send—An output on a mixer or other audio device to route signals to an external effect or other device. Examples include aux (auxiliary) sends, and tape sends. Usually paired with a matching return.

sequencer—Hardware or software designed to record and play back MIDI data.

sibilance—The high-frequency parts of some vocal sounds, such as s and sh.

signal—An electronic current that represents audio.

signal chain—The path through which an audio signal travels. For example, an input signal chain might include a microphone preamplifier, mixer channel strip, and an audio interface. Also called a signal path.

SMF—Standard MIDI File. A universal exchange format for MIDI files.

SMPTE—Society of Motion Picture and Television Engineers. Used as shorthand for a kind of mechanical time code to synchronize audio recorders with film. MTC, or MIDI time code, is essentially SMPTE translated into MIDI language.

snapshot automation—A type of mixer automation that involves saving and then recalling a virtual "picture" of all of the settings at a given point in time.

sound design—The art of creating sound effects and synthesizer patches.

SoundFont—An extension of the MIDI standard that includes instructions necessary to create sound effects and musical instruments using wavetable synthesis.

spaced pair—A stereo microphone technique using two widely spaced mics.

synthesizer—A device for creating and modifying audio waveforms electronically.

system bus—The signal path in computers connecting the CPU to the RAM. Faster is better.

T

tablature—A form of musical notation using numbers (and sometimes letters) to indicate where to place your fingers on an instrument. Most common with guitars.

take—A recorded performance.

TAO—Track at Once. A CD-R recording scheme for adding one track at a time. TAO discs must be finalized before they can be played. See DAO.

tape—What we used to record on before digital audio. Many people still think it sounds better.

tape delay—A delay effect created with loops of audiotape. Most digital effects use modeling to re-create the sound.

TDM—Digidesign's plug-in format for Pro Tools. TDM requires Digidesign hardware for digital signal processing (DSP).

tempo map—A series of tempo changes recorded into sequencers and DAWs to set the playback tempos of a song.

track—A legacy of tape-based analog recording, a track is a single "stripe" of audio data. A hard disk track may consist of one audio file or many. Also used as a verb, as in, "Dim the lights. It's time to track the vocals."

transient—The loud, quickly occurring portion of some audio signals, such as the attack of a drum or the sound of a vocal consonant.

tremolo—An effect that varies the amplitude (loudness) of a signal over time.

TRS—Tip-ring-sleeve. A ¼-inch audio plug with three isolated sections. TRS connectors are used for signals requiring two conductors plus a ground, such as balanced equipment, stereo headphones, and insert cables.

TS—A ¼-inch audio connector for unbalanced signals. Also called a phone plug.

tweeter—The smallest speaker (or transducer) in a multispeaker cabinet. The tweeter reproduces the high frequencies while the woofer takes care of the bass.

U

unbalanced—An electrical circuit with only two conductors (called legs). In unbalanced circuits, one leg carries both the signal and the ground while the other carries only the signal. Unbalanced lines are prone to noise. Hence, cable runs should be kept to under 25 feet.

undo—A feature of most computer programs that keeps track of all of your changes and lets you reverse a previous action. Multiple levels of undo are very useful.

unity gain—The point at which a device or gain stage setting neither adds to nor diminishes the signal level.

USB—Universal Serial Bus. An expandable, hot-pluggable connection between computers and external gear such as printers, scanners, and audio and MIDI interfaces. USB 1.1 supports data transfers up to 12MB per second, which is too slow for serious multichannel audio work. USB 2 pushes it up to 480MB per second.

V

VCA—Voltage-controlled amplifier. An amplification circuit controlled by external voltage. Used in synthesizers as well as some automated mixing consoles.

VCF—Voltage-control filter. Like a VCA, only the control voltage affects a filter. Used in synths and samplers to modify sounds.

VCO—Voltage-controlled oscillator. Similar to VCA and VCF—an oscillator where the frequency is controlled by voltage.

velocity—A MIDI message pertaining to the speed with which a key was pressed (and released, though note-off velocity data is almost universally ignored). Usually relates to the volume of a MIDI note, but also might affect the attack time or other parameters.

virtual instrument—A software instrument that emulates the characteristics of a digital or analog synthesizer. Sometimes called a soft synth.

virtual track—An audio track that is saved but not currently assigned to a mixer channel in a digital audio workstation (DAW).

vocoder—An effect in which the characteristics of a human voice are used to filter the output of another sound. Yes, your guitar really can talk.

voice—Another name for the sounds played on a synthesizer or sampler. A 64-voice instrument can play 64 notes simultaneously.

VST—A host-based plug-in protocol for effects and virtual instruments developed by the audio and media equipment maker Steinberg. VST is widely supported.

W

WAV—Sometimes spelled WAVE or .wav. A standard audio file format for Windows applications.

wavetable synthesis—A type of synthesis where complex sounds are created by cross-fading and modifying waveform parameters stored in memory.

wet–Refers to the character of a sound plus any effects added to it. A 40 percent wet signal is made up of 60 percent of the unaffected signal and 40 percent of the output from the effects device. The opposite is dry.

woofer–A speaker for reproducing low frequencies. A subwoofer is a separate speaker enclosure to reproduce the very low frequencies found in movie and video game sound effects.

word–A complete sample of digital audio. A word is a group of bits, so 16-bit audio contains words of 16 bits to describe each sample.

word length–Refers to the resolution, or dynamic accuracy, of digital audio. All things being equal, the greater the word length, the more detail.

workstation–A term to describe a device or software suite that combines many music production tasks in one interface.

X–Y–Z

XLR–A type of three-wire audio connector. XLR jacks are round with three pins; the plugs have three corresponding holes. XLR connectors are used for microphones operating at mic level and for some +4 dBu equipment.

Y cable–A cable used to split a signal into two parts, such as an insert cable.

Z–The symbol for impedance. Also, the mark of Zorro.

ZIFF-socket–Short for zero insertion force. A type of connector found on some computer circuit boards. ZIFF sockets make changing electronic chips a simple task.

Appendix B

Buying Used Gear

Outfitting a computer music system with all the latest equipment can be an expensive proposition if you buy everything at full retail. But just as you can retrofit your existing home computer system with a new hard drive, more memory, and an audio interface, you also can make use of older gear to fulfill your music needs. Just about everything in your home studio—synths, samplers, audio and MIDI interfaces, mixing control surface, digital multitrack recorders, effects, and even your desk—can be purchased used for a fraction of the retail cost. You can even find software on the used market, though there are special precautions you'll need to take.

These days, online auction sites and online classified ads are probably your best bet—but don't overlook your local newspaper and specialty papers. In spite of the urban legends, buying online is as safe as any arm's-length transaction, as long as you follow a few simple guidelines. One quick point: There is a world of difference between "vintage" and just plain used. The word "vintage" is used to describe gear with a certain level of desirability, function, and class that goes beyond just age. For example, certain vintage microphones command prices far in excess of their modern counterparts. So unless you know the vintage market well, leave it for the experts.

What to Buy and What to Avoid

It's a fact of life that some things we use for making music hold up better over time than others. A complex, finely tuned multitrack recorder needs frequent maintenance just to operate properly. If it's been neglected for several years, driven hard for countless hours, and shoved around in a smoky remote-recording truck, the chances are good it won't work by the time it gets to your door. On the other hand, a rack-mounted digital effects module doesn't have a lot of moving parts to wear out, so a five-year-old one will probably work as good as new.

Generally speaking, digital gear and stuff with few moving parts—effects units, solid-state compressors, direct boxes, synth modules, and the like—tend to be fairly safe bets. Barring a serious electrical accident or outright stupidity, they'll keep operating long past the point of obsolescence. A dead battery can be replaced, a burned-out LED or LCD may not affect the operation, and tubes are easy to change. The problems you do encounter tend to be mechanical—excessive noise at the outputs, crunchy pots and switches, and obvious shorts, for example. Some of these are easy fixes, and some aren't.

Buying used microphones takes a bit more care. Condenser and ribbon microphones can be very fragile, so try to learn how and where they were used before agreeing to purchase. If the mic was used onstage, it may have been drop-kicked by an overly enthusiastic fan or used as a hammer by some roadie. Studio mics may have been well cared for—or maybe not. Ask for a trial period and test as thoroughly as you are able. Make sure you are getting all the accessories—clips, power supplies, form-fitted cases—that you bargained for.

As I've suggested above, the more moving parts something has, the greater the chance for trouble. Recorders and mixers require periodic maintenance to operate properly. The membranes that run under the keys on keyboards can wear out. Computers have many delicate parts that all must work together. Even something as simple as a broken fan may cause serious problems.

That doesn't mean you shouldn't buy used recorders, mixers, or computers. In a few moments, I'll talk about some steps you can take to make sure the used gear you buy won't end up holding down a stack of papers somewhere. But first I want to talk about buying used computers.

Used Computers and Software

Every couple of months a whole raft of new computer models hits the market. They're bigger, better, faster, and far more capable than anything currently available. So you should trash your present system and run out and buy the next big thing, right? Not so fast.

Last year's model may be exactly what you need. And it may sell for 40 percent of what it did when it was new. As I've said repeatedly, unless you are doing cutting-edge audio and video production, practically any computer made in the past five years is more than up to the task of desktop music making. In many cases, all you need to bring a used machine up to snuff is more memory or a larger internal drive. Both USB and FireWire cards are easy to add. Sometimes you can even pop in an accelerator or new motherboard to bring the machine up to current specs.

Not only that, but many of the basic components—memory, drives, monitors, keyboards, mice, and monitors—are available on the used market.

If you do go this route, be sure that the original machine will handle the new parts. You may need to get some tech advice about data transfer rates and the like before you crack open the case. Check online discussion groups, or ask the neighborhood whiz kid.

The best place to buy a used computer and used parts is from a retailer specializing in pre-owned equipment. Often these machines will have been thoroughly checked and any problems repaired. And you can usually get some kind of exchange period and warranty. If you buy from an individual, insist on a trial/exchange period.

Used software is a gray area. With very few exceptions, software licenses are nontransferable. At the very least, that means you will not be eligible for tech support or upgrades. Sometimes you can purchase a license for used software directly from the manufacturer, so it pays to check. If you do buy used software, always ask for the original discs and manuals. Under no circumstances should you accept software that's been copied to CD-R or installed on the hard drive without the original disc—it may mean that someone is trying to sell you a stolen copy. Piracy is cool only in the movies.

Do Your Homework

It's always best to know what you want and why you want it before you start shopping. Take the time to dream a little—write down what your ideal setup would be. Maybe you'd like to have a big 88-key weighted-action controller to replace the little plastic job next to your computer. Or perhaps you thought you'd have to settle for a basic two-in/two-out audio interface because of the price when you really need a full-featured multichannel box with all the bells and whistles.

Then find out what's out there. A good first step is to subscribe to a music and recording magazine and read the gear reviews and how-to stories. *Electronic Musician*, *EQ*, and *Future Music* all are aimed at people who make music using home computers. Instrument-specific magazines such as *Guitar World* and *Keyboard* often feature articles and tutorials about music technology. And don't overlook the ads—there's nothing better than a little gear lust to inspire you to make a wish list.

Once you've got a handle on what you want, fire up your Web browser and do some research. Online user groups are a great resource. Most manufacturers maintain links to official—and sometimes, unofficial—groups. Or simply run a search on the name of the product. Be sure to bookmark any useful sites in case you need them again after your purchase. The best user groups are moderated by technicians who work with the products every day. Above all, don't be shy about asking questions. Subscribe to some news groups. Many have extensive searchable archives. (See Appendix D,"Resources.")

Visit the manufacturer's Web site to read about the product and to view technical reports. Even equipment and software that's been off the market for years may still be supported. Look for downloadable updates, user tips, FAQs, and more. Try to learn whether something's recently been orphaned—dropped from the development process. Such dead-end gear may look like a bargain, but it's not if you can't get support or supplies.

Incidentally, many manufacturers are in the habit of "blowing out" their inventories of soon-to-be orphaned equipment. Large retailers pick up the stock and sell it at a fraction of the retail price. Sometimes it's hard to tell whether a sale item is simply last-year's model whose newer version has minor cosmetic changes or a true dead-end kid destined for doorstop duty.

Obsolete technology that has built up a large user base is another story. Just because the buzz is now all about 24-bit, 192kHz digital audio and surround sound doesn't mean you should pass on a perfectly good older interface or modular recorder if it fits your needs and budget. Remember, CDs tracked at 16 bits and 44.1kHz have sold millions of copies.

Use PrePal.com to get an idea of the prices for used gear, including synthesizers, samplers, interfaces, and other studio staples. The free service tracks all of the major online auctions and posts daily updates for more than 3,500 different products in its database. Keep tabs on items sold on eBay and get in the habit of checking out the various online classifieds sites.

By the way, it's not uncommon for the used price of an item auctioned online to be *higher* than the new price from a discount retailer. That's another good reason to do your homework.

Buying Online

There are two main ways to buy gear online.

Many user groups and special-interest Web sites maintain extensive classified-ad sections. Classifieds are great places to pick up used gear. You can usually take the time to ask questions, negotiate price, and work out details of shipping and payment. User groups, forums, and news groups often allow members to post ads—a great resource when you're looking for something specific. Some, such as the classified section at VintageSynth.com, can be quite focused. Other sites, such as retail giant Sweetwater's Trading Post, cater to a wide range of musical and recording interests.

Dedicated classified sites range from huge international listings to tiny pages with a few specialized ads. A number of online retailers and informational sites host independent classified sites as well. Most classifieds work the same way—you contact the seller directly to make the deal. At some sites you post your offer for a set amount of time, during which the seller can either accept it or pass.

And then there's eBay.

Sooner or later, just about everything you can think of shows up on this huge online auction site. eBay has spawned a mini-industry of books, Web sites, and articles aimed at helping you reap huge profits. It's supremely user friendly—just log on and follow the prompts. eBay offers a small amount of protection through its system of rating buyers and sellers, but trust is the order of the day. Think of it like a giant virtual garage sale.

The safest way to buy on eBay, or anywhere else online, is to use an escrow service. It works like this: Both the buyer and seller agree to use the service and negotiate the terms. Once you win a bid, the escrow service holds onto your payment until you've received and inspected the gear. If it doesn't work out, you can return it for a full refund, less a small handling charge. eBay maintains a list of recommended escrow service. Or check out http://www.escrow.com and http://www.afterson.com/escrow.

Unfortunately, the Web is rife with fraudulent escrow services. Be sure to do your homework and check out the escrow services suggested by the buyer thoroughly. Avoid services that ask you to use nontraceable payment services such as Western Union. The Auction Guild (http://www.auctionguild.com) has tips for spotting fraudulent escrow services. For a small fee, they will research a service for you. e-Bay's Safe Harbor Service helps protect you against fraud as well.

If eBay's size gives you the willies, check out InstrumentExchange.com. The service deals only in musical instruments and gear and offers guaranteed 48-hour inspection and FedEx shipping.

Regardless of which site you choose, the secret to auction success is to know your price and stick to it. Don't get caught in a bidding war; you'll end up spending far more than the item was worth. It's common for a seller to watch the action and list a similar item immediately after the one you were bidding on closed. Usually, the second one will sell for less.

You can also let the auction site make proxy bids for you. You post a range that you want to spend, and the software does the rest. If someone tops your minimum bid, the software automatically posts a new one. Slick.

If you'd rather participate, most of the action happens toward the closing time, so set your alarm. Sometimes it all comes down to who's quickest at the final gun.

Avoiding Pitfalls

Before you commit to a purchase, ask the owner for details about where and how the unit was used. Find out whether it was installed in a nonsmoking facility—cigarette smoke leaves residue that can damage electrical and mechanical parts. Learn about regularly scheduled maintenance and service. Always ask the seller about the user's manual and supplemental paperwork and whether the unit comes with any add-ons or accessories such as power supplies, rack hardware, or extra sounds. Depending on the site, you either post your questions using a query form or contact the seller directly for a confidential reply.

Ask whether the owner has the original box and shipping materials—not just because these ensure that the unit will be packed safely, but also because it suggests that the gear has been well cared for. Be wary of people using generic e-mail accounts such as Hotmail or Yahoo! They are impossible to trace if something does go wrong. Always make sure you get a verified phone number as well as a valid street address.

When you have completed the deal, ask the seller to insure the shipment for its full value. Be sure to get the tracking number. Inspect the package when it arrives; shippers are liable for merchandise damaged in transit only if it was properly packaged and you file a claim promptly. Sometimes an unscrupulous person will try to pawn off damaged goods by shipping them with inadequate packaging. If you receive something that was obviously underpackaged, refuse the shipment and get your money back.

If you feel that the unit is not what was advertised, contact the seller and arrange a return. Most sellers insist you pay the return shipping to cut down on frivolous returns.

It is often possible to replace a lost or missing manual. Many manufacturers maintain downloadable archives; others will sell you a hard copy. Some retailers specialize in out-of-print and hard-to-find manuals. User groups are another great resource.

Finding parts and service for obsolete equipment is more of a challenge. The first step is to check the manufacturer's tech-support pages for service policies or a nearby service center. The Musical Instrument Technicians Association maintains a membership list sorted by state.

No matter what you may have heard, fraud is pretty rare in the world of online auctions. It does happen sometimes—another argument for using an escrow service. Most auction sites can lead you through the steps for filing a claim with the proper authorities. You may also be covered for purchases made with a credit card.

PayPal is a great way to move money around. You can send money to anyone with an e-mail address. The service is free to the sender; it charges the recipient a small amount—about equal to a bank's charges for accepting a credit card. Use PayPal to get the fraud protection built into your credit card without the risk of giving a stranger your personal information.

Despite the legwork involved, building your home studio with used gear is a terrific option for the cash-strapped musician. And that pretty much describes all of us, doesn't it?

Appendix C

Manufacturers

Here's where you'll find Internet home pages for the manufacturers mentioned in the book (as well as some that weren't). Some companies maintain separate Web sites for their various product lines. Many have user groups, technical FAQs, and other helpful information. Demo software may be available, so you can try out a product before you commit.

Please be aware that things can change rapidly on the Web—a product may change names or even company affiliations—without notice. So if you can't find something on the pages listed here, try entering the name in your search engine of choice.

I've included short descriptions of what the companies make where necessary.

A

Ableton Software—Live 5 music-production software

http://www.ableton.com

AKAI Professional Products—Studio electronics, recorders, hardware

http://www.akaipro.com

AKG Acoustics—Microphones, headphones

http://www.akgusa.com

Alesis Corporation—Studio hardware, recorders, mixers

http://www.alesis.com

AMD: Advanced Micro Devices—Integrated circuits

http://www.amd.com

Antares Audio Technologies—Plug-in processing software

http://www.antarestech.com

Apogee Digital—Hardware converters

http://www.apogeedigital.com

Apple Computer—Computers, software

http://www.apple.com

Applied Acoustics—Software and virtual instruments

http://www.applied-acoustics.com

Arboretum Systems—Audio restoration software, plug-ins

http://www.arboretum.com

Argosy—Studio furniture

http://www.argosyconsole.com

Ars Nova Software—Education and scoring software

http://www.ars-nova.com

ART (Applied Research and Technology)—Studio processors, hardware

http://www.artroch.com

ARTURIA—Virtual-instrument software

http://www.arturia.com

Audio Ease—Plug-in software, virtual instruments

http://www.audioease.com

Audio-Technica—Microphones, headphones, studio electronics

http://www.audio-technica.com

Auralux Acoustics—Acoustical treatment products

http://www.auralux.com

B

BBE Sound—Direct boxes, studio electronics

http://www.bbesound.com

Behringer—Mixers, studio hardware, microphones, electronics

http://www.behringer.com

Belkin Corporation—Electronic products, cables

http://world.belkin.com

BGW Products—Custom computers, amplifiers, studio products

http://www.bgw.com

Bias—Music production and restoration software

http://www.bias-inc.com

Blue—Microphones, preamplifiers

http://www.bluemic.com

Boss Music Products—See *Roland Corporation US*

Brian Moore Guitars—"iGuitar" MIDI guitars

http://www.brianmooreguitars.com

C

Cakewalk—Production and effects software

http://www.cakewalk.com

Compaq (United States)—Desktop and notebook computers

http://h18000.www1.hp.com/

Creative Technology—SoundBlaster audio cards

http://www.soundblaster.com

Cycling '74—Plug-in and virtual-instrument software

http://www.cycling74.com

D

dbx Professional Products—Studio processors and electronics

http://www.dbxpro.com

Dell Computer Corporation

http://www.dell.com

Digidesign—Recording software and hardware

http://www.digidesign.com

Digigram—PCMCIA audio interfaces, studio networking

http://www.digigram.com

DigiTech—Effects and studio electronics

http://www.digitech.com

E

EastWest—Virtual instruments, romplers, samples

http://www.soundsonline.com

Eccentric Software—"A Zillion Kajillion Rhymes" songwriting tool

http://www.eccentricsoftware.com

Echo Digital Audio Corporation—Sound cards and digital audio interfaces

http://www.echoaudio.com

ECSMedia—Music education software

http://www.ecsmedia.com

Edirol Corporation North America—Home and project studio products, electronic musical instruments

http://www.edirol.com

eMedia Music Corporation—Educational software

http://www.emediamusic.com

E-MU Systems—Audio hardware, samplers

http://www.emu.com

Event Electronics—Studio monitors

http://www.event1.com

Evolution Electronics—MIDI controllers

http://www.evolution.co.uk/

EZQuest—Hard drives

http://www.ezq.com

F

Fatar—Studiologic keyboard controllers

http://www.studiologic.net

Fender Musical Instruments—"Roland-ready" MIDI guitars

http://www.fender.com

Fostex—Studio equipment, headphones, recorders

http://www.fostex.com

Furman Sound—Power conditioners

http://www.furmansound.com

G

Garritan Personal Orchestra

http://www.personalorchestra.com

Gateway Computers

http://www.gateway.com

Gefen Inc.—Computer and AV connectivity products

http://www.gefen.com

GenieSoft, Inc. —Scoring software

http://www.geniesoft.com

Glyph Technologies—Hard drives

http://www.glyphtech.com

Godin Guitars—Synth Access MIDI guitars

http://www.godinguitars.com/godingman.htm

H

Hewlett-Packard—Desktop and notebook computers

http://www.hp.com

I

IBM—Computer technology

http://www.ibm.com/us/

IK Multimedia—Music production, plug-in, and virtual instrument software

http://www.ikmultimedia.com

See also

http://www.amplitube.com

http://www.groovemaker.com

http://www.t-racks.com

http://www.sonicsynth.com

http://www.sampletank.com

Image-Line Software—FL Studio 5 looping and production software

http://www.fruityloops.com

Intel Corporation—Computer chips

http://www.intel.com

Interactive Media Corporation—Kanguru Solutions. Removable computer storage, backup, accessories

http://www.kanguru.com

J

Jana Software—Personal Ear Trainer software

http://www.janasoftware.com/pet.php

JL Cooper Electronics—Studio hardware and controllers

http://www.jlcooper.com

K

Kinesis Corporation—Ergonomic computer keyboards

http://www.kinesis-ergo.com

Korg—Electronic musical instruments, studio electronics

http://www.korg.com

L

LaCie USA—Hard drives, CD and DVD recorders

http://www.lacie.com

LE Studio Racks

http://www.lashen.com

Lexicon—Studio processors, software, audio hardware

http://www.lexicon.com

Line-6—Guitar-amplifier modeling products, amplifiers, electronic guitars

http://www.line6.com

http://www.guitarport.com

Linux Software

http://www.linux.org

LyricPro—Songwriting software

http://www.lyricpro.com

M

Master Writer—Songwriting software

http://www.masterwriter.com

M-Audio—Audio and MIDI interfaces, keyboards and controllers, studio gear

http://www.m-audio.com

Mackie Designs—Mixers, studio hardware, software

http://www.mackie.com

MakeMusic Software—Educational and scoring software

http://www.makemusic.com

See also

http://www.finalemusic.com

Marathon Computer—Rack-mount computer products

http://www.marathoncomputer.com

Mark of the Unicorn—DAW software, virtual instruments, audio interfaces

http://www.motu.com

Maxtor Corporation—Computer hard drives, mass storage

http://www.maxtor.com

McDSP (McDowell Signal Processing)—Plug-in effects

http://www.mcdsp.com

MiBAC Music Software—Music-education software

http://www.mibac.com

Microboards Technology—CD- and DVD-duplication hardware

http://www.microboards.com

Microsoft Corporation—Software

http://www.microsoft.com

Mixman—DJ and looping software

http://www.mixman.com

Monster Cable—Cable and electronics products

http://www.monstercable.com

Moog Music—Company founded by analog synth pioneer Robert Moog

http://www.moogmusic.com

Muse Research—Receptor hardware VST player

http://www.museresearch.com

Musical Computers—Custom computers for music

http://www.musicalcomputers.com

MusicXPC—Custom computers for music

http://www.musicxpc.com

N

Native Instruments—Plug-ins, virtual instruments

http://www.native-instruments.com

Noteworthy Software—Scoring software

http://www.noteworthysoftware.com/composer/

Novation Music—MIDI controllers and audio interfaces

http://www.novationmusic.com

Neumann USA—Microphones

http://www.neumannusa.com

NVIDIA Corporation—Computer graphics enhancement

http://www.nvidia.com

O

Omnirax—Studio furniture and rack systems

http://www.omnirax.com

P—Q

PG Music, Inc—Band-in-a-Box, composition, educational, and production software

http://www.pgmusic.com

Presonus Audio Electronics—Studio hardware, audio interfaces, microphone preamps

http://www.presonus.com

Primera Technology—CD and DVD replicators and printers

http://www.primera.com

Pro Co—Cable and audio connectivity

http://www.procosound.com

Propellerhead Software—Reason audio-production software

http://www.propellerheads.se/

R

RMC Pickups–Hexaphonic pickups for MIDI guitars

http://www.rmcpickup.com

RME Audio–Audio interfaces, studio electronics

http://www.rme-audio.com/english/

Rode Microphones

http://www.rode.com.au/

Roland Corporation US–Electronic musical instruments, studio hardware, music technology

http://www.rolandus.com

Royer Labs–Microphones

http://www.royerlabs.com

S

Samson Audio–Studio and live sound equipment

http://www.samsontech.com

SDG Soft–Music-instruction software

http://www.sdgsoft.com

Seagate Technology–Computer hard drives

http://www.seagate.com

Sennheiser–Microphones and headphones

http://www.sennheiser.com

Shure Incorporated–Microphones and audio electronics

http://www.shure.com

Sibelius USA, Inc.–Scoring and educational software

http://www.sibelius.com

SKB–Cases and studio racks

http://www.skbcases.com

Sonnet Technologies–Computer-enhancement products

http://www.sonnettech.com

Sony Electronics—Computers, home entertainment, recorders, media, software

http://www.sony.com

http://www.sonystyle.com

Soundcraft—Spirit mixers

http://www.spiritbysoundcraft.com

SoundTrek—Jammer software

http://www.soundtrek.com

Starr Labs—MIDI guitar controllers

http://www.starrlabs.com

Steinberg Corporation—Music-production software

http://www.steinberg.de/Steinberg/default5b09.html

http://www.steinberg.net

Stewart Audio, Inc.—DIs, amplifiers, studio products

http://www.stewartaudio.com

Symantec Corporation—Computer-utility software

http://www.symantec.com

T

Take Note Publishing, Ltd.—C.A.T.S. music-instruction software

http://www.takenotepublishing.co.uk/cats

TASCAM—Professional and consumer electronics, studio hardware, software

http://www.tascam.com

http://www.tascam.com/indexTASCAM.html

TC Electronics—Studio hardware and software plug-ins

http://www.tcelectronic.com

Tech 21—Sans Amp DIs, guitar and bass amps and effects

http://www.tech21nyc.com

U

Ultimate Support Systems—Speaker and microphone stands, studio furniture

http://www.ultimatesupport.com

Universal Audio—Studio hardware and software plug-ins

http://www.uaudio.com

V

vanBasco Software—Karaoke software and MIDI files

http://www.vanbasco.com

W–X

Wave Digital—Custom computers for music

http://www.wavedigital.com

Waves—Effects, restoration, and mastering software and hardware

http://www.waves.com

Whirlwind Music Distribution—Studio cable and accessories

http://www.whirlwindusa.com

Y–Z

Yamaha Corporation of America—Electronic musical instruments, studio hardware and software, consumer electronics

http://www.yamaha.com

http://www.yamaha.com/yamahavgn/CDA/home/YamahaHome/

Appendix D }

Resources

The world of computers and music is large indeed. But don't fret—help is just a mouse click away. Here's a handy list of resources to help ease the way. This is by no means exhaustive—I googled "music and computers" and got 57 million hits! These are some of my favorites. Most have links, too.

Happy surfing!

Magazines
These fine print magazines have online editions with searchable articles, tutorials, gear reviews, and more.

Computers and Computing
There are hundreds of magazines dedicated to various bits of the computer world. Here are four of general interest.

MacAddict—A Macintosh magazine with edge. http://www.macaddict.com

MacWorld—"The Mac Product Experts." A huge magazine dedicated to all things Mac. http://www.macworld.com

MaximumPC—A proven favorite. Reviews, advice, and techniques. http://www.maximumpc.com

PC World—"Technology Advice You Can Trust." http://www.pcworld.com

Music Technology and Home Recording

Acoustic Player Magazine—It has a nice online article about home recording for the acoustic musician. http://www.acousticplayermagazine.com

Computer Music—A great offering from across the pond. http://www.computermusic.co.uk

Electronic Musician—For the project studio owner and home recordist. http://www.emusician.com

EQ—A magazine for recording enthusiasts and home studio owners. http://www.eqmag.com

Future Music—The American version of the great British dance music tech zine. http://www.futuremusicmag.com

Keyboard Magazine—More than just a resource for keyboardists, although it's one of the best. *Keyboard* really covers the digital music world. Good tutorials, top-rate reviews. http://www.keyboardmag.com

Mix—For the professional audio engineer. Find out what the big dogs are up to. http://www.mixonline.com

Music Education Technology—For educators and anyone interested in the field. http://www.metmagazine.com

Music Tech Magazine—"Your complete guide to creating, recording and editing music." Great tutorials on specific software, step-by-step lessons, raps about vintage gear, and techniques. This British magazine is well worth searching out on newsstands. http://www.musictechmag.co.uk

Recording—The name pretty well sums it up. http://www.recordingmag.com

Remix—Music technology magazine for the dance world. http://www.remixmag.com

Sound on Sound—A British magazine billed as "The World's Best Music Recording Magazine," it is very good, indeed. http://www.soundonsound.com

Computers and Computer Mods

Peruse one of these helpful sites before you dig inside your computer. Most computer and hardware manufacturers maintain active tutorials on their Web sites. See Appendix C, "Manufacturers."

http://www.cpushack.net—The CPU Shack is "a microprocessor museum of CPU history for Intel CPUs, AMD processor history, Cyrix microprocessors," and more. Photos, details, specs, how-to articles, and a store for the serious collector of vintage parts. Weirdly compelling, in a William Gibson-ish sort of way.

http://www.ehow.com—The "how to do everything" site. Good, basic information on buying computers and hardware, operating them efficiently, and upgrading them yourself.

http://www.pcmech.com—The PC Mechanic. Another great resource for PC users wanting to get the most out of their computers.

http://pcsupport.about.com/od/upgradetutorials/—A listing of tutorials and articles on About.com. Excellent resource.

http://www.pctechguide.com—The PC Technology Guide. A terrific resource with tons of info, first-rate tutorials on upgrading your PC, price comparisons, and more. Bookmark this site.

http://www.xlr8yourmac.com—Accelerate Your Mac. Get it? Loads of info on improving your Mac's performance, memory, hardware mods, CPU upgrades, and more.

Desktop Recording

Here's a generous sampling of Web sites dedicated to home recording and desktop music making. Most have extensive links to other sites. Happy surfing!

http://www.audioforums.com—Audio forums for PC and Macintosh digital audio hardware and software. Mainly aimed at professionals.

http://www.digido.com—Links, technical papers, tutorials, and more. For pros and home recordists who want professional results. This site just keeps getting better and better.

http://www.geeknoize.com/—"Mr. Geeky and his staff are working 24/7 for the digital audio revolution." Lots of info and links.

http://www.harmony-central.com—The biggest and possibly the best online musician's resource. Tutorials, gear reviews, and oodles of links.

http://www.homerecording.com—Just what the name implies. Check out the Web ring for online collaborators, tutorials, and more. Good message board.

http://www.homerecording.about.com—Tutorials and more.

http://www.musiconmypc.co.uk—"Sound Advice on Music Software." Highly recommended.

http://www.pc-music.com—An extremely useful site. Host Robin Vincent is tech director of Carillon Systems, a company specializing in custom PCs for the music biz.

http://www.pcrecording.com—FAQs, tips, and reviews.

http://www.prorec.com—Industry news and discussion. Pro, semipro, and amateur. Classifieds and discussion forum.

http://www.sweetwater.com/insync/word/letter/A—Excellent glossary of audio terms. While you're there, check out the Technical Tip of the Day archives. Affiliated with retailer Sweetwater.com.

http://www.tape.com/Bartlett_Articles/stereo_microphone_techniques.html—Great info on stereo miking.

Recording History

Learn more about the early days here.

http://www.recording-history.org/HTML/technology.htm—Technical history of recording.

http://www.tcd.ie/Music/recordingevents.htm—History of recording.

Looping and Dance Music Production

These three sites will get you connected to the huge world of dance, trance, and electronic music. You'll find links to software and samples, how-to articles, DJs and producers, clubs, recordings, reviews, and much more. See also Web sites for specific software and hardware.

http://www.dancetech.com—Gear reviews, tutorials, links, free plug-ins, and lots more to help you get up to speed with digital DJ and dance music production.

http://www.ivibes.nu/—The i:Vibes online presence dedicated to everything dance. Some good tutorials.

http://www.trugroovez.com—TruGroovez maintains a directory of links in the dance music world. Check out the forum.

Gear Reviews and Resources

It seems as if everybody and his uncle posts online gear reviews. In addition to the sites listed here, check out those in the "Desktop Recording" section.

http://musicians.about.com/index.htm?terms=Musicians—Informational site with subsections on buying used gear, links to auctions, reviews, and more. See also www.altmusic.about.com.

http://www.digitalprosound.com—Gear reviews, tutorials, opinion, and links dedicating to digital audio.

http://www.headwize.com—Everything you need to know about headphones.

http://www.musicgearreview.com—Reader reviews of new and used gear. Affiliated with retailer Musician's Friend.

http://www.tweakheadz.com—Reviews gear picks and advice on buying used gear. Affiliated with online retailer zZounds.com.

Synthesizers and Electronic Musical Instruments

Here are some cool sites with info and links. Most brands have their own official Web site as well as unofficial sites. I'm not going to list sites for synth patches and sample collections—there are simply too many. You've got a search engine, don't you?

http://www.kvraudio.com—They bill themselves as "the Internet's number one news and information resource for open standard audio plugins." If it's a software instrument that runs under VST, DirectX, or AU, you'll find info here. Affiliated with Muse Research, the company that makes the Receptor hardware VST player.

http://www.localcolorart.com/search/encyclopedia/Robert_Moog/—Article about synthesizer pioneer Robert Moog.

http://www.obsolete.com/120_years/links/links.html—120 Years of Electronic Music: Links.

http://www.sequencer.de—The Moogulator's synthesizer and sequencers page. Huge amounts of useful info on digital and analog synthesizers, sequencers, tips, and techniques. In English and German.

http://www.sonicstate.com/synth—They bill it as "The World's Greatest Synth Site." Reviews, tutorials, links—if it has to do with synthesizers, start your search here.

http://www.synthony.com/museum.html—Online synth and MIDI museum.

http://www.synthzone.com—Good general site for info and links—mainly synthesizers, naturally.

http://www.vintagesynth.com—Vintage synthesizer explorer.

Software: Freeware and Shareware

Another enormous category. Here are a few places to start.

http://www.audiomelody.com—All music freeware, all the time.

http://www.download.com—Dozens of shareware and freeware audio programs.

http://www.hitsquad.com—Also known as SharewareMusicMachine.com. Big site dedicated to music software. Mac, Windows, Linux.

http://www.tucows.com—Huge site for shareware and freeware. All platforms, user rating system, good search engine.

Songwriting and Music Publishing

Some useful links for you.

http://www.cdbaby.com—The independent recording artist's best hope in a huge, impersonal world.

http://www.copyright.gov—Everything you need to know about US copyright, straight from the source.

http://www.musesmuse.com—The Muse's Muse is an online business dedicated to songwriters. Forums, info, links, Artist's Spotlights.

http://www.taxi.com—The independent A&R (artist and repertoire) site. Get your music heard.

http://www.themusiciansresource.com—Info on indy radio, promo, downloading, gear, and more. Links plus Internet radio that accepts indy submissions.

Organizations

Some sites to check out.

http://www.aes.org—The Audio Engineering Society is the only professional organization dedicated to audio technology.

http://www.ascap.com—American Society of Composers, Authors and Publishers. Performing rights organization for songwriters and music publishers.

http://www.bmi.com—Broadcast Music International, the other big performing rights organization.

http://www.cnmat.berkeley.edu—Berkeley's Center for New Music and Audio Technologies is dedicated to "promoting the creative interaction of music and technology." Always something interesting going on here.

http://www.midi.org—The MIDI Manufacturers Association.

Lotsa Links

These two sites are dedicated to the idea that putting all of your links in one basket is a good idea.

http://dmoz.org/Arts/Music/—"The Open Directory Project is the largest, most comprehensive human-edited directory on the Web." Links, links, and more links, arranged in a hierarchical fashion for easy browsing. This page takes you directly into the music links.

http://www.somusical.com—SoMusical! maintains extensive links to all things musical.

And Finally...

http://www.mark-o.com—The author's personal Web site. Yes, he has a life.

http://www.courseptr.com—Thomson Course Technology's home. You know them—they published this book. Check out the industry resources and complete listing of Course Technology's books on music technology.

http://www.coursedirect.com—The Thomson Course Technology online bookstore. Find expert help with most of the music software and recording techniques mentioned in this book.

Index

INDEX ♩

INDEX ♩